DATE DUE

PEOPLES OF A SPACIOUS LAND

Gloria L. Main

Peoples of a Spacious Land
Families and Cultures in
Colonial New England

HARVARD UNIVERSITY PRESS

Cambridge, Massachusetts, and London, England   2001

Library of Congress Cataloging-in-Publication Data

Main, Gloria L. (Gloria Lund), 1933–
    Peoples of a spacious land : families and cultures in colonial New England / Gloria L. Main
      p.   cm.
    Includes bibliographical references and index.
    ISBN 0-674-00628-3 (alk. paper)
    1. Family—New England—History   2. New England—Social life and customs.
  3. Indians of North America—New England—Social life and customs.
  4. Narragansett Indians—Social life and customs.   5. New England—History—Colonial
period, ca. 1600–1775. I. Title

    HQ535 .M347 2001
    306.85´0974—dc21

To Jackson Turner Main, beloved mentor

Contents

Preface

This book is about families living and working on the land in southern New England from 1600 to 1775. Although its main focus is how English immigrants and their descendants adapted to their New World environment, the book utilizes archaeological and historical materials on the native peoples of the region, particularly the Narragansetts of modern Rhode Island, to provide an essential counterpoint. *Peoples of a Spacious Land* takes the second half of its title from a *Mayflower* passenger's description of New England to friends at home. The sudden dying-off of coastal native peoples from a mysterious epidemic disease just before the arrival of the first English persuaded them that God was with them and intended the land to be theirs. This perception of a wild and heathen place waiting for hard-working settlers to subdue and transform it into a productive Christian commonwealth served as justification for its peaceful appropriation. The central story of the book is the intertwined processes of family formation and town founding by which the English took the land and displaced its original inhabitants. Crucial to this story is the evolving nature of the relationship between children and parents and between wives and husbands as English family practices adapted to New World conditions.

This story of the dynamic impact of New England's unique environment on English family values, and of English culture and technology on that environment, unfolds through the voices and actions of the people themselves in their diaries and records. Early chapters describe native New England and the arrival and dispersion of English colonists, after which the book turns to the laws, customs, and experiences of family life, using stages of the lifecycle to explore such issues as courtship and marriage, pregnancy and childbearing, childhood and childrearing theories, youth and old age. Each chapter compares English to native ways in order to explore the influence of cultural values. The final chapters take the story of Narragansetts and English through the terrible tragedy of King Philip's War and into the eighteenth century, when the family lives of both peoples underwent significant change. The Seven Years' War stimulated the region's economy, and the series of political confrontations with the British leading up to independence reawakened English descendants' sense of separate, and superior, identity. Most important of all, perhaps, was the creation of a new nation that promised perpetual accessions of new lands, enabling the old compact between parents and children to advance and flourish. By the close of the colonial period, their myriad descendants had established towns across the face of southern New England, begun developing its northern parts, and were expanding westward into New York and Pennsylvania. The expansion of New Englanders across the northern half of the United States was to plant New England family culture in New York, Ohio, the prairie states, and ultimately all the way to the Pacific.

The long gestation of this book created many debts. I am grateful to the American Antiquarian Society, the American Council of Learned Societies, the National Endowment for the Humanities, and the Council for Research and Creative Work at the University of Colorado for their financial support over the years. I also want to thank the highly professional and helpful library staff at the American Antiquarian Society, the New England Historic Genealogical Society, the Massachusetts Historical Society, the Connecticut State Archives, the Connecticut Historical Society, the Rhode Island Historical Society, the New Hampshire State Archives, and the Peabody Institute of Salem.

All teachers learn from their students, and mine have taught me much. I am deeply grateful to them and to the University of Colorado for giving me the opportunity to exchange ideas with them. The works of Edmund Sears Morgan and Darrett Rutman continue to inspire me even as I move in a direction very different from theirs. I have also benefited over the years from the kindness of many scholars. Conversations with Robert Charles Anderson, Jon Butler, Lois Green Carr, David Hall, Ruth Herndon, Jackson Turner Main, John McCusker, George Freeman Sanborn Jr., Melinde Lutz Sanborn, Kevin Sweeney, Laurel Ulrich, and Lorena Walsh have helped me in ways these kind people could not have anticipated. Among my colleagues at the University of Colorado I wish particularly to thank Fred Anderson, Virginia DeJohn Anderson, Ann Carlos, Lee Chambers-Schiller, Philip Deloria,

Susan Kent, and Marjorie McIntosh for many helpful comments. The friendship of Patricia and Jeffrey Limerick has nourished my spirit and broadened my horizons. My greatest debt is to my husband, Jack, my beloved mentor and companion for close to half a century. He has read at least twice every word of every article and chapter I have ever written, and he seems still to thrive in spite of it all.

PEOPLES OF A SPACIOUS LAND

Native New England

We weare no Cloaths, have many Gods,
And yet our sinnes are lesse:
You are Barbarians, Pagans wild,
Your Land's the Wildernesse.

—Roger Williams, *A Key into the Language of America*

When Giovanni da Verrazano sailed near the shore of what is now Narra-gansett Bay in 1524, his ship was approached by about twenty boats filled with curious but friendly people. His men threw them trinkets, assuring them of their peaceful intentions, and many ventured to come on board. He pronounced them the "most beautiful and have the most civil customs that we have found on this voyage. They are taller than we are; they are a bronze color . . . the face is clean-cut; the hair is long and black . . . the eyes are black and alert, and their manner is sweet and gentle . . . Their women are just as shapely and beautiful; very gracious." These exquisite creatures proved interested not in the European tools, guns, or cloth showed them, but only in the jewelry.[1]

Verrazano's ship had approached from the west, by way of Long Island and Block Island Sounds, and news of its progress had probably preceded it along well-trodden paths. Southern New England was well populated by descendants of people who had arrived many thousands of years before. It was far from being a vacant wilderness, but neither was it a rustic countryside of small villages organized on the European model. Its landscape was unique.

The subregion known as southern New England encompasses the southernmost part of Maine, including the Saco Valley, the estuary of the Piscataqua River in southeastern New Hampshire, all of Massachusetts, Rhode Island, and Connecticut, plus the offshore islands and the eastern half of Long Island. The area extends 136 miles from north to south and roughly 155 miles from the Taconic Range in the west to the ocean's edge at Cape Cod in the east. With the exception of the Connecticut, none of the region's rivers provides deep-water navigation more than a few miles into an interior dominated by rolling hills, ridges, and highlands. Most of eastern Long Island is quite flat, but the only level areas on the mainland are those lying along river valleys and on the relatively narrow coastal plain. Southern Rhode Island, between Narragansett Bay and west to the Pawcatuck River, represents a substantial exception.

Eons of volcanic activity shaped this landscape, but its soil cover is the product of relatively recent glaciation of the bedrock. The final retreat of the Wisconsin ice sheets took place about 13,000 years ago, leaving gravel, sand, and silt soils lying in a complex topography of moraines, drumlins, till plains, and glacial lake strand lines. The glaciers scoured the land as they withdrew slowly and erratically northward; hence the rivers flow southward between parallel spines of hills. Given the geologically short interval since then, soil layers outside of river floodplains have accumulated little depth and are still acidic from the earliest evergreen tree cover. In well-drained, undisturbed sites, such topsoil that has developed over the past 8,000 years is markedly shallow and filled with rocky debris. Pristine topsoils in New England are only two to four inches deep, in contrast to the fourteen-inch soils of the midwestern prairies.[2] Because the land was created by the grinding down of mantle rock with the weight of thousands of feet of moving ice, New England's surface soils reflect the chemical properties of the parent rock. As a consequence, they are less fertile than those of the midwestern prairies, but they respond well to applications of lime (calcium oxide) and readily absorb nitrogen from legumes, potassium from potash, and phosphorus from bones.

Soil is composed of particles of worn rock that come in a range of sizes. The larger the particles, the sandier the soil, and the faster it dries out. Silt and clay consist of smaller particles, and these make the earth sticky and waterlogged. The surface water evaporates faster than the subsurface, leaving the ground compact and cementlike. The ideal texture for growing plants is loam, which is made up of sand, silt, and clay in equal amounts. Soils formed at higher elevations and on slopes tend to drain fast, the surface runoff can be quite rapid, and the water table is often more than six feet below the surface. Land at lower elevations receives runoff from higher elevations and has a water table less than six feet down. Soils lying in depressions or adjacent to drainage-ways may remain highly saturated. The best land for raising crops has loamy, deep, and friable soil, is not frequently flooded during the growing season, drains well but not too fast, slopes less than 7 percent, and is free of rocky debris. Outside of the Connecticut and Thames River Valleys (the latter in southeastern Connecticut), such soils and conditions are scarce in southern New England and are widely dispersed.[3] Because good, tillable, level deposits lie in scattered pockets rather than in broad swaths, the region is better suited for small-scale gardening than for extensive farming. The stones and boulders make plowing difficult, and when the land slopes too sharply, plowing becomes a nightmare. Despite culling of the ground through centuries of use and the construction of hundreds of miles of rock walls in New England, winter freezes and spring thaws continue to bring rocks and boulders to its surface.

The landscape of southern New England is highly variable because of its very uneven topography and the often contrary effects of sea and wind. The diversity of local soils and microclimates form a patchwork of species habitats across the land and along the coasts. Natural open areas and meadows are rare in New England outside the extensive Narragansett country visited by Verrazano. The absence of grazing animals may account for this peculiarity of the region. Without their selective feeding to keep back the trees and to encourage the more nutritious species, the small patches of indigenous grasses would make poor fodder for the livestock that the English would bring.[4]

Climate since the Ice Age has warmed and dried the landscape, raised sea levels, and encouraged the proliferation of species among the flora and fauna. The early postglacial forests in New England consisted of northern conifers such as spruce and hemlock. Later, the slower-moving southern species made their way into the region, trailed by the deciduous hardwoods. Thus, the forests of New England were mixed in composition and in a constant state of flux resulting from the dynamic action of wind and fire. For humans living there, the most important trees were those that bore nuts, especially hickory, oak, and chestnut. Nuts support fauna of high caloric value such as deer, bear, raccoon, turkey, and squirrel and supply supplemental protein and fats to human diet. Hard-shell nuts keep well, so gatherers can store them for later use. Nut trees also help to build up soils and reduce their acidity.[5]

Trees and food crops, such as corn and beans, require ample amounts of rain and sunshine, and the frost-free season must last long enough for fruits and seeds to ripen. The current northern limit for reliable harvests of corn lies somewhere between the Saco and Kennebec Rivers in Maine, at about 44° latitude. That boundary marker dips sharply southward as one moves inland, except for a jog northward in the Connecticut River valley. Average annual temperatures vary widely over this mixed terrain, the products of latitude, elevation, and proximity to the ocean. The distance from Portsmouth, New Hampshire, to Norwalk, Connecticut, is two degrees of latitude and a two-week difference in growing season. Inland, the growing season varies more directly with elevation than with latitude, but cold Canadian air masses may end the growing season as early as late September, whereas killing frosts may not come to the coast until November. Yet ocean effects also delay the arrival of spring. Barnstable, on Cape Cod, well to the south, has a growing season no longer than Portsmouth's in New Hampshire. The Cape lies exposed to almost constant winds in winter, and the ocean warms up more slowly than the land, so spring comes later.[6]

Modern temperatures are higher and growing seasons longer than they were during the "Little Ice Age" of the seventeenth century.[7] The first European visitors to New England came in summertime, which can get uncomfortably hot and humid, so they judged the climate to be like that of southern Spain, which lies in the same latitude. The length and harshness of New England winters took colonists by surprise, but they soon came to understand that the severity of winter was due to the region's position on the eastern edge of a large northern land mass. Roger Williams explained the situation to an English audience in 1644: "It may bee wondred why since *New-England* is about 12 degrees neerer to the Sun, yet . . . Winter . . . is there ordinarily more cold than here in England: the reason is plaine: All Ilands are warmer . . . Englands winds are Sea winds . . . The NorWest wind (which occasioneth *New-England* cold) comes over the cold frozen Land and over many millions of Loads of Snow . . ."[8]

Although tree rings show that there have been frequent droughts and periods of unusually cool temperatures, the generally moderate climate of southern New England would still make the area hospitable to horticulture were it not for its rough topography and thin, acidic soils. In normal years the growing season is sufficiently long for cold-weather-adapted flint corn as well as for wheat and rye. Rainfall is normally ample early in the growing season, averaging forty to forty-five inches a year, but declines in late summer and early fall. Edward Winslow of Plymouth reported a "great drought" in 1623 that brought the little colony to the edge of despair. But Edward Johnson, writing in 1651, observed that "the Country is naturally subject to drought" in the summer.[9]

The first humans arrived in New England 10,000 or more years ago. They did not merely browse nature's bounty, but actively reshaped their new home. Their selective interaction with the plants and animals helped to guide the region's ecological development. For example, people burned enormous quantities of wood year round to warm themselves in winter, cook their meals, smoke-dry meat, fish, and shellfish, and fire their pottery. They also set fires in the late fall to clear away the dead leaves and underbrush for easier hunting in the woods, and, when women began raising corn, they burned their fields each spring before sowing. The forests appeared to European visitors as "naturally" clear and open, in contrast to those at home.[10]

Long before corn arrived, the women had already modified the region's plant life by selective gathering. They dug ground nuts, Jerusalem artichokes, and other tubers; encouraged plants with large, nutritious seeds, such as sunflowers; and discouraged plants that offered little of value.[11] The great majority of New England's people probably lived along coastal estuaries and riparian ways where they could harvest a rich assortment of flora and fauna all year round. For those living inland, the forests, rivers, swamps, and ponds yielded enough to eat, so long as the ice did not become too thick nor the snows too deep. The women's close study of plants and persistent experimentation gradually extended their stores of medicines and tools as well as of foods. Bulrushes and cattails, for instance, supplied fibers with which women wove mats for house coverings and wall hangings as well as baskets and sandals. Hemp provided fibers for fashioning into cordage, nets, and coarse cloth.

About 1,000 years ago the climate went through a long warming interval, bringing longer growing seasons. Shorter winters encouraged women gatherers to experiment with the seeds of nonnative plants obtained through trade.[12] In more favored regions to the west of New England, such as Ontario and northern New York, the improved growing conditions led to the widespread adoption of the maize-squash-beans complex from growers in the Ohio Valley. The greater stability of food resources, in turn, led to population growth, larger and more permanent settlements, and more elaborate political and social systems. Because of New England's inadequate soils the adoption of corn there did not have these consequences, although people living in small inland villages along the Connecticut River did become dependent on the grain.[13] Coastal peoples took up corn-growing relatively late in the precontact period, but the scattered nature of suitable sites prevented them from congregating. When corn became important in their diets, they moved onto individual homesteads. Hence throughout most of the region there were no real villages, only dispersed, impermanent habitations.[14]

Expert knowledge of terrain, plants, and animals, coupled with the purposeful use of fire and selective harvesting, continued to modify New England's landscape and resources to make it a more productive environment for humans. The introduction of maize growing expanded the populations of deer, rabbits, and other small animals by creating edge habitats that enhanced the volume of plant materials for browsing. Burning the woods in the fall also increased the food supply of grouse, pigeons, and turkeys.[15] Yet the cumulative impact of thousands of years of human activity in the region did not diminish the reproductive capacity of their faunal prey. Salmon and shad did not fail in their spring runs up the rivers; striped bass and mackerel returned every summer to coastal waters; passenger pigeons and aquatic fowl migrated through every spring and fall. Europeans visiting New England in summertime were astounded (and misled) by the abundance of game and fish, unaware of its seasonal nature.[16]

Kathleen Bragdon outlines four principal ecological environments in southern New England that supplied subsistence to prehistoric and early modern peoples: upland woods, riparian ways, estuaries, and rivers and coastal waters.[17] The woods furnished herbs, berries, nuts, roots, and edible fauna such as deer, bear, raccoons, rabbits, and squirrels. The riparian lowlands provided the only tillable soils in New England that were level and had good drainage. The estuaries were the richest environments in terms of biomass. They supplied resting places for migrating waterfowl and were home to fish, frogs, and shellfish. Shellfish seek out clean salt marshes and these require shelter from storms, which they find in the lee of strategically situated headlands. In turn, birds, crustaceans, and fin fish feed on the shellfish. Oysters, clams, mussels, and whelks are tasty and easier to harvest than deep-water fish, but the payoff is poorer: a pound of shellfish meat yields only about 400 calories and is deficient in key nutrients. Cod is far more sustaining. Shellfish, then, provided emergency food in seasons when other sources dwindled.[18] The coastal waters furnished quantities of fish in season, and eels made regular spring and fall migrations in the riverways.

One ought to add the offshore islands as a fifth form to Bragdon's ecological environments, because these were among the earliest areas to be developed by native peoples as agricultural preserves. The islands of Narragansett Bay, for instance, totaled some 75,000 acres in area, 5,000 of which were rich silt loam. The rest would be especially attractive to the English for apple orchards and safe pasture.[19] The open, stony soils of the Narragansett country west of the Bay formed a subset of this environment; the absence of woods not only made fewer deer available but also pushed inhabitants further into maritime pursuits and into trading with more northern peoples to obtain the furs and hides so necessary to their way of life.[20]

When people exhausted the local stocks of what they needed, such as firewood, they moved. They also shifted with the seasons, from snug winter homes to early spring fishing sites, to late spring planting fields, to summertime gathering and fishing, to fall hunting grounds, and from old fields to new fields.[21] Moving was an efficient response to diminishing returns, but its necessity dramatically shaped life-styles and material values. The native peoples kept their houses small and portable, and their furnishings simple, for precisely this reason.[22]

The supply of natural resources accessible to human exploitation slowly expanded over the centuries even as their biological makeup altered, all in consequence of purposeful human activity. Because of the risks from early and late frosts, people of the interior uplands never dared to give over their subsistence activities in order to farm. The gradual growth of population, however, may have induced the extension of corn-growing in the late Woodland period among coastal dwellers, who had begun to disperse into hamlets and individual homesteads for this purpose.[23]

Favored dwelling sites had always been those within safe reach of both aquatic resources and stands of nut-bearing trees. When good soils for growing corn were also nearby, especially where there was full southern exposure for extending the growing season, such places became all the more desirable and worth defending against rivals.[24] These are the places where archaeologists expected to find signs of permanent Indian villages, but they have found none.[25] The absence of such sites is no mystery given modern soil maps, but signs of increasing dependency on corn-growing raises questions about political dynamics in the region prior to contact. If growing population created pressures that substantially altered human relationships with the land, differential access to the most desirable sites would have created new tensions among kin groups while exacerbating those between bands. Some peoples had always benefited more than others, and so the arrival of European trade goods merely introduced one more factor into the competitive brew.[26]

Although the concept of "carrying capacity" is useful for imagining the workings of environmental constraints on population size in any given area, it unfortunately turns out to be impossible to estimate. Consequently, one cannot calculate the maximum sustainable numbers of human beings that southern New England could have supported with native technology. If one is to judge by the observations of early European visitors, the native peoples—"Ninnimissinouk," as they came to call themselves in opposition to the English—had not reached the saturation point.[27] The visitors describe a population that was robust and well nourished, and the skeletal evidence from burials supports this impression. It is clear that no famine was then stalking the land, but they may have been moving closer to a boundary.

As many as 100,000 people may have lived in New England prior to contact. Given the region's scarcity of farm land suitable to slash-and-burn technology, lower rather than higher population estimates seem more likely. Dean Snow has compiled a useful summary of the numbers suggested by English observers and has calculated the size of each of the territories occupied by one or another group of Native Americans.[28] Only a small fraction of those extensive tracts contained tillable land, perhaps as little as 10 percent in Connecticut and Rhode Island, if one is to judge from modern soil maps, and even less would have been true for Massachusetts Bay Company and Plymouth Colony.

At the time of English colonization, the Narragansetts of Rhode Island constituted the largest confederation of bands in New England. They were traditionally allied with the powerful and greatly feared Mohawks of the Five Nations. Neighbors of the Narragansetts to the west, the Pequots of the Thames River Valley formed a rival confederacy that included their less numerous kin, the Mohegans. The villages of the middle Connecticut River Valley never succeeded in developing a strong counterconfederacy, although they were customary allies of the Mahicans of the Hudson Valley, who in turn were archrivals of the Mohawks. As Mahican strength diminished in their contest with the Mohawks, the Connecticut villages were forced to pay tribute to the Pequots.

To the east of the Narragansetts, on the opposite shore of Narragansett Bay, lived the Pokanoket Wampanoags with their tributaries and allies on Cape Cod, the Nauset. Northward along the Atlantic coastal plain lived the Massachusetts, another populous confederacy whose members included the Pennacook of the lower Merrimac basin. All of these various Indian groups practiced the same economy of gathering, hunting, and fishing, supplemented to greater or lesser degrees by maize horticulture and with local variations in the relative importance of one or another food source.

North of these groups lived Indians who practiced little or no horticulture and whose principal means of survival came from hunting, fowling, fishing, and gathering. Birch forests provided the material for their lighter and more mobile canoes, but such fragile craft were vulnerable in open seas, where dugouts had the advantage. Maritime Indians were quick to adopt masts and sails once they were able to procure cloth suitable for this purpose, and became excellent sailors. One group of Micmac spotted by English crewmen early in the seventeenth century had somehow obtained a Basque fishing boat and were observed to be operating it successfully. Traditional coastal raiding by Micmacs became even more fearsome when they were able to employ both sails and guns.[29]

Alliances and group identities larger than kinship networks were fluid among the Ninnimissinouk. Their languages were all of the Algonquian family, but they formed a distinct subgroup composed of Loup, Massachusetts, Narragansett, Mohegan-Pequot-Montauk, and Quiriipi-Unquachog.[30] Speakers of any one of these could understand those speaking another tongue, but the level of understanding faded with the geographic distance separating their home territories.

Evidence from archaeological sites suggests that during the sixteenth century coastal peoples began to give corn-growing more attention, dispersing into separate "homesteads," each occupied by a nuclear family.[31] If population growth forced greater dependence on corn despite the scarcity of good land for the purpose, farming would have had to become much more intensive, with greater attention given to weeding, and preferably with annual applications of some kind of fertilizer, especially in the sandier soils along the coasts. Obviously, time spent at the planting ground was time taken from other productive pursuits such as gathering shellfish, smoke-drying fish for later use, and making trips to the woods to gather greens, herbs, and berries. A diet increasingly dependent on stored corn, moreover, would have required hours of daily pounding at the mortar, a tedious, tiring, and altogether mind-numbing task when done alone. The dispersion into separate homesteads tended to isolate women, making it more difficult to share monotonous tasks. Pounding corn replaced making a stately pot or weaving an intricately patterned mat to hang on the wall or sewing supple and durable deerskin moccasins. More-intensive farming, combined with hand-grinding the hard corn, added greatly to the already heavy labors of women. They could not have welcomed the change.

The sixteenth century brought exciting times for the men, however, as they engaged in trading, high politics, and military ventures. Narragansett and other Ninnimissinouk men living along Long Island Sound made shell jewelry called wampum from specific species of small mollusks that lived nowhere else. The men formed the shells into small cylinders for stringing by tedious drilling and polishing. The purple wampum was made from a hard-shell clam species, *Mercenaria mercenaria,* named by Linnaeus for its use among humans. Shore Indians manufactured the white beads from the inner columellae of two species of whelk, *Busycon carica* and *Busycon canaliculatum.*[32] Key shellfish beds were not uniform in richness and density and were found only at certain sites having the requisite shoreline conformation and water temperatures.[33] Hence rival Indian groups fought for access to specific stretches of coastline. Women strung these colored cylinders on long hempen strings and sewed them together to make decorative bracelets and necklaces.[34] Wampum beads were originally ritual objects worn only by the most powerful or high-ranking individuals as symbols denoting spiritual power. The scarcity of these purple and white beads further enhanced their value. The beads circulated throughout a wide trading area extending to the Micmac of the Gaspé Peninsula, west into the Hudson River Valley, along the waterways of the Great Lakes, and down the Ohio. They moved just as readily along the Atlantic coast south to the Florida keys. When specially assembled for the purpose, wampum belts became central to the increasingly important condolence ceremonies of the Iroquois. As demand for the beads rose sharply, the growing area of these species of whelk became exceptionally valuable. The inhabitants of adjacent coastal territories who traditionally gathered the shells and turned them into beads were pressed by more powerful neighbors to pay annual quantities of wampum as protection money in the form of gifts. Narragansetts were in prime position to corner the market on wampum because they were located near excellent shellfish beds and were numerous enough to compel strategically situated Long Islanders to deal their beads through them. The Narragansetts, in turn, paid annual tribute to their allies, the awesomely ferocious Mohawk, easternmost of the Five Nations, who considered southern New England a subsidiary trading territory. The Narragansett alliance gave the Mohawk guaranteed annual supplies of the precious wampum, strengthening their negotiating position within the Five Nations and making them more attractive partners in military alliances.

When the Dutch introduced the fur trade into the Hudson Valley and learned of wampum's role among Native Americans, they struck up business with Pequot traders to acquire quantities for the purchase of pelts. Wampum thereupon became a means of exchange and assumed the role of money, used by traders for selling European goods as well as acquiring furs. Colonial governments designated wampum as money for tax purposes and set its official value in terms of European currencies. The exchange value of wampum must have risen sharply as a consequence, making producers such as the Narragansetts momentarily rich in European goods. However, the introduction of European steel drills greatly speeded up the manufacturing process, leading to an expansion of the supply of beads in circulation, and inevitably lowering their exchange value. It was a brief reign of glory for the wampum producers, but it thoroughly disrupted customary political relationships and heated up long-standing rivalries both among and between Narragansetts and their neighbors.

Ninnimissinouk modes of dealing with family, friends, neighbors, trading partners, and enemies can be glimpsed only haphazardly from descriptions by European visitors going all the way back to Verrazano. Because of the credulity, confusion, prejudice, and self-interest of their writings, they require the more objective data from archaeological sites as correctives. These digs provide invaluable material evidence of life-styles, funerary practices, and settlement locations and size. In addition, modern linguistic analysis of seventeenth- and eighteenth-century documents generated by the Ninnimissinouk furnish previously unavailable information that helps to correct the European impressions as well as to supplement the evidence from the ground. Recollections and folk stories recited by more recent Native Americans offer their versions of their past, often providing uniquely valuable insights into the indigenous point of view. Each type of source has strengths and weaknesses, and all stand silent on many important questions. Putting them together to make a coherent and compelling story is not a straightforward task. When these incomplete scraps are set in the full context of ethnographic field studies now available, however, some patterns of social relationships emerge as far more likely than others.[35]

All stable relationships in human societies are formed and maintained by reiterating processes—the mutual performance of subsistence-related duties, accompanied by social gestures continually offered and accepted by each to each.[36] In Ninnimissinouk society, relationships were not egalitarian, and the gestures of reinforcement were those of deference and petition on the one side, obligation and generosity on the other, all couched in terms of parental or brotherly affection. In describing Massachusetts' burial practices in 1632, Thomas Morton wrote: "they put a greate difference between persons of noble, and of ignoble, or obscure, or inferior descent."[37] Power and authority were claimed and exercised unevenly. The sexes were not equal. The elders were arbiters to the young. Families claimed rank through their lineages as royal, noble, or commoner. A good part of the future career of a newborn infant, then, pivoted on its gender and who its parents were. But despite the inequality of rank and opportunity that permeated Ninnimissinouk society, there was sufficient ambiguity about individual status to make assertion and rivalry perpetual ingredients of daily interactions. Heirs to chiefly status vied among themselves to become sachem, and sachems competed with one another for supremacy. Scholars have not fully sorted out the intricacies of kinship and lineage among the Ninnimissinouk, but it appears that neither matrilineal or patrilineal kinship clearly dominated family affiliations. For instance, Uncas, sachem of the Mohegans, claimed rank through his wife as well as his parental lines. Postcontact records of land decisions by the native council on Block Island suggest that rights to land passed through the mother's line.[38] If land rights belonged to women, their value as marital partners must have risen as horticulture became increasingly important to their economy.

That women should control the land was natural, because they did the agricultural work. The basic division of family responsibility between the sexes was one familiar the world over: women stayed close to home in order to care for small children while men protected the women and children from enemies and kidnappers. Women carried out tasks that did not take them far from the family hearth, the kinds of jobs that could be picked up and dropped without danger or loss. Because women took care of things at home, men were free to travel and therefore were the traders and diplomats as well as warriors and hunters. Under traditional circumstances, however, the hearth and its attendants often accompanied the men. When men went hunting in a body, the women and children usually went along, too. When men tended circuits of traps, each in his own territory, his women and children set up housekeeping at a location convenient to the traps. Women did most of the carrying when they were on the move, because men had to keep their hands free for using their weapons.

All food gathering and preparation lay in women's domain except for big game hunting and large-scale fishing, activities reserved to men. Women did the planting and weeding of corn, beans, and squash, although men helped with the clearing and the harvest. Women also gathered and prescribed herbs for medicine, but they seem not to have acted as spiritual healers, or conjurors, or councilors to sachems. Men raised the tobacco that was used in rituals and in group smoking, a ritual that not only promoted sociability but also contributed importantly to the lengthy process of patient consensus-building that characterized decisionmaking among men.

As necessary tools of their trade, Ninnimissinouk men of coastal New England wove the fish weirs and stout deep-sea fishing nets that brought in the catch. They also made the long dugout canoes in which they went out to sea for cod and bluefish. Dugouts were fashioned out of the trunks of chestnut trees, with their centers very gradually charred by slow-burning coals, then scraped clear to make a hollow. Members of both sexes were strong swimmers and paddlers, handling boats with practiced ease.

Men past their physical prime and no longer able to keep up with the hunt or the war parties had the leisure to carve a variety of useful utensils such as bowls from burl wood and smoking pipes of steatite, in addition to making the usual array of necessary tools and weapons. Their most artistic efforts went into weaving gala ceremonial cloaks of turkey feathers, which were as warm and comfortable as they were beautiful.[39]

Most sachems were men. Other than the occasional sachemship, women held no public offices. Those who were of royal lineage may have influenced political decisions, but if they did so, their activity was not public. Public demeanor by commoner women was modest and retiring, and at meals they waited on the men. Men and women of commoner status could not marry within their lineages but were otherwise relatively free to marry whom they chose. The traditional specifications and boundaries that defined one's lineage among the Ninnimissinouk are not known. Men were free to divorce their wives, but it is not clear that ordinary women could divorce their husbands, although the Pocasset squaw sachem Weetamo did so. Husbands were free to chastise wayward wives and their illicit lovers, but wives had no equivalent right. Men could take as many wives as they could support, although few had more than one; but women had only one husband at a time.

In societies around the world, goods buried with the dead often include tools or their effigies, pertinent to each sex, such as weapons for men and pestles for women, symbolizing their separate realms of responsibility among the living. It is interesting, therefore, that among all the Ninnimissinouk grave sites known to archaeologists, those of the Narragansett from the early seventeenth century contained the most of such gender marking items. If the shift to greater concentration in corn-growing was altering the balance of power between men and women among the Narragansett, the greater emphasis on customary difference displayed by this funerary furniture suggests that the division of labor had become a source of tensions between them.[40]

The divisions between the sexes furnish vital clues to the marriage and kinship systems that underlay their political structures. Sachemships were composed of multiple lineages rooted in traditional territories. These larger and vaguer kin-based agglomerations organized themselves into what might be provisionally identified as clans. Body and facial tattoos described by the English, and archaeological recovery of animal figures incised on pebbles and rocks, may have been totemic symbols of clan membership.

Whether or not true clans existed among the Ninnimissinouk, larger groups of kinship affiliations certainly existed and were subsumed under the leadership of the sachem, who acted as a kind of uncle to all. Some were "great" sachems, overlords or great-uncles of other sachems. Sachems and their councils controlled territories and access to land within those territories. They may also have allocated hunting rights and fishing sites. In exchange for such "gifts," they expected shares in the harvests, catches of fish, and bags from the hunt. They also received labor services from their subjects in their corn fields.

The sachem symbolically embodied the group of which he was head. Deference and obligation formed a mutual relationship governed by the ideology of reciprocity. The infants were born indebted to their parents for their life and well-being. Children owed their parents love and loyalty, but they owed these things even more to one another. Brothers and sisters were responsible for guarding one another's honor and the honor of their parents.

Kin shared with one another and exchanged gifts on an ongoing basis. No one in the family must want so long as any member had what was required. Families were more important than individuals because families assumed the obligations of their members. Sons could not obtain brides without their families' help in negotiating with the brides' families and in donating the gifts that secured their consent.

Families also shared with others, observing rigorous rules of hospitality. Hosts courteously saw to the comfort of their guests and offered whatever food there was. The host's honor and the family's prestige rested on their ability to be generous and hospitable. Individuals gave feasts, and guests sang their praises. Wealth and food signaled abundance and well-being.

Making gifts and holding feasts constituted both a sharing of joy and an encompassing of the recipients within the community of families. Giving was also getting, however. The act of giving initiated an obligation on the part of the recipient to return the gift's value and more, if possible. In the meantime, the recipient remained a debtor under continuous duty to appear grateful and respectful. The proud man could no longer strut if his rival gave him more and better gifts.

The rules of reciprocity were truly coercive: not only must one pay back, but one was not free to decline a request. If someone asked for a nice-looking knife, the owner must give it freely and joyously. Failing to do so was a mark of bad manners and an ungenerous heart. The catch to this system of rewarding begging was that the recipient must be equally prepared to surrender the new toy.

Demanding and deference went hand in hand. The expectation that people who commanded others would respond to their petitions underpinned the legitimacy of hierarchy and authority among the Ninnimissinouk. Good leaders cared for their followers and were bountiful. They were beseeched to be their petitioner's advocate in disputes with others, to intercede on their behalf. The exercise of influence reinforced one's reputation as a good man who could get things done. *Being* big was being *big*.

The surprise is that apparently anyone could beg without losing face. The Narragansett sachem Canonicus freely and frequently begged sugar from his English friends. Roger Williams would write on his behalf to John Winthrop in Boston, arguing that making such gifts was crucial to keeping good relations between them. This habit of asking for things, and of showing up uninvited at people's houses expecting to be entertained, annoyed the English sense of propriety. The failure of the English to reciprocate with appropriate gestures of largesse marked them, so far as the Ninnimissinouk were concerned, as shirkers, ill-mannered ingrates, selfish, and therefore unreliable.

The religious ideas and ceremonies of the native peoples in southern New England never received the kind of close, sustained study that the French missionaries applied to the Algonquian, Huron, and Five Nations Iroquois. Roger Williams' *A Key into the Language of America* supplies most of what we know. He traded with Algonquians north of Salem while living there, then lived with the Pokanoket in the winter after he eluded his impending deportation. He negotiated for land at Providence with the elder sachem of the Narragansett, Canonicus, and became their interpreter and advocate with the United Colonies. Williams also set up a trading post on the western edge of Narragansett Bay and gradually became well acquainted with these peo-ple and their customs. He especially admired Canonicus' intelligence and leadership abilities. Williams found Native Americans and their customs fas-cinating and genuinely liked them, but he was first and foremost an ardent Christian, deeply steeped in the Bible. As a seventeenth-century intellec-tual, he was also a close student of millenarian ideas and something of a mystic. He had no question that the evil that Christians personified as the devil ruled Native American minds and religious practices. Fear of encoun-tering Satan kept him from attending their rituals in person, and Reformed Protestant theological ideas barred Williams from calling upon any magical protection.[41]

As a consequence of Williams' avoidance of key Narragansett rites, mod-ern scholars must work around significant gaps in the available information to glimpse elements of Ninnimissinouk cosmology. Anthropologists such as William Simmons and Kathleen Bragdon have placed clues from Williams himself, and from writers such as Edward Winslow, William Wood, and Daniel Gookin, in a broad ethnographic context in order to reconstruct their underlying order.[42] Ninnimissinouk religion was spirit-centered rather than deistic or personified, so they did not erect images or build temples. The fun-damental tenet of this cosmology was the belief that a divine force, Manitou, permeated the universe and everything in it. This force was neither uni-formly distributed nor always benign.

Manitou was impersonal and autonomous, but it could be accessed and its powers utilized for human purposes in a variety of ways. Learning how to call up and manipulate Manitou was the object of secret, private, intensive practice. Only a gifted few could hope to employ Manitou powers to harm or influence others, to heal the sick, protect the vulnerable, or foresee the future.

The Ninnimissinouk believed that nature observed the rules of reciprocity. The natural world was composed of manifold animate agencies with which humans conducted exchanges and observed proprieties by using deference and acting the role of humble petitioners. Every animal, bird, place, and tree apparently had its spirit, and each species had a master spirit that directed their actions. These spirits and others that were active in human affairs required respectful acknowledgment and small gifts. In return, they were morally bound to share with humans.[43]

In response to European questions, some groups did identify a great spirit—Catantouwit among the Narragansett—who lived to the southwest and presided over an afterworld to which most people were destined to go. In early seventeenth-century Narragansett cemeteries bodies were buried in a flexed position with their heads pointing in that direction and were accompanied by relatively few funeral goods of mixed origins. Later, postcontact graves had substantially more in the way of goods, which were of decidedly eclectic derivation. Narragansett and Pokanoket stoutly resisted Christian missionary efforts, but their weaker, less numerous neighbors, such as the Nauset, Massachusetts, and Nipmuck, proved more amenable to the preaching of the English evangelicals. Christian burials among these peoples show a great mixing of funerary goods and styles, but the bodies were neither flexed nor headed in a southwesterly direction. Hence it seems likely that this mode of positioning the body among traditional, non-Christian peoples was religiously motivated and, among the Narragansett, associated with Catantouwit.

Funerary practices of the precontact Ninnimissinouk actually trace a long history of change, from community ossuaries, to unadorned individual burials in shallow cavities located near camp sites, to community cemeteries of individual graves containing well-adorned bodies accompanied by grave goods. Whereas earlier burials exhibit little distinctiveness or attention to social rank, those from the middle of the seventeenth century display the greatest degrees of such differentiation and include quite a few European goods such as glass beads and metalware.[44] Particularly striking are graves of children and adolescents, who were accompanied by the most valuable of all the objects found in the cemetery.

This rather bald outline of the historical changes in Ninnimissinouk mortuary practices suggests that their lifeways and social structures had undergone a long-term evolution from a relatively simple, communal, and egalitarian society composed of mobile hunter-gatherers to a less mobile, more territory-based, hierarchically organized society that then evolved further into one even more marked by distinctions of rank and in which, perhaps, the nuclear family had superseded ties to lineage and clan. The presence of ostentatious burial goods for children of affluent families in the decades after contact further suggests that social rivalries among the living had heated up to an unprecedented degree.

What the people themselves were thinking cannot be known, and scholarly interpretations are not much more than knowledgeable hypotheses offered for consideration in an ongoing discourse.[45] When, however, one sets the changes in funerary practices in the context of long-term economic development, their evidence of increasing social complexity appears causally associated with population growth and ecological pressures. They not only had preceded the arrival of European goods, but had long preceded the Europeans themselves. Contact and trade, therefore, seem merely to have turned up the heat under an already simmering pot of political rivalries, social competition, and tensions between the sexes. It is true that the ethnicizing of group loyalties would eventually follow the Westernizing of material culture. The Narragansetts, however, would triumphantly remain Narragansett for centuries to come. Moreover, they parlayed their geographic situation into decades of strong diplomacy in the contest unfolding in southern New England.

2

Newcomers

But some will say, what right have I to go live in the heathens' country? This then is a sufficient reason to prove our going thither to live lawful: their land is spacious and void, and there are few and do but run over the grass, as do also the foxes and wild beasts. They are not industrious, neither have they art, science, skill, or faculty to use either the land or the commodities of it, but all spoils, rots, and is marred for want of manuring, gathering, ordering, etc.

—"R. C." [Robert Cushman], *Mourt's Relation*

The first Europeans to visit the southern coast of New England were explorers like Giovanni da Verrazano, many of whom, including Verrazano himself, did not hesitate to kidnap a few natives as souvenirs to take home. Then came fishermen and mariners looking for furs and other commodities for trade. They offered the coastal peoples metal, jewelry, and cloth—knives and kettles, hatchets and fish hooks, blankets, fancy jackets, and glass beads. They also left behind less visible souvenirs of their visits: germs capable of wreaking terrible havoc among a populace never before exposed to the common contagions of Europe.

One such visitation hit southeastern New England in 1616 with so devastating an impact that other diseases piggybacked on them to overcome already weakened victims. English visitor Thomas Dermer in 1619 reported: "I passed alongst the Coast where I found some antient Plantations, not long since populous now utterly void; in other places a remnant remaines, but not free of sicknesse. Their disease the Plague, for wee might perceive the sores of some that had escaped, who described the spots of such as usually die." Daniel Gookin, writing many years later about this epidemic, reported: "Some old Indians, that were then youths . . . say that the bodies all over were exceeding yellow, describing it by a yellow garment they showed me, both before they died, and afterwards." Such reports have drawn the attention of modern medical scholars who debate diagnoses.[1]

Whatever the exact identity of the disease organisms, these epidemics scythed through the native population along the Atlantic coast of New England from the Merrimac River in the north to Cape Cod in the south, and from the coast overland to the shores of Narragansett Bay. Patuxets simply disappeared, and the Massachusetts declined to less than one-tenth of their former numbers. The first documented visitation of the region by smallpox came with immigrants in 1633, finishing off most of the rest of the Massachusetts. The pestilence reached far inland, extending into the countries of the Narragansetts, the Pequots, and the Connecticut River Valley tribes. It followed old trade routes to poison the populations living in the St. Lawrence, Richelieu, Hudson, and Mohawk Valleys and along the lower Great Lakes, to the country of the Iroquois and the Huron in upper New York and Ontario.[2]

The English coming to New England in the 1620s and 1630s with the intent to settle found a human wasteland where grieving survivors were unable to bury all their dead. Both the Pilgrims and the Puritans were convinced that God had deliberately sent these plagues among the heathen to clear a place for themselves.[3]

The Ninnimissinouk must often have wondered how it was that they should sicken and die while less fit outsiders flourished. One group, however, escaped with minimal losses and became convinced that faithful performance of sacred rituals had given them spiritual protection while their enemies were being punished for their sloth. These were the Narragansetts, the extensive, loosely organized confederacy living west of the bay that bears their name. They had escaped the killer epidemics of 1616–1619 and were only lightly affected by the smallpox epidemic of 1633. Curious about the outlandish foreigners arriving on their shores, they pressed their new neighbor Roger Williams to explain English motives for settling so far from their own country. Since they themselves were accustomed to shifting their habitations, several suggested, only half in jest, that the English must have run out of firewood back home. Williams laughed at the idea, but their guess was a good one. England's population was indeed outstripping its available resources, including its trees, but material incentives alone did not suffice for an answer. Williams struggled to explain how it was that Christians of the same nation were willing to fight one another over the meanings of their shared religion.[4]

The people whom history calls the Pilgrims, for instance, worshipped separately from England's spiritually flaccid national church and had fled to

Amsterdam in 1606 to escape the wrath of ecclesiastical authorities. From Amsterdam they had moved to Leiden, and from there, ten years later, they began negotiating with the group in London that held royal patents to New England. These English refugees worried that Dutch materialism and their toleration of dangerous religious ideas were endangering their children's commitment to the purity of their church. Concerned parents feared to stay on in Holland, and for the same reasons they did not want to live in a Dutch colony in the New World. Moving to English territory overseas with the permission if not the blessing of the bishops would solve the problem: they would be free to raise their children in the pure faith without corrupting influences threatening them from all sides.

After numerous setbacks, the overloaded vessel carrying a few "saints" from Leiden and many strangers from England began its crossing in the late autumn of 1620, a dangerous time in the north Atlantic. John Howland was an indentured servant on board the *Mayflower*, "a lusty younge man," as William Bradford termed him, who ventured out on deck during a severe storm. He was washed overboard as the ship wallowed amid the huge waves whipped up by the winds. In Bradford's words, "It pleased God that he caught hold of the topsail halyards which hung overboard and ran out at length. Yet he held his hold (though he was sundry fathoms under water) till he was hauled up by the same rope to the brim of the water, and then with a boat hook and other means got into the ship again and his life saved."[5]

On November 9, 1620, Captain Christopher Jones sighted Cape Cod, which he recognized from accounts by John Smith and other previous visitors. Contrary winds prevented them from getting around the Cape. William Bradford's history and a description of Plymouth Plantation published in London in 1622 describe the dangerous shoals and rocks of Monomoy Point. Given the lateness of the season, they wisely backed off and anchored in Cape Cod Bay, sending scouting parties ashore to find a good site for the winter.

Locating such a site proved unexpectedly difficult: the Cape was sandy, windblown, and with scanty supplies of fresh water. Moreover, the people living there—the Nauset—clearly didn't want them. After locating Plymouth harbor to the north and exploring the abandoned Patuxet village and fields adjacent, a few of the passengers at last went ashore. There, on Christmas Day, they commenced building their first habitation.[6]

Although all but one had survived the long and difficult passage from

England, half of the *Mayflower* passengers were to die in the months ahead, not from hunger or a hard winter, but from scurvy and exposure. Wading through cold waters in the icy wind between shore and boat at Cape Cod had so deeply chilled the bodies of many that they never recovered from the shock. Scurvy may have killed even more. Had they understood the serious vitamin deficiencies in their food supplies, especially of vitamin C, they could have avoided it. Scurvy imparts a deep lassitude long before the complete exhaustion and death that is brought about by internal hemorrhaging of the soft tissues.[7]

They glimpsed only a few native people during the first few months after their arrival. One day in March, as they were out in their fields preparing them for planting, an Indian man emerged from the woods and spoke to them in English. It was Samoset, an Abenaki native of Maine who had learned the language from visiting fishermen. Although he did not say so at the time, he was reconnoitering on behalf of the Pokanoket sachem, Massasoit. He apparently found the prospects reassuring, for he soon returned to Plymouth to prepare them for Massasoit's arrival with his guard of honor and accompanied by the "last" of the Patuxet, Squanto. Squanto stayed on to help them and to provide a communications link with the Pokanoket.[8]

They would need help getting through the next few years, and would have been in dangerous straits had they not been able to buy corn from the Pokanoket. Massasoit hoped to make them a useful ally against his Narragansett enemies to the west and an aid in his navigation of the unsettled politics of the much-depleted peoples living around Massachusetts Bay. The handful of English at Plymouth, even after additional people arrived on the *Fortune* and later ships, posed no obvious threat to his interests.[9]

Massasoit was no better at reading the future than the rest of humankind. Plymouth, once built, would be capable of resisting anyone lacking long-range cannon. *Mourt's Relation* describes the laying out of the town along two sides of a single broad street ascending the hill above the bay. By the time the Dutch visitor Isaac de Rasieres saw the town in 1628, it contained a few hundred inhabitants with a cross street bisecting the community halfway up the hill. De Rasieres admired the well-built houses of hand-sawn planks covering the heavy timber frames, each with its neat, well-tended garden in the rear. At the intersection of the two streets stood a square stockade with four mounted mortars capable of firing along all four streets. Next to the stockade stood the governor's house. At the top of the hill sat the fort, a square structure with a flat roof on which were poised six cannon capable of sending balls out into the harbor below and the country behind. The lower part of this building was used as a meeting house. The entire settlement was enclosed by a tall, stout fence with gates at harborside and at each end of the cross street. Plymouth had made itself secure from Indian attack and would not be an easy target for casual raids from the sea.[10]

History books celebrate the Pilgrims for their sturdy courage, their simple faith, their democratic polity, and their peaceful relations with Massasoit's people. Seeking only to be left alone to worship God as the Bible directed, they had fled persecution at home only to encounter the sinful temptations of their worldly Dutch hosts, so they fled again, this time to a place far away. Although their story carries undeniable drama, the people themselves have elicited scant interest among leading scholars of the colonial period. C. M. Andrews observed from Yale in the 1930s:

> In their simplicity and humble-mindedness they had no other aim than to live decently and righteously and in accord with what they believed to be God's purpose in directing their course . . . They rejected some of the richest of human manifestations, in literature, art, music, and the drama, as in no way belonging to the world to come . . . Hence in all save his religious sincerity the Pilgrim never rose far above the ordinary round of daily toil and the meeting of the ends of material existence . . . away from the moving stream of American civilization.

To Andrews and others, the story of the Pilgrims provides a heart-warming narrative of America's beginnings, useful in countering the image of ignoble greed projected by Virginia's first planters, but one that warrants only a few pages on the way to the "Puritans."

The true meaning for history of this small settlement derives not from its failure to generate the wealth that would support the high arts prized by Andrews, but for its early conversion to the very "American" pursuit of private property in land. This was a drive that destroyed all chance for peaceful coexistence with the Ninnimissinouk, brought about a terrible war that ended in the enslavement of thousands, and turned hitherto ethnocentric English into confirmed racists. The virtues of the original Pilgrims were real enough, as were their struggles to make a living and pay off their debts, but the Separatists from Leiden were never in the majority even of their own company, on board the *Mayflower* or on shore. The Mayflower Compact, drafted before disembarking at Cape Cod, was signed by forty-one men; nineteen were from Leiden, sixteen were from London and environs, four were servants, and two were sailors. Nine did not sign, of whom all were servants except one, and probably all sick at the time. Ten years later, émigrés from the Leiden congregation made up no more than a quarter of all emigrants to the "Old Colony."[11] The majority of Plymouth's settlers, including many of the colony's leaders, were mainstream English.

Nor were they all the poor simple rustics described by Andrews. No one has yet sorted out the complicated international dealings of merchant Isaac Allerton, but Edward Winslow, another *Mayflower* passenger who later died in the service of Oliver Cromwell, surely ranks among the movers and shakers of the English world of his time. As for their presumed indifference to the things of this world, probate inventories show that before King Philip's War, Plymouth residents were no poorer and lived no more meanly than their Puritan neighbors. More of them, proportionately, owned books than was true of the residents of Boston, rural Suffolk, Essex, Hampshire, and Hartford Counties. Only the inventories of New Havenites among the probated decedents surveyed were more likely than Plymouth colonists to list books. Old soldier Miles Standish, himself no Pilgrim, possessed a considerable library, including Homer's *Iliad*.[12]

Historians' politely benevolent views of Plymouth necessarily rest heavily on the writings of its chief boosters: Edward Winslow, the anonymous authors of *Mourt's Relation*, Nathaniel Morton, and, most important, Governor William Bradford himself, whose lengthy historical memoir and surviving letters provide an insider's view of events. In his writings, Bradford sought to justify the Pilgrim leaders' every action and continually laments the colony's poverty and vulnerability. The modern reader takes note of Bradford's self-righteous defensiveness and hostility, even duplicity, toward all outsiders and critics, regardless of ethnic background. He and the others did not like "Indians," nor did they ever make any effort to understand them, even Massasoit, their neighbor and staunchest ally. Doughty Miles Standish, the professional soldier they hired as their military commander, seems to have taken Captain John Smith of Virginia fame for his role model, never trusting any "savage" and standing ever ready to make the first strike, postponing questions for later.

Separatists shaped their church and their government in forms little different from those the Puritans were later to build, and for these innovations one must candidly concede the strong creative role of their ideology. Their apprehensiveness toward their adopted land and its peoples, however, were if anything even stronger than those of other English settlers in the New World, regardless of religious persuasion. All practiced "separatism" from heathens, and all sought to extract profitable commodities from them and their land.[13]

Plymouth's self-imposed isolation, along with much of its cohesiveness, came to a crashing halt when the Winthrop fleet arrived in the early summer of 1630, bringing nearly 1,000 cash customers avid for Plymouth's cattle and corn. These potential customers for Plymouth farmers continued to arrive by the thousands for the rest of the decade. Looking back from 1653, Edward Johnson counted 198 ships that had left England for Massachusetts between 1630 and 1643, at a cost he estimated of 200,000 pounds sterling and carrying, he thought, some 20,000 people.[14] They made quite a market for those who had preceded them.

Important as these immigrants were to New England's history, their numbers pale in the larger context of England's mass exodus: close to 500,000 people left their home country between 1600 and 1700, mostly male and mostly young, some going to the Netherlands and Germany, a substantial number to Ireland, more than 100,000 to the Chesapeake, and well over 200,000 to the West Indies.[15] The peak period of emigration from England began in the late 1630s, when an estimated 11,000 to 12,000, on average, began taking ship every year for twenty-five years.[16] The coming of England's Civil War, which abruptly ended the emigration to New England, fueled an even greater outpouring to colonies in the more southern latitudes.

Not too surprisingly, the population of England fell substantially in the second half of the seventeenth century, but only three-fifths of the drop can be attributed to net outmigration. The rest of the decline came from a paucity of births resulting from postponed marriages and because a quarter of the adult population stayed single. The proportions never marrying among men and women in England began rising in the second half of the sixteenth century, from 55 per 1,000 born in 1561–1571, to a peak of 270 in the years 1636–1666. The English have not experienced such high ratios of never-married adults since that time.[17]

There seems little doubt that this pattern of heavy emigration and delayed or forgone marriages stemmed from a deep, long-term economic crisis that was further exacerbated by civil war and local unrest. Population and food prices had begun rising in the sixteenth century, forcing down real wages and putting ever greater pressure on the limited supply of agricultural land.[18] Landlords sought to raise productivity through enclosure of open fields, woodlands, and common "wastes," evicting tenants and small-holders. In sheep country, landowners illegally increased the size of their flocks at the expense of others. When developers cut down woods and drained swamps, they turned out cottagers and deprived poor people of resources on which they depended.[19]

This early stage of England's agricultural revolution, which in the long run raised productivity and lowered food prices, drove people off the land and created hunger and homelessness. The crimes and oppression committed by many "improvers" violated people's sense of justice and fairness, and when courts failed to control their trespasses, victims and sympathizers retaliated. Criminal acts committed by both sides in the unequal struggle undermined the mutual trust on which the old system had depended, vitiating the efforts of reformers and damaging morale.[20]

It seemed to many in England that God was punishing the nation for its sins. Plague repeatedly swept the country, then smallpox took its place as principal scourge. Harvests failed repeatedly from the 1580s through the 1660s. The 1590s and the 1620s were particularly brutal decades, with back-to-back harvest failures. Starving people in the countryside stole sheep, and ate dogs and rats if they could catch them. Malnourished people suffered from debilitating diseases like scurvy while employers blamed them for laziness.[21] Hard times evoked impulses among the "haves" to control the "have-nots," not only to protect property but to relieve their anxieties over losing it.[22]

For poor, struggling England, troubles came in crowds. Pirates infested the shipping lanes, and England's inglorious involvement in the Thirty Years' War swelled taxes and wounded national pride. The country's clothing manufacturers faced a long-term depression in their overseas markets during the early part of the seventeenth century, partly as a result of changing fashion and foreign competition but also as a result of governmental bungling and the disruptions of international wars. The broadcloth industry in Suffolk in East Anglia fell into terminal decline. Unsold cloth piled up in warehouses, putting whole families and entire communities out of work. When harvests failed three years in a row, in 1628–1630, many of the unemployed starved to death.

It is no wonder, then, that people of property saw England as over-crowded, burdened with too many poor who had nothing to do but make trouble. The answer was to put them to work, but since there were no jobs at home, why not ship them overseas, where they could feed themselves and find plenty of work? Richard Hakluyt the elder had laid it all out as early as 1584: colonies would make England rich and solve the unemployment problem. They would produce exotic goods in great demand in Europe, employ ships and merchants to transport and sell them, and the people living in the colonies would buy large amounts of English manufactures, boosting employment at home. Meanwhile hard-working emigrant laborers could save enough to buy their own land, employ their countrymen, and enrich themselves. One of the aims in Hakluyt's program included sending missionaries to the Indians, so Christians could feel good about making money while spreading the gospel and civilizing poor savages. This was a win-win plan—for the English.[23]

After several false starts, English emigration to the New World began in earnest early in the seventeenth century. The costs of colonizing the regions left open by Spain and Portugal proved too great even for wealthy individuals to carry out alone, as Raleigh had tried to do in Roanoke and Guiana, but the joint-stock company offered an institutional means for mobilizing large sums of capital and recruiting proven managers. The Virginia Company purchased Raleigh's patent to an enormous territory stretching from the Atlantic to the Mississippi, and won a charter from the king giving the company sole rights of government there as well as a monopoly of its trade. Of course, patents and charters were only pieces of paper, no matter how impressively embossed. It would be up to the colonists themselves to do the job.

The Company naturally hoped to make money quickly, but when that didn't pan out, they resorted to selling lottery tickets to the English public. Their marketing campaigns played simultaneously on patriotism and greed, not unlike modern state lotteries. The strategy sold well for a few years, but the Company eventually went down because of mismanagement and embezzlement by its own employees. Ironically, though, their pipe dream did go up in smoke: the production of tobacco leaves, dried and cured, produced a cheap, pleasant, and addictive narcotic. The English, the Dutch, the French, the Germans—all became consumers of Virginia tobacco. Virginia's economic success encouraged the Pilgrims to make their own Lilliputian effort as well as the much grander schemes that financed colonizing ventures to various Caribbean islands such as Barbados and Providence Island.[24]

Among the hundreds of thousands leaving England for the New World in the seventeenth century, those we call Puritans formed only a small minority, but they organized and participated in multiple colonizing and trading companies, and they went to all the colonies, south as well as north. At

Providence Island they formed the majority of the planters as well as the company directors.[25] Wherever they went, Puritans made deals, launched enterprises, started plantations. They scouted for dye woods, searched for salt, looked for mines. Those going to warm climes were prepared to raise whatever crops would sell well: tobacco, sugar, or cotton. Labor-intensive crops such as these required an enormous supply of English workers, given the heavy mortality rates and the brevity of their contracts. Whereas in England an adult farm worker normally hired out from year to year, such an arrangement could not work for overseas employers. A single year's earnings would not cover the costs of recruiting, feeding, and transporting employees from England, especially after absorbing the loss of their time during months of debilitating "seasoning." A laborer's death wiped out this investment, and modern studies suggest that no more than half of those going to the Chesapeake survived even five years.[26] Such a high death rate doubled the real cost of servant labor.

Given the costs and risks of acquiring and maintaining a sufficient supply of labor in the staple-producing colonies, it is not surprising that filling the demand became a lucrative business in itself, in which the workers signed contracts, known as indentures, stating the conditions under which they would work and the term of service. These contracts were then sold or auctioned to planters in the colonies, who regarded servants more as property than as fellow citizens.[27]

Despite the thousands of indentured servants emigrating abroad every year, especially during the Civil War and Interregnum, the supply proved inadequate to meet the demand, particularly in the rapidly expanding sugar colonies. From the planters' point of view, Africans enslaved for life provided a better source of labor. They cost at least twice as much up front but almost certainly outlasted the average Englishman, who was not only malnourished but also entirely lacking in genetic or acquired immunities against warm winter diseases, and who would soon be freed. Africans possessed other advantages: there were many more of them, and their ethnic diversity and mutually unintelligible languages made them easier to control and to capture if they ran away. Moreover, their status as heathens set them apart from Christian servants, readily persuading many planters that they need not extend to them the rights claimed by Englishmen.[28] Puritan colonists, along with the other English, bought, used, and abused African slaves. Puritans of Providence Island, in fact, began systematically importing them in the 1630s, before those on Barbados did so. And when the Providence Island planters became apprehensive of Spanish attack, they did not hesitate to sell them away rather than lose their investments. Among the first to go were a group taken back to New England by Captain William Peirce, who had brought a cargo of Pequot captives (Ninnimissinouk from Connecticut) for sale on the island.[29]

None of the lucrative warm-climate crops would flourish in the northern latitudes where New England lies: this much became clear in the accounts appearing after 1620. Yet of the thousands of propertied families who joined the floods of emigrants from England, by far the great majority chose to go to New England instead of to Ireland, the Netherlands, Virginia, or the West Indies. Indeed, the demographic makeup of the those moving to New England contrasted sharply with those going elsewhere. The majority of both free and unfree immigrants to southern climes were male: the ratio among those going to the Chesapeake was six males to each female in the early years, gradually easing to a slightly better-balanced three to one in later decades. The sex ratio among immigrants to New England was more like three to two; in fact women and children together outnumbered the men. In the Chesapeake, a small minority of colonists paid the costs of economic development in order to benefit from the labor of the majority. More than three-quarters of newcomers arrived there as servants, whose fare and keep were the responsibility of the planters who purchased their time. Most of the people going to New England paid not only their own way but those of their dependents, as well.[30] Moreover, free immigrants had to bear freight charges on the supplies of tools, wearing apparel, and bedding to last them until their first crops came in, and in the meantime they spent money for food and shelter. A family man who proposed to move to New England required substantial financial resources to do so, something most of England's people simply did not have.

How did these families expect to make a living in New England? The region's only known commercial attraction was its proximity to some of the world's finest fishing grounds.[31] Individual entrepreneurs and joint-stock companies, including Plymouth's, had made a number of efforts to plant colonies on the coast for the specific purpose of exploiting that proximity. The Massachusetts Bay Company, in seeking a charter from the government, explained that it, too, intended to try fishing. If one is to judge from their previous occupations, however, those going over in the 1630s had no intention of fishing for a living themselves. Indeed, very few of the men who settled New England had any maritime experience in the north Atlantic. Among

those whose occupations are known, 11 percent were involved with ma-
rine-related work in the 1620s, 10 percent in the early 1630s, and only one
percent in the late 1630s. Nor were there many capable of building boats for
the purpose. Immigrant leaders might hope to provision a fleet once somebody else built it and manned it, but they vastly underestimated the resources and experienced manpower required to create a flourishing fishing
industry. At the same time, they overestimated New England's agricultural
potential, swayed by the optimistic reports of summertime visitors such as
Captain John Smith. After a few winters' residence, they undoubtedly modified their expectations. However, newcomers continued coming over each
year by the thousands, bringing with them money, tools, and textiles to exchange for food, shelter, and livestock. Their demand put local prices at levels that were fabulous by old-country standards, so the earliest settlers were
in fact becoming rich. Colonizing New England worked like a Ponzi scheme:
so long as sufficient numbers of newcomers arrived every year prepared to
spend, the English already there would sell and prosper.

Because most did stay, and because the majority ended up on small fam-
ily-operated farms, historians have understandably inferred that the settlers
had intended things to be that way. By going to New England, after all, they
were *choosing* not to go to Virginia or the Caribbean. Ergo, they were spurn-
ing plantation societies. Moreover, their letters said that they did not want
crowds of irreligious young male servants roistering about, swearing and
blaspheming, and abusing the sabbath. Like the Pilgrims, according to this
interpretation, the immigrants to Massachusetts of "Puritan" persuasion
would be content to work hard and live frugally. Their paramount concerns
were religious, corporate, and deeply traditional.

Such reasoning attributes intentionality to the newcomers for what in fact
came later. Not only does it assume that they achieved that for which they
had crossed an ocean, but it denies the possibility of discovery, experimentation, and adaptation. In fact, whatever moved them to leave England, they
had to alter their sights after arriving in a place so un-English. The virtues
attributed to them—frugality, hard work, and minimizing (not avoiding)
risk—were fundamental to successful pioneering, but so are such qualities
as adaptability and a willingness to learn from one's surroundings. The goal
of establishing a more God-centered, God-fearing society did not compete
with the practical concerns of making a living and getting ahead.

Religion did play a formative role in the English settlement of New England, just as it did in Catholic Maryland and Quaker Pennsylvania; however,
the economic outcomes were in each case the result of English adaptation to

local environmental resources and constraints. That the leaders of the Massachusetts Bay Company intended to create a holy commonwealth is well established, but the same was also true of the Puritan leaders of the Providence Island Company. That the latter failed, wiped out by a Spanish squadron in 1641, and the former flourished had nothing to do with the quality of their Puritanism.[32]

Though heavily influenced by continental theologians, particularly John Calvin, Reformed Protestantism in England followed a distinctive historical path. It grew out of the frustrations engendered by a stalled reform movement. The word "Puritan" was itself a sneering pejorative applied by conservatives to their political opponents; hence there is no necessary consistency in the application of the term, nor did Puritans apply it to themselves as a distinguishing term. Moreover, the movement evolved over time, and "Puritanism" evolved with it. Those who came to New England in the 1630s, therefore, did not share a well-defined ideology, nor was there a common commitment to a single ecclesiastical program.[33] It seems safe to say only that most immigrant heads of households were dissatisfied with the Church of England, were distressed over the moral laxity of English society, and were hungering for a more rewarding spiritualism for themselves and their children.

Since the English, especially in the southeastern part of the country, were in the throes of early capitalist development, Puritan discipline effectively combined with an already active orientation toward viewing the natural world and its nonhuman inhabitants as mere commodities to be bought and sold. This potent combination stimulated not only private accumulation but active search for the productive reinvestment of one's capital, the *sine qua non* of real economic growth.[34]

Historians know tantalizingly little about the Puritan movement among laymen. They have no idea of their numbers, nor can they identify more than a few conventicles. Members did not talk about their activities in public and wrote sparingly, often in code, in order to evade detection by ecclesiastical spies. Yet it seems probable that the founders of the Massachusetts Bay Company organized the first stage of the migration to New England by means of a network of Puritan laymen, helped by the "Spiritual Brotherhood" of Puritan ministers.[35] Historians believe that the geographic heart of the movement lay in the southeastern triangle of England, home to a large proportion of the country's cloth manufacturers and the most populous, literate, "urbanized," and technologically advanced region of the country. One of the strongest clues to the social and religious identity and possible motivations of the immigrants to New England, therefore, lies in where they came from and what they did for a living. Passenger lists of ships sailing for the New World offer one means for exploring these issues, although few authentic ones survive. Most in print are reconstructed from other sources using methods that are unclear and often unacceptably freewheeling. Many scholars, for instance, have relied on Charles Banks' *Winthrop Fleet of 1630* because it is so comprehensive in scope, believing that errors would somehow cancel each other out.[36]

A more comprehensive route to identifying the immigrants to New England is that taken recently by Robert Anderson, who has surveyed a wide array of sources in order to identify everyone arriving in New England during the years 1620 through 1633, an enormous but manageable project that yielded the names of more than 900 individuals who came over alone, as servants, or with dependents. He then traced these people through secondary sources, particularly genealogies, to find out where they came from and what happened to them. He also supplies information on their children, when and where they were born, whether they survived to adulthood and married and where. There are many holes and palpable biases in the resulting data, but it is, nevertheless, the richest single resource on the people who colonized early New England.

Table 1 supplies an overview of the geographic origins of the early comers arriving before 1634 surveyed by Robert Anderson.[37] Anderson could not identify the origins of more than three-fifths of the individuals in his file. Of those whose county of residence he did discover, two-thirds came from the southeastern triangle—East Anglia (Cambridgeshire, Norfolk, and Suffolk), eastern Essex and the counties of the southeast (Kent, Surrey, and Sussex), and the West Country (Devon, Somerset, and Dorset). Another quarter included (forty-three) Londoners and (thirty-one) Pilgrims and their fellow congregants from the Netherlands, some of whom were originally from Yorkshire. There was no significant difference in the regional origins of those who came before the Winthrop fleet of 1630 and those who came in 1630–1633.

Although Virginia Anderson does not provide a regional breakdown of those identified as passengers on the seven ships in her sample, she does note that out of 590 whose English residences were recorded, 364 (62 percent) came from market towns, 200 of them from sizable towns of 3,000 or more.[38] Table 2 shows the status and occupations, where known, of male immigrants age fifteen and above based on the two samples described above:

Table 1 Regional origins of immigrants to New England, 1620–1633
(N = 409)

Region	Percent
North, Northwest	2.4
West, Southwest	21.8
Midlands, Central	17.4
Southeast	40.3
London	10.5
Netherlands	7.6

Note: North, Northwest = Lancaster (3), York (6), Cheshire (1); West, Southwest = Shropshire (3), Gloucester (2), Devon (18), Somerset (24), Dorset (27), Wiltshire (3), Berkshire (1), Hampshire (7), Warwick (4); Midlands, Central = Worcester (7), Nottingham (4), Leicester (5), Lincoln (26), Northampton (4), Oxford (1), Buckingham (1), Hertford (11), Bedford (8), Derby (2); Southeast = Norfolk (14), Suffolk (54), Essex (55), Kent (15), Surrey (16), Sussex (1), Cambridge (6), Middlesex (2), Huntingdon (2); London = 43; Netherlands = 31.

Source: Robert Charles Anderson, *The Great Migration Begins: Immigrants to New England, 1620–1633*, 3 vols. (Boston: New England Genealogical Historical Society, 1995).

Table 2 Occupations of male immigrants, age 15+, to New England, 1620–1638 (%)

Occupation	1620–1629 % (N = 94)	1630–1633 % (N = 300)	1635–1638 % (N = 219)
Gentry	13	16	0
Professions	12	8	2
Commerce	26	20	1
Marine	11	10	1
Cloth manufacturing	5	7	16
Other manufacturing	19	27	21
Agriculture	4	5	22
Servant	10	8	37

Sources: Robert Charles Anderson, *The Great Migration Begins: Immigrants to New England, 1620–1633*, 3 vols. (Boston: New England Genealogical Historical Society, 1995); Virginia DeJohn Anderson, *New England's Generation: The Great Migration and the Formation of Society and Culture in the Seventeenth Century* (Cambridge: Cambridge University Press, 1991), p. 224.

those found arriving before 1634 according to documents on this side of the water and passengers on seven ships sailing in 1635–1638.

When placed in comparative perspective, the outstanding common characteristic of men immigrating to New England is the small proportion of servants.[39] Among those going to the Chesapeake, as shown in Table 3, servants outnumbered free emigrants by three or four to one, whereas among those heading to the northern region, free men outnumbered servants by ten to one in the early list and a bit less than three to one in the later list.

If we look just at the free adult male immigrants to the two regions, however, New England looks less different. The greatest revelation is that artisans moved in large numbers to both colonies as both free and indentured immigrants. Fewer gentry and more maritime-oriented men went to the northern destination, but neither region attracted many free emigrants from England's agricultural sector. Those engaged in farming who could afford to go were those who had rights or freeholds in land, yet these were precisely the people who had the most stake in staying. Given the probable occupational structure in England, one may infer from all these lists that agricultural workers, as a rule, were less likely to emigrate in proportion to their numbers than were those working in manufacturing. The degree of their attraction to the tobacco-growing colonies is more a measure of their economic straits at home than of any predisposition as a class to the Puritan cause.

Table 3   Occupations of free adult male immigrants to New England (1620–1633) and the Chesapeake (1607–1699) (%)

Occupation	New England (N = 361)	Chesapeake (N = 431)
Gentry	16	31
Professions	10	8
Commerce	24	28
Marine	11	4
Cloth manufacturing	7	10
Other manufacturing	28	16
Agriculture	5	3

Sources: Robert Charles Anderson, *The Great Migration Begins: Immigrants to New England, 1620–1633*, 3 vols. (Boston: New England Genealogical Historical Society, 1995); James Horn, *Adapting to a New World: English Society in the Seventeenth-Century Chesapeake* (Chapel Hill: University of North Carolina Press, 1994), p. 27.

The two New England migration lists in Table 2 reveal striking differences, partly attributable to the retrospective nature of the reconstructed list, for whom occupational identity prior to first appearance in New England records can be elusive, but also partly attributable to time-related changes in the composition of the migration itself. The later immigrants were older and included proportionately more females. More of them were associated with the cloth trades and farming, and fewer were merchants and seamen. If all the servants on the second list were in agriculture, as is probable, that category would rise to 58 percent, an even greater proportion than among the Bristol servants.

Changes in the composition of migration before and after 1633 presumably reflect corresponding alterations in the nature of the forces in England propelling it. In the late 1620s the calamities hitting the country were physical, stark, and immediate—a string of harvest failures, gross unemployment and starvation in the cloth trades, and, for the reform-minded elites, the dissolution of Parliament. The immediacy of the economic crisis faded when harvests improved, but a new political threat against Puritans emerged with the advent of their archenemy, William Laud, first to the bishopric of London, then to the episcopal see of Canterbury, the highest office in the Church of England. Laud belonged to a small band of clerics who disliked Calvinism and adopted Arminianism as a theologically respectable alternative. Charles I's Catholic sympathies and belief in the divine right of kings led him to favor this group as a means of stalling or reversing the course of the Reformation in England. The Arminians launched a campaign to restore church ritual and adornments, cut back on preaching, restore the Book of Common Prayer to its central place in the liturgy, and reissue the Book of Sports, which encouraged sports on Sundays after services, anathema to those anxious to protect the sabbath from sacrilege. Laud aggressively enforced conformity in order to flush out his ideological enemies, the subversives who, by flouting constituted authority, would further undermine his own. It seems reasonable to speculate that rising persecution in England stimulated many Puritan families to leave who would not otherwise have taken so drastic a step.[40]

No one denies the importance of religious persecution or of deepening despair over the declining state of church and country as powerful incentives for emigration in the Laudian period, 1634–1641, but many historians assert the concurrent importance of economic motives.[41] The occupations of immigrants provide some clues to assessing the competing degrees of importance of these two sets of motives. If depression in the cloth trade, for instance, was the immediate motive for weavers and others to debark, more should have appeared on the list of earlier immigrants than on the later one, but the contrary is true: their proportions were reversed, 5 percent then 16 percent. Furthermore, the decline in the relative numbers of risk-taking merchants and seamen suggests they were finding more exciting opportunities in the rapidly expanding West Indies. This changing composition of emigrants to New England suggests a shift in the balance of the mix of motives, from more economic and less ideological in the period before 1635 to more ideological and less economic in the period afterward.

There is still another dimension to emigrant character, beyond the simple dualism of presumably competing motives, and that is the personality and temperament of those who endured the early privations and did not return to England. These were the true "Builders of the Bay Colony," insofar as they created a workable polity and demonstrated the feasibility of the enterprise to the more cautious folk back home. Those arriving later had not participated in the creation and so had to accept or reject what they found. With each year's arriving passengers, it would become more difficult to reverse the direction of the colony.[42]

The alterations in the social origins of immigrants visible in Table 2 can also be read as lending support to Stephen Foster's argument about the ongoing evolution of English Puritanism as a movement: that the people who came earlier had exited from a stream whose course continued through a changing landscape. The sudden ascendancy of the Laudians publicly polarized the contestants, politicizing religious priorities for many. Men who conscientiously but quietly opposed the Laudian reforms were forced out of the closet, so to speak, and this experience jolted their accustomed deference to constituted authority. People whose primary reason for selling all they had and pulling up stakes was religious in nature would, one suspects, be *more* inclined to guard their freedom of conscience and therefore be less trusting of ministers and magistrates than those who had preceded them to New England. Whether newcomers after 1633 actively exacerbated tensions between individualism and corporatism already present in New England politics or simply responded to them remains an open question.

The writings of individual ministers who chose to emigrate throws considerable light on their reasons for doing so, as do the works and correspondence of Massachusetts Governor John Winthrop. Although all emphasize the opportunity to live under God's ordinances and the greater freedom from sinful temptations, their writings also premise the capability of New England to sustain them and their children in an *English* life-style. No one wanted to surrender a material standard of living that literally defined Christian civilization. No Puritan wanted to live as the natives did. Winthrop and other leaders were not fools: they knew that the colony was subsisting on immigrants' capital, but they had no reason to believe the immigrants would suddenly cease coming. Moreover, they placed their trust in quickly finding the "means," such as fishing, that would earn the sterling credits necessary to keep supplies coming from England. Meanwhile they intended to live in English style houses, not wigwams, to sit on chairs (or benches, stools, and trunks) and not on floor mats, to use metal tools and utensils and not stone-age implements, to sleep on sheets and mattresses, not bear rugs, and to wear body-covering suits and gowns made of the familiar woven textiles of England. (Ninnimissinouk went naked.)[43] Passengers brought cows and goats for dairying, swine for meat, and horses to ride. They brought seeds of herbs and "salats," including dandelions, to the everlasting sorrow of lawnkeepers. They planned to make their bread of wheat and to grow barley and hops for beer. They brought apple seeds and honey bees. Those who could afford servants brought them to do the hard physical work. They would make it a new England, a better England, and they invested their lives and fortunes in the process.

What may prove of greater interest to the history of New England, and of America, than the emigrants' initial motives for leaving is what they did after they got there. They reproduced at a mighty pace and forged a work culture oriented toward investing for future returns. They created an economic and demographic juggernaut that, by the time of the American Revolution, had created a "world of fields and fences" in place of the forests, deer parks, and hamlets of the Ninnimissinouk whom they supplanted. And in their dealings with Indians, few sincerely hewed to the first three protocols of Roger Williams' sound advice: "First kisse Truth where . . . your soule see it: 2 Advance Justice, though upon a childs eye: 3 Seeke and make peace if possible with all men 4 Secure Your owne Life from a revengefull malicious Arrow or hatchet."[44]

3

Taking the Land

God hathe hereby cleered our title to this place.

—John Winthrop, *Winthrop Papers*

The economic problems facing immigrants to New England were twofold: the local supply of land suitable for plowing was usually insufficient to support the desired density of inhabitants, that is, enough people living close together to be able to defend themselves against attack and to support a college-educated minister. The second problem was keeping their animals alive through the long winter. European cattle needed vast amounts of good grass to sustain them. Natural meadows scarcely existed in New England, and the native grasses supplied more bulk than nourishment. Hay made from these grasses was scarcely worth the labor required. Livestock struggled every year to survive the four or five months without fresh provender. The tidal salt marshes fringing estuaries became the most highly prized acreages in the region because the grasses there were more nutritious, began growing earliest in the spring, and ceased growing latest in the fall. Salt hay was worth three times as much as fresh.[1]

The first priority in 1621 and 1630, however, was getting newly arriving humans onto the land quickly so that they could build shelters for winter and start growing food crops. Hence settlement of the first English "towns" in the Bay Colony appears to have proceeded rather haphazardly; surviving records provide little insight into the actual process. Plymouth's experiences were described retrospectively by William Bradford, Edward Winslow, and Nathaniel Morton.[2] The Pilgrim leaders settled at Plymouth because it had fresh water, a good harbor, albeit too shallow for really big ships, a defensible hillside site, and old Ninnimissinouk fields ready to plant in the spring. Defense was a major priority. New France, for instance, might send a gunboat to challenge an English settlement, and there were sufficient numbers of native survivors in Massachusetts Bay, on Cape Cod, and to the west to pose a threat to security.

The expectation had been that the men of Plymouth would fish as well as farm, since all the explorers' accounts had described the abundance of fish and the ease of catching them. The century-long success of the Newfoundland fisheries, carried out in summertime by large, well-manned boats from European ports, attested to the reliability of this resource. To succeed at the business in Plymouth, the Pilgrims needed capital to buy the ship and equipment and to provision the crew and, most important, vast quantities of salt to preserve the catch for transport to European markets. The Pilgrims had no salt, no seines, no experience, and but one small boat. Their first efforts were calamitous, and they soon turned to trading for furs with natives at Kennebec. Furs yielded a far more valuable commodity than fish, pound for pound, and required neither labor nor salt. The would-be trader had only to present attractive wares to his Native American customers. For these, the Plymouth colonists sent Isaac Allerton, an experienced merchant, to England to buy an assortment of trade goods and to sell furs on their behalf. Allerton somehow managed to lose money for them while making money for himself, or so Governor Bradford complained.³

The fur trade began paying off after the Dutch told them about wampum, and with the proceeds the Pilgrims bought out their creditors. Meanwhile the majority of the people at Plymouth concentrated on the number-one priority facing them: feeding themselves. This they learned to do, gradually weaning themselves from dependency on Massasoit's people and building up surpluses to trade at their Kennebec post along with wampum, in exchange for furs.

But Plymouth could not feed or nurse the thousands who in 1629 began coming to settle in the Bay. The original plan of the Massachusetts Bay Company was to put everyone onto a single, large, fortified site, as at Plymouth, with planting fields close by and meadows at the outskirts. Neither Governor John Winthrop nor Lieutenant Governor Thomas Dudley liked Salem for this purpose, nor were they entirely satisfied with an alternative site at Charlestown. Nevertheless, they forced the passengers to walk overland from Salem in the July heat to crowd together on a peninsula between the Mystic and Charles Rivers, where they remained until the leaders could make up their minds. The colonists soon began to suffer from scurvy and dysentery, and the situation threatened to deteriorate into another James-town fiasco. When rumors circulated that the French were about to attack, the frightened leaders quickly dispersed the colonists, undoubtedly saving lives and possibly the enterprise itself.

As the 1630 immigrants fled the sickly tent town on the Charles, they sought out cleared fields along the ocean littoral and inland along the Charles and Mystic Rivers. There were many abandoned sites available. Most of the hundred or so surviving Massachusett welcomed the English, regarding them as a source of protection against their predatory neighbors.

How the other Ninnimissinouk perceived English purposes is less clear. None had challenged the presence of the English at Plymouth, because the few survivors of the epidemic had fled westward to take refuge with Massasoit. Although Chickataubet of Naponset, north of Plymouth, felt secure enough to continue to live on the coast, two Massachusett sagamores, brothers called "John" and "James" by the English, had actively sought settlers in their area to help screen their people from the "Tarrantines." These raiders were probably Micmac from the Gaspé Peninsula who, one day in 1633, fearlessly swooped in to surprise the Massachusett and murdered several in their own homes.[4] It was easy, therefore, for the English to regard themselves as protectors and guardians of "their" Indians, and when smallpox hit later that year, they nursed the native victims as tenderly as their own. Thus, in the first years of the English occupation, the native occupants of the land were too few and too precariously situated to do anything but make the best of the situation. No one on either side could have predicted that the 400 or 500 English households then in eastern New England would soon increase by many thousands. Neither could any have anticipated how quickly they would fan out to occupy the harbors, estuaries, offshore islands, and river valleys of southern New England.

Nor could anyone have predicted the devastation that would visit the Ninnimissinouk when smallpox first hit the Northeast in 1633.[5] Governor Winthrop reported in a letter to England a year later how "the greatest part of them," over an area of 300 miles, "had been swept away by the small pox," which was then still raging among them. Particularly hard hit were the villages of the Connecticut River Valley. Those remaining "have put themselves under our protection." Winthrop declared that "God hathe hereby cleered our title to this place." In answer to Roger Williams' argument that the English had no just claim to the land, he asked: "if God were not pleased with our inheriting these parts, why did he drive out the natives before us? and why dothe he still make roome for us, by deminishinge them as we increase?"[6]

Such a response was not insincere, although it was, of course, self-serving. God, in his providence, directs all things. It needs repeating that no one of the time knew about microbes and how they were communicated. The human mind demands explanation for why illness and accidents strike without warning, inflicting pain and taking innocent lives when often sparing the guilty. There must be reasons why such things happen; there must be agents making them happen. Europeans and natives alike had a horror of witches, who made bargains with demons and secretly employed magical powers to hurt their enemies. Both peoples believed in ghosts and specters. Both felt themselves at the mercy of cosmic forces they did not understand and could not control. What else but the deliberate workings of a great god could explain the timing, the scale, and the unambiguous selectivity of the killing diseases that afflicted the Ninnimissinouk? To the Puritans, God in his providence had prepared a place for his persecuted people, just as the Bible describes the history of the Israelites, who fled persecution in Egypt to find a land of milk and honey in Palestine. Despite the prestige that Christianity won among the Ninnimissinouk as a result of this epidemic, the sachems and powwows (medicine men) of the surviving Pokanoket and Narragansett firmly resisted the Christian interpretation of their predicament.[7]

In 1630, the arriving passengers of the Winthrop fleet had other things on their mind than the welfare of Indians. They had assumed that a commodious settlement at Salem or Charlestown would be waiting for them, furnished with ample supplies of fresh water and broad fields of growing crops. They had expected fresh food for sale when they stepped off the boats and sufficient stocks of grain and dried legumes to get them through their first winter. Instead, when their leaders finally released them from their death camp on the Charles, they were forced to seek out their own accommodations and to get in crops promptly wherever they could. With only small stores of food brought over on the ships and no shelter, they scattered to likely-looking Indian fields and, at each, gathered themselves together into cooperative communities with scant ceremony. It is little wonder there are few records of this headlong process.

Hundreds died before the end of the year and "scores more" that following winter before the arrival of a ship in February brought provisions. Among the dead were some of the most notable, whose presence and wealth had lent prestige and credibility to the enterprise. Thomas Dudley explained the mortality as, in general, due to "want of warm lodging and good diet," but more specifically, for those landing in June and July, the heat of a New England summer, fevers associated with summer, too much salt meat, and scurvy among the "poorer sort." Other families, notable and otherwise, had taken one look around that terrible summer and booked return passage home.[8]

Despite the deep gloom of that first winter, the new residents of Massachusetts Bay did not abandon their project. They bought what corn they could from Plymouth farmers and area Indians and were resupplied from England in 1631. Since relatively few new immigrants joined them that year, they escaped the burden that hordes of hungry newcomers would have imposed. Winthrop and Dudley, meanwhile, did their best to cultivate optimism on both sides of the Atlantic, and interest in the plantation remained high in England. Hundreds more immigrants arrived in 1632 and 1633, bringing the total number of English living in New England to about 1,800; the birth rate was high and deaths among adults relatively few, despite the smallpox.[9]

Until 1634 newcomers to New England settled in one of the nine original plantations: Plymouth, Salem, Charlestown, Medford, Watertown, Boston, Roxbury, Dorchester, and Weymouth. All lay on the coast or along the tidal stretches of rivers emptying into the bay. Except for Plymouth, these settlements had grown spontaneously and with little oversight. People bought, sold, and exchanged land informally. In the absence of competing institutions, the church meeting became the dominant forum for local decision-making, segueing from ecclesiastical to town matters without missing a beat. Most male heads of households were readily accepted as voting members in both church and town, although rank and status continued to structure their interactions in familiar ways. The shared experience of living and working in raw, unfamiliar circumstances, without wells or streets, without shops or mechanics, without municipal services—all placed a premium on cooperation and mutual aid.[10] Town and church institutions supplied flexible, responsive means for problemsolving in these first years.

The General Court underwent a more visible evolution as a governing body when townsmen took actions that challenged the authority of the governor and his assistants. A series of strategic compromises enabled the assistants to regain the initiative just as the trickle of yearly immigrants swelled to flood tide at mid-decade, and the Court successfully reasserted its authority over the settlement process. In legislation passed in 1636, the Court began defining town powers. New towns were to be chartered by the General Court in a formal procedure that granted land within designated bounds to groups of petitioners, who in turn agreed to abide by rules, especially those pertaining to paying taxes and hiring "orthodox" ministers. The General Court appointed a committee to distribute the new town's land to settlers, with the intention of preventing early arrivals from grabbing all the best sites for themselves. This town-based mode of distributing land was a constitutional innovation probably unique to New England. It created corporate entities resembling joint-stock companies in which "inhabitants" of the town formed the body of shareholders. These consisted principally but not solely of the male heads of settler families who had been accepted as "inhabitants," either initially by the committee appointed to distribute the land or later by the body of inhabitants as voters.[11] A family could not just walk into a town and expect to receive an allotment. They might rent a house and make friends with their neighbors, but the husband/father would not become an "inhabitant" without the vote of the town's "inhabitants."

From the point of view of those already living in a town, some potential settlers were more desirable than others. Families with animals, tools, and cash would be able to pay taxes as well as to exchange work and equipment with their neighbors. Town promoters openly competed for men who were well heeled and well connected or for men with special skills such as blacksmiths and millers, shipbuilders, miners, and iron smelters. Meanwhile, the press of new immigrants often alerted prior inhabitants to the insufficiencies of their original sites. The Massachusetts General Court received numerous petitions from early towns asking for an enlargement of their boundaries or for grants of "colony" towns where their surplus inhabitants might be more comfortably accommodated.[12]

The eagerness of new arrivals to pay cash for a standing cottage and a patch of cleared ground made selling out an attractive proposition to earlier settlers. Roughly three-fifths of immigrants identified by Robert Anderson as arriving before 1634 did not stay on at their original habitations, many moving several times. That year there began a surging roundelay of population movement among old and new towns that did not cease with the end of large-scale immigration in 1641 but continued for decades, halted only in 1675 by the sudden hardening of Ninnimissinouk resistance.[13]

Residents might find themselves having to deal with strangers very unlike themselves despite their common nationality. England's southeastern triangle whence so many came was much more populous, mobile, and "progressive" than the rest of the country, yet even there, villages quite close to each other in terms of distance could be miles apart culturally. The two areas most often contrasted by American writers are East Anglia (usually identified as the counties of Norfolk, Suffolk, and Essex) and the "West Country," a more vaguely defined region traversing parts of counties south of the Midlands, east of Cornwall, and west of Kent, Surrey, and Sussex. Although both these areas were Puritan strongholds, their economies, cultures, and ethnic origins were strikingly different. East Anglia lay open to continental influences and had been repeatedly colonized from there, most recently by highly skilled Dutch artisans of strong Reform principles. The West Country, on the other hand, was more rural, more conservative, and slower to enclose its open fields. Both areas supported cloth industries employing families who worked up the wool supplied them by merchants, but the West Country's may have been smaller in scale, less well funded.[14]

Puritans from both areas shared many values and religious ideas, so it may have been that the differences they saw in each other were a matter more of style than of substance. For instance, open-field communities had to be highly regulated and closely integrated because decisions about what to do and when to do it affected everyone. Negotiations proceeded in a carefully orchestrated fashion that promoted consensus among major property holders. In such places, ambitious men had to accommodate themselves to everyone who controlled a piece of land. Patience, courtesy, the habit of listening respectfully to others—all were traits that brought material rewards in open-field agriculture. Many East Anglian communities, on the other hand, had begun enclosing fields as early as the thirteenth century and featured active markets in land. Landowners in these areas were among the first to adopt progressive Dutch horticultural practices that gradually revolutionized English agriculture.[15]

When less corporately inclined East Anglians began arriving in large numbers in Salem, Dorchester, and Hingham, for instance, these towns' earlier settlers reacted negatively. It was a bit like modern New Yorkers invading Tennessee. In Salem, most of the early settlers had come from a single area in the west of England. Imagine their dismay when they were joined by seventeen interrelated families from Great Yarmouth in Norfolk who formed a faction, leveraging their votes in the annual negotiations over crop choices, fences, and field allocations. They also held more radical ideas than the old residents about church doctrine and standards for admission to church membership. Similarly in Hingham, families from Norfolk began arriving in small numbers as early as 1633, but their numbers swelled every year with new arrivals. The decisive moment came when the *Diligent* docked in 1638 with more than 100 East Anglian passengers. Surely it was no coincidence that West Country officeholders were replaced by East Anglians the very next year. In an acrimonious affair that ensnared the General Court, they flagrantly employed their voting strength to replace the current captain of the militia with one of their own. They also warded off sanctions aimed at their Presbyterian-minded minister.[16]

Many old planters chose to leave rather than live with obnoxious newcomers. The group departing from Dorchester in 1635, most of whom had been passengers on the same ship in 1630, had formed a sizable share of the town's population, if one is to judge by the town's proportion of the provincial tax assessment, which fell from 13.5 percent in 1635 to 9.2 percent by 1638. The emigrant party, led by minister John Warham, headed for the newly opened Connecticut River Valley, where they founded the town of Windsor, just north of Hartford.[17] In Cambridge and Watertown, East Anglians were the ones who felt themselves crowded out. The spacious and populous settlement at Watertown became a favorite first stop for newcomers just off the boat. Old-timers there understood all too well that there was not enough meadow and marsh to support everybody's cattle, whereas inexperienced strangers saw plenty of open space that needed only hard work to develop. In 1634 the town's freemen (male church members) began to enact formal regulations pertaining to property and voting rights separately from church business, with which previously they had apparently been intermixed. In January 1635 they voted "that no foreigner [coming out] of England, or some other plantation, shall have liberty to sett down amongst us, unless he first have the consent of the freemen of the Towne." They then proceeded to restrict voting rights in town matters to those freemen who had previously received grants in "commonage"—that is, rights of use to the common lands of Watertown—and they elected selectmen to make all future allocations of ungranted lands. Most striking, however, was their decision to turn public land into a jointly owned stock, with themselves the shareholders. "In consideration there be too many inhabitants in the Towne, & the Towne thereby in danger to be ruinated, that no farrainer comming into the Towne, or any family arising among ourselves, shall have any benefit either of Commonage or Land undivided, but what they shall purchase." Thereafter the only way to become a recognized "inhabitant" in Watertown was to purchase somebody else's home lot and commonage.

These actions came too late for many early residents, who began an exodus that continued even into the nineteenth century, with the town's numbers being continually replenished by children coming of age and by outsiders purchasing the home lots of those departing. Watertown was not only a gateway community but also a seed town for others—Concord, Wethersfield, Sudbury, and Dedham—and in a later phase of expansion numerous Watertown families joined in a westward movement that pioneered Groton and far-distant Lancaster. The vast mobility that characterized Watertown is summed up by the fact that only one out of eight heads of households whose names surfaced in its records up to 1645 actually died there.[18] Everyone else had moved on.

Dislike of "foreigners" or perhaps demotion to minority status was not the only reason why firstcomers would pull up stakes. Like Watertown, Roxbury was a first-generation town that saw a large turnover of settlers, but in this case newcomers shared with firstcomers the same relatively homogeneous origins in East Anglia. More than two-thirds of its settlers in 1630–1645 came from an area north and east of London in Essex and east Hertfordshire. Chelmsford was the major urban center; others included Colchester, Braintree, and Nazing in Essex and a market town just across the border in Hertfordshire, Bishops Stortford. The earliest to arrive in Roxbury came from Chelmsford, led by the Pynchon family from adjoining Springfield. There was also a sizable group from non–East Anglian Kent, but historian Sylvia Bugbee has discovered that even these people had ancient ties to Bishop Stortford.[19]

Not surprisingly, given their propinquity in the old country, most Roxbury settlers were closely related by kinship and marriage. Some of these kin networks were of very long standing, made up of families that had lived in their old-country neighborhoods for a century or more. Despite such coziness, people moved in and out of Roxbury at a dizzying rate. Children moved away from parents; brothers who had emigrated together or within a few years of each other dispersed. Sisters more often stuck together, whether they stayed on in Roxbury or moved elsewhere. Bugbee argues that the special needs of childbearing and women's culturally assigned roles of nursing the sick probably made them value intimacy and close relationships more highly than men. She believes that sisters were more inclined to stick together, in order to have each other's support during such recurrent family crises, as was true for nineteenth-century women involved in the westward movement.[20]

The ties of kinship and neighborhood helped pull people across the Atlantic and directed where they went once they arrived, but kinship or friendship does not explain why people moved again.[21] In Roxbury one finds a congenial community of neighbors, friends, and kin who had not been invaded by "foreigners" yet who appear to have been just as inclined as any to move on. Why this urge to move? One possible motive was religious disagreement. It took Roxbury two years to form its church, and fewer than half its residents became members, a decidedly low figure among early towns.[22]

Although Roxbury resolved its ecclesiastical problems by hiring a favorite son from home, doctrinal disputes erupted elsewhere in New England and undoubtedly promoted musical chairs among the founding generation. One of the emerging characteristics of Massachusetts Bay orthodoxy was to separate and distinguish the converted from the unconverted by restricting admission to formal membership in the locally gathered congregation. In England the national church was comprehensive in its scope. All Englishmen were born into it and paid taxes to support it. Heretics and criminals might be expelled, but all upright citizens were free to partake in the church sacraments. What became "the New England Way" followed a more restricted path. Each town organized its own church, which was independent from all others. Each congregation hired its own minister and made its own rules with respect to membership. Nonmembers were expected to attend church and to pay taxes to support the minister, in whose selection they had no say. They could not share in the sacraments and had no voice in the dispensing of church monies. Nor could nonmembers hold provincial office or vote for town representatives to the General Court. Potential members had to pass a public examination concerning their understanding of Christian doctrine and their personal spiritual experiences. Some towns were more rigorous than others in their admissions standards, and the more inflexible the standards, the smaller the proportion who could qualify. In those circumstances, members became a minority elite who risked arousing the resentment of the majority.[23]

Religious factionalism could wreak havoc in communities struggling to establish firm grounds of trust for carrying on the cooperative work of building a town and a church. Towns founded by already-formed congregations and led by already-ordained ministers had the best chances for success. Rowley, founded by the congregation from that town in England and led by their minister, Ezekiel Rogers, furnishes an outstanding example of such a town. But neither religious consensus nor common geographic origins kept everybody home in early New England. In Watertown, Ipswich, and Roxbury, for instance, the majority of original settlers moved on, church members and nonmembers alike.[24]

Their destinations provide some clues to their motives for moving. Thomas Weld went back to England as a representative of Massachusetts and, along with many other returning ministers, became caught up in the momentous events leading to the triumph of Parliament. Robert Cole, who was excommunicated by Roxbury Church within a year of its founding, moved in succession to Ipswich, Salem, and Providence within half a dozen years, finally ending up in Warwick, Rhode Island. His wife, Mary, "lived an afflicted life," mourned minister John Eliot, "by reason of his unsettledness & removing from place to place." Of the sixty-four free adult male immigrants to Roxbury identified by Robert Anderson as arriving before 1634, and comprising both church members and nonmembers, we know that at least thirty-four moved on. Seven, including the aforementioned Cole, ended their days in Rhode Island and one in Exeter, New Hampshire, settlements formed by religious dissidents. Three others went to Salem and environs, and nine traveled west to the Connecticut River Valley or southwest to the shores of Long Island. Two died in the West Indies: one at Providence Island, the other in Barbados. Thus, at least one-fourth moved for reasons that probably included religious conscience. The diversity of their destinations is striking, however.[25]

How do we explain all these comings and goings in ethnically homogeneous, neighborly Roxbury with its agreeable minister? First of all, the town was not poor. Its location was convenient to Boston, and it gradually became a weekend resort for the city's well-to-do. Moreover, the people who stayed on in Roxbury did well economically: probated estates show Roxbury among the wealthier rural communities in New England before 1676. Of the twenty towns generating sufficient numbers of estates in this period to make meaningful comparisons, Roxbury was fifth in average total estate value. Roxbury may have faced a critical shortage of land suitable for cattle. As Thomas Hooker's petition to the General Court in 1634 explained, he and his fellow petitioners from Newtown wished to remove to Connecticut "for want of accommodation for their cattle," a situation that made it impossible for them to "receive any more of their friends" from England.[26] In other words, Hooker's congregation and followers could not complete their settlement in Cambridge or in any other of the existing towns, because they needed far more hay ground for their cattle than could be supplied by even the most spacious plantations in Massachusetts Bay.

The answer to the shortage of land for cattle in Watertown and Cambridge was to move, in small groups following a leader westward, or to found new towns elsewhere. Watertown founded Sudbury, and Watertown residents crossed the Charles to found Dedham. Roxbury did not found its own western extension, Woodstock, until the 1660s, but groups of Roxbury people joined the westering trekkers from Cambridge in 1635. It is possible in this case that they were lured more by the charisma of Hooker than by economic prospects in Connecticut. Despite the petition's language about "crowding," historians have speculated that Hooker felt personally crowded by John Cotton, who had swept Boston (and Winthrop) off its feet the year before Hooker arrived. These two brilliant preachers were natural rivals for the spiritual leadership of New England, and they disagreed over ecclesiastical matters, although they were more like each other than either was to Roger Williams, Salem's holy terror. Cotton played a key role in the development of strict admission requirements for church membership (see his advice to Richard Mather after the collapse of the first effort to form a new church in Dorchester).[27] Since Massachusetts had already limited the franchise to church members, tightening the screws on such membership could only mean an even greater exclusion of otherwise qualified men from participation in public life. Hooker disagreed with the rigor of both innovations, and when the river towns of Connecticut came to frame their government, they deliberately ignored church membership in defining who had the right to vote.

William Pynchon led another group from Roxbury to the Connecticut Valley in 1635. These, too, were pursuing the opportunity to acquire good meadow land that had been made available by the smallpox epidemic among the River Indians. Pynchon's location at Springfield, moreover, cut off the more southerly English settlements from direct trade to the north and west for furs. That Pynchon and his son, John, went on to create a real-estate empire in the valley, made up of some of the best farmland in all of New England, has tended to obscure the enduring power of the elder Pynchon's religious convictions. He, like Hooker, did not agree with the emerging orthodoxy of John Cotton and his disciples in Massachusetts. In both cases, religion and economic interests "jumped together."[28]

Other emigrants from Roxbury headed in the opposite direction, geographically if not politically or religiously. Several moved to Ipswich in 1634, then on the northern frontier of Massachusetts Bay settlements, a town founded to forestall a feared land grab by New France and for its potential as a seaport. Early founders included men of wealth and prominence, such as the merchants William and John Payne and the governor's own son, John

Winthrop Jr. Ipswich quickly overtook Salem in wealth and numbers, taking second place behind Boston in Massachusetts' provincial assessments. Besides the rich and famous, however, Ipswich also drew "multitudes of idle and profane young men, servants and others." This trend alarmed the town's first minister, because, he said, New England had "neede to be strong and of a homogeneous spirit and people, as free from dangerous persons as we may."[29]

As these remarks indicate, not everyone who came to New England had come for conscience' sake, and the arrival of godless multitudes may well have driven the more religious-minded to move again in order to take their children even further out of reach of the corruptions of old England. Clearly, the post-1633 migration into Massachusetts Bay was too vast and too mixed for the old settlements to absorb. It would be wrong, however, to depict all those who moved on as primarily motivated to seek sanctuary from intolerant neighbors or "profane young men." The strength of economic ambition is too patent among too many to ignore. As William Pynchon's example illustrates, men could comfortably combine good business instincts with strong religious principles. Take the case of one young gentleman from Roxbury who moved a good deal, Mr. William Perkins. According to Anderson, Perkins was a Cambridge graduate whose father was a merchant tailor of London. He arrived as a twenty-five-year-old single man on the *William & Francis* in 1632 (one of only two arrivals in Roxbury that year who chanced *not* to be related to minister John Eliot). He settled there, and a year later "Sergeant Perkins" was ordered to "carry 40 turves to the fort, as a punishment for drunkenness." He was promoted to ensign of the militia company the following year, so all must have been forgiven until alcohol again got him into trouble. This time his punishment was more spectacular: he was to stand for one hour in public view at the next General Court with a sheet of white paper on his chest bearing a "great D" for drunkard.[30]

Either the punishment or his marriage in 1636 proved efficacious, because Perkins continued up the ladder of success, albeit not by staying in Roxbury. After going to Weymouth in 1643, "Lieutenant" Perkins was elected deputy to the General Court in 1644 and then appointed "Commissioner to end small causes," equivalent to a justice of the peace. He also taught school and eventually made captain. Weymouth had been good for his career, but in 1651 William answered a call from Gloucester. He and Elizabeth and their four children moved there so he could become the town's new minister, but then they moved again, four years and one additional child later, to Topsfield, where he again would serve as minister and Eliza-beth bore four more children. This time Perkins had climbed to a rung less suited to his talents. His years in the pulpit there were marked by congrega-tional turmoil and court suits, and he was eventually turned out of his post. He got into debt and lost much of his property. In 1666, when he was no longer minister, he was fined for excessive drinking again. Perkins died in 1682 without making a will, perhaps because he had no land left to be-queath. After expenses and debts, his remaining personal property scarcely sufficed to support his widow.[31]

Perkins' life is instructive. Although he had the advantages of a college ed-ucation and came from a prosperous, well-connected family, making his way even in the New World required a succession of moves. That he was shadowed by recurrent personal problems may testify only to the poor fit of his talents with his ambitions.

Roxbury, meanwhile, was not visibly affected by the departure of William Perkins or of all those others who left. Because of the enduring set of old ties among the remainder, and the common background of newcomers, Roxbury probably came as close as any of the original towns to fulfilling immigrants' expectations. Most, like Charlestown, had been accidental communities thrown together by circumstance, at first pulled together by common needs and dangers, later pulled apart by religious differences or the desire for "more room" or to escape "foreigners" and "profane young men."[32] In contrast, towns settled in the second half of the 1630s would be planned with more forethought.

From 1634 through 1641, nearly forty new towns were planted, from Fal-mouth (Portland) in Maine to Greenwich in southwest Connecticut on the New York border. All located themselves on waterways, both salt and fresh. Some, like New Haven, were started by newcomers to New England; others, like Dedham, were begun by more seasoned colonists. A few, such as Row-ley, Windsor, and Milford, were founded by congregations from old England parishes. Excommunicants and dissenters formed their own places of ref-uge, as did Exeter in the north and Rhode Island to the south. New England towns were indeed varied places, partly because of their founders' multiple origins and heterogeneous religious principles, partly because of the pecu-liarities of location and resource endowments, but perhaps most impor-tantly (certainly most elusively for historians) because of the dynamics among those early families who stayed after the rush was over, especially those with numerous healthy children. Because almost no personal accounts from ordinary people survive, historians can only speculate how communities came together and evolved.

It is easy to imagine how a small group of men on board ship or as residents in an established town might discover in one another a like mind on church matters and a common desire to improve their estates. Kinship, friendship, and intermarriage might leaven and sweeten common self-interest. In order to found a town of their own, however, they would have to move beyond the small circle of their kin, friends, and neighbors in order to amass the significant number of signatures required for their petition to win the acquiescence of the General Court. They would also do well to recruit famous men among their petitioners as well as a well-known legislative figure to support them, who would attest to their respectability and to the sufficiency of their estates to start a town and to purchase Indian titles.[33] Among the conditions attached to grants of land for new towns was the settlement of some minimum number of families by the end of the probationary period. In addition, the petitioners had to promise to secure a minister acceptable to the other ministers of the Bay Colony, to build a meeting house, and to see that some competent person was available to teach children how to read. The largest towns were required by law to ensure that a qualified individual would be present to offer boys (not necessarily girls) advanced skills such as writing, mathematics, and Latin. By failing to meet the provisions of their grant, the new town ran the risk of losing the entire enterprise. The General Court set the minimum number of productive families in order to ensure that the town would have a tax base sufficiently large to bear all the mandated charges as well as to supply ordinary town services such as keeping pounds for stray animals and building roads and bridges. After a grace period, the town also had to pay its share of periodic provincial assessments.

Friends in high places who could certify the petitioners' credibility would help speed matters along. If the land they hoped to develop lay in a militarily or diplomatically strategic location, the process moved expeditiously, especially if someone acting for them could negotiate good treaties and titles with proprietary Ninnimissinouk. In the event of the success of their petition, the new town's champions at the General Court would be rewarded with town land for their services not only as a courtesy but to add their names to the roster of property owners and thus enhance their own reputation in the colony as founders of a very desirable settlement. No one at the time saw these awards as bribes or sources of corruption, only as pay to busy men for valuable services rendered.[34]

Once a town opened its doors for business, no one could be sure who would come knocking. Strict Congregationalists might want to exclude all others, but those of more latitudinarian principles (or out of practical considerations) asked only for willingness to work, sufficient resources, and good character. Even these would ban the more notorious religious radicals such as Antinomians, Familists, and Baptists, especially if they couldn't keep their opinions to themselves. Such people found a welcome in Rhode Island so long as they didn't look like future welfare applicants. No one wanted the indigent, and Catholics need not apply. Irish, Indians, and blacks were tolerated only if they were servants under the control of a strong, respectable master. Later on, in the 1650s, Indians who agreed to convert, dress like Christians, settle down, and farm like Christians also became welcome, but only in their own towns, specially set aside for them. For most English settlements in New England, the exclusionary rule apparently ran: "out of sight, out of mind, out of trouble."

Even if the General Court was willing to grant land to the petitioners, they had to settle title to it with its native owners before they could move there. Finding the right sachems and getting them to affix their marks to a deed cost time and substantial gifts. It also required an experienced negotiator who knew the language and was trusted by them. Benedict Arnold of Rhode Island, for instance, lent his services to Massachusetts speculators on numerous occasions, but when he incurred the enmity of the Narragansetts, he dared not even enter their country and so lost his usefulness (though not his livelihood).[35]

One of the first problems faced by founders was how much of the land to give out and to whom. Virtually all the towns made the earliest settlers proprietors by admitting them to "inhabitancy," and gave each family a house lot and shares in the common meadows and planting lots. The committees charged with distributing the land did not hand it out in equal amounts, however. Both within towns and between towns, land allotments ranged widely in size, each town applying its own criteria in its own way. New Haven's ranged from 10 to 1,000 acres per shareholder, Hartford's from 160 to less than 10. Families arriving after the initial distributions might or might not receive shares. Hartford, for instance, voted to award such shares only as a "courtesy," and these did not carry any automatic rights to future distributions.[36]

Dedham, Massachusetts, is typical of the generality of New England towns settled in the second wave of immigration, and its history illustrates how much alike were the parallel processes of founding both town and church.

Dedham was originally one of the larger towns in Massachusetts, though less than half the size of Ipswich or Salem, and it was neither richer nor poorer than others. Dedham relied more heavily on farming than some of these other towns, having soon lost its more commercially minded men to Boston. About thirty families, mostly originating in Yorkshire and East Anglia and finding one another in Watertown, crossed the Charles in the late summer of 1636 to take possession of an enormous tract of land stretching southward from Boston and Roxbury to the northeastern border of Rhode Island. Their leaders set about organizing both town and church with impressive care. They adopted a town covenant that "simultaneously set forth their social ideal, outlined the policies by which they would attempt to bring that idea to reality, and pledged themselves to obey these policies." The second clause announced their intention to "keep off from us all such as are contrary minded, and receive only [those who] walk in a peaceable conversation."[37]

The covenant was signed, the town organized, and land distributed virtually overnight. Organization of the church, on the other hand, would take time. The precedent had been clearly laid out the previous winter when Thomas Shepherd and "divers other good Christians, intending to raise a church body at Newtown" (Cambridge, after the departure of Hooker and company), "sought the approbation of the magistrates" and the assistance of the neighboring churches in constituting their body. John Winthrop avidly set down in his journal every phase of the elaborate, daylong ceremonies. A similar effort in Dorchester just two months later ended in the public humiliation of the minister, Richard Mather, and his associates when the invited ministers and magistrates judged their public testimonies of faith both inadequate and misguided.[38]

With the contrasting experiences of Cambridge and Dorchester churches available as object lessons, Dedham's residents began a series of weekly meetings late in 1637, in which they gradually hammered out a series of doctrinal propositions for their proposed church. Once they had completed that part of the work the following spring, they commenced a long, drawn-out process whereby the most exemplary among them would, by lengthy mutual testing, winnow themselves down to a small group of mutually assured saints. These would serve as the first "pillars," who would sign the covenant, ordain the minister, and judge the qualifications of applicants for admission. According to their chronicler, pastor John Allin, they met weekly and prayed together, recited their experiences, and submitted to each other's

searching examinations. They did this for nearly half a year, finally present-
ing eight well-rehearsed and utterly convincing men to the town for their
approbation. When that was forthcoming, the town sent out invitations to
the churches and magistrates to witness and judge the qualifications of the
pillars and the soundness of their covenant for the inaugural church. The
fact that the ceremonies apparently went off without a hitch must have
brought intense satisfaction to the community at large.[39]

Dedham enjoyed some celebrity for this conscientiousness, and the relative peacefulness of its covenanted community has caused historians to regard it as a model "Puritan" town. The church was a success: most of the
first generation became church members, thus enabling the baptism of most
of the children born there.[40] Church, town, and minister were happy with
one another until the minister died in 1671. Filling his shoes did not prove
easy.

As Dedham's historian, Kenneth Lockridge, has made abundantly clear,
the town was corporate as well as Christian. Founders admitted only whom
they wanted as shareholders and as church members, but they did take care
of one another. There were rich and poor in town, but traditional bonds
of obligation and deference kept them reasonably united. When it came
to town land claims, however, the proprietors closed ranks against everybody else. The separation of Medfield in 1649–1651 and later subdivisions
prompted ill-tempered outbursts and occasional displays of intransigence.[41]

The town handed out its acres parsimoniously: less than 3,000 over
twenty years, by the end of which time seventy-five heads of households
had signed the town covenant. The distributions thus averaged 40 acres
apiece. By comparison, Salem had allocated 50 acres per proprietor, Roxbury over 100, and Watertown over 700 (distributions in Connecticut towns
varied just as widely, from 8.5 acres in Derby to 110 in New Haven). Seventy-five owners sharing Dedham's undistributed land seemed far too many
to one group of original residents, who protested that "in the infancy of this
plantation . . . the first planters agreed that they would entertain only sixty
persons to the privilege . . . of divisions . . . in the town commons." The town
responded by thereafter closing the door to all prospective shareholders, and
placated the complainants by enlarging the sizes of their shares.[42] The sizes
of individual shares also varied, from just a few acres to several hundred. Puritans were no more egalitarian in worldly matters than were any other
English Christians of their time. They believed that people got what they
earned or what God intended them to have.

Much of the land was not very good, but since it was virtually all they had in the way of capital and security, Dedhamites husbanded their undistributed land carefully. The acres in common were like savings in a bank, gradually increasing in value as the population increased, untaxed yet available to draw on for apportioning to their children and grandchildren. Many were willing to help finance the development of Medfield and Wrentham in order to make their own shares in the land there appreciate in value. This attitude toward land as a long-term capital investment made sound economic sense, but a less attractive, more speculative stance emerged in Dedham's dealings with Deerfield. In 1663, the same year it was distributing lots in the first division at Wrentham, the town of Dedham applied for, and received, a grant of 8,000 acres in the upper Connecticut River Valley. Acting on Dedham's behalf, William Pynchon acquired the Indian title in 1666, picking up a "right" in the new town for himself as compensation for his service. Pynchon had no intention of moving there, nor, as it happened, did any resident of Dedham. Instead, Dedham proprietors voted themselves shares in Deerfield equivalent to their shares in Dedham's common land and proceeded to buy and sell these in a lively land market open to all comers. Pynchon acquired enough through purchase to become one of the largest landowners of Deerfield.[43] People who actually made the move to Deerfield either purchased or rented their lots from these nonresident owners, whose absentee status hindered the town's progress and defense. After King Philip's War devastated the town in 1676, survivors attempted to rebuild the town. They petitioned the General Court in 1678, complaining that nonresidents owned the best lands yet would neither move to the town nor surrender their titles. The General Court said it was sorry and urged nonresident proprietors to be more helpful to the struggling community.

Dedham's behavior with respect to land was not out of the ordinary. The inhabitants there were no more venal than their neighbors and peers. The town met its challenges pretty successfully, and it was exceptionally fortunate in its first minister. As in other towns, the inhabitants controlled access to their land, kept out the undesirable, and those who were dissatisfied were free to move away. They kept a higher-than-average proportion of their land as commons and took longer than usual to distribute it all, but keeping this large bank of undistributed land enabled many shareholding fathers to help their sons when they came of marriageable age, although division land inevitably became ever more remote from the old town center as the decades passed.

All newly founded towns faced questions about what to do with their land. All adopted rules to restrict the number of shares in the undistributed land, some earlier than others. After making the initial distributions, however, many towns founded between 1634 and 1644 failed or refused to adopt explicit rules about how future allocations were to be made. In many cases, the town proprietors didn't want to bind themselves too soon before they had a chance to consider the matters of equity that might arise. In one unusual case, the town of Barnstable, on Cape Cod, voted that the sons of all the present inhabitants "shall successively be received as Inhabitants and allowed equal privileges as belong to the present inhabitants" on the day of their marriage or at age twenty-four.[44]

Initial failure to clarify the nature of property rights in the town common lands often led to trouble later. Some town leaders avoided the question because they wished to retain power over the grant decisions. Others avoided making any decision because it was potentially so divisive. In the case of the town of Sudbury, the problems that ensued from leaders' deliberate ambiguity were compounded by the rapid growth of population and a contest over the town's open-field system. The issues came to a head when sons who had lived in the town since its inception and worked in its common fields felt themselves justified in pressing for land allotments for themselves.

Sudbury was founded in 1638 from Watertown. Forty-three families located themselves at the site ten miles west of Watertown, where it lay in a great grassy meadow on the banks of the Musketaquid River, a tributary of the Merrimac. The only Native Americans in the area lived miles away and were amenable to granting title. At least half of the early settlers came from open-field villages, although they represented twelve different English counties. Most early new towns adopted open fields at the outset because they reduced the amount of fencing necessary to protect crops and meadow grass from marauding beasts. Once the pioneer stage had passed, however, proprietors in many towns bought and sold shares in a process that gradually consolidated their strips into convenient holdings, which they then got permission to fence off from the rest. Large allotments to favored individuals were often granted as farms on the peripheries of towns. Farmers who chafed at the inconveniences of the open-field system often pressured their town meetings to make new dividends in the form of such farms or at least to adopt policies that made it easier for individuals to enclose their plots. Such enclosures not only complicated the management of the open fields, but their removal from public control undercut the authority and prestige of the town elders. Young men who had grown up amidst New England's plentiful acres had no special yearning to continue living and working under the thumb of town elders, but they needed land of their own in order to vote as well as to marry. As their numbers in town increased, the discontented young could shake the meeting house floor with the pounding of their boots.[45]

In Sudbury, each settler family got a 4-acre house lot along the edge of the meadow, but the sizes of their shares of meadow ranged widely, from John Loker's single acre to the minister's 75. The land to be distributed was divided into 848 strips that were then numbered and drawn by lot, so the location of one's meadow strip(s) depended strictly on chance. In 1640 the town petitioned for an additional 3,320 acres on its southern border, raising the total acreage to nearly 20,000 of upland and meadow. The town then distributed 751 acres of upland to its inhabitants, ranging from the 76 acres given to Edmund Pendleton to 4 for John Wood, most lying together in great fields. Rights to the use of the commons were strictly tied to the number of acres of meadow received in the first division, although the initial numbers of cattle were too few to pose any immediate threat of overuse. One could add rights by buying meadow from neighbors, so long as "liberty of commonage" was made explicit in the deed. Only those holding rights in commons could be designated as "free townsmen" with the right to vote. The substitution of this term for "freemen" suggests that church membership would not be a prerequisite for voting on town matters as it was in Watertown. Absentee owners apparently were not included in this definition, although their exclusion was nowhere stated in the town book. When they made new grants out of the common land, the elected representatives of the free townsmen could and did leave out free townsmen at their discretion. There was thus no automatic property right in the town's undivided land, nor were the sizes of dividend shares determined by a fixed formula.[46]

Hindsight counsels that Sudbury's land policy was fraught with danger, and so it happened. The blowup came after the town had successfully petitioned the General Court in 1649 for yet more land on its western border, a tract two miles in width containing 6,400 acres. The ever-cautious selectmen postponed apportioning the new grant, whereupon the entire land policy of the town came under public discussion. A party of older men, including one of the selectmen, took up the cause of the younger men in the town, at least twenty-six of whom were sons of the founders who had come of age yet had received no meadow and hence could not vote. In addition, there were present in the town about eighteen men who were not on the original list of meadow grantees, only a few of whom had bought meadow land with commonage rights.

According to Massachusetts law, all free adult males could attend town meetings and ask questions, even if they could not vote. At one such meeting in 1651, someone who *could* vote moved a resolution: "When the two miles shall be laid out, that every man shall enjoy a like quantity of land." This was a radical position not only because it was flagrantly egalitarian but also because it would give nontownsmen a dividend and would undercut the selectmen's treasured prerogative to reward and punish through the granting or withholding of dividend land. The motion did not pass that year, but it provided a public opportunity to challenge the traditional leaders on their politics with respect to land. The popularity of town meetings became so great that the town soon needed a new and larger meeting house. In order to build it, voters passed the heaviest single tax in Sudbury history, to which, of course, the largest land owners had to pay the largest shares. Some interpreted the vote as a deliberate punishment of certain selectmen for resisting the pressure to distribute the new land.[47]

From the modern perspective, the outcome was foreordained: a clash between conservatives—who would strictly limit proprietary privileges while threatening selectively to withhold shares in future divisions, a position that put heavy pressure on fathers with adult sons—and the "liberals," for lack of a better word—those who wanted the town to grant land and voting privileges to all deserving men in the town. The fight over allocation of the new grant brought all these issues to a head, and the radical position triumphed in an open vote. The wily but stubborn selectmen then began a series of maneuvers, including the imposition of the first stints on use of the commons. These went against the spirit of the vote and pitted half the town against the other half. At the next town meeting, angry residents challenged one another's rights to vote. One of the smaller holders in town warned: "If you oppresse the poore, they will cry out; and if you persecute us in one city, wee must fly to another." And so it came to pass. After years of bitter fighting, disaffected Sudbury townsmen petitioned successfully in 1657 for a new town grant to the west, to be called "Marlborough," and moved away.[48]

Only Lyme, Connecticut, ever granted town land directly to the children of proprietors, and they included the daughters. Barnstable awarded it to sons of shareholders as they married or turned twenty-four. As we have seen, Sudbury almost came to blows over this issue. Watertown and Roxbury may have distributed all their land early just to avoid this problem. Yet in Andover, founded in 1642, fathers reveled in their control over town land because of the leverage it gave them over their children. Not only did they keep the proprietorship of the land among themselves; they even withheld the deeds of the land they "gave" their sons.[49] So Lyme's participation in the "portioning" of its children meant the surrendering of a customary means of parental control: the threat of disinheritance. Given the poor quality of the land there, the worst in the entire colony, the gift was more symbolic than real.

This parade of examples demonstrates that local stories both illuminate and complicate the story of English settlement. Despite the heterogeneous backgrounds and mixed motives of the immigrants, common patterns emerged as a result of the rapid development of a new institution in English experience, the township. "Towns," as they were called, promoted the rapid acquisition of native land in large chunks by groups of proprietors who controlled the pace and patterns of its distribution among themselves and their heirs. The towns varied widely in their resource endowments and in the decisions they adopted, but the fundamental mode of acquiring land remained in place until all the land in New England had been taken up or set aside by central authorities. The first towns situated themselves on old Ninnimissinouk sites, where farms were easiest to establish. The natural landscape of New England tended to disperse pockets of good land and furnished few natural meadows for the pasturing of domesticated livestock. Hence, the need for spreading out quickly manifested itself early even though the colony's leaders preferred compact villages for protection and to enable residents to attend religious services on a regular basis. The establishment of farms was a paramount consideration, however, and human labor thus became a far more valuable resource than it had been in the old country. The cheapest and most reliable source of labor was children. Farms were small businesses run by cooperative production units—families—with implied contracts between children and parents as well as between husbands and wives.

Having made the initial break from home in England, colonists found that subsequent moves came more easily. There was plenty of land, but yet there wasn't. Town after town refused to share its land with later arrivals or with its own children. Many sent petitions to the legislature begging for more, complaining of crowding. Meanwhile, like a time bomb quietly ticking, the settlers kept on producing more and more children, who survived in vast numbers and grew to adulthood. "Give us land! It is our due!" These were the expectations of the rising generation, an enormous multiplication of arms, mouths, wombs, and souls, all raised in the good clean air of the New English Canaan, inured to hard work and baked beans, who had earned the right to share their fathers' land, the right to marry, and the right to have their children baptized against Satan and his minions.

These demands placed often unbearable burdens on their parents and, by extension, on the towns' remaining fund of land. Their native neighbors gradually retreated, not at the point of a gun but to escape the incoming traffic, preceded as it was by a vanguard of foraging livestock.[50]

4

Sexuality, Courtship, and Marriage

If Robert had that gierl which there was a talke about she would not give him a penny.

—Abigail Young, 1692

Chapter 3 described how the New England township system became a land-gobbling engine of growth. It was fueled by an enormously successful family regime that produced hordes of healthy, long-lived, hard-working children. The founders did not tamper much with English laws and customs regulating marriage and childrearing but were unprepared for the ways in which their new environment—particularly the high price of labor—would affect how families functioned. This chapter and the next three analyze the dynamics of family life in early New England.

Before the advent of modern contraceptive technology, sexual intercourse between a man and a woman had a high likelihood of making her pregnant. Bearing a child outside accepted social and legal conventions raised the odds against that child's survival or success in adult society. In a world without hormone pills or condoms, most societies chose to regulate sexuality itself in order to minimize the births of such children. Some form of marital arrangement for the sexual partners, with binding obligations to provide for their offspring, has been humanity's most common solution to the problem of unwanted children.

Men and women contemplating marriage hope for affectionate companionship spiced with sexual pleasure, and their parents and friends hope for their economic well-being and emotional compatibility. In societies that allow women to go out in public, such as the Ninnimissinouk and the English, courting pairs have some opportunity to size up each other as prospective mates: she, or those who have her in charge, look for a good father for her offspring, a protector and co-provider. He and his family, in turn, seek a healthy, good-tempered woman young enough to bear, nurse, and rear strong, intelligent children, *his* children.[1] Both gauge each other in terms of physical attractiveness but also in terms of social "quality."[2]

In most societies of the past and present, social rank and control over resources are highly correlated and therefore furnish primary concerns for the families of prospective wedding partners. Among the Ninnimissinouk, status considerations were particularly important for members of the chiefly lineages, but power and prestige were not tied to ownership of material possessions as they were among the English. Making a good match brought not wealth but political clout. For commoners, on the other hand, economic considerations did play an important role. Women had greater economic value than men in native society, because they produced most of the food and did most of its processing. As a result, it was incumbent upon the hopeful young man to offer a large present to his prospective bride's family as consolation for their loss.

Roger Williams says of the Narragansett, "Generally the husband gives payments for a dowry [brideprice] to the father or mother or guardian of the maid . . . if the man be poor, his friends and neighbors contribute money toward the dowry." Men unable to give prestigious goods were at a disadvantage in the competition for a desirable woman, but those who were expert hunters or fishermen would make valuable connections for her kin-group.[3]

Ninnimissinouk men could have more than one wife, though only the powerful could afford them. Sachems of rival groups, such as Uncas, the Mohegan, and Miantonomo of the Narragansetts, competed for women of chiefly lineages in order to make strategic political alliances.[4] Marriage was serious politics. Roger Williams' *A Key into the Language of America* provides a succinct summary of Narragansett marriage rules insofar as he understood them, but he casts them in English, male terms:

> Their number [of wives] is not stinted . . . [although] the Narragansett generally have but one wife. Two causes they allege for their many wives: first desire of riches, because the women bring in an increase of the field, etc, the husband only fisheth, hunteth, &c. Secondly, their long sequestering themselves from their wives after conception until the child be weaned, which with some is long after a year old.
>
> God hath planted in the hearts of the wildest of the sons of men, an high and honorable esteem of the marriage bed, insomuch that they universally

submit unto it and hold the violation of that bed abominable . . . Single fornication they count no sin, but after marriage (which they solemnize by
consent of parents and public approbation publicly) then they count it heinous for either of them to be false. In [case of adultery] the wronged party
may put away or keep the party offending. Commonly, if the woman be
false, the offended husband will be solemnly revenged upon the offender,
before many witnesses, by many blows and wounds, and if it be to death,
yet the guilty resists not, nor is his death revenged.

Williams does not say what would happen if it was the man who proved
"false." The aggrieved wife clearly had the option of divorcing him and remarrying: "They put away [divorce], as in Israel, frequently for other occasions beside adultery, yet I know many couples that have lived twenty,
thirty, forty years together."[5]

Marriage was universal among the Ninnimissinouk, and sexuality was
prized. They did not expect any but the most dedicated holy people to ab-
stain for long from the pleasures of the flesh. Even children were free to explore and enjoy their bodies. Christians of this era, in contrast, believed that
sexual intercourse was intended by the Creator for reproduction and was
not to be indulged purely for its own sake. Nor should its sacred biological
purposes be subverted or controverted. On the other hand, both sexes expected to enjoy God's gift. Women's pleasure was part of the divine plan, because, according to English ideas, a woman could not conceive without an
orgasm to release her seed. When Martha Richardson of Stamford, in New
Haven Colony, denied that she had engaged in sexual relations with her
husband before marriage, despite bearing a full-term child rather too soon
after their nuptials, the court replied firmly, "No woman can be gotten with
child without some knowledge, consent and delight in the acting therof."[6]

Thus Puritans enjoyed and respected their sexuality, contrary to modern
stereotypes, but they did seek to channel it within the bounds of Christian
marriage. Their goal was to integrate and refine sensuality with spiritual
love and faithfulness, but unlike the Ninnimissinouk, they also believed that
sex outside marital ties was abominable in the eyes of God. Sexual union for
devout Christians was a sacred act hedged about with many taboos.[7]

Engaging in sex with anyone other than one's lawfully wedded spouse
was also a crime, but the degree of criminality varied with the status and sex
of the partner. When both were unmarried and of the opposite sex, their offense was "fornication," which, if prosecuted, was punishable by fines or

flogging or both, and the miscreants were strongly urged to marry. If a woman bore a child out of wedlock, the child was "illegitimate," and the father had to marry her or pay child support. Both parties could be prosecuted for fornication, and she for bearing a bastard. If she were already married to another man, however, the charge became "adultery," a much more serious affair—in early Massachusetts, punishable by death for both parties. It was the married state of the woman that defined the crime as adultery. Because her children were her husband's legal heirs, her deception and disloyalty trespassed on the twice holy ground of property and honor.[8]

If both partners were male, their act constituted a heinous crime against God and the state, termed "sodomy," also punishable by death. If a man forced his member into a resisting woman, the act was "rape," and he could receive the death penalty as well, but the law required two witnesses to convict for any capital crime, and so would not take her word solely against his. Although this is a reasonable argument in theory on behalf of justice for the accused, in practice it meant that no legal recourse was possible for children and women facing repeated abuse by men in their own households.[9]

Although Christian women and men could have only one spouse at a time, they were free to remarry if their spouse died. Legal separation was possible but not easy to obtain, and divorce was not normally available, although in post-Reformation England, Parliament could pass bills of divorcement. Church authorities in England and on the continent granted petitions for annulment of marriages on technically defined grounds of incest, or in cases in which one of the partners was incapable of consummating sexual intercourse. Given the emphasis on reproduction and patriarchal control over women, it is somewhat surprising to discover that women who proved infertile could not be divorced for that reason nor could their marriage be annulled.[10]

In New England all these matters were decided by civil, as opposed to ecclesiastical, authorities, with some slight reduction in the strictures on separation and divorce. Deserted wives could petition the legislature for divorce in Massachusetts if witnesses reported their husbands living with another woman. Anne Clarke, for instance, was granted a divorce by the Court of Assistants on just such grounds. Her husband had refused in writing to return to her and, according to witnesses, was living with another woman by whom he had already had two children.[11]

Unlike other British colonies, Connecticut refused to grant separations from bed and board, only divorces.[12] Divorce was legal even for couples liv ing together if either partner could be proven to have "violated the marriage bed." The "guilty" party was not permitted to remarry, whereas the injured partner was free to do so. A husband who ran away or disappeared on a voyage could be declared legally dead after seven years, thus freeing the wife to remarry. The total number of recorded divorces in either colony was paltry, because the law restricted the principal bases to desertion and/or sexual misbehavior. Cruelty alone did not become sufficient grounds for divorce until the end of the eighteenth century. For colonists generally, divorce was not a practicable route of escape from the marriage bond.[13] Even in colonial New England, then, marriage vows were almost irreversible, the ties dissoluble principally by death alone.

Despite their rarity, cases of divorce illuminate the meaning of marriage among the English in New England.[14] One of the first divorces in Massachusetts was masterminded by Thomas Dudley, sometime governor, on behalf of his daughter Sarah (sister to Anne Bradstreet), who presents to posterity every appearance of having been the guilty party. She ran away from her husband, Benjamin Keayne, according to a letter by Keayne to Dudley dated from London, March 18, 1647. Another letter from Keayne to John Cotton earlier in the same month stated, "I have spent my estate to maintaine my strength to content, & hazarded my health & life, to satisfy the unsatiable desire & lust of a wife that in requitall impoysoned my body wth such a running of the reines that would, if not (through mercie) cured, haved turned into the french Pox & so indangered my life." They were divorced that year. Boston's First Church excommunicated Sarah for ill behavior in church and for "odeious, lewd, & scandalous uncleane behavior." Although she had been adjudged the guilty party, Sarah married again but had no children, perhaps as a consequence of the venereal disease she had previously shared with Benjamin.[15]

Benjamin's sister, Anna, petitioned the Massachusetts Court of Assistants in 1658 to be freed of her husband, Edward Lane, for not "performing the duty of a husband." When the court called him in and put the question bluntly, he replied that "the truth was" he had not. The court declared the marriage null and Anna free to remarry.[16]

Another case that throws considerable light on the relationship between sexual competency and a valid marriage in English common law appeared in New Haven Colony in 1657. Hannah Foote won a divorce and a settlement of thirty pounds from her husband, John Foote, on the grounds of impotence. She then remarried. When Foote got his father's maidservant pregnant, he was charged with fornication and forced to appear in the same court that had granted the divorce. Members of the court were understandably perplexed. They reminded him that they had permitted his divorce because he had confessed himself "not fit for that relation . . . [nor] never shall be fit, which was also confirmed by his father." He desired the court to consider: if his wife "had caryed it toward him as she ought he might in time have proved sufficient." When the court inquired of the servant, Martha Netleton, if she hadn't got pregnant by another, since Foote was divorced for self-confessed impotence, she firmly denied it, persuading the court that Foote probably was capable of marriage. The judges punished them both with fines for fornication and gave them permission to marry.[17]

Then they called in John's former wife, Hannah. They confronted her with the palpable evidence of John's potency and recited John's complaint that while married to him, Hannah had "refused all his advances and scorned him." Further there was report that she had vowed on her wedding day "to keep herself a maid for one year." John's parents testified that they had tried to persuade her to try harder with their son, but "she wound him around her finger" so he confessed impotence and fault. The court listened to the testimony of these and other witnesses and concluded that it had been a great sin to have permitted the divorce, fined Hannah ten pounds plus court charges, and ordered her to return the thirty-pound settlement to Foote.[18]

Not only must a man be able to fulfill his "duty" to his wife, people also believed that he owed her sustained physical intimacy, for to deprive her of sexual gratification was inhumanly cruel. This becomes clear in a case that came before Middlesex County Court in 1666 when Edmund Pinson complained that Richard Dexter had slandered him, saying "that he Brock his deceased wife's hart with Greife, that he wold be absent from her 3 weeks together when he was at home, and wold never come nere her, and such Like." Gossip among the neighbors was suggesting that Pinson's wife was driven to an early grave by the coldness of her husband and condemned him for it. The records are silent on the outcome of the case, but it is notable that men gossiped about men who did not "take care" of their wives.[19] They may not have got all the facts straight in this case, but their ideas about the sexual needs of women and the reciprocal obligations of husbands illuminate the fundamental role of sexuality in Puritan marriages.

In return for husbandly performance of their duties, wives owed them loyalty and should not cheat. In most societies studied by anthropologists, male members have shown more anxiety about the sexual fidelity of their women than have the women about their men. This difference is probably due to the fact that only the woman can be sure of her baby's paternity. It is therefore in men's interest to control their women if they can. Otherwise they may end up supporting another man's brat without knowing it, or they might suspect it but cannot know for sure. Paternity thus becomes an extremely sensitive matter of honor. In societies in which women have successfully eluded male control and retain full rights over their bodies, as was true among the Five Nations Iroquois of colonial New York, men compensated by forging strong bonds with their sisters' children. With these, at least, their blood relationship was certain. Consequently, among the Iroquois the role of uncle superseded that of father.[20]

In countries granting men considerable dominion over women, however, such as those of early modern Europe, masculine self-esteem pivots on female submission. One of the worst things that can happen to a man in these circumstances is to have a wife who cheats on him; her bearing another man's child and passing it off as her husband's is his ultimate humiliation. Even by keeping company with another man, she makes her husband the butt of malicious gossip, a laughingstock, shaming him and all his kin.[21] Patriarchy thus endowed English women with the power to destroy male honor, and fear of women made all questions of female moral character in seventeenth-century England center upon this issue. That this is so becomes clear in the cases brought before courts in both Englands in which slanders against men disparaged their honesty, but slanders against women impugned their chastity or sexual loyalty.[22]

Masculine honor for Europeans, then, required effective dominion over women's sexuality. The laws regulating marriage in early modern England and its colonies sought to protect and empower husbands by guaranteeing them an "absolute property" in their wives. Religious authorities, moreover, justified male control of women by citing pertinent biblical passages. Women were the heirs of Eve, who committed the first sin in eating the forbidden fruit of the Tree of Knowledge, and because she then tempted Adam with the fruit, she was not only the weaker of the two but imperiled his own salvation. Women represented danger not only because of their susceptibility to the flatteries of others, but because they aroused lust, and lust could destroy a man more quickly than drink. "Give not thy Strength to Women."[23]

Englishmen further believed that women more readily fell prey to their passions than men, were less rational, and were subject to hysteria.[24] Clearly, such poor, undependable creatures should not be trusted with responsibilities beyond their limited capacity. Governor John Winthrop of Massachusetts Bay made this clear when he reported in 1645 that the wife of the governor of Connecticut had lost her reason, "by occasion of her giving herself wholly to reading and writing, and had written many books . . . For if she had attended her household affairs, and such things as belong to women, and not gone out of her way and calling to meddle in such things as be proper for men, whose minds are stronger, etc., she had kept her wits, and might have improved [utilized] them usefully and honorably in the place God had set her."[25]

From this perception of male superiority and female deficiency flowed all the concerns that shaped the rules regulating sex and marriage in early modern England and its colonies. The ideal Christian marriage was one based on mutual love, in which the man was a wise master, gentle but firm, and the woman submitted lovingly to his leadership. Submission was not supposed to ruin either her character or her disposition but to lend her the strength to carry out her duties. Although the good wife never wore the breeches, she did take charge of the house, the children, and the servants. Ideally, she exercised her authority under her husband's lead and did not tyrannize over them or him. As one author sums it up, men wanted women to be chaste, silent, and obedient, but above all obedient.[26]

Not surprisingly, most Englishmen intensely disliked bossy or assertive women and scorned as "momma's boys" men who allowed themselves to be led by their wives' apron strings. Such feelings are well expressed by the lyrics of a ballad popular in early seventeenth-century England, titled "Married Man's Complaint":

> I wash the dishes, sweep the house,
>   I dress the wholesome dyet;
> I humour her in everything,
>   because I would be quyet:
> Of every several dish of meat,
>   she'll surely be first taster,
> And I am glad to pick the bones,
>   she is so much my Master . . .
> And when I am with her in bed,
>   she doth not use me well, sir;

> She'l wring my nose, and pull my ears,
>   a pitifull tale to tell, Sir.
> And when I am with her in bed,
>   not meaning to molest her,
> She'll kick me out at her bed's-feet,
>   and so become my Master.[27]

How much worse was it for the woman who must submit and obey the man whom all society enfranchised as her personal overlord? Hear the words of Mary Astell, written in 1706:

> They only who have felt it, know the Misery of being forc'd to marry where they do not love; of being yok'd for Life to a disagreeable Person and imperious Temper, where ignorance and Folly . . . tyrannizes over Wit and Sense: to be perpetually contradicted for Contradiction-sake, and bore down by Authority, not by Argument; to be denied one's most innocent Desires, for no other Reason but the absolute Will and Pleasure of a Lord and Master, whose Follies a Wife, with all her prudence, cannot hide, and whose commands she cannot but despise at the same Time that she obeys them.[28]

Despite the risks to both sexes of entering into a permanent relationship, most people in seventeenth-century New England took marriage vows at some point in their lives. As in England, parents or others had no right in law to prevent a couple from marrying so long as both were free, single, of age, and willing. Also as in England, custom and decency frowned on elopements, and public opinion continued to prefer that the couple be "suitable" for each other, compatible in body, temperament, age, and estate. But religious concerns played a clearly more notable role in New England. Nathaniel Warren of Plymouth directed the overseers of his will to supervise the marriage matches for his children, "that they be matched with such as may be fitt for them both in reference to their spiritual and outward estate."[29] Yet no laws prevented a poor young girl from marrying a rich old man, or a rich widow from taking a handsome young suitor. Gossip alone remained the guardian of propriety.

In seventeenth-century England, a quarter of the population remained single all their lives. Unmarried women in England were called maids, and those who had passed the usual age at marriage without acquiring a husband were derided as "old maids." They were thought to be soured by disappointment, envious of young maids, and in the process of drying up physically as well as metaphorically. Young widows, on the other hand, might be pitied if poor, but would remain under suspicion as potential home wreckers because they were presumed to be especially libidinous, having been awakened to sex and then deprived. Young maids, living at home under the watchful guard of their parents, were presumed to be dewily innocent of the pleasures of the body, but young (and not-so-young) widows might go mad under the rigors of enforced celibacy. The best solution, for the peace of the community, was to marry them off quickly, preferably to a widower in order to reserve the younger men for the virgins.[30]

Whereas single women in Christian Europe were defined by the fact that they had no man, the single male was not yet a man but still a boy. "A person becomes a man when he is married," because he then fulfilled his role in the recreation of life. Males who were legally of age but unmarried were deemed not yet socially competent and were supposed to live in the household of a married couple, preferably parents or an employer, and under their supervision. Ideally, then, young, unmarried adults would remain under the guardianship of responsible citizens and be prevented from harming themselves or society.

Since marriage among the English was forever, the advice of ministers and others was that partners should love each other, be well suited to each other, and be compatible in age, temperament, and upbringing. All very sensible, given the unlikelihood that passionate love would endure, although compatibility as to estate was probably more important to family and friends than to the partners, at least initially. Choosing a spouse involved some of the same considerations that beset commoners among the Ninnimissinouk, but rank and economic resources were far more closely related in England and far more unequally distributed. When the English Puritan minister Ralph Josselin was approached by a potential suitor for his daughter, he recorded in his diary: "Jonathan Woodthorp of our town, a Tanner, asked my consent to come to my daughter Jane and had it, on this ground especially that he was a sober, hopeful man his estate about 500 pounds."[31] What predisposed Josselin in Woodthorp's favor was not only his good character and temperament, but that he also possessed substantial capital and prospects for more.

For English of the better sort, tasteful displays of wealth were necessary to reassure everyone concerned that there were sufficient resources backing a nominee to finance the new and separate household that an English marriage demanded. For those of the lesser sort, similar displays were also necessary, albeit at a more modest level, because the economic concerns were the same. Making a good match was first and foremost an economic decision in English society.[32]

Well-to-do parents were especially interested in ensuring the economic viability of a proposed match, because they had more to lose from a bad bargain. Parental consent was not required by the English church for those aged twenty-one or above, and ecclesiastical courts there never dissolved marriages made without such consent. Parents simply had no legal recourse if their children got themselves involved in contracts of marriage, no matter how ill considered. This problem was only partially rectified in the colonies by prohibiting the clergy from performing marriages and placing that power solely in the hands of magistrates. Marriage was defined in Plymouth Colony and elsewhere as a civil contract based on "the mutuall consent of two parties with the consent of parents or guardians if there be any to be had and a solemne promise of marriage in due tyme to eich other before two competent witnesses," with a magistrate in charge.[33] Magistrates in all the New England colonies were obliged to refuse marriage to underage couples who could not provide evidence of such consent.

Although parents could not dictate their children's marital choice or overturn it once consummated, sons and daughters hoping for good portions would take care to seek their consent before embarking on an active courtship. Men and women who had few prospects of an inheritance were freest to make up their own minds. As one young London woman put it, "I can make my choice myself." Another insisted, "I am past twise 7 yeares old And therefore will take my choise where I shall like."[34] An independent-minded female under the age of eighteen in New England would not be able to find an agent of the state willing to grant her that choice.

Given the danger in England that children might marry clandestinely, parents of property there were especially concerned to guard them against fortune hunters. Because people believed that women could not adequately protect themselves from predatory males and were susceptible to male charms, daughters and maids could not be left alone safely with any man who was not their kin, employer, or guardian. Their presumed vulnerability tended to enhance the value of female virginity, but one should not exaggerate its appeal. It was more important to the reputation and honor of both partners that wives maintain sexual fidelity to the husband after marriage, than that they be virgins beforehand.

Nonetheless, guidelines of respectability and the danger to parental pocketbooks required that courtship of a young, unmarried woman in England and the colonies be conducted in public and follow certain rules. Courtship formally began only when the suitor had first obtained the consent of her parents or master to approach her. No son who was counting on his father's largesse would dare take even that step without first obtaining his own parents' consent.

As far as the limited records from seventeenth-century New England permit any statements concerning actual courtship practices, they do not contradict prevailing English rules of etiquette. Only widows living in their own households were free to negotiate on their own behalf, but since polite society frowned on "forward" women, the cautious widow guarded her reputation by securing the "protection" of a male relative, through whom the hopeful suitor would make his initial approaches.

There are colorful folk myths about courtship practices of the early Puritans, many based on family stories passed down through the generations and not recorded until the nineteenth century.[35] Letters and diaries from the times are remarkably silent on the topic. The following anecdote appeared in a town history published in the nineteenth century and purports to describe the humorous genesis of a marriage proposal made in the 1640s.

> During a visit to the household of Edmond Tapp, Esq., where young Robert Treat was frequently made welcome, he took Tapp's only daughter Jane upon his knee and commenced "trolling" her. "Robert," said she, "be still that, I had rather be Treated than trolled," upon which he proposed marriage, "which was immediately consented to by all concerned."

They married sometime in the mid-1640s. True or not, it makes a nice story, especially in light of the fact that Treat later became governor of Connecticut.[36]

One colorful form of courtship presumably used by Puritans was bundling, "a European custom which became widespread in New England," according to David Hackett Fischer. "The courting couple were put to bed together, 'tarrying' all night with a 'bundling board' between them. Sometimes the young woman's legs were bound together in a 'bundling stock.' "[37] These images are reminiscent of the 1950s games in the United States of "necking," "petting," and "making out" engaged in by dating couples in parked cars at night. The young woman must not, under any circumstances, lose her virginity, for that made her "easy," diminishing her value in the marriage market. She might also get pregnant, an eventuality that would destroy her reputation, dishonor her family, and pose the problem of an illegitimate child in an age when abortion was illegal. In the 1950s the job of policing the degree of intimacy was hers, but in late eighteenth-century New England the propinquity of parents, plus the board between the couple, helped the girl resist her suitor, if this was what she wanted, and thus avoid pregnancy.

Although the stories about bundling are titillating, it is most unlikely that seventeenth-century parents would have intentionally sponsored or orchestrated physical intimacy between unmarried couples. Couples whose full-term babies were born too soon after marriage were in technical violation of the laws against fornication and were prosecuted. Judges as well as churches required guilty couples to confess their sin and beg forgiveness for their "filthyness." Penalties for fornication in the General Laws of Massachusetts (1648) included fines and corporal punishment. New Haven magistrates were perhaps the strictest of any.[38] Furthermore, illegitimate births were rare before 1675, and the rate of bridal pregnancy was far below contemporary England's or what it came to be in the eighteenth century.[39]

In practice, of course, people will bend, stretch, and redefine social rules as their own self-interest dictates. When two people meet and find each other interesting, they will find ways to see each other again. The English courting game could support quite elaborate plots, subplots, and counterplots. The intricacies and delicious nuances that so deeply fascinated England's upper-middle classes may not have troubled the dreams of more ordinary people. Yet the rules served as a bulwark for any family who thought they had something to lose from the susceptibility of an innocent daughter or from the independence of a stronger-minded one.[40]

Even quite properly conducted courtships could go awry. English Puritan minister Ralph Josselin had a daughter, Mary, who was being courted by a minister who was well settled in an affluent parish. "Mary quitted Mr. Rhea. Her exceptions were his age, being 14 years older, she might be left a widow with children. She checked at his estate being not suitable to her portion . . . he seemed to her not loving. It was no small grief to me, but I could not desire it when she said it would make both their lives miserable."[41]

Sons seeking to gratify a domineering father might find themselves betrothed to a woman of their father's choice, only to find the prospect distasteful. Then what? Breaking the engagement would not only bring down Father's wrath and humiliate her and her family; he might also become the object of a lawsuit for breach of contract. Andrew Pepperrell, son of William, of Kittery Point, Maine, became engaged in 1746 to Hannah Waldo, daughter of Samuel Waldo, of Boston. Both families were eminent and wealthy. He repeatedly postponed the wedding on the grounds that business kept him away, and people understandably grew concerned. In 1750, some four years after proposing to Hannah, Andrew still had yet to set the date. His brother-in-law, Nathaniel Sparhawk, wrote pointedly to him: "The country, especially the more worthy and better part of it, are very much alarmed at, and apear quite exasperated with your conduct relating to your *amour* . . . what you may imagine will pass still for a justification of your conduct, that you 'intend nothing but honor in the case and will be along soon' is perfectly ridiculed." Not surprisingly, the marriage never took place. Perhaps Hannah herself broke it off with the relieved consent of the Pepperrells.[42]

Hannah would have hesitated to do so. Society in New and old England required a marriageable woman to play a waiting game in the business of choosing a mate. Any show of aggressiveness on her part would compromise her reputation and diminish her "femininity." The business of waiting for suitors to appear offered scant opportunity to show off one's talents, whereas to many young men, the demure damsel may have reminded them of a spider waiting on a very sticky web. Aspiring young women could only hope to attract the notice of those they found attractive, and to discourage the attentions of those they did not. Imagine the mix of emotions in large social gatherings as eligible individuals on each side covertly studied each other.

As a general rule, parents in New England seem not to have "arranged" matches, but to have negotiated with their counterparts after the couple had agreed between themselves.[43] Parental consent was not mandatory if both bride and groom were free and of legal age, but banns were to be posted three times in a public place, such as a meeting house, to warn of an impending marriage.[44] Magistrates qualified to perform the marriages might refuse couples whose parents' opinions were adverse or unknown to them and definitely would do so if either party were underage. In Charles Manwaring's notes from Connecticut probate records, one finds the following certificate of consent, dated 1657: "These are to certify any to whom it may come, that our Children John addams & Abigail smith have our full Consent to be marryed together . . ." signed Rich: Smith, Jer: Addams. Both John and Abigail were underage.[45] In Providence, Rhode Island, Lawrence Clinton and Mary Woodin published their intentions in 1681 according to law and showed members of the town council the written consent of her father,

John Woodin of Beverly, Massachusetts, dated February 1, 1681. Furthermore, John Rament Jr., a resident of Beverly, testified to the council that he knew to certain knowledge of father John's consent, so the marriage was allowed to go forward.[46] Since no consent was required of Clinton in this case, one presumes that he was of age and she was not.

Consent was not always forthcoming, of course, but the parents could not lawfully prevent the marriage if their children were adults, nor could they force them to marry against their will. Marriage vows were not binding, after all, unless freely made. In his will of December 28, 1643, John Jenney, "Gent.," of Plymouth expressed his anxiety over the proposed marriage of his eldest daughter, Abigail. Her grandmother had left her "somewhat," and one Henry Wood was now paying suit. Possibly Jenney suspected Wood of being a fortune hunter, but whatever the grounds of his apprehensions, Jenney did not threaten to cut her off. He asked only that she delay tying the knot. If she would live one full year with the minister of Scituate before her marriage, he would give her two cows and his full consent. "And in case mr Chauncey be against it then I would have her dwell with Mistriss Winslowe of Careswell the said term of one year further."[47]

Some parents did not hesitate to withhold both their consent and their money if their children chose against their will. Richard Dexter told his new son-in-law: "As you married her without my consent, you shal keepe her without my help." Toward the end of the seventeenth century, widow Abigail Young lay on her sickbed worrying about her youngest sons, still "undisposed." She confided to her two older sons that "Shee was Troubled that henry and Robert was so much hindred about her . . . shee Intended for to Leave al to them when her head was Laied." But "if Robert had that gierl which there was a talke about she would not give him a penny."[48]

Portions enabled both sons and daughters to get a head start on adult life. For the girls, they provided dowries to marry; for boys, they provided the means of making a living and seeking a wife. Such seemed to be the thinking of widower Joseph Clarke, who, in his will dated 1641, from Windsor, Connecticut, begged the deacons and elders of the church to take charge of his small estate and of his two little children, using the income from the estate to support them. He asked that when they become old enough, they be put out to service and the income from the estate saved to become a portion or dowry for the daughter at age twenty-one. Then the estate itself was to be turned over to the son as *his* portion.[49]

Since both partners were expected to bring property to the marriage, parents negotiated with each other what each was to give. Thomas Minor announced in his diary that a match had been made between his son Ephraim and Hannah Avery. "I gave the two horses to Ephraim and Joseph to buy their wedding suits." And just one year later, he referred to the completion of a settlement for his son Joseph before his marriage to Marie Avery. It is worth noting that his diary had made no equivalent reference prior to his son Clement's marriage some five years earlier. At that time, Minor wrote only that Clement had "published" his intentions to marry Frances Willie on September 21, 1662, whom he married on November 26. According to Minor's diary, their daughter, Marie, was born on January 19, 1663. As was typical, Minor did not reveal either his or his wife Grace's reactions to this notably early arrival, and one wonders why the couple waited such a dangerously long time before tying the knot. Did Clement get cold feet? Was either set of parents against the match?[50]

Historian Margaret Hunt observes that in England "Marriage was, for all ranks, the main means of transferring property, occupational status, personal contacts, money, tools, livestock, and women across generations and kin groups."[51] The same was true in New England farm communities, where portions from both families enabled the couple to set up housekeeping and begin a new and independent enterprise. Along with the land and material goods thus pooled, each acquired a new set of relations whom they could call on for labor, tools, or credit when needed. Relatives and in-laws shared food, stood surety for each other, provided witnesses in lawsuits, and smoothed negotiations for business deals. A man who "married well" and pleased his wife and her relatives could go on multiplying his capital, credit, and opportunities. Similarly, the well-endowed farm wife could hire maids to do the drudge work and devote more of her time to the profits of dairying. Husbands who did not win or keep their in-laws' favor could find themselves cut out of future gifts and bequests. Such seemed to be the case in the Providence town records for December 8, 1670, when a father made over deeds of gifts of land to his children, including one to a married daughter, worded as though she were *femme sole,* even though her husband was alive and present.[52]

The customary portions that sons brought to a marriage consisted of land. Brides generally brought all kinds of personal property, including cattle as well as utensils and furniture. Governor William Bradford of Plymouth Colony gave his son William both land and cattle before his marriage in 1650: "half my farm at stoney Brooke, 4 or 5 cowes and when we part our employment I am to leave 4 young bullocks or other oxen. He's to have the whole after my and my wife's decease."[53]

But fathers gave their daughters real estate when they had little else, as Godbert Godbertson did in 1633 for his wife's two daughters by a previous marriage. In families without sons, daughters became heirs to the whole estate. On January 9, 1639, Elizabeth Warren, widow, in consideration of a marriage already consummated between Anthony Snow and her daughter Abigail, signed over to Anthony her house near Hobbs Hole, with the eight acres of land adjoining.[54]

Under English common law, freehold land that a woman brought into a marriage came under the management, but not the ownership, of her husband. Rights of inheritance in that land belonged to her children, although her husband could continue to benefit from it if he outlived her. These rules carried over to New England. The widow of William Harris, who died in Boston in 1684, had owned a valuable piece of property in town before her marriage, and Harris' inventory made careful note of the fact that he had "merely enjoyed it" during the marriage. One way of ensuring that the real estate given a married daughter would go to her children was to entail it, as Captain Hutchinson did for the daughter who became the wife of Edward Winslow.[55]

Later, as land prices rose and livestock prices declined, women's dowries more often came to consist solely of household goods, including linens and coverlets of their own making. Mindwell Lyman, daughter of John of Northampton, married John Montague Jr. of Hadley in 1712. Her "setting out" included a feather bed, bolster, pillows and pillowcases, coverlets, curtains and valence, table and bed linens, one spinning wheel with "flyers, spindle, and quill," fireplace equipment and cooking utensils, thirty-five pieces of pewterware, including a chamber pot and a beer pot (one-quart size), five alchemy (metal alloy) spoons, candlesticks, eighteen pieces of wooden tableware, a few pieces of earthenware, a looking glass and a drinking glass, a cupboard, a carved chest, a plain chest, a trunk, a table, and eight chairs. This was the equipment of an upper-middle-class household, worth almost twenty-eight pounds sterling, roughly equivalent to the seventieth percentile of consumption values in both New England and Maryland probate records.[56]

Although parents in New England may have wanted to have more say concerning whom and when their children married, most also sought to avoid even the appearance of favoritism when deciding on the portion they would give. If the match was especially desirable in the eyes of one set of parents, they might make an exceptionally favorable offer, but strive to make up for it with the other children later. As the language of their wills makes clear, testators strove hard to give every son and every daughter shares in their estates equivalent to what they gave their other offspring of the same sex.[57] The most common reason offered by those making wills was to prevent jealousy and quarreling among the children after parents' deaths. For these parents, the great goal was to have their children love, honor, and support one another in the vicissitudes of life.

The overwhelming evidence for this parental evenhandedness, combined as it was with parity in age at marriage among brothers, sorely undercuts darker images of paternal despotism in Puritan New England. This is not to deny the reality of patriarchal power there, but rather to emphasize the real-life constraints hedging it in—such as the high cost of labor because of the magnetic effect of the frontier (that is, the founding of new towns), but also an emerging public opinion that adult sons had certain rights vis-à-vis their parents. In the minds of the men writing these wills, a man of property ought not to postpone his sons' admission into the full rights and responsibilities of adulthood.[58]

New Englanders made marriage into a civil ceremony to be performed by a magistrate instead of a clergyman. Puritan distaste for "popish" ceremonies led to all sorts of efforts at simplifying English rituals. In early New England, both weddings and funerals remained solemn and important occasions, but they were brief, sedate, and understated. They were intended to express sincerity and to testify to the respectability of the parties involved. These worthy sentiments gradually gave way to the universal human impulse to use such occasions to support family honor by displaying rank, wealth, and cohesiveness. The cost of funerals rose faster than weddings, however, which remained primarily family gatherings until the middle of the eighteenth century, when these, too, went public (with occasional disconcerting consequences). When the daughter of minister John Ballentine of Westfield, Massachusetts, set her wedding day, her father confided to his diary: "I gave a general invitation, some stayed away because they thought some had a more particular invitation, some stayed away because they thought there would be too many for comfort." Gifts arriving the day before the wedding included rum, brandy, joints of mutton, two pigs, five fowls, a piece of veal, flour and suet, butter, cranberries and apples, cabbages, and potatoes. A large party had come from Sheffield, the groom's home town, to attend the wedding, and they stayed on. They dined with the Ballentines again the day after the party, after which Ballentine's daughter and her consort set out for Sheffield accompanied by her brothers, two young women, and six young men, all from Westfield, for part of the journey, some going all the way there. The next day, "our folks got up well and seasonably," suggesting some little surprise on the part of the father of the bride. At another wedding at which Ballentine was officiating, some young men "gathered together and raised a dead creature on a pole, and made a fire under it to show their resentment that they were not invited." He remonstrated with them, and they dispersed.[59]

The demands of the agricultural calendar largely determined the timing of discretionary events such as weddings. The majority of weddings took place in the "off" season, November and December, with the Twelve Days of Christmas the most popular of all. Given the heavy demands of haying and harvest in the summer months, few would have chosen these times to get married, unless, of course, they had to. For maids who discovered themselves pregnant, the sooner the wedding, the better. Figure 1 shows the seasonality of marriage in the seventeenth century for brides who were presumably not pregnant, and for those whose babies arrived less than eight and a half months after the wedding. Counting back nine months from the date of birth reveals that April and May in New England were particularly dangerous months for unmarried youth.[60]

Because English custom demanded that married couples set up housekeeping independently of their parents and kin, average age at first marriage was a barometer of economic welfare. Hard times in seventeenth-century England prevented or postponed marriage for many, and a quarter of the population never married at all. The mean age at first marriage there was 28 for men and 26 for women. The New World was to be a wholly different demographic story. Land was cheap and wages high, so the marriage market boomed, and an unbalanced sex ratio in the earliest years gave women the advantage. The mean age at marriage in New England for sons hung steady at 26 through most of the colonial period, except during King Philip's War and its long aftermath (1675–1691), when it rose to 27, and most men who married did so while still in their twenties. Marriage age for women was at a mean of 20.5 until 1675, then between 22 and 23 thereafter.[61] Thus the difference in age between husbands and wives narrowed substantially in the eighteenth century.

Almost three-fourths of the daughters marrying before 1675 were under age 22, and one out of ten was less than 18. The heavy pressure on women to marry, so unlike conditions in the old country, astonished and alarmed the leaders in the new settlements, not least for its potential effects on women's attitudes. In 1633 the Massachusetts court ordered Joyce Bradwick to pay twenty shillings to Alexander Becke "for promising him marriage

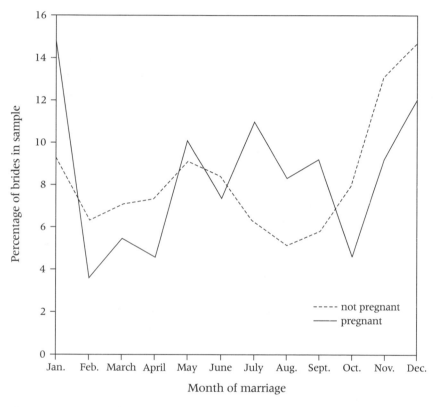

Figure 1. Seasonality of marriage in rural New England: brides who were pregnant vs. brides who were not (Source: Published genealogies and vital records of Guilford, Windsor, and New Haven, Connecticut; and of Rowley, Salisbury, Watertown, and Weymouth, Massachusetts; also Elizabeth Pearson White, *John Howland of the Mayflower*, 2 vols. [Camden, Maine: Picton Press, 1990–1993]; General Society of Mayflower Descendants, *Mayflower Families through Five Generations*, 5 vols. [Plymouth, Mass., 1975–1991]; and profiles of immigrants in Robert C. Anderson, *The Great Migration Begins: Immigrants to New England, 1620–1633*, 3 vols. [Boston: New England Historic Genealogical Society, 1996])

without her friends consent and nowe refuseing to pforme the *same*." New Haven magistrates censured one young maidservant who violated her contract in order to marry. "Ann Small was asked what she said to it that having hired herself a servant for a year, she should within a month enter a treaty of marriage with a man without consent of parents or master . . . having got a suit of clothes of her master . . . She thinks her mother is living and would be grieved to hear of her irregular proceedings."[62] Plymouth Colony tried to restrict financially unwise marriages and to guard very young girls from the rigors of precocious courtship by passing a law stating: "Whereas divers psons unfitt for marriage both in regard of their yeong yeares as also in regard of their weake estate . . . any that shall make any motion of marriage to any man's daughter or maid servant must first obtain consent."[63]

Men of property who could use the promise of valuable wedding gifts as bait were the only fathers with sufficient leverage to mold their children's marital choices. The extent to which they used their power is hard to assess, but the relative homogeneity of men's and women's ages at marriage and the fact that roughly two-thirds of sons and daughters generally married in order of birth militate against the idea that they used whatever power they had in an arbitrary fashion. If parents habitually dictated whom and when to marry, there should have been much greater variation in the ages at which siblings left home to marry than was the actual case. Moreover, this pattern of marrying sequentially by age showed no tendency to weaken in the eighteenth century, even though Puritan patriarchy had by then supposedly relaxed its grip. Why, then, this enduring pattern of sisters and brothers marrying in order of birth? First, parents owned their children's labor until they came of age: eighteen for women, twenty-one for men. Second, members of both sexes needed time thereafter to accumulate the necessary wherewithal to set up housekeeping—land, tools, housing, furnishings, and livestock—in order to make a proposed match attractive to potential partners. They could earn this capital by working for their parents—in which case the parents gave them their portions or promised to do so within some period—or they could work for others for wages. To be physically pleasing and have charming manners helped, of course, but without this capital, there could be no house and no farm.

Obviously, children of poorer parents in New England could not expect as much of a marriage portion as their better-off peers. Parental contributions toward a marriage settlement were always welcome, but not necessarily crucial for young men in a frontier society such as early New England's, where land was cheap and wages high. Eighteenth-century diarists John May and Samuel Lane managed to accumulate their own portions through a combination of farm labor and craftwork. In new towns with plenty of undeveloped land, sons whose fathers had moved there would get a share of parental land, as Joseph Minor did. His father negotiated Joseph's portion with the parents of Joseph's intended, who offered a portion with her.[64]

Although sons could find plenty of farm work in season to earn money, there was little opportunity for young women to do so during the first century of English settlement in New England, and they remained dependent on their parents until they married. On the other hand, the marriage market in the seventeenth century valued women highly for their intrinsic worth as helpmeets and future mothers. As population grew in the older towns, young men emigrated, and marital chances declined for women. On the other hand, opportunities for nonfarm employment grew, and eighteenth-century account books show payments to unmarried women for their products entering local exchange networks.[65]

Growing numbers of women elected not to marry in the eighteenth century, but they could not expect to live independently and still retain their respectability. They could work as maids in others' houses or stay home and spin, weave, quilt, or sew shirts, for pay. Maids' wages were less than half what a farm laborer could earn, but women got good wages at harvest time, and weaving became a popular trade for women in the second half of the eighteenth century. If working as a maid or living at home palled, they could move to new settlements with their siblings or cousins and help them with gardening, housework, and childcare. There would be no shortage of suitors on the frontier, to judge from the sex ratios in new towns.[66] Depending on their diligence and gumption, then, young women anxious to marry and set up housekeeping might accumulate enough to attract a young man of prospects. Otherwise it was a life without power or privacy, dedicated to filling other people's needs.

When widows and widowers thought about remarrying, property considerations played an especially important role, because of the interests of their children from the previous marriage. Negotiations were usually between the prospective partners themselves. Although prenuptial agreements appear only very occasionally in public deeds, references to them are common in probate accounts and wills.[67] There was a legal pitfall in all such agreements. According to English common law, a married woman had no separate legal identity from her husband. He was their spokesman as well as her boss. This merging of the two into a single "interest" was called coverture, and its logic meant that she could not bind him to any promises other than their marriage vows, so long as he was alive. Thus an agreement made between them *before* marriage was null *during* the marriage. Zephaniah Smith, who wrote a very useful treatise on Connecticut probate law in the early nineteenth century, explains:

> In respect to contracts made between the husband and the wife, prior to their marriage, the general rule is that all which are to take effect during the coverture are annulled by the marriage, but all which are to take effect after the dissolution are valid and binding on the husband . . . Contracts by the husband with the wife before marriage containing duties not to be performed till after the dissolution, which were entered into with a view of providing for the wife, or his issue by her, are binding on him both in law and equity.[68]

Prenuptial agreements, then, focused on property concerns, especially what he would guarantee her and her heirs in his will.

Given the one-sided nature of coverture, the question naturally arises, why would any woman marry or marry a second time? The answer, as we have just seen, is that the alternatives were no less constraining. So long as she was single, a woman was under the parental roof at her mother's beck and call. Alternatively, she lived in her employer's house under circumstances even more confining or with a married sibling as an old-maid aunt. Widows of means, on the other hand, were heads of their own households and managed their own affairs. They were the only females in English society who were not beholden to a man. If they could support themselves and their dependents, why should they surrender both their freedom *and* their property? Besides the desire for love and companionship, there were other good reasons for reentering coverture, however. A woman could not run a farm by herself (neither could a man), so she would either have to hire someone to do the work a husband would or else rent out the farm and go live in a city like Boston. She could not sell the farm without legislative dispensation, because it belonged to her children and she had only a life interest in it. Moreover, there were few competent men willing to rent in the seventeenth century because it was so easy to buy. Consequently, if a widow had more children than money, and they were young, she would most likely marry again. More than three-quarters of widows under the age of forty in the seventeenth century did so.[69]

John Betts of Connecticut married one such widow whose former husband's estate was beset with heavy debts. In order to avoid liability for those debts, he followed an old English tradition by forswearing any "interest" in her estate, debts or credits, and marrying her "in clothes of his own providing." Before the wedding, she was stripped to the skin by female witnesses and reclad in items of apparel he supplied, as a graphic demonstration that she brought him nothing.[70]

Widowers were even more likely to marry again than widows, regardless of age. They had everything to gain by remarrying: the new wife's property and her services as housekeeper and sexual partner. Hear the plaintive note in the deposition of John Knight, widower, who deposed that he had warned his servant, Sarah Crouch, against "sitting up" at night entertaining friends and threatened to tell per parents. But, sure enough, "my child that lay with her cryed out. I called to her severall times but she gave no answer . . . I went downstairs . . . and found her and another girl with two men." The useless girl got herself pregnant, his washerwoman was unreliable, and his household was in disarray.[71] He needed a wife.

What were the drawbacks of remarrying for the widower? A new wife immediately acquired a one-third interest in his real estate (called "dower," not to be confused with dowry), of which by law he could not deprive her unless she had signed a prenuptial agreement to the contrary. The administrator of Nicholas Wood's estate acknowledged a debt to Wood's widow of 150 pounds, per "marriage agreement." Older widowers might find themselves under heavy pressure from their grown children to try to make such a settlement in order to protect their inheritance. The children might even try to shame their father into confining his search to women safely beyond childbearing age, so as to prevent the birth of rival heirs. If the widower's children were still young, however, he was freer to choose a younger woman who might then bear him a second set of children (and heirs). Clement Grose, for example, signed a contract with trustees for his children by his first wife in order to protect his second wife and the children he would have by her.[72]

Remarriages by people with children from a previous marriage greatly complicated the devolution of property. Timothy Baldwin, for instance, was the second husband of his wife, and she, in turn, was second wife to him. She was executor of her former husband's estate, which was not yet settled because her children were still minors. Baldwin's will navigates carefully and precisely among his children, her children, and the grandchildren on both sides. Without such documents, their claims and counterclaims could tie up estates in the courts for years.[73]

A particularly egregious example of what could happen in a second marriage if the survivor did not make a careful will is provided by the very eminent and greatly revered Reverend Samuel Willard. The court appointed his young second wife, Eunice, administrator of his estate. There were eleven Willard children, seven by Samuel's deceased first wife and four by Eunice. The ample inventory came to over 1,000 pounds sterling in goods, money, and credits. Eunice's mother had given her 100 pounds for her children, but he had made no will, and the law would treat that sum as part of the estate that would be divided among *all* the children. Eunice therefore had to prove that the sum, plus accumulated interest, belonged only to her children by Willard and not to the others. The court finally agreed to apply the gift of Eunice's mother solely toward her children's portions, plus interest, but the judgment was on shaky legal ground.[74]

Most prenuptial agreements that have come to light are those mentioned in the wills of previously widowed men who had remarried.[75] Yet widows contemplating remarriage were no less anxious than widowers to protect their property and/or the inheritances of their children. An example comes from the Essex County probate records in 1647, wherein that court required Joseph Bixby, the intended husband of widow Sarah Heard, to give bond for thirty pounds that her two sons by Luke Heard be well brought up, taught to read and write, and apprenticed by the age of thirteen "at furthest." He was to pay them sums of money when they turned twenty-one and to give them their father's books. He agreed also that if Sarah died first, he had no right in her inheritance in land on account of their marriage.[76] In another example, Thomas Rowell of Salisbury agreed he would take the children of Margery Osgood, widow, two sons and two daughters, "as his own" and pay them their inheritances as their father had outlined in his will. In addition he would give Margery half of his estate at his decease besides the estate she would bring to their marriage.[77]

Perhaps more telling is a case in which the widow did not obtain a prenuptial agreement before remarrying and lived to regret it. John Benham told his wife after the wedding that he had already given half the house to his son John Jr.; the other half would go to him after he died. But "some of her friends in the Bay hearing of, being troubled, spake to him about it, upon which he promised to leave her a house and lot" worth twenty pounds. Son Joseph testified after John Sr.'s death that his father had promised to provide his new wife a house. Father had spoken to son John about selling back his part of the house, but the son had put it off since he was going to Virginia. He was still there when his father died and was now the legal owner of the house in which his stepmother was living. There would then be nothing left of the estate for the widow after she paid off the creditors. The court appointed commissioners, as the law directed for insolvent estates, and directed the commissioners to meet with the creditors and seek an abatement on their claims in order to relieve the widow. An attorney for John Jr. meanwhile submitted his claim to the other half of the house. The creditors would not agree to accept fifteen shillings on the pound for the help of the widow, unless that half of the house was mortgaged to them. John Jr.'s attorney could not agree to this without John's explicit consent, which never arrived. The widow was, in effect, left homeless.[78]

By law, a widow had dower rights in her deceased husband's estate, but since wills occasionally contained a penalty clause revoking dower if she remarried, any widow whose dower was so encumbered would have been foolish to marry unless her prospective new husband offered her a truly lucrative financial inducement couched in an iron-clad prenuptial agreement. Widows who retained an interest in the estates of their deceased husbands with no strings attached were freer to remarry, but, as we have seen, their husbands-to-be would take control of that interest and of the estate itself if the children were under age. Hence the attraction of a prenuptial agreement. And if she did not feel up to the demands of negotiating on her own behalf, she could call on male relatives who could try to woo or intimidate the suitor, depending on his attractiveness to her family's interests.[79]

Given all these property considerations, it comes as no surprise that negotiations before a second marriage were often brazenly mercenary. The niceties of courtship could not disguise the priority of business-first in these cases. The diaries of Judge Samuel Sewall and minister Cotton Mather describe their pursuit of well-heeled widows, some of whom appeared less than pleased by their attentions.[80]

Not all marriages are happy, of course, but an unhappy spouse had little legal recourse in the English family system. And this problem was compounded by patriarchy.[81] Society and religion not only gave husbands and fathers license to dominate their wives and children; they demanded that heads of households take responsibility for the moral development and public behavior of everyone living under their roof, including their wives. Ministers urged submissiveness, patience, and obedience on women, who had scant protection against abusive husbands. The father and brothers of an abused wife might intercede on her behalf and reason with, cajole, or threaten her husband. Church members might try to ameliorate the discord between a couple and urge greater lovingkindness on both sides. But neighbors, by and large, held back from intervening in "private business." The wife of an abuser or an alcoholic or a ne'er-do-well could find herself very much alone in a community that hesitated to threaten the rights of all husbands by taking action against one.[82]

That tension is particularly well illustrated in an agonizing case discussed in correspondence between Roger Williams and John Winthrop. Joshua Verin had moved to Providence from Salem with his wife. He was "a young man, boysterous and desperate," who beat his wife for attending worship services, "she and we long bearing though with his furious blowes she went in danger of Life." They finally "disfranchized" him, and he vowed to "have Justice . . . at other Courts." His wife was forced to accompany him back to Salem. Many of the male heads of household at Providence, who alone had voting rights, had opposed the disfranchisement of young Verin and refused to intercede on behalf of Verin's wife, because a woman's first duty was obedience to her husband, even if he kept her from divine worship.[83]

The high social status of one abusing husband so intimidated neighbors that it took a grand jury to bring in a formal complaint. Henry Sewall had been ordered by the Massachusetts Court of Assistants in 1635 to give his wife, Ellen, separate maintenance. She was to be "at her own disposal for the place of her habitation and that her said husband shall allow her, her wearing apparel and [twenty pounds] pr annum to be paid quarterly," as also a bed and furniture. This arrangement did not solve the problem, to judge from the jury's subsequent indictment of Sewall for beating his wife.[84]

Although law, courts, and custom backed up men's authority over their wives, they also came to support, and even enforce, the right of women (and men) not to be physically abused by their spouses. Massachusetts' legislators declared in 1650 that "no man shall strike his wife, nor any woman her husband."[85] Plymouth and Rhode Island followed suit more than twenty years later, but Connecticut, ever the maverick in matters of family law and the rights of women, abstained on this issue.[86] These laws represent a continuing evolution in Englishmen's ideas concerning the location of the boundaries between the rights of heads of families and society's rights as asserted and defended by the state. The quid pro quo, however, was the parallel and compensatory trend in property law toward restricting widows' autonomy. This topic is taken up in more detail in Chapter 9.

Despite the patriarchal nature of English society in New England, women could, and did, take advantage of frontier circumstances to alter their domestic arrangements to suit themselves. Take, for example, Herodias Long.[87] On March 7, 1645, John Hicks of Newport, Rhode Island, was bound by the court there for ten pounds to keep the peace for beating his wife, "Harwood" (Herodias). He abruptly left Newport and moved to Flushing, Long Island, then within the bounds of New Netherlands, taking their two children with him. Despite appearances, Hicks was not entirely at fault. He wrote to John Coggeshall at Newport on December 12, 1645, asking if there was some way to "untie that Knott, wch was at first by man tyed . . . for the Knot of affection on her part have been untied long since, and her whoredome have freed my conscience." John finally secured a divorce ten years later from Governor Peter Stuyvesant on the grounds that she had deserted *him*, marrying another man by whom, Hicks claimed, she had five or six children.

Herodias' side of the story comes out in a petition she presented to the King's Commissioners in 1665, who were then in Rhode Island, asking for a separation from her *second* husband, George Gardiner. She stated that upon her father's death, she was sent to London by her mother

in much sorrow and griefe of spirit, and there taken by one John Hicks unknowne to any of my friends, and by the said Hicks privately married . . . and . . . brought to New England, when I was between thirteene and fourteene years of age, and lived two years and half at Weymouth [twelve miles from Boston], and then came to Rhode Island about the year 1640 and there lived ever since, till I came heare to Pettycomscutt. Not long after my coming to Rhode Island, there happened a difference betweene the said John Hicks and myself, soe that the authority that then was under grace, saw cause to part us, and ordered that I should have the estate which was sent mee by my mother, delivered to me by said John Hicks; but I never had it, but the said John Hicks went away to the Dutch, and carried away with him the most of my estate; by which meanes I was put to great hardshipe and straight. Then I thought to goe to my friends, but was hindered by the warres, and the death of my friends. My mother and brother loosing their lives and estates in his Majestyes service, and I being not brought up to labour, and young, knew not what to do to have something to live, having noe friend; in which straight I was drawne by George Gardener to consent to him soe fare as I did, for my mayntainance. Yett with much oppression of spiritt, judging him not to be my husband, never being married to him according to the law of the place; alsoe I told him of my oppression, and desiered him, seeing that hee had that little that I had, and all my labour, that he would allow mee some maintainance, either to live apart from him, or else not to meddle with mee; but hee always refused. Therefore, my humble petition to your honours is, that of that estate and labour hee has had of mine and that the house upon my land I may enjoy without molestation, and that he may alow mee my child to bring up with maintainance for her, and that he may be restrained from ever meddling me, or troubling mee more.

The King's Commissioners were understandably befuddled by the petition and handed it on to the governor, who in turn sent it to the General Assembly. That body summoned Gardiner along with Robert Stanton as witness, a friend of both George and Herodias. George admitted that they had never married before a magistrate, but Stanton testified that "both of them did say before him and his wife that they did take one the other as man and wife." The Assembly agreed to pass an act of separation, but did not give Herodias quite what she had asked for.

Whereas Hored Long, heretobefore the wife of John Hicks, and since the reputed wife of George Gardener of Newport in Rhode Island, by a petition presented unto the Right honourable His Majestyes Commissioners did most impudently discover her owne nakedness by declaring therein unto their honours, that although she had lived for a long space of time with the aforesaid Gardener, as in a married estate, and had owned him as her lawfull husband, yett she was never lawfully married to him, neither could owne him in such a relation, and so consequently that she had lived all this time in that abominable lust of fornication, contrary to the general apprehension of her neighbors, she having had by the aforesaid Gardener many children . . .

The Assembly fined them twenty pounds apiece and commanded them to live lawfully thereafter, "lest they feel the extremest penalty that either is or shall be provided in such cases."

This is not the end of the story. At that same session, the Assembly granted another petition, that of Margaret Porter, wife of John Porter, who had deserted her and left her destitute. The Assembly directed that all deeds and conveyances made by Porter since he left her be void and of no force in law. This legal blackout had its intended consequences. Porter made a provision for his wife that was acceptable to her, and so he was released and they were divorced. Soon afterward John married Herodias.

As the career of Herodias Long Hicks Gardiner Porter indicates, the customary exercise of public authority in family matters in early Rhode Island was rather lax. Laws might proscribe and threaten, but women and men lived there as they chose, more or less, without molestation. Herodias' first husband had to move to New Netherlands to win his freedom, after she had moved in with George Gardiner. When the King's Commissioners came to Rhode Island on imperial business, Herodias saw her chance to dump George and move in legally with John Porter.

As we have seen, court cases amply document the existence of marital unhappiness in colonial New England communities, but the story of George and Rachel Potter is a happier one. Sometime before the end of 1699 Rachel separated from George and moved from Providence, Rhode Island, to the great city of Boston, where life came to seem not so rosy. She and George decided to patch things up. "She removed to Boston with my consent & now finding it uncomfortable so to live & I being desireous to Come together again," they made an agreement between them in the form of a contract. Since she had given away some of his estate to her children, he made note of his consent to it. Furthermore, if he died first, she was to have their house and land during her widowhood, but if she married again, she would receive only her dower thirds for life. He promised not to deed away any real estate without her consent, a right she would have had in neighboring Massachusetts (but not in Connecticut). Finally, the whole of the personal estate would go to her outright. Interestingly, George put his mark to this document whereas Rachel signed it. The discrepancy between their signatures and the whole tone of the agreement suggests that Rachel was of higher social status than her husband but had few economic resources of her own. Yet she had given things to her children (they were from a previous marriage, apparently, since he does not refer to them as "our" children), so she had not been down and out while living in Boston, and therefore made desperate. Whatever had influenced her to change her mind and return to George, the agreement she signed indicates that goodwill on both sides could work things out to their mutual satisfaction.

*   *   *

That there were many mutually satisfying marriages in colonial New England seems well substantiated. Manifest tokens of loving relationships emerge during times when couples are unwillingly separated, when they write sweet, longing letters to each other. Such was the case of John and Margaret Winthrop and Simon and Anne Bradstreet.[88] Unfortunately, few diaries of the colonial period include any enlightening statements about personal relationships. When diarists do speak, it is usually out of grief for the recently departed, as in 1766, when the wife of Daniel King of Marblehead died, and he wrote in his diary, "My dear Companion is left me." More movingly, on the anniversary of her death he continued to mourn her: "a whole years Experience has Taught me the dreadfull Truth how hard it is to live alone how hard it is But God is Just and Holy." This sad plaint was followed by a lengthy poem.[89]

One diary that speaks at length about relations between men and women is by Colonel Joseph Pitken, of East Hartford, Connecticut, who died in 1762 at the age of sixty-seven. Pitken left a diary-memoir describing two events in his life. The earliest pages depict a time of "mortal sickness" in 1712 when "multitudes" died. He, too, came down with the disease and became terrified of dying. His father and his minister spoke to him concerning the condition of his soul. There was much prayer and exhortation to throw himself on God's mercy. This section closes with his recovery and heartfelt gratitude. The experience clearly changed his life.[90]

The middle pages of Pitken's book are blank; then there begins an extended memoir of his search for a wife. "The comfort of this life much depends upon persons being suitably match'd," he said of his rather priggish thoughts as a young man, and, more fervently, went on to maintain that spouses should be faithful to each other, keeping "the bed undefiled." He resolved, therefore, to live a chaste life and wait for God to send him a wife.

> One of the first I pitched my mind upon designing to make a wife of, was the same I married. The motion was pleasing to my parents and hers but many difficulties intervened before the time that God had set came about. For want of encouragement from her I offered myself to some others which [God caused?] surely to be prevented. Sometimes I think that I was slighted because I gave myself so much liberty in carnal mirth . . . Those disappointments I met with all in looking a wife were a considerable trial of my faith . . . [compares himself to Job of the Bible] . . . My wife and I could both see the finger of God most plainly in reserving us for each other . . . after near

seven years . . . and the time much delayed through needless misunderstanding between ourselves . . .

After marriage in general we could conform to each others temper but in some small matters I could plainly see the Evil one seeking to kindle fires of strife . . . by Divine assistance we got well over such differences. But now a new trial came on for after marriage it was about 12 months before my wife was like to have a child which was to her especially a great trial and she had difficult work as Rachel had to keep in submission to the will of God. [Genesis 29–30: Rachel was the beloved second wife of Jacob, whose first wife was her sister, Leah. Leah bore six sons and a daughter before the anxious Rachel was able to conceive. They held a day of fasting and prayer together and she soon became pregnant.]

When my wife went with her first child and grew towards her time she was much distressed about the difficult hour which put us constantly upon seeking mercy and grace from God for Mother and child and God heard us as to safe delivery of a son but my wife was after within a stopp of death but God in mercy raised her again but the child after a little time fell into sickness and great pain and distress and died in its 7th week. Here was a new trial of our faith, patience, and resignation.

He goes on to tell of other children and other afflictions and of their continuing efforts to "wait on the Lord." Unfortunately, she developed a postpartum fever and died on October 10, 1740. He found some relief for his profound grief in reading pious literature: "my weary soul is at rest and safe in the Bosom of this Blessed Covenant." Pitken married again in March 1742, sixteen months after his first wife's death, but the diary thereafter says little about the new wife or their marriage. The compelling urge to confide his innermost thoughts about marriage had perhaps subsided along with his grief over the loss of his first, and greatest, love.

By comparison with Ninnimissinouk practices, marriage for the English in New England was a very different institution. Its basic purposes were the same for both societies: to form a stable new economic and sexual partnership capable of supporting and nurturing the children born to it. Individuals exercised considerable choice in both societies, but were sensitive to the rank and resources of prospective spouses. Among the Ninnimissinouk, an unhappy spouse was free to leave and marry again, and a man was free to take additional wives if he could attract them. For the English, all sexual intercourse was ideally confined to the monogamous pair; husbands' rights and wishes superseded their wives'; and parents exercised a great deal of influence over their children's choices through their control over family assets, although the high value of labor and the availability of undeveloped land undercut that power. The English style of marriage joined the two parties together for the duration, which could be galling or spiritually nourishing, but the deliberate design of the marital yoke was to place women at a significant legal and social disadvantage.

5

Bearing and Losing Children

Ah me! conceiv'd in sin, and born in sorrow,
A nothing, here to day, but gone to morrow.

—Anne Bradstreet

Early in the seventeenth century, Margaret Marre of London, "bygge with childe," accidentally encountered her brother-in-law in the street. He had not known she was pregnant, and when he inquired in some surprise about her condition, she replied that she was "about to go into the cuntrey, to my fathers to be browght a bedde." He wondered why his brother would not "kepe you to lye home, or that you be ashamed." To go away to have the baby suggested that there was something shameful about her situation. In response to his embarrassing question, she confessed that the child was not her husband's, but the fault was not hers. He "did not deserve therefore," for he "was never able to gett a child of her." Marre is blaming her husband for the fact that she is carrying another man's child, yet had he been impotent, an ecclesiastical court would have readily freed her from the marriage. What she was telling her brother-in-law was that his brother had failed to give her sexual pleasure, and she had had to go elsewhere to get both satisfaction and a baby.[1]

Belief of the time held that female orgasm was necessary for conception to take place. Conception and pleasure went together. If husbands could not give pleasure, they could not father children. Although experience must often have disproved this maxim, it is easy to understand how dissatisfied wives might deem their husbands undeserving of children. On the other hand, people also believed that God punished the adulteress by denying her children. Parenthood, therefore, must be earned, and for the English of the seventeenth century, fatherhood required a giving as well as taking of pleasure.[2]

The customary division of labor between the sexes throughout human history has, until recently, assigned childrearing to the childbearers. It is an onerous responsibility because it is everlasting. Human infants take far longer to mature than all other mammals, and unlike other adult primates, humans continue to protect, care for, and feed even juveniles and sub-adults.[3] All this childcare generally falls on the females and is not actively assumed by adult males until the growing youth can be useful to them or requires their deliberate intervention to defuse a potential threat to their hegemony.

Even when mothers and their female kin form cooperative groups to share the burden of childcare, they must stay within constant communication for the group to function successfully.[4] As a consequence of childcare responsibilities, women have not ordinarily enjoyed the freedom to take long journeys or to withdraw their services in order to work at long-term projects. They must stay "home" and watch the kids, unless they live in a society that allows some to force others to raise their children for them.

Since in most traditional societies women were already tied down by childcare, they shouldered the chores that fitted their circumstances: housework, gardening, and gathering herbs, berries, and nuts. They made the kinds of things, such as baskets and clothing, that can be picked up and put down at a moment's notice because children are their primary concern.

Women may, of course, reject motherhood, but in past times such a decision could be implemented only through sexual abstinence, an extreme form of self-denial that usually entailed a degree of alienation from the normal round of human relations. In early modern Europe, moreover, a woman's womb was thought to have certain needs that must be met or she would sicken. People believed that the womb must be used to be healthy, and it required refreshment by regular orgasms, "which feed it with seed" and regular pregnancies. Given such ideas about the body, women who went without sex were in danger of going a little crazy. It is not surprising that women accepted the idea that they would be unhappy without children and most unnatural if they did not want them.[5]

The rewards for childbearing have always been substantial: babies are lovable and adore their caretakers. A young woman who believes herself homely knows that she will be beautiful to her child. A lonely woman expects that a baby will give her unconditional love. The expectant mother, especially if she is safely married, will find her parents and siblings and neighbors all smiling at her. She has become somebody important; pregnancy justifies her, sanctifies her. Even women who have already borne children feel a certain smug satisfaction when they get pregnant again. English-woman Hester Thrale confided to her diary: "This is a horrible Business indeed: five little Girls too, & breeding again, & Fool enough to be proud of it! Old Idiot! What should I want more children for?"[6]

In seventeenth-century England, a village physician who took notes on his patients' mental symptoms described the anguish of women who were unable to bear children.[7] There were no prestigious and satisfying alternatives to marriage and motherhood, and most women believed that children were vital to their happiness.

As a woman's pregnancy becomes visible, people cannot help noticing. In many cultures, however, pregnancy is a very personal matter that concerns only the woman; no ceremonies mark the first unmistakable signs of conception or the quickening of the fetus; the expectant mother says nothing, going on matter-of-factly about her business. Among Native Americans of the Northeast, women took a special pride in their physical and mental toughness and regarded pregnancy and labor as mundane activities to be handled without fuss.

Among the English in rural New England, married women under forty were seldom free of the cycle of pregnancy and nursing, and so they, like the Ninnimissinouk, became inured to constant hard work while carrying a child in the womb. The diary of a young eighteenth-century country minister, Justus Forward, noted that on May 3, 1762, he plowed "my garden; helpt my wife garden." Within five days his wife delivered their third daughter.[8]

In other New World cultures, such as the Aztec, childbirth was a momentous occasion because the life forces of the universe were focusing and concentrating within the mother. She became dangerously, terrifyingly potent. The safe emergence of the baby out of the womb and into the world diffused that energy while marking the end of one journey and the beginnings of another.[9]

In some societies, then, the birth of a child can be a profoundly religious event, one perceived as fraught with danger to the mother and child and calling for the intercession of a wise being, one capable of mustering and directing the help and support of family and friends. For both Aztecs and English, that special person was the midwife, whose role among the Aztecs was as much priestly as it was functional.

The ceremony of childbirth in England did not require priestly intervention to protect the all-female attendants from spiritual violence, but their sexual exclusivity was nevertheless accompanied by ritualism. English males probably feared pollution rather than volatile spirits, but in any case they stayed well clear of the goings-on. Adrian Wilson describes the preparations: "In the later months of her pregnancy, the mother-to-be would issue invitations to her female friends, relatives and neighbours." Presumably she'd already contracted with a midwife. "When the mother's labour-pains began, there fell upon her husband (perhaps assisted by a servant or neighbour) the duty of what in East Anglia was known as 'nidgeting': that is, going about from house to house to summon the midwife and the other women to the birth." Similarly in New England, minister Peter Thacher noted in his diary that the household was making preparations for his wife's lying-in, brewing a special beer to serve the guests. On May 7 he "fecht old Mrs Dummick ye midwife to bee with my dear till she Lay in." She was not delivered until the evening of May 16, more than a week after the first signs of labor. It was only then that Thacher borrowed a cradle. Would it have been bad luck to bring the cradle into the house beforehand?[10]

According to Wilson, the custom was for the women to assemble in the mother's bedroom, or the inner room of the more common two-room house, to which she had withdrawn for the occasion. Such gatherings were convivial: the Thachers served their specially prepared "groaning beer." The father-to-be took care to stay out of the way—Samuel Sewall of Boston sat out in the "hall," the equivalent of the modern living room, with his father-in-law, as they awaited the first child together.[11]

The midwife was in complete charge of the process, and for her services she was paid by the father (and in England "tipped" later at the christening ceremony by the godparents). Unless the mother herself called for a physician, the midwife's authority over the lying-in was total and overrode all distinctions of rank and status. No other occupation open to women invested its practitioners with such power.[12]

The midwife and her helpers would close up the bedchamber, even blocking keyholes, with candles providing the only light. Darkening the room was supposed to prevent convulsions, but the tradition probably originated as a means of blocking entry of evil spirits. They would keep a fire going in the fireplace, perhaps for the same purpose, where the women prepared the mother's "caudle," her special ritual drink of ale, or wine warmed with sugar and spices if she could afford it. As the diaries of Peter Thacher and Samuel Sewall attest, colonists generally settled for beer.[13]

Different midwives had their chosen methods for delivering the babies who "presented" themselves in a variety of ways, some far easier than others. If labor continued beyond twenty-four hours without delivery, the midwife might try intervening in some direct way. Peter Thacher described one particularly dangerous delivery for his wife in which "the child was turned" so they had "great trouble getting her out."[14] Sarah Stone, an English midwife writing in 1737, described a breech delivery in which she had to reach into the womb in order to turn the baby before pulling it out. As she did so, it "suck'd my fingers," which "concern'd me, fearing it impossible for the poor Infant to be born alive."[15] Martha Ballard, midwife of Hallowell (Augusta), Maine, occasionally faced similar emergencies, but only once did she call in a doctor for help, and even then she safely performed the delivery, and both mother and child were well. A shaken Ballard confided to her diary: "The life of the [infant] I dispard off for some time," and in the margin she added: "The most perelous sien I Ever past thro in the Course of my practice."[16]

The local minister would be called if the situation got desperate, to pray with the mother, to remind her of her soul's duty to God, and to comfort her. The intensity of the experience and the minister's sense of helplessness encouraged many of them to learn "physic." Peter Thacher once was sent for to attend a parishioner, Mary Jones, who was "in travell & like to dy," so he brought along his "travell powder," which he gave her, and "she was delivered of a son in a quarter of an hour after."[17]

Once the child had been delivered, the "navel-string" tied and cut, and the child washed, the midwife swaddled the child, wrapping its body tightly, and presented it to the mother. Adrian Wilson believes that swaddling may have been efficacious in sending the baby to sleep.[18] The Reverend Mr. Torrey of Weymouth, who died in 1707 at the age of seventy-six or seventy-seven, claimed in a memoir that he was born prematurely and kept in warm lambskins "till the full proper time came."[19]

English mothers did not normally begin breast-feeding the newborn child until their "milk came in." They did not know that the colorless colostrum produced by their mammary glands was naturally designed for the newborn child, containing agents that stimulate and support the child's immune system. Instead the mother employed a neighbor or relative to wet-nurse the child for the first day or so, thus postponing her own restorative process, which would be stimulated by the child's suckling.[20]

"Up sitting" after the birth and a rest was an important social occasion and inaugurated the period in which it was proper for individuals to call and be served some of the special drink. Esther Burr paid a visit to a friend newly brought to bed, carrying her own two-year-old daughter with her. "There was a house full of people (as there always is as soon as a woman is a Bed)." Eight days after the birth of her thirteenth child on a cold January afternoon, Hannah Sewall treated her midwife and fifteen other women to a dinner of boiled pork, "very good" roast beef, fowls, turkey pie, and tarts. "A good fire in the Stove warm'd the Room," Samuel Sewall noted in his diary.[21]

Sexual activity between husband and wife was suspended during the lying-in and for some time after, during which time they slept apart. When Peter Thacher's wife became ill two weeks after the birth of a child, he got up to help her. When she felt better, he went back "into my owne bed again and slept."[22]

Although affluent women with plenty of help might continue their lying-in for as long as a month, most women probably got up and back to work within the week. Martha Ballard's Maine mothers did so within a day or two. Abigail Foster of Boston took longer to recover: her bill of charges for lying-in, dated 1695, included five shillings for the midwife, six shillings for "entertainment" of the women at her labor, thirty shillings for "the nurse" and her food, twenty shillings for firewood and candles for five weeks, and twenty shillings for Foster's own keep during the period.[23]

The end of lying-in was marked in England by the ecclesiastical rite of "churching." Originally the purpose of this ceremony had been ritual purification, but after 1552 it became the "thanksgiving of women after childbirth" in the Book of Common Prayer. In theory the mother could not go outdoors until she was churched; so for the trip to church, she wore a veil and was accompanied by her midwife and female friends. In parts of London in the seventeenth century, as many as 90 percent of recent mothers were churched, according to one estimate. Ministers in the more austere environment of New England churches also made a special occasion of a mother's first appearance after the birth. Ebenezer Parkman, eighteenth-century minister of Westborough, Massachusetts, occasionally noted in his diary the dates when his second wife, Hannah Breck, returned to church after giving birth. After her first successful delivery (she had had two miscarriages) she was able to make it in twenty-six days, but she required longer recoveries thereafter: thirty-six to fifty-one days for six of her eleven children. The infants themselves, by contrast, were usually baptized in church on the first or second Sunday after birth. Samuel Sewall's firstborn was carried to the church by the midwife. The minister prayed over the baby, Samuel named him, and then the minister baptized him, presumably with water, "in the name of the Father, Son, and H. Ghost." For the baptism of a later son, Sewall noted that "His brother Sam. Shew'd the Midwife who carried him, the way to the Pew."[24]

Anthropologists would have little difficulty interpreting English childbirth rituals. Because both menstruation and giving birth involve the passage of corrupt matter through women's "secret parts," many traditional cultures require women to seclude themselves during these occasions and then to purify themselves and their infants before reentering society. This is what the native women of New England did, although their withdrawals were interpreted by European male observers as graceful gestures of modesty. The men also commented approvingly on the physical fortitude and quiet demeanor of these women, contrasting their cool self-possession with the "coddling" demanded by European women who were undoubtedly spoiled by civilization. Englishman John Oliver, writing in the late seventeenth century, agreed with expectant mothers that their dangers were many, but asked that they "abate somewhat those dreadful groans and cries which do so much discourage their friends and relations that are near them."[25] These men understood that childbirth was painful, but, not having to experience it themselves, they believed that women could take it in stride if only they gritted their teeth and got on with it. They also understood that the coddling that women gave themselves was not only a respite from onerous duties but also a vacation from men. Churching represented not purification after pollution but a triumphal celebration. The entire process, from calling in the midwife and friends to the churching, was created by women for women as a show of support during a time of danger, accompanied by festive socializing that reinforced their common bonds. The ceremony of childbirth inverted the normal pattern of English conjugal relations; the wife's bodily energies and sexuality belonged to herself alone, for the space of that "month." Hence the collective female character of the ritual. Men, meanwhile, probably welcomed their exclusion from the birthing chamber and found the secretive hustle and bustle a small price to pay for not having to see their wives' suffering.

The separation of the sexes, with members of each attending to their own "business," helps to explain the indifference or condescension of men toward female concerns. Consider the case of Henry Sewall of late eighteenth-century Maine. His wife, Tabitha, had eight children, all of whose births were attended by midwife Martha Ballard. Sewall's diary mentions Ballard's presence on only four of these occasions, and only twice did he take any notice of the other attendants, all of whom were named by Ballard in her own diary.[26]

Another source of male discomfort with the traditions surrounding lying-in was the displacement of himself by the midwife. Midwives were powerful figures in the seventeenth century. They carried great prestige as witnesses in court.[27] They were generally more literate than most women, and that fact, combined with their experience in crisis situations, gave them a self-assurance that suffused their entire demeanor. Such "carriage" could offend judges and ministers, who were accustomed to a public show of meekness by women, thus exposing midwives to male complaints that they were "stubborn, defiant, willful, self-sufficient, and self-assertive." Midwife Anne Hutchinson of early Boston, who had been explicating weekly sermons for mixed audiences in her home, was accused of all these things and worse at her church trial in 1638: "You have stept out of your place, you have rather bine a Husband than a Wife and a preacher than a Hearer, and a Magistrate than a Subject," charged the Reverend Hugh Peter.[28]

Midwives normally acquired their skills through informal apprenticeships. In England the church licensed midwives as it did physicians and surgeons. To get a license, a midwife had only to bring in testimonials, swear an elaborate oath, and pay a substantial fee. Their lack of formal training came to be perceived as a public health problem by physicians and physician-trained midwives. A new genre of books beginning in the late seventeenth century attempted to rectify what their authors viewed as ignorance and lack of skill among "country" midwives, especially in handling difficult births.[29]

During the eighteenth century, college-trained medical doctors created the discipline of obstetrics, which emphasized knowledge of the reproductive anatomy of women and of the processes of pregnancy, labor, and birth. The evolution of this new science not only resulted in the substitution of "scientists" for midwives but also banished the ceremonies associated with lying-in along with the company of women. By physically isolating the parturient mother, they could more easily exercise their own oversight and authority. Their newly acquired knowledge of female anatomy, moreover, began to replace old ideas about the nature of sexual differences with entirely new ones. They now emphasized a dichotomous polarity in place of gradations from perfect (and superior) maleness to weaker, inverted female beings, inferior because their emotional weakness made them more suscep- tible to passion and irrationality. New attitudes toward women in the eight- eenth century not only emphasized their differences from men but attrib- uted to them an absence of sexuality, quite a reversal from their previous image as lustful and devouring. This newer, friendlier depiction supposedly imbued them with special moral attributes that could counter and soften men, whose masculine drives to succeed in business supposedly made them less sensitive to human suffering.[30]

The new physicians' manuals of the eighteenth and early nineteenth cen- turies provided graphic representations of the birth canal with illustrations of the range of fetal positions within the uterus. They prescribed internal and external means for easing the birth and avoiding the problems associ- ated with difficult presentations. Feeling themselves scientific practitioners of a field hitherto in the hands of ignorant and superstitious laywomen, these male midwives aggressively sought not only to reform childbirth prac- tices but to put themselves in charge. In London they created lying-in hospi- tals where expectant mothers would be treated as individual patients in a queue of beds among whom doctors could more efficiently deploy their tal- ents, bustling from one active womb site to the next. Since they did not wash their hands, or their forceps if they used them, they not only isolated these women from comforting circles of friends but became remarkably ef- ficient agents for spreading puerperal fever.[31]

At the end of the eighteenth century, however, traditional midwives still held sway in the New England countryside. Martha Ballard was probably unusual in that she had an uncle and two brothers-in-law who were physi- cians, and two of her brothers were college graduates. She also had the benefit of growing up among older women. From some or all of them, she acquired a formidable set of skills that brought most of her nearly one thou- sand patients successfully through their ordeal. She did not pass on her skills to her own daughters, however, perhaps because the women of their gener- ation had already begun to transfer their trust to doctors.[32]

Probably most midwives were qualified by experience to attend normal births, and these, after all, made up the vast majority (estimated to be roughly 96 percent of human births). Women may not have enjoyed preg- nancy, probably dreaded labor, and had genuine grounds for fear during the ordeal, but remarkably few Anglo–New England women actually died in childbirth. Martha Ballard, for instance, lost only 5 mothers out of the 998 births she attended, of which there were only 14 stillbirths. Estimates for seventeenth-century England range from 10 to 29 deaths per 1,000 women giving birth.[33] The rate of maternal deaths in a large, diversified sample of New England genealogies was under 11 per 1,000 births and may have been even lower. The greatest risk to mothers was with the first baby: 13 per 1,000 women died the same year in which they had their first child. For later births, the risk declined to below 10 per 1,000 and stayed there through the ninth delivery, rising sharply thereafter. Thus, most mothers and infants never needed the skills that country midwives were said to lack.

Among women who lived into their sixties, childbearing and nursing took up a big chunk of their lives. Marrying at twenty-one, bearing their last child twenty years later, marrying off their youngest twenty to twenty-five years after that—women lived much of their lives as actively involved mothers. Such numbers are not astonishing in themselves: the average family in sample genealogies bore slightly more than six children. Women who married in their early twenties and lived with their husbands to age forty-five generally bore more than eight children, and many had ten or more. The cumulative impact of universal marriage, biennial babies, and low mortality, generation after generation, was to double the population about every twenty-two years.[34]

The median interval between births of the first six children was twenty-six months, a seemingly leisurely pace until one realizes that Native American women probably spaced their children at three to four years. The duration and intensity of breast-feeding are crucial. If her baby dies or she cannot nurse, a woman's ability to conceive could return as early as six weeks postpartum. Were she to conceive quickly, within a month of the return of menstruation, and should a normal pregnancy then ensue, the interval between two full-term babies could be as short as eleven months, not much less than that characterizing mothers of the 1950s in the United States who bottle-fed their babies and didn't use contraceptive devices. Modern studies using both ethnographic and historical data indicate that breast-feeding can postpone the resumption of the menstrual cycle for a year, even two years, but the actual time lapse depends directly on the strength, duration, and frequency with which the child suckles.[35] Since breast-feeding practices vary widely, even within cultures, their effect on fecundity varies too. Women who put their babies out to wet nurses, who put their babies down for long periods and make them wait to be fed, or who supplement their breast milk with other food will find their menstrual cycles returning many months sooner than mothers who nurse their babies on demand and without supplementation.[36]

The Native American mother nursed her child more exclusively and for far longer than her English counterpart. One reason for doing so was that clean, digestible, high-fat foods were not available as substitutes. The very young child does not thrive on cereal gruels low in fat. It will become malnourished and susceptible to gastrointestinal infections, and the resulting diarrhea will quickly lead to fatal dehydration. The older the child when weaned from the breast, the better its chances of surviving, not only because it can then get adequate nourishment from a broader range of foods, but because constituents in mother's milk have helped the child's body develop its own immune system and improve its cognitive functions.[37] In order to maximize the chances of each child, Ninnimissinouk women probably tried to space their children fairly widely apart. Such spacing and long-term breast-feeding would have brought life-saving benefits to the unweaned child and minimized competing demands on mothers' attention. A woman on the move could comfortably carry only one child at a time in addition to all her other porterage responsibilities. She also probably paid attention to the timing of the next pregnancy and birth, to ensure that an abundance of appropriate food would be available for the child she must wean.[38]

After the resumption of her period, a mother's chances of getting pregnant again depend on the timing and frequency with which she engages in sexual intercourse, because menstruating women can conceive within only a short window of time each month of their cycle. The monthly ovum has a life span of only forty-eight hours. Furthermore, a significant proportion of all human conceptions fails to survive. If she wants another baby but does not understand the ovulation process or its timing, then frequent sexual intercourse is the only means for getting pregnant faster. So, depending on the wait to conceive again of, say, six months, plus the ensuing nine months of gestation, the resulting interval between births could be about twenty-eight months for well-nourished mothers who breast-feed with no supplementation.[39]

When babies cry all night or when adolescents turn fractious, parents may wonder why they ever wanted children in the first place. Given all the trouble and cost of having children, why *do* otherwise rational adults let themselves in for twenty years or more of disruption and anxiety? Yet the proportion of adults who choose not to have them remains low even today. Evolutionary biologists, unromantic scientists that they are, argue that all animals reproduce in order to perpetuate their genes and will sacrifice even their lives to ensure the survival and success of their offspring. Economists, equally cold-eyed in their assessment of human reproductive choices, argue that parents in traditional societies bring up children to exploit their labor and to be taken care of in old age. When governments assume the cost of old-age security (if not the responsibility), they remove the last economic reason for having children. Yet people continue to do so, having fewer of them but investing a great deal more time and resources in each. The benefits of children then become purely psychic; or, in the jargon of the economists, children share in their parents' utility function. By extension, pets function as cheap substitutes.[40]

One may grant all these motives for having children in the first place, but still ask why New England farm families went on having them in the numbers they did. There is no statistical evidence that they tried to stop. The median interval between births was the same before the seventh and eighth children as it was before the sixth. If parents had lost one or more children, of course, they might decide to have a few more to play safe. But those having numerous surviving children also continued to produce right up to the end of the wife's reproductive span.[41] Stopping would not be easily achieved, in any event, because there were no contraceptive devices available, and abortificants were painful and dangerous. Moreover, religious ideology frowned on behavior that was "unnatural." Christian folk wisdom taught that unimpeded (and uninterrupted) sexual intercourse between spouses lying face-to-face promoted marital bliss in the way God intended. Children were God's blessings and, as such, should be humbly welcomed. Besides, why would a man forgo the means of sexual pleasure God had given him solely to ease his wife of so natural a burden?[42]

So the question comes down to whether parents of many children actually wanted all of them. (Probably not.) Perhaps they went on having children as insurance in case of an epidemic. They also probably tended to exaggerate the risk of premature death for their children. Many ministers and town clerks kept records of the numbers of births and deaths each year, but when they remarked about such things, it was only to exclaim over the unusual—the very old, the promising young man cut off in the prime of life, the virtuous young mother dying in childbirth, the simultaneous deaths of brothers, the loss of whole families of children to diphtheria, or the horror of death at the hands of heathen savages. They did not notice or understand that adults were living longer than had been usual back in the old country, and that a greater proportion of their children were surviving to adulthood.[43] Even so, only half of John Winthrop's sixteen survived to adulthood, and two more died before reaching their thirties. Winthrop's repeated widowhood and the deaths of so many of his children provided stark evidence of the reality and unpredictability of death.[44]

People may have found it unthinkable even to try to stop having children, whether or not they had already achieved numbers that should have provided an ample margin of safety against the risk of losing them all. Although the care of so many children must have been burdensome and, for the women, just plain punishing, children were obviously valuable long-term investments: they supplied cheap, docile, trained labor on family farms, and one or another might be expected to take care of the parents in their old age in return for the farm itself. Having more of them did not materially add to the cost of running the farm, and the older ones took care of the younger ones. If the oldest was a girl, she was already an experienced "nanny" by the time she was nine or ten, having helped shepherd two or three younger siblings through toddlerhood.[45] In the process of growing up together, siblings forged enduring ties of affection and loyalty, ties that are movingly visible in their habit of naming their own children after one another.

Choosing the name of the new child is fraught with significance in all cultures. Aztec priests used astrological maps to advise the parents in choosing a name that provided protection from evil spirits even as it embodied the fortune and destiny their calculations revealed.[46] Names and naming were so central to individual identity among Native Americans of the Northeast that good manners required one to avoid speaking these names aloud except under ceremonially controlled circumstances. People did not keep their birth names for life but assumed new ones when they were initiated into adulthood or into secret societies or when they changed roles. War captives who were adopted into their captors' families took new names with their new identities, often as representatives of deceased relatives. Adoption signaled rebirth, perhaps even reincarnation.

The conventions of naming children among the English had altered with the initial conversion to Christianity, again with the Norman invasion, and then again after the Protestant Reformation. Throughout these upheavals, there persisted a steady current of favorite English names such as Agnes and Henry. Before the Reformation, parents frequently gave their children saints' names in the hope of invoking their spiritual protection. When the

Protestant iconoclasts banished saints' statues from church sanctuaries and directed worshipers to pray directly to God, saints' names were replaced by favorites from beloved Bible stories, resonant with moral meaning.[47]

Family culture was Bible-centered, and its pages supplied a bountiful store of names for their proliferating children. A second source of names, for Puritans in particular, came from the ministers' hortatory preaching. For instance, Elizabeth Tilley and John Howland of the *Mayflower* did not give their firstborn, a daughter, her mother's name or the good English names of either of her grandmothers, Joan and Margaret, nor did they select any of the popular biblical choices. Instead they named her Desire, probably in tribute to the young woman who had taken care of Elizabeth after her parents died in the winter after they landed at Plymouth. To modern ears, Desire connotes yearning of a very carnal kind, but to the Puritans "desire" signified a spiritual hunger for God. Other names, of a hortatory nature, were intended to remind both child and parent of their duty to God. Faith, Hope, and Charity, from 2 Corinthians 13, are familiar examples of those given to girls, but Mercy, Patience, and Thankful were actually far more common, followed by Desire, Experience, and Grace. Less familiar to us are those occasionally allotted to boys, such as Hopestill, Hatevil, and Deliverance. In some New England families the name Hatevil reappears every generation well into the nineteenth century.[48]

The traditional naming ceremony among pre-Reformation Christians was part of the sacrament of infant baptism administered by a priest within the sacred confines of the church sanctuary. Baptism welcomed the new arrival into a universal community of worship, and godparents stood up on its behalf to make holy vows that they would oversee its religious instruction. Parents used the institution of godparenthood as an extension of kinship obligation. It both honored and committed these adults, as they pledged themselves for the sake of the child. To express their gratitude, the parents often bestowed the forename of one of the godparents on the child, erecting a flattering as well as enduring symbol of her or his commitment.

Immigrants to New England dispensed with the custom of godparents but retained the rite of baptism. Popular belief endowed baptism with a kind of magical prophylaxis against witches' curses as well as damnation, but its appropriateness and efficacy were matters of sharp dispute among theologians. That there was widely shared anxiety among laypeople to obtain baptism for children is well demonstrated by the very short lapse of time between birth at home and baptism at the meeting house, usually on the following

Sunday. Given the alacrity with which it was carried out, postpartum mothers did not attend the ceremony.[49]

No one has fully described one of these baptisms, but Samuel Sewall's diary provides clues. Sewall stood alone or with other fathers at the font before the minister, each bearing his infant in his arms. The father announced its name in response to the minister's query, but how and why that name was chosen is a tantalizing mystery. Sewall seems to have chosen them without any consultation with his wife, Hannah, because he always says "I" named "my" child, and on several occasions in the diary he explains why he chose that name and not another. If he consulted with anybody, it was with his minister.[50]

The names given by parents to their sons and daughters provide clues to attitudes toward themselves as parents and toward their children as their lineal offspring and as creatures of gender. For instance, members of the two sexes rarely shared the same name; Frances and Francis are an exception, as are some hortatory names such as Experience and Deliverance. One has to see whom they married to be sure of their gender. Another common rule was that siblings of the same gender did not bear the same name, except that when a child died young, the next to come along of the same sex would often receive the dead child's. Similarly, if a man died without leaving a child bearing his name, his siblings might rush to fill the void, passing on his name and memory to the next child of the same sex born to themselves.[51] These were not hard-and-fast rules, but they were popular practices.

The most popular naming convention in early modern England was naming the first son for the father's father and the first daughter for the mother's mother, customs often reinforced by choosing these same individuals to serve as godparents to their grandchild-namesakes. Birth order forms a natural hierarchy for a people accustomed to ranking everybody, such as the English, and they strongly tended to privilege first over second and older over younger among their offspring.

Often parents in England who called their firstborn after a grandparent would name the second of the same sex for themselves, affirming the primacy of lineage over individuality. This core pattern reappeared at once in tidewater Virginia.[52] In much of New England, however, this time-honored convention was supplanted by parent-centered naming: the selection of the father's and mother's own names for the first son and daughter. Moreover, among those naming their first for themselves, only 15–20 percent went on to call the second after a grandparent. Naming firstborn daughters after their mothers instead of one of the grandmothers had been so uncommon in England as to amount to a virtual taboo.[53] The distinctiveness of parent-centered naming in New England emphasizes the prescriptive position of the parents in the Puritan household. This was a powerful theme in religious advice manuals and suggests the importance, among the immigrants and their children, of the mother in upholding the father's moral and spiritual authority over their children.

Puritan baptismal practices may also have encouraged the emergence of parent-centered naming. As noted, they dispensed with godparents in the baptismal ceremony and placed the responsibility for the children's spiritual upbringing squarely on the shoulders of the parents. Infant baptism was available only to the children of church members, however. Many churches in New England, particularly in Massachusetts, were quite strict in the admission standards. The effect was to withhold the rite from numerous children wherever such standards prevailed. Church membership seems to have declined over the seventeenth century, although there is some dispute about this.[54] If it did, the proportions of unbaptized children grew, and the spiritual roles of their unchurched parents must inevitably have weakened as a result. Insofar as the popularity of parent-centered naming was religiously inspired, the fact that it waned with time comes as no surprise. But the shift away from naming the first daughter for her mother came earlier and more markedly than it did for first sons with fathers' names. Thus, the early and distinctively New England practice of maternal naming failed to take enduring hold, falling victim, perhaps, to the same political forces that moved to deny speaking and voting rights to female church members.

Historians used to think that high mortality among children in pre-industrial countries hardened parents, forcing them in sheer self-defense to adopt a deliberately stoical attitude toward the earthly fate of their young children. Affectionate, attentive childrearing had to wait, this notion went, until improvement in the child's chances of surviving merited such investment on the part of parents. Evidence such as diaries, however, contradicts this idea. For instance, the unusually detailed physician's journal of Richard Napier, who practiced for close to forty years in a seventeenth-century English village, recorded 134 cases of "disturbing grief," 58 of which were directly associated with the deaths of children. The journal's editor explains that the women of the village "formed deep and enduring bonds with their children and were forced to suffer again and again as disease slew one child after another." Levels of infant and child mortality were certainly high by modern standards: approximately one English child in six did not survive his or her first year, and only slightly fewer, proportionately, died in infancy in New England. These rates are roughly the same as those prevailing in the late nineteenth-century United States, when Victorian sentimentality over children and childhood was at its apogee.[55] Since Victorian attitudes coexisted with the same or worse rates of child mortality as prevailed in the deeper past, there are no logical grounds for inferring opposing attitudes as resulting from them. Moreover, child mortality was probably higher among Native Americans in the early period, and no European observer ever suggested that they were indifferent to or unmoved by the death of a child.

One particularly moving story of a mother's grief for her dead child comes from minister John Hale in 1702. According to Hale, Mary Parsons of Springfield was accused in 1651 of possessing the two daughters of the local minister. In her confession she reported that "she had lost a child and was exceedingly discontented at it and longed, Oh that she might see her Child Again! And at last the Devil in likeness of her Child came to her bedside and talked with her, and asked to come into the bed to her and she received it into the bed to her that night and several nights after, and so entered into covenant with Satan and became a Witch."[56]

New England diarists' reactions to the loss of a child not surprisingly yield a range of emotional expression. Generally speaking, diarist-fathers register more emotion over the illnesses and deaths of children who are no longer infants. It does not seem to be true, however, that the older the child is, the greater the grief. Differences among the diarists' responses reflect temperament more than changing times.

Thomas and Grace Minor of Stonington, Connecticut, lost two children during the period covered by his extant diary, which begins in 1654. The first was Marie, born in 1651, who died on January 24, 1661. Minor's diary first announces she is sick on the eighth of that month, and a week later describes her as "very sick" and states that he went out to fetch honey. On the fatal day, he wrote only that "Marie died abt six o'clock." The other child to die was Thomas, his second son and namesake, who died fifteen months after Marie, at the age of twenty-two. He had fallen sick while trying to retrieve runaway horses in the Narragansett country in late March. People sent word to the Minors on the eighth of April, but it was not until the seventeenth that the father finally rode to Narragansett, arriving in time to be with his son before he died on the nineteenth. Minor wrote nothing in the diary about his feelings on this or any other occasion.[57]

A letter written in 1669 by Josiah Cotton's maternal grandfather to

Josiah's parents reported in similarly straightforward fashion the death of his daughter, sister to Josiah's mother. His wife, however, was so overborne by grief that she refused to eat and died less than three weeks later.[58]

Boston diarist Samuel Sewall, born a generation later, also offers a strong contrast to Minor. He was a warmhearted and loquacious gossip, sensitive to slights but studiously modest in the face of praise. Like his brilliant young contemporary Cotton Mather, Sewall was also exceedingly earnest and scrupulous in all matters of religion. Sewall married his boss's eighteen-year-old daughter Hannah Hull early in 1676, and together they had fourteen children, including one stillborn, of whom only six survived. Sewall supplies occasional choice details on his wife's lyings-in and other feminine matters, giving us glimpses into family affairs not otherwise available. He names the midwife, the women who first suckle the newborns, the nurses who attend them, the difficulties of getting the firstborn to suck successfully, the baptisms, the illnesses, and the deaths.

Here is a sample vignette. On the sabbath day when the minister was to baptize his sixth child (and fourth son), "Nurse Hill came in before the Psalm was Sung, and yet the Child was fine and quiet." The text of the sermon that day could not have been more satisfying to father's ears. "Mr. Willard preached from John 15th 8. 'Herein is my Father glorified, that you bear much Fruit, so shall ye be my Disciples': which is the first Sermon my little Son hath been present at."[59]

The baby became seriously ill a week later: "Mr. Willard Prayes with my little Henry, being ver ill." Next day he sends notes to the two ministers of his church to pray for Henry. "Monday, about four in the Morn the faint and moaning noise of my child forces me up to pray for it." When the minister arrives that evening, "I get him to go up and Pray with my extream sick Son." Early the next morning, "Child makes no noise save by a kind of snoaring as it breathed, and as it were slept." He reads aloud from the Bible to comfort his wife and the nurse. "And so about Sun-rise, or little after, he fell asleep, I hope in Jesus, and that a Mansion was ready for him in the Father's House. Died in Nurse Hill's Lap. Nurse Hill washes and layes him out." That night Sewall read to himself the part of the Bible "out of which Mr. Willard took his Text the day Henry was baptized."[60]

As Henry lies dying, Sewall can write of little else but this unfolding tragedy, although his affection for all his children is confirmed by his noting that the night before he has taken into bed with him his eighteen-month-old son, "little Hullie," who is suffering from convulsions. He and his wife carried Hullie to Newbury the following April, probably to stay with Sewall's mother in the hope that the air there would clear away his convulsions as it did earlier for their previous son, Samuel. But early one Saturday morning word reaches them that Hullie has fallen ill the previous morning and died that night. They race off within the hour to Newbury, arriving only just in time for the funeral.[61]

There were more births and deaths to follow, and Sewall's diary brings us into the center of events, even if not quite clarifying their emotional meanings. The next of Hannah's and Samuel's children to die was Stephen, born seven months after Hullie's death. "My wife sent not for the Midwife till near 7 at night . . . The child large, so my wive's safe delivery is much to be heeded, considering our former fears." Six months later, little Stephen becomes very sick and the minister arrives to pray with him. "About Nine aclock" the next day, "my dear Son Stephen Sewall expires . . . died in his Grandmother's Bed-Chamber in Nurse Hill's Arms. Had two Teeth cut, no Convulsions." The next evening they carry his coffin down into "the Tomb" at the burial ground, the entire family attending in formal procession, including cousins and the surviving Sewall children, two by two, a male to "lead" each female. The opening of the tomb brought its own horror: "Sam. and his sisters cryed much coming home and at home, so that could hardly quiet them. It seems they look'd into Tomb, and Sam said he saw a great Coffin there, his Grandfathers."[62]

Son Joseph, born a year later, flourished: he took both degrees at Harvard, became minister at his father's Old South Church, married the daughter of a major general, and became a doctor of divinity at Glasgow. But Hannah Sewall bore six more babies after Joseph, five daughters of whom only two survived, and a stillborn son. The first, in order, was little Judith: "I . . . held her up for Mr. Willard to baptize her. She cried not at all, though a pretty deal of water was poured on her by Mr. Willard . . . I named my Daughter Judith for the sake of her Grandmother and great Grandmother, who both wore that Name, and the Signification of it very good." Sewall then launches into a heartfelt panegyric upon his mother-in-law: "Her Prayers and Painstaking for all my Children are incessant, voluntary, with condescension to the meanest Services night and day: that I judg'd I could in justice doe no less than endeavour her remembrance by putting her Name on one of her Grand-Daughters."[63]

Only a few weeks later, "My little Judith languishes and moans, ready to die, and she did. Between 1693 and 1696 daughters Jane and Sarah were born a little over a year apart, followed by their little unnamed brother. Jane lived only five weeks. Not long after Sarah was born, Sewall had a terrifying dream in the night, after a "sore" snowstorm, in which all his children were dead except Sarah, "which did distress me sorely with Reflexions on my Omission of Duty towards them, as well as Breaking oft the Hopes I had of them. The Lord help me thankfully and fruitfully to enjoy them."[64] By way of consolation, a classmate of Sewall's at Harvard, Reverend Edward Taylor of Westfield, Massachusetts, sent two verses that he had written on the death of one of his own children, which express grief but also joyous comfort in the thought that they had gone Home: 'Take, Lord, they're Thine . . . may I sweet flowers for glory breed.'[65] Sewall published the verses with the funeral sermon preached by Cotton Mather.

Cotton Mather has been characterized by Philip Greven as a controlling Calvinist who sought to break the will of his children. Certainly Mather's diary shows that he regularly indulged in the favorite Puritan pastime of scaring them with visions of hell and damnation. Yet Sewall himself imparted much the same doctrine to his own children, then rushed to comfort them when they became fearful.[66] Mather's diary reveals him to have been even more deeply involved in the religious education of his children than was Sewall, especially as they got older, but he shared with Sewall similar degrees of love and affection toward them, and great sorrow over their illnesses and deaths. Early in 1688, his and his wife's five-month-old child, "perhaps one of the Comeliest Infants that have been seen in the world," died of convulsions. He preached that very afternoon about the nature and purpose of such afflictions, using his experience in this way to "quiet my own tempestuous, rebellious heart." He had looked often on this baby's "Lovely Features and Actions," he says, and groans that "few outward, earthly anguishes are equal to these. The dying of a Child is like the tearing of a limb from us."[67]

Sewall and Mather were urban intellectuals of the second and third generations of Puritans, and their relations with their children were shaped and framed by horizons broader than even Boston's Atlantic reach. Diaries written by men elsewhere, removed as they were from the city's excitements, verge more toward the stiff-jawed accounts of Thomas Minor in style but not in feeling. New Hampshire minister John Pike recorded the death of his "dear son, Samuel" in his diary on November 29, 1702. Samuel had "lived seven years, seven months, twenty eight days," his father tells us, "the joy of my heart." In contrast to Minor, Pike is able to convey both his love and a sense of loss. Reciting the precise age, date, and time was a common way for men of this period to focus their thoughts and yet gain perspective on them. It may have helped them deal with life's passages, including those terrible griefs and great joys that their cultural vocabulary silenced.[68]

Daniel King of Marblehead was a godfearing, warmhearted husband and father who, most of the time, managed his apprehensions and grief in the composed and manly style worn by Minor. Yet when his wife had a hard delivery in the early 1730s, King paused to say so and to give thanks to God for her safety and the child's. When his daughter Tabitha died, he called himself accountable to God for her. When, in 1738, his little son Daniel also died, "a pleasant babe," he felt ashamed of his resentment for "another affliction." Then, in March 1739, his son Samuel began having ominous "fits." The father describes him as a "delightfull pleasant chld about four years old" and expresses his sense of "great gilt" over questioning why a child should suffer so and begging God to "have mercy." The vicissitudes of life were undermining his ability to accept God's chastening hand.[69]

Even more striking are the words of John Ballantine, minister at Westfield: "my child is dangerously sick, she is greatly distressed. Righteous art thou O Lord, yet let me plead with thee." He struggles to understand and submit but asks why the Lord would hurt a little child who can gain no benefit from the experience. He and his wife had already lost two children and had named this one for a previous one who had died at "age two and a third years."[70]

After a long and terrible ordeal with his father's final illness, young country minister Justus Forward recalls the death of his own son by drowning the previous year. Then, as he helps settle his father's estate, he happens to notice that it is the anniversary of that son's death, and grief wells up suddenly and overwhelms him as he realizes that "the days of mourning are not ended." As though to rub salt in still-open wounds, his brother's infant son then dies, the very child whom they had "called Joshua to bear our son's name."[71]

Experience Richardson was the wife of a man of property and standing. She was a woman much troubled by religious anxieties. She yearned for signs of God's love yet felt herself under his punishing hand for insufficiently resigning herself to his will. Hers is an exceptionally sad and dreary diary, a case study in clinical depression. Her son, Luther, was born in 1748, when she was forty-three—her previous child had been born many years before, and she had not wanted this surprise. Then he died, "aged 4 yrs 2 mos 11 days old." A week later she reflects: "I was willing to have this child I have lost for God tho I had no mind to have it for my own pleasure and altho I Loved the child two well I am afraid yet this day I thought I was willing to part with it for God and was willing to have a nother for God tho I have no desire to have another for my own pleasure." And she thought maybe having a child die might be better than seeing him grow up to be wicked: "if my heart dont deceve me I was made more contented still by haveing two men come which I Looked upon very wicked thinking how dreadfull it would have been if he had lived to have seen him a man grown and been like them."[72]

Repeated entries bear on her children's fates. She wonders if they are saved and questions the state of her dead child, whose loss continues to haunt her. In July comes a glimmer of warming comfort: "as I was Riding to meeting it came to my mind how I had given my child Luther to God many and many a time . . . I do believe he is gone to rest." And on October 6, 1753, she can write calmly, "a year since my son Luther died."[73]

Although it is difficult to understand Richardson's persistent sense of guilt, not for her child's death but for the danger to his soul, there is no question that she loved him deeply and felt his loss strongly. Surely most parents in old and New England felt such love, although it usually becomes evident only when the diarist fears or experiences a child's death. The question, then, is not whether these New Englanders loved their children but how they treated them. For most parents then as for most parents now, the trick was to find, and maintain, the right balance between loving encouragement of the faltering child and firm enforcement of wholesome rules. These are the topics of the next chapter.

6

Childrearing and the
Experience of Childhood

They no sooner *step* than they *stray,* they no sooner *lisp* then they *ly.*
—Cotton Mather, *Diary*

We humans are not solitary atoms, spinning in our own private spheres. We are social beings and inhabit a universe of our predecessors' making, one structured by hierarchies and stamped by patterns. Because we are mortal, the continuity of this cultural universe relies on the successful socialization of our children. How we rear our children plays an important part in how they socialize each other, and understanding childrearing practices tells us much about the parents. The English brought a long-functioning family system with them to New England and fully intended to bring up their children as English and Puritan. Native Americans offered a perfect counterimage of what they didn't want to be.

Socialization is a two-way street, however. Children do not passively absorb their lessons but respond selectively while actively shaping their world and one another. They do not recreate but reform culture in a lifelong interactive game with their parents and grandparents, with their siblings and cousins and peers, and then with their own children and grandchildren. Meanwhile they have been adapting to whatever changes have come along. Human society is malleable, susceptible to shifts in environmental opportunities and constraints. Tradition is something we choose to remember, for our children's sakes. Culture, therefore, is a dynamic process, not a fixed, inflexible organism. Modifications that promise to improve the success of their children will be quickly incorporated by parents into the cultural corpus of ideas and values. But it is the young who are the most open and imaginative in reaching out to new ideas; they are innovators by nature. Parents, therefore, tend to exaggerate the degree to which they can affect their children's development.[1] Such was the case in Puritan New England.

In most societies, mothers raise the younger children, and men take over the boys when they reach the stage when they can begin to learn the skills pertaining to men. In between these two stages, children socialize one another.[2] Only recently have fathers in our own society become actively involved with their offspring during their most formative years. Among neither the English nor the Ninnimissinouk in early New England did men customarily participate in the care and feeding of infants and toddlers, nor would they even handle them except for ritual purposes such as naming ceremonies. Thus, childrearing for both peoples was in the hands of the women until the child reached age six or seven, after which boys might begin to spend a little time in the company of men. Then as now, from the point of view of the children themselves, the most influential people in their lives, once they have begun to free themselves from their mothers, are other children.

Some developmental biologists define five stages of human growth from birth to reproductive maturity: infancy, childhood, juvenility, adolescence, and adulthood. In this scheme, "childhood" comes after weaning, but teeth, digestive tracts, and immune systems are still immature, and the child's rapidly growing brain continues to place heavy demands on its metabolism. As a result, the young child requires a special diet and protection from predators and disease. This prolongation of the close parental care and oversight that all other species of primates provide only to their nursing young may help to account for the fact that human parents raise a greater percentage of offspring to adulthood than any other species. In their overview of a collection of essays titled *The Evolving Female,* the editors have drawn on multiple field studies of primate and human societies in order to characterize human females and their lives. Humans live and raise their young in a social environment. "To become a viable human adult, the acquisition of social abilities is often of greater importance to future reproductive success than physical size or age at sexual maturity." Learning how to get along in the group, how to give as well as to take, how to seek help and make use of instruction are skills that can only be learned, not inherited.[3] "Culture" comprehends these acquired traits, and humans have crafted an amazing variety of cultural patterns over the centuries and around the globe.

As new parents quickly come to realize, infants and children go through many developmental stages on their way to adulthood. They are partly genetic in origin, but also culturally and environmentally influenced. For instance, mothers in one modern Mayan village of the Yucatán employ a detailed scheme to classify babies at different ages: "very little babies" nurse and sleep on demand; "lap babies" have sufficient control of their heads and backs to be held safely on the hip, at which point they accompany sibling caretakers wherever they go; when "lap babies" get better at sitting up, they are often placed on the floor to sit, sometimes propped up; "scooter babies" have learned to scoot around on their behinds from a sitting position and become mobile and endangered (babies in this village do not learn to crawl). "Upright babies" have learned to stand and then to walk, amidst concerns the child will stumble and fall, so the child is often picked up and carried; mothers believe babies at this age are capable of learning and eager to do so. "Talking babies" (eighteen to twenty-four months) are thought to learn automatically, without deliberate coaching. Mayan children who can follow simple instructions, who consistently obey simple directives, and who can focus on a simple task are no longer viewed as babies but as "beginning-to-start-understanding children." At their own pace, and by watching other children, they learn to take care of themselves, to dress and feed themselves, to follow proper etiquette for elimination of body wastes, to wash themselves, and to put themselves to sleep. They are gradually given chores that benefit the family and not just themselves. They follow older siblings and neighbor children, often carrying a younger sibling with them.[4]

Anthropological psychologists utilize a simpler but similar classification scheme. They differentiate the stages of development as "lap babies," "knee babies," and "yard children," ages four to six. Yard children have boundless energy and are constantly pushing the boundaries of independence from their mothers. They seek out other children to play with, and in most traditional cultures they are socialized by older children who exercise dominance over them, and whose authoritative position in the pecking order is silently ratified by the parents, who do not interfere in children's games or quarrels. Age, size, strength, and "moxie" stratify children in the local "gang," and almost every child has the experience of working his or her way up the prestige ladder.[5]

The spatial density of the local population significantly affects the size and makeup of the child's play group. Agricultural societies, especially those practicing animal husbandry, are usually village based, with sufficient numbers of children present that they can separate into older and younger groups, and the older ones may also divide along gender lines. Hunter-gatherers are generally too few in number for children to divide by age or gender, and the children tend not to differentiate much in their behavior patterns until puberty. Modern Western societies are unique in dispatching their children to school every day, where from prekindergarten through college they attend classes in the company of their age peers. As a result Western children experience far less dominance by older children.

Since it is not possible to observe parent-child and child-child interaction in the households of either the Ninnimissinouk or the English in early New England, the bits and pieces of information that survive in the documents will take on greater meaning if one interprets them in the light of other societies. This approach entails risks: one may miss significant differences. And since cultures are constantly evolving, any practice noted by an observer may be either new, old, or evanescent. Nonetheless, observations of a modern, exceptionally well-studied population, such as the Ache (pronounced "Ah-chaay") of eastern Paraguay, can be helpful in identifying the sequence of choices faced by all parents and children as they deal with one another on a daily basis.[6]

During the first year of her life, an Ache baby is never put down. Someone is holding her at all times, usually but not solely her mother. She sleeps across Mother's knees as Mother sleeps semiupright, to ensure that her baby will be warm, protected against the rain, and not smothered. The baby nurses on demand both at night and during the day. Mother wears nothing at all over her breasts, giving Baby prompt, unobstructed access. Mother may or may not go out to work during the day, "work" being gardening or gathering. She relies on her husband and other adults to help her older children get enough food. At some time before Baby turns a year old, Mother begins to sleep lying down, usually with a man who may not be Baby's father but who helps provide food for herself and Baby's siblings. Baby continues to sleep with Mother and to nurse at will. She spends almost half the daylight time in Mother's arms or lap, but is allowed to sit or stand next to her some of the time. Ache children are late walkers as a consequence of this close restraint, the average age of achievement being twenty-one to twenty-three months, nine months later than the mean for modern American children.[7]

Mother will get pregnant sometime after Baby has turned three and will begin to wean her. Nursing has continued to be frequent throughout the day and night, so the weaning process now proves extremely unpleasant for both. Baby demands to nurse, and Mother refuses, even putting something bitter on her nipples to discourage her. Baby cries, screams, throws terrible tantrums for several weeks, even hitting Mother in angry frustration, and she keeps trying to nurse every time Mother is within reach.

Only after Baby is three will she begin to spend significant time more than a foot away from Mother, who continues to monitor her movements almost constantly. Mother may tie her to her ankle to ensure that she doesn't fall into the open fire or under falling arrows when the group is on a hunt. The floor of the rain forest is a dangerous place for a small person because of the abundance of venomous snakes, spiders, and stinging insects. Ache children are so unused to free walking that they resist it even when the group is moving on to another campsite. Adults will carry children up to the age of five or six on their shoulders for long distances, but when the children are about five they try to put the child down, and at this point there begins a contest of wills over whether or not the child will get carried. "Children scream, cry, hit their parents, and try everything they can think of to get adults to continue carrying them. Often, they simply sit and refuse to walk, prompting older band members to leave them behind. This tactic leads to a dangerous game of 'chicken' in which parents and children both hope the other will give in before the child is too far behind and may become lost . . . A small child cannot survive long in the Paraguayan forest, and if not found within one day is unlikely to survive."[8]

Older children form groups to forage under the eyes of the adult women. The children stay within a few yards of the women, although they readily climb trees for fruit. They also learn to follow the trail signs made by the adults such as bent leaves, twigs, and shrubs. There is no segregation by gender until the boys are old enough to be invited along with the men, at which point they begin to carry a bow that has been given them. (They will not learn how to make their own weapons until they are in midadulthood.) Girls stay with the women and spend a good deal of time babysitting and running errands. They do not begin to carry a burden basket until after they marry, nor will they learn how to make one until then.

Boys begin breaking away from their mothers at an earlier age than their sisters. When as young as eight or ten, they begin living with a male relative or neighbor for lengthy periods.[9] This is particularly the case among those whose biological father no longer resides with their mother or who has died. Boys also go off on extended trips, visiting other bands. They learn hunting, shooting, and forest lore through these self-chosen apprenticeships, during which they learn how to ingratiate themselves with older men and avoid antagonizing them.

This outline of the stages of Ache childhood highlights the long period of close dependency of the child on its mother, interrupted by two abrupt and traumatic transitions: forced weaning and forced walking. Once the child has survived these psychological blows, she joins the world of children, helps to find food, and receives the joint protection and guidance of all the adults in the band. Kinship, real or fictive, continues to play a role. Although sharing is always the rule, successful hunters give the best portions to their own families, and orphans must beg from family to family to get enough to eat.[10] It is no wonder, then, that fatherless boys try to attach themselves to other men, especially because they have already in a sense been thrice sundered from their mothers if they have been displaced by a younger sibling. Girls do not have the option of following a man but must stay with the women, who do not encourage them to be venturesome. Females remain heavily dependent on male providers and protectors for most if not all of their lives. Gender is destiny in this society as it is in many others.

The Narragansetts of precontact southern New England lived in larger bands than the Ache, so the women could call on more kinswomen for help. Parentless children were less likely to risk rejection and go hungry. "There are no beggars amongst them, nor fatherless children unprovided for," observed Roger Williams.[11] Both shellfishing and maize horticulture were under Narragansett women's control, making them less dependent than Ache women on the men's contribution to their diet. The floor of the temperate forest is not nearly so dangerous for the crawling infant or toddling child as the teeming surfaces of the rain forest, so Narragansett babies probably began to walk at an earlier age, making the danger from open fires all the greater.

There are some useful similarities between the modern Ache and the Woodland peoples of northeastern North America, including the Narragansetts, as described by European observers. For instance, Pierre de Charlevoix, writing of the native peoples of New France in the eighteenth century, praised the mothers' care of their young children: "They never leave them, they carry them every where about with them; and even when they are ready to sink under the burthen with which they load themselves."[12] There would be far more danger from the cold in northern winters than in tropical Paraguay, but the Narragansetts could support themselves with stores of maize and dried beans when they took refuge in snug quarters during the coldest season of the year.

A Narragansett mother most likely began weaning her child when she found herself pregnant again. If she hadn't already begun to do so, she would begin feeding the child semiliquid corn mush, but at some point not too far along in her pregnancy she would cease letting the child come to her breast.[13] The distress experienced by the child probably paralleled that of weanling children among the Ache. The Narragansett child would also face the same demand at a similar age that she walk rather than be carried when the families made one of their many seasonal moves. Annual destinations included fishing sites at river falls in early spring, then to their cornfields, to the seashore in summertime, back to the cornfields in the early fall, then on to hunting territories in the late fall, and finally back to winter quarters when the nights turned bitter cold. Women had a great deal to carry from campsite to campsite, including the materials for their houses besides their cooking and sewing tools and other gear.[14] The young child would also have to walk when her mother began carrying the new baby. The fact that she had been consistently freer than her Ache counterpart to run about and develop her muscles probably lessened the shock of no longer being carried when she demanded it.

Babies in English settler families started life like babies among the Ache: they slept with their mothers and nursed freely night and day. Wet nurses were usually neighbors with plenty of milk who helped out the first day or two after birth but thereafter only if the mothers became sick or unable to nurse. Courtesy suckling was part of the mutual aid mothers expected to give each other. Putting out babies to hired wet nurses was not common among the colonists. An overwhelming social consensus from the start favored mothers' breast-feeding their own children.[15]

Ache children wear nothing. Narragansett babies wore only dried moss, and their mothers placed them in cradleboards to make their backs straight.[16] English babies wore cloth diapers, called "clouts." Their mothers swaddled them, presumably for the same reason, and laced them into cradles with rockers. The swaddling clothes were loosened after a few months, at which point cradles ceased being safe repositories for increasingly active infants.[17]

Most babies in all three cultures continued to sleep with their mothers until they were more than six months old and may have done so until weaning. Young children did not have to sleep by themselves after being ejected from the parental bed, but usually moved in with a sibling or cousin. No one slept alone in either society.[18]

Young English babies who slept with their mothers, sisters, or maids were at risk of accidental smothering during the night. A coroner's jury in Plymouth Colony was called to determine the cause of death of a six-month-old baby, "being found dead in the morning in the absence of its parents, lying in bed with Waitstill Elmes and Sarah Hatch, the child's sister." Jurors heard testimony from Daniel Prior, who had lain in the house that night. He confirmed the others' testimony to the effect that "the child had not been well a day or two before, troubled with a cold, and that it was found dead on its face at a distance from those that then lay with it, yett by view finding it to be very blacke about one syde of the head and soe parte of the body, wee, according to our information and best understanding, judge that either it was stiffled by lying on its face or accidentally overlayed in the bed, as a cause of its death."[19]

Likewise, the son of Mary Fiske was found dead lying on his mother's arm as she lay in bed at her brother's house in Providence in November 1708, "& none in ye Howse Sencible of its being Sick." The town called a jury of inquest of twelve men, who pronounced the death an act of God. A few months later in the same town, a young child, son of Lieutenant James Olney and his wife, Halelujah, died suddenly in the night, and another jury of twelve men brought in a similar verdict of natural death.[20]

Parents or nursemaids in New England must also have spent a good deal of time carrying their little charges about in their arms or on their hips, since there are no references to slings or backpacks or cradleboards or high chairs, although rare inventories mention a "child's chair." Crying babies were rocked in cradles, walked about, sung to. When they became mobile, scooting or crawling, or started walking, they were tied to their caretakers by "leading strings," to keep them out of trouble. Some parents made go-carts for their toddlers, but these were dangerous.[21] To give their mothers time to do their many chores, older siblings or cousins probably took charge of the babies as they proceeded through their developmental stages, from "lap," to "scooter" or crawler, to "knee," to "yard."

Only very rarely do probate inventories mention nursing bottles. Most children were weaned directly from the breast to spoon food such as corn mush made with milk, the timing probably being determined by the availability of fresh milk from cows. A few diaries allude explicitly to weaning, usually in pained tones because the young child was complaining noisily and persistently. Some mothers even moved out of the house for a few weeks in order to accomplish the weaning.[22]

Weaning and replacement by a new rival came at a much earlier age for English children than for the Ache and the Narragansetts, but whether their loss was any the less stressful on that account seems doubtful.[23] When they got "too big," they too were no longer picked up and carried on family treks, such as the walk to church on Sundays. They confronted toilet training some time after learning to walk, an event that may have brought its own share of anxiety, but there is no mention of it in the diaries. Children under the age of seven wore skirts and no underwear, and floors were bare boards, so "accidents" were less troublesome than they are today. Like the unclothed and undiapered Ninnimissinouk children, English children probably "toilet trained" themselves, as many modern Swedish children are encouraged to do.[24]

As children move from infancy through childhood, they generally become more sociable, more verbal, more competent in motor skills, and more able and eager to acquire cultural information. They seek attention and approval for performing chores or completing self-care tasks, for sharing information about events that they observed or heard about, and for remembering to ask permission to leave home to explore or to join social activities. Out-of-doors, they may spend less time under direct adult supervision and more time with other children of mixed ages. They universally become much more self-conscious about who they are and where they fit in the world beyond the doorstep. They learn that age and gender structure that world, as does kinship. Older children tend to dominate them, and they, in turn, dominate the lap babies and knee babies. At some point in this process, depending on the culture, their mothers give them clothes or adornments that help them define who they are, and they come to identify more specifically with other members of the same sex.[25] They observe the gender division of labor that prevails among adults and see the status differentials between men and women that are associated with their work responsibilities. They come to understand that their own tasks, at home or in school, are more or less honorable in terms of age and gender and so are early encouraged to strive for more demanding and more responsible assignments. All of this learning is mediated through the children's own group dynamics. Just as children must accommodate themselves to the will of powerful adults, so parents find their power diffused and refracted by their children's siblings and peers.

"Culture" shapes how parents view these stages and what they understand of the child's competence and its limits. In some cultures, parents regard the early experiences of babies and very young children as unimportant to their later development. They therefore hand them over to cheap help until they become more articulate. In other cultures, parents view their own roles in raising even very young children as of central importance to their happiness and future careers. Much depends on how parents perceive children's personality development, whether they think it is governed more by innate tendencies or by external influences. If the latter, parents will intervene regularly in their children's daily lives in order to control their environment and mold their characters and habits. If, on the other hand, children are to be allowed to grow up according to their own internal clocks and temperaments, the parent's task becomes one of merely supplying them with appropriate means and skills at the right time and, in the meanwhile, preventing them from doing harm to themselves and others. These viewpoints fall into two familiar opposing camps: nature versus nurture. How much one trusts or fears human nature determines how far one is willing to go in trying to change it.[26]

Native American parents of the seventeenth and eighteenth centuries "indulged" their children in behaviors that Europeans often found rude, indeed intolerable. Father Gabriel Sagard remarked that Huron and Algonquian fathers loved their children dearly even though they were "for the most part very naughty, paying them little respect, and hardly more obedience . . . and parents, for failure to punish their children, are often compelled to suffer wrong-doing at their hands, sometimes being beaten and flouted to their face . . . Bad example, and bad bringing up, without punishment or correction, are the causes of all this lack of decency."[27] The Europeans and the natives had clearly different styles of childrearing, and Europeans reacted strongly against any overt demonstration of childish independence.

Roger Williams remarked on Narragansett fathers' indulgent love for their children,

> I have knowne a Father to take so grievously the loss of his childe, that hee hath cut and stob'd himselfe with griefe and rage. This extreme affection, together with want of learning, make ther children sawcie, bold, and undutifull. I once came into a house, and requested some water to drink; the father bid his son (of some 8 years of age) to fetch some water; the boy refused, and would not stir; I told the father, that I would correct my child, if he should so disobey me, &c. Upon this the father took up a stick, the boy another, and flew at his father; upon my persuasion, the poor father made him smart a little, throw down his stick, and run for water, and the father confessed the benefit of correction, and the evil of their too indulgent affections.[28]

The father in this case must have been confused by Williams' advice as well as embarrassed at his son's bad manners. Normal courtesy prevailed, however, as the host made himself and his boy agreeable to this strange guest.

Jesuit priest Pierre de Charlevoix explained Miami and Potawatomi parenting styles in the eighteenth century as a deliberate effort to foster sturdy independence. "Nothing can exceed the care which mothers take of their children whilst in the cradle; but from the moment they have weaned them, they abandon them entirely to themselves; not out of hard heartedness or indifference, for they never lose but with their life the affection they have for them; but from a persuasion that nature ought to be suffered to act upon them, and that they ought not to be confined in any thing."[29] Like the mothers in the Mayan village, these Native American mothers saw little point in exercising parental control over the individual development of children once they became "yard" children.

The comments of Sagard, Charlevoix, Williams, and many others show that Europeans expected parents to apply physical force if necessary to compel obedience and respect from their children. Native Americans, on the other hand, expected children to develop self-discipline and good manners through interaction with their peers. In their view, it was up to each individual to meet and overcome challenges by close study of the environment and, for boys, by constant striving in competition with peers and through the emulation of heroes. In contrast, Europeans placed the responsibility for these attainments squarely on the shoulders of the parents, who believed they must overcome the naturally willful and slothful nature of their children through continuing supervision and correction.

Handing on "Christian civilization," then, was up to the parents, an obligation of awesome proportions. To help them in their task, the God of the Europeans had commanded his people to honor "thy father and thy mother," and children were judged by their demeanor toward their elders. To all orthodox Christians, whether Protestant or Catholic, the necessity for punishment arose out of the sinful nature of humankind since Adam's fall from grace. Children are born with the stain of original sin inherited from Adam, and their nature naturally inclines towards evil. Anne Bradstreet of colonial Massachusetts put this into rhyme:

> Stained from birth with *Adams* sinfull fact,
> Then I began to sin as soon as act;

> A perverse *will,* a love to what's forbid,
> A serpents sting in pleasing face lay hid:
> A lying tongue as soon as it could speak,
> And fifth Commandment do daily break.[30]

Original sin condemned even babies to eternal damnation unless God redeemed them. Christian baptism would remove the stain temporarily and forestall that terrible fate should they die. Baptism protected only the very young, however. It could not remove an individual's inherited tendencies toward evil, so as the child grows older, the threat of damnation increased. Christians of the early modern period believed, therefore, that because young children were naturally and sinfully willful, their willfulness must be curbed early and consistently in order for them to feel authentic contrition, the necessary first step toward salvation. Parents were not to be seduced by their affections or by the apparent innocence of their little children but were to maintain strict vigilance against sinful acts.[31]

English beliefs about children and childrearing should be understood in the context of Christian ideas about the purpose of human life, which was to glorify God and seek personal salvation. The Christian's journey on earth required a persistent seeking of God's will and an active striving to avoid temptation to do that which God abhorred. The earnest Christian reviewed his conscience daily to discover sinful thoughts and acts, to repent of them, and to pray to God for forgiveness. Without forgiveness, one died in a sinful state, at great risk to one's soul. Prior to the English Reformation under Henry VIII, the English shared the religious culture of their contemporaries on the continent. As Catholics, they had believed that penance imposed by a priest for a sin was efficacious toward receiving absolution, whereas Protestants were arguing that only God, not good works, could absolve the sinner of her sins. Because sins were odious in the eyes of God, both branches believed that sins should be punished in this world, whether or not the sinner repented. Hence punishment for a child's misbehavior may have been seen as a form of atonement, although it was also used to shame the child and to change her or his behavior. Corporal punishment served as warning and negative reinforcement.[32]

Ideas about how children learn and the functions of punishment did not alter as a consequence of the advent of Protestantism in England or of its evolution into Puritan forms. Attitudes toward children began to change only in the eighteenth century, and even then were primarily restricted to the educated classes. Comparisons of Catholic and Protestant manuals yield much the same advice with the same explanations. A pre-Reformation English essayist, Richard Whytford, published in 1530 a book of Christian advice to "householders," in which he instructed fathers and masters how to regulate their families. Most importantly, they were to require their servants and children to assimilate the rules of Christian morality by means of memorizing prayers and lessons. Parents were to begin instruction of children "as soon as they could speak. For it is an old saying, 'The pot or vessel shall ever savor or smell of that thing wherewith it is first seasoned.'" Similarly, "the young cock crows as he hears."[33]

As Whytford's use of these proverbs suggests, he believed that very young children learned most easily and that conscientious parents could imprint on them the forms of correct behavior. Learning would "take" through imitation and repetition: "Bringing up and learning do make manners . . . The plover by sight will follow the gesture and behavior of the fowler. And the ape by exercise will work and do as she is taught, and so will the dog . . . learn to dance. The children therefore that by reason do far exceed other creatures will bear away what they hear spoken . . . as they be taught, so will they do, and in many things they may be compelled unto a continual custom which alters and changes natural disposition."[34] Children, in this view, were like potter's clay. By the command exercised by their parents over their daily routine, so would they be shaped. But let them go unsupervised and uninstructed, and they would quickly fall into bad company, endangering their souls. For those of strong religious bent in early modern England, Christian nurture should work to overcome evil nature in the education of children.

These are precisely the same concerns expressed by Ezekias Woodward a hundred years later, who warned that parents must not suffer the child to be idle, nor to swear oaths, and the parent likewise must not swear. If parents were careful always to keep their word, the child would be less likely to lie. Children should not be allowed to quarrel among themselves or to bully the servants. Compelling obedience was the best lesson for children.[35] Faithful parents were activist parents; faithful children, unlike Pinocchio, must not disregard their teachings. Yet, as Pinocchio discovered, evil companions lay in wait to entrap them, for Satan and his minions stood ever poised to snatch their souls away.

Evil-intentioned spirits also abounded in Native American societies of the Northeast, but one could generally "buy them off" by observing customary taboos and making appropriate gestures of respect and sacrifice. The penalty for disrespect could be bad luck in hunting or even death for oneself or one's kin, including children. Such placatory gestures were abominable in the eyes of the practicing Christian because God tolerated no rivals. Only the steady inculcation of obedience, good habits, and the fear of God would protect children from Satan's clutches. When they erred, Whytford's advice to parents was that the punishment should be swift and well laid on. He makes this clear in offering this "pretty lesson to teach your children":

> If I lie, backbite, or steal,
> If I curse, scorn, mock, or swear,
> If I chide, fight, strive, or threat,
> Then am I worthy to be beat.
> Good mother or mistress mine,
> If any of these nine
> I trespass to your knowing,
> With a new rod and fine,
> Early naked before I dine,
> Amend me with a scourging.

Whytford counsels the parent to scourge for the sake of the child. "Think it not cruelly but mercifully done. For the wise man sayeth, who spares the rod hates the child."[36]

Christian chastisement was nevertheless to be combined with gentleness and applied for the good of the child. "Whosoever do the correction, whether it be in lashes or words, let it be done with the charity of our lord and with a mild and soft spirit that ever it be done for the reformation of the person rather than for the revenge of the fault." Whytford goes on to advise the parent to defer all correction if "vexed, chafed, troubled, wroth, or angry for any cause." The parent should explain the nature of the offense and the reason for punishment before applying it, and afterward "forgive them clearly and gently"; for "if you rebuke or strike with hastiness to revenge your own cause or appetite, you shall render them more stubborn and stiff-hearted and engender in them an hatred toward you." Love and concern for the child will cleanse the violence of its anger and ugliness, transforming it into a positive, clarifying experience.[37]

In his "pretty lesson" Whytford assigned the office of correction to the mother or the master's wife, "for commonly they do take the labor of that ministry and service." Women, then, were the usual disciplinarians in

Whytford's England. In his explication of the Ten Commandments, he expounds the commandment "to honor thy father and thy mother." He advises parents to require the children to ask for their blessing every night, "kneeling before they go to rest." And if the child resists, "let it surely be whisked with a good rod and be compelled thereunto by force. And if [the child is too old for] such correction and yet will be obstinate, let them have such sharp and grievous punishment as conveniently may be devised, as to sit at dinner alone and by themself at a stool in the middle of the hall with only brown bread and water." Whytford here is advocating shaming and deprivation as more effective for the older child than hitting or striking. As for the oldest recalcitrants, he tells parents to put them out to service or otherwise banish them because of the bad example they set for others.[38]

Whytford stresses the Christian duty of parents, masters, and mistresses to instruct, restrain, and punish their wards for their own good, and the earlier they start, when the child is just beginning to talk, the more compliant and obedient the child will become. Submission to authority, obedience, and dutifulness were central virtues to be imparted, and parents who could not exact such behavior from their children by one means or another were failing in their duty and should turn them over to another better equipped to do the job. Indeed, when their children reached age eleven or so, English parents were not loath to pass on the task to others. Those of middling status apprenticed them, laboring folk bound them out as servants in husbandry, and even upper-class parents sent them off to serve in elite households. The legislature of colonial Connecticut required that children who were unruly be placed with a master until they turned twenty-one (girls at eighteen), and if ever convicted of "stubborn or rebellious carriage," they were to be committed to the house of correction for hard labor and severe punishment.[39]

Using physical means to coerce obedience was endorsed by all sides in a society anxious to secure good order. How commonly, and with what restraint, did English parents "whisk with the rod"? Historian Linda Pollock searched a large sample of British and American diaries and correspondence for clues to childrearing among people born between 1500 and 1900. She reports that in every generation some children were beaten regularly and heartlessly, whereas others were gently nurtured. She concludes that methods of discipline have always varied among parents and that "no century was or will be notably cruel or kind." Such a view apparently asserts the primacy of inherited temperament in shaping parenting styles despite changing fashions of childrearing advice, although Pollock herself stops short of theorizing about human nature or the role of religion and culture in child development.[40]

Authors of New England diaries and memoirs of the seventeenth and eighteenth centuries ruthlessly censor personal expressions of emotion except those ritually prescribed sentiments on occasions such as the illness and death of one's parents and children. At these moments, however, the door of the heart sometimes opens up further than the diarist perhaps intends. Fathers who made note of the death of a child in their diaries often supply some seemingly irrelevant detail, such as the exact time of day when the child was born and when he or she died, even calculating the precise number of the child's days on earth. Recounting apparently trivial facts may have provided some small relief, sticks of reality to which to cling to avoid going under in a stormy sea of anger and grief. By contrast, in the late eighteenth and the nineteenth centuries, an expanding vocabulary of emotional expression registers itself in the diaries and correspondence. Pollock suggests that the growing use of such language may mislead modern scholars into seeing a greater contrast between earlier and later times than their actual behavior warrants. Yet, acquiring socially acceptable phrases to express one's feelings probably makes one more aware of them, and this would have been a positive step toward greater self-realization and better parenting in Anglo-American society.

Although early diaries are a difficult genre to interpret because they are so terse, their writers bound by conventions of spiritual piety and strict emotional control, they provide useful evidence on the role of physical punishment in childrearing. The earliest English diarist identified by Pollock was Henry Machyn (1498–1563), a Catholic tailor, who reported that he had seen a woman set in the pillory for beating her child with rods. He does not say whether she was being punished for hitting her child or for beating it with rods or for beating the child too hard. The last seems to be indicated by another entry in which Machyn reports that a young apprentice had been beaten so severely by his master that the skin was taken off his back. For that, the master was also set in the pillory and whipped until "blude ran downe." From these two entries one can reasonably infer with Pollock that, for Machyn, physical punishment of the young was acceptable only in moderation.[41]

John Dee (1527–1608), teacher, mathematician, astrologer, and father of six, offered no insight into his own reaction when he reported that

"Katharin [eight years old at the time] by a blow on the eare given by her mother did bled at the nose very much, which did stay for an houre and more." The potential seriousness of the injury is probably what caused him to write it down, but Dee neither interfered with his wife nor expressed criticism of her in his diary. He may have had good reason to trust her judgment, since all six of their children survived to adulthood.[42]

Memoirist Grace Mildmay (1552–1620), gentlewoman, recalled that she was often whipped as a girl, to "inculcate virtuous principles." Richard Norwood (1590–1675), surveyor, wrote that as a child, "often on a Lord's day at night or Monday morning I prayed to escape beating that week." Henry Newcome (1627–1695), a Puritan minister and father of five, acted more in conformity with Whytford's advice when he "discharged my duty of correction to my poor child, prayed with him after." Yet others recall no harsh regimen and speak only of parental love. Oliver Heywood (1630–1702), another Puritan minister, tried to be severe with his boys: "on Saturday morning my sons having not made their latin in expectation to goe to Halifax, were loath to goe to schoole, yet I threatened them, they went crying, my bowels workt and I sent to call them back."[43]

Among the English there appears to have been a close relationship between degree of religious conviction and depth of concern for the proper upbringing of children, especially boys. Ralph Josselin and Adam Martindale, in addition to Henry Newcome and Oliver Heywood, were pious Puritan clergymen who kept rich, informative diaries, and all four had trouble with at least one of their sons. Family historian Ralph Houlbrooke remarks, "It is in this group that we find the most intense brooding over boys' moral development, though they also worried about early accidents and illnesses." "Lord," asked Oliver Heywood in 1676, whose two sons were then away at college in Scotland, "Shall children of so many prayers and teares miscarry?"[44]

Pious English parents felt the weight of their responsibilities and feared that any indulgence would endanger their children's souls. But they, like Heywood, must often have found their hearts yearning toward them. Stern admonitions, consistent application of rules, and the use of physical chastisement were all part of the recommended package; but for many parents, as the diaries and memoirs show, love and tenderness infiltrated the system at every pore.

The advice literature and the sermons may have preached a single philosophy of childrearing, but Pollock's survey of English diaries has disclosed a variety of practices. The same holds true for the records in New England and its Puritan society. Modern writers on the subject of Puritan childrearing ideas tend to disregard the pre-Reformation origins of this tradition and to treat parental implementation as straightforward applications of what was a very complex and dynamic religious ideology.[45] The English in New England were not all of one mind, and their ideas about families, children, and gender evolved as they adapted to the New World environment, including the presence of large numbers of non-Christian neighbors. Furthermore, descendants idealized the immigrants and their motives, creating a mythological "Puritan" ideal type to which standard they sought to hew, and were inevitably disappointed and concerned for their children. Failure to appreciate these generational shifts in the religious psychology of parenting in seventeenth-century New England will only lend further support to the old stereotype in Americans' minds of "stern" Puritan parents freely and unfeelingly applying the switch. A favorite piece of evidence often adduced in this regard is a printed sermon by John Robinson, the pastor of the Pilgrims' church in Leiden, who never set foot on these shores. "And surely there is in all children," he avowed,

> a stubbornness, and stoutness of mind arising from natural pride, which must, in the first place, be broken and beaten down, that so the foundation of their education being laid in humility and tractableness, other virtues may, in their time, be built thereon . . . For the beating, and keeping down of this stubborness parents must provide carefully . . . that the children's wills and wilfulness be restrained and repressed, and that, in time; lest sooner than they imagine, the tender sprigs grow to that stiffness, that they will rather break than bow.[46]

This advice goes beyond both the Catholic Whytford and the Protestant Woodward in the harshness of its imagery. Robinson here is recommending that the child not be allowed to have a mind of its own but be made spinelessly submissive in order to be educated. "Break the will, by force if necessary." Probably no one outside the Separatist community ever read this tract, but the question remains, did New Englanders follow this kind of advice in raising their children? Certainly a long succession of New England ministers stressed the importance of inculcating obedience very early in the child's development and of doing this so consistently and so calmly that children would understand the necessity, and harsh punishments would not then be necessary.

How demanding and punishing—how repressive—were the Puritans to-ward their children? Like Pollock, Edmund Morgan searched his sources but found no evidence that seventeenth-century parents were any more likely to strike a child than were parents of later times.[47] Philip Greven agrees that the most successful evangelical parents did not need to use physical punish-ment because they watched and corrected the young child so intensively and consistently that they won the battle early. He judges them repressive, nevertheless, because they did not allow the child to grow emotionally and psychologically.[48] Like the Reformed Protestants in old England, Puritans in New England believed themselves weightily endowed by God with respon-sibility toward their children as well as with his authority, and, as in old Eng-land, there were parents who felt their better judgment occasionally over-whelmed by their affections. Third-generation minister Cotton Mather wore both hats: "They go astray as soon as they are born. They no sooner *step* than they *stray,* they no sooner *lisp* then they *ly.* Satan gets them to be proud, pro-fane, reviling and revengeful as *young* as they are." He also confessed rather disarmingly, "Lord we know, we know, wee that are Parents feel it so, that if one of our Children should come to us and say unto us, 'Fathere there is one thing that would make us perfectly and forever Happy and it is a thing that you can do us, by Speaking of on Word; will you please to do it?' Wee could sooner dy, than deny that thing unto them."[49]

The evidence on parental discipline in colonial New England is scanty. Early diarists say nothing about the forms and frequency of punishments meted out to their own children, and court records refer to cases of servant-beating but not to the excessive chastisement of one's own children. The English continued to support the right and obligation of the father to "cor-rect" his wife and of both parents to correct their children. Thus the absence of comment in the records about child-beating does not mean that physical correction was spared.

The probable goal for Puritan parents in New England, as it has been for most modern parents, was to balance love and gentleness with consistent discipline. Most likely, physical enforcement played its most crucial role in bringing up very young children, who were, after all, under the care and di-rection of their mothers. If the mother did her job well, the children would already have been thoroughly habituated to cheerful obedience by the time their father took closer notice of them. Both Samuel Sewall and Cotton Mather greatly preferred speaking to their children in private and praying with them to spanking or whipping. A reminiscence written much later by an adoring grandson describes the disciplinary style of Sarah Pierpont Edwards, wife of the great theologian Jonathan Edwards.

> She had an excellent way of governing her children; she knew how to make them regard and obey her cheerfully, without loud angry words, much less heavy blows. She seldom punished them; and in speaking to them, used gentle and pleasant words. If any correction was necessary, she did not administer it in a passion; and when she had occasion to reprove and rebuke, she would do it in few words . . . with all calmness and gentleness of mind . . . Her system of discipline, was begun at a very early age, and it was her rule, to resist the first, as well as every subsequent exhibition of temper or disobedience in the child, however young, until its will was brought into submission to the will of its parents: wisely reflecting, that untill a child will obey his parents, he can never be brought to obey God.[50]

Esther Edwards Burr, daughter of this consummate Puritan mother, moved from Northampton, Massachusetts, to Princeton, New Jersey, in the early 1750s with her new husband, Aaron Burr. There he took charge of the new Presbyterian college, and Esther led a busy life as hostess, housekeeper, and mother. She wrote a series of letters to her closest friend back home, and these furnish stunning glimpses into her feelings about her children and herself. Daughter Sally was about nine months old when Esther reports: "You my dear cant immagine how much pleased of late Mr. Burr is with his little Daughter. He begins to think she is good to kiss, and thinks he sees a great many beauties in her, that he used to be perfectly blind to. He complains she is another temptation to him, to spend two [sic] much time with her—he does love to play with her dearly." Only one month later, Esther is explaining:

> I have begun to govourn Sally. She has been Whip'd once on Old Adams account, and she knows the difference between a smile and a frown as well as I do. When she has done any thing that she surspects [sic] is wrong, will look with concern to see what Mama says, and if I only knit my brow she will cry till I smile, and altho she is not quite Ten months old, yet when she knows so much, I think tis time she should be taught. But none but a parent can conceive how hard it is to chastise your own most tender self. I confess I never had a right idea of the mothers heart at such a time before.[51]

Teaching right from wrong requires more than frowning, Esther is thinking, but by this point she has used physical means once only. By the time

Sally was two years old, using such means had become frequent enough to make Esther wince in shame as she recalls times when she overdid it. "I feel as I do after whping Sally prety hard, and am affraid I have whiped her more then was needfull."[52] That Esther can write so freely about hitting her toddler shows that she does not question her right and duty to do so; she questions only whether she is doing it with proper restraint, as Richard Whytford had advised some two centuries earlier.

Older children who had not sufficiently absorbed the lesson of obedience when young—whether because of too-soft or careless parents or their own stubborn temperament—were the ones most likely to challenge and anger supervising adults. Young servants, in particular, often felt the sting of a master's or mistress' anger. Minister Peter Thacher, for instance, says nothing about spanking his children, yet reported in 1679: "I came home & found that my Indian girle had like to have knocked my Theodora in the head by leting her fall wherefore I took a good walnut stick & beat ye Indian to purpose till she promise never to do soe anymore." Picking up "a good walnut stick" to "beat to purpose" gave vent to Thacher's fear and anger and perhaps to something uglier.[53] Despite this one violent outburst against a despised and helpless outsider, Thacher's diary shows him to have been a good person who clearly loved his wife and children.

Two incidents in early court records illustrate the several dimensions of the Puritan attitude toward parental responsibility. Judges of the Essex County Court in 1660 admonished Francis Urselton and his wife "for leaving their children alone in the night in a lonely house, far from neighbors, after having been warned of it." The New Haven town fathers charged a parent in 1656 who allowed his children to engage in "disorderly walking" on the sabbath, and stealing apples and eggs from neighbors instead of going to sabbath services at the meeting house. "The said children are not nurtured and brought up as children ought to be," they huffed. Their father was required to post bond that his children would behave "well and righteously amonge their neighbours," and that they would attend church regularly. If the family did not reform, the magistrates warned, they would be banished.[54]

Nobody among the French or English liked "spoiled" children. What they wanted was a respectful, obedient, courteous, cooperative child. What Native Americans wanted was a physically and mentally tough, bold, adventuresome, and independent child, and they achieved their goal by turning their children loose to teach one another. Native boys in the Northeast learned through self-directed practice how to draw the bow and shoot the arrow, to throw spears, and to play competitive sports in order to develop their bodies and perfect the skills that would bring them success as men. "But if a mother asks her son to go for water or wood or do some similar household service," complained Father Sagard, "he will reply to her that this is girl's work and will do none of it."[55]

All societies tend to raise boys differently from girls, although the age varies at which distinctions between them formally manifest themselves. The differences center on the division of labor, but adults seem also to believe there is a divergence in the *way* boys and girls learn as well as in what they should learn. According to many studies, boys and girls come to regard each other as different on their own and at quite an early age, and when given the opportunity to do so will choose others of their own sex as friends and playmates. Whether or not mothers actively discriminate in their child-rearing modes, the young boy soon transfers his learning model to other males because he prefers their company. He strives to be noticed and sufficiently liked by older boys and young men so that they will tolerate his presence and teach him things while his sisters continue under the direction of their mother or other female kin. Just as boys prefer to be with other boys, girls tend to regard boys as too assertive and boisterous. Girls "grow into" their mother's roles through early immersion in them, receiving continual reward from one another as well as from her for their hearty cooperation and team spirit. The precise way in which boys become men in each culture depends on what it is that most distinguishes men's work from women's. The path of their trajectory may be easy and painless, or it may be deliberately beset with obstacles and ordeals.[56]

Although Pierre de Charlevoix made no distinction with reference to gender in describing the freedom Native American mothers gave their children, it is doubtful that their daughters experienced anything like the same degree of encouragement toward independence as their sons. Boys' games and rivalries excluded girls, and mothers needed their daughters' help. As soon as the little girls learned to walk "they have a little stick put into their hands to train them and teach them early to pound corn, and when they are grown somewhat they also play various little games with their companions, and in the course of these small frolics they are trained quietly to perform trifling and petty household duties."[57]

Little girls in England were also supposed to stay close to their mothers and learn domestic tasks, but social class clearly affected the degree of parental oversight. Girls of the lower classes were not as strictly supervised as girls in higher social ranks. For instance, a London artisan's daughter, aged less than four, went out "with a nother little childe to play as we had thought but it semes my dafter Sarah left the other childe and went herself as far as [the] fell." Once she was missed, her father went out to search, with no success, but she was brought home safely by a neighbor, to his vast relief. Rural children were also given a great deal of freedom, although boys enjoyed more than girls, to judge by Barbara Hanawalt's findings from medieval coroners' records: the most common causes of untimely deaths among children aged two or three were falling into wells or ponds, and scalding. She noted that the boys' accidents generally took place *outside*, unlike the girls'.[58]

"Growing up" comprises all those changes, physical, mental, and emotional, that normal children undergo between birth and adulthood. "Adulthood" is as much a cultural and legal condition as it is a biological state. The English defined it as the ability to make and keep contracts, and interpreted it as beginning at the age of eighteen for women and twenty-one for men; but in practice, unmarried persons were treated as dependent, incomplete, and subadult. Under the law, "infancy" ended at age seven, followed by "childhood" (seven through thirteen) and "nonage" (fourteen through seventeen for females, fourteen through twenty for males). Until age seven, English boys and girls were given similar tasks and clothing, but upon reaching age seven, the boys were "breeched," donning the garment distinctive to men. Girls, meanwhile, continued to wear skirts and aprons. It was only after their boys had begun wearing breeches that English fathers took a more active role in their upbringing, encouraging their sons toward greater independence and self-reliance. A striking example comes from the eighteenth-century diary of Massachusetts minister Ebenezer Parkman, who proudly reported dispatching his seven-year-old son on horseback alone to the gristmill with a sack of grain.[59] It was typical of the culture and the times that the opportunity Parkman offered his young son was a work task.

Work was what most people did most of the time in early modern England and its colonies. Except among a few, school was not yet the principal means of socializing and educating children. Until age twelve or fourteen, most English children lived at home, worked at home, and played with their siblings and friends in the neighborhood. Outside urban areas, it was rare for a young child to have others of the same age to play with. Older children were responsible for younger ones: they taught them how to behave and how to play by rules. Most likely they were not gentle and did not teach by explaining.[60]

Few English children in the seventeenth century went to school on a regular basis, and if they did, it was for only a few weeks in the year. Although Protestants everywhere in early modern Europe actively espoused the teaching of the Bible, the process of educating the common people, particularly females, was to be a halting one. The English at mid-seventeenth century were still overwhelmingly rural and "massively illiterate," according to David Cressy, who estimates that more than two-thirds of the men and over nine-tenths of the women were unable to write their names.[61]

English immigrants to New England, on the other hand, were an especially determined lot, intent on creating a Bible-centered, godly society free of blaspheming and sabbath-breaking. Popular literacy was a vital key to achieving their utopia, and they were cheerfully willing to mandate, and pay for, near-universal availability of schooling in the townships despite soaring costs as the population dispersed. Massachusetts passed laws as early as the 1640s that required towns above a minimum size to maintain schools and support school masters: those with fifty families were to ensure that reading and writing would be taught by someone in the town, and those of a hundred or more were to support grammar schools taught by college graduates to prepare qualified boys for college and the ministry. Connecticut and Plymouth soon followed suit.

Passing laws does not ensure compliance. Who was to pay the teacher, maintain the building, supply the firewood? Who would teach? Before the 1670s, grammar-school teachers were never in short supply. Harvard began graduating young men at a good clip by the end of the 1640s, and despite the founding of so many new towns, they were not hiring ministers at a rate fast enough to absorb them all. Meanwhile established pulpits seldom went vacant, because their occupants usually lived to a ripe old age. So a steady stream of hopefuls entered the job market for grammar-school masters, hoping to earn their keep and pick up invitations to preach as they jockeyed for a pastorate.[62]

Teaching contracts ran for a year at a time, and students were of all levels, many wholly unprepared. In the town of Hampton, New Hampshire, John Legat agreed in 1649 "to teach & instruct all the children of or belonging to our town, both male & female (which are capable of learning) to write & read & cast accounts (if it be desired) this yeare insuing, as the weather shall be fitting for the youth to come together to one place; also to teach & instruct them once in a week or more in some orthodox Catechism provided for them by their parents or masters." Watertown, on the Charles River west of Cambridge, prescribed similar duties in 1651 for a prospective schoolmaster, adding, however, that "it is in the liberty of any inhabitant to send his sons or servant for a week or two and to take them away again at his plea-sure." The teachers could not count on any kind of continuity: they came and went, these shy and awkward strangers, and how could a teacher ever know what each understood in terms of words, meanings, and concepts? Watertown leaders also directed the schoolmaster to accept girls "that have a desire to learn to write." They did not seem to anticipate much demand, but at least the girls were welcome, as at Hampton, New Hampshire. There is no indication whether the girls were taught along with the boys or separately. For learning English only, the tuition in Watertown would be three pennies a week; for those learning how to write or to learn Latin, the tuition would be four pennies.[63]

These early laws and contracts were optimistic, and a few generously in-cluded girls, but modes of financing became highly contentious. At no time did leaders seriously contemplate the complete package we now associate with public schools: compulsory attendance financed entirely out of taxes levied on the whole community of landowners. New Haven town records give some idea of the nature of the debate over public education. The town meeting appointed a committee to discuss where to have a school and how much salary to allow the teacher, whether the town should bear part of the charges, whether "the parents of the children [should also be?] taught apart," and "whether parents shall be compelled to put their children to Learning, at least to learne to read English & to write." It would have been illuminating to hear that discussion.[64]

A man with a master's degree from Harvard was clearly overqualified to teach basic reading skills. It would not have been cost-effective to employ him for this purpose, but neither New Haven or any of the other towns ap-propriated public funds to hire women for the purpose, a choice that would become common in the eighteenth century. As a consequence, private dame schools appeared wherever towns hired writing schoolmasters and set admission standards. These dame schools were unregulated private enter-prises, and parents took their chances. The daughter of a Captain How was hauled into court, along with her mother, for swearing. Her mother said her daughter had learned "ill carriage" at Goodwife Wickam's where she went to "scoole." The court sentenced the daughter to be whipped "suitable to her yeares."[65]

The larger towns found it possible at first to comply with the school laws, but the challenge of pioneering ultimately proved too great a financial burden for the majority of the towns to support this keystone in the arch of Puritanism. As early as 1660, the court in New Haven Colony confessed itself "deeply sensible of the small progress" made "of late yeares in the colony and of the great difficulty & charge to make pay etc for the maintaining children at ye schools or colledge in the Bay [Harvard, in Massachusetts Bay Colony]." The following year New Haven did succeed in hiring a grammar-school master. All prospective students would be screened for competency. The master was to have one week's vacation each year, to be free from taxes, and to have free lodging "in a settled habitation." His pay was to be forty pounds from the colony and ten pounds from the town, to be paid mostly in country produce: wheat, pork, beef, Indian corn, pease, oats, flax, and butter.[66]

Where no writing school existed, ministers such as Peter Thacher took in boys for instruction in language and arithmetic, occasionally in exchange for their labor. Thacher's diary also records teaching a girl how to write. Mothers, too, were sometimes qualified to take on the task of teaching their children how to write as well as read. At the Hartford district court in 1668, the widow of Thomas Brooks agreed to a court-arranged settlement of his estate, "she maintaining and bringing up the Children & teaching the daughters to read and sew and the son to read and write." The more scattered nature and small populations of newer towns discouraged efforts to maintain ministers, much less teachers; and colonial governments found themselves struggling against a widening failure to comply with the laws. The ability of even the older towns to maintain grammar schools was already faltering before King Philip's War in 1675–76, the destructiveness of which tends to be blamed for so many of New England's difficulties in the final quarter of the seventeenth century. For one thing the supply of teachers had dwindled sharply. By 1670 the numbers of students entering Harvard College had dropped almost to the vanishing point.[67] Thomas Shepard, minister at Cambridge, lamented in 1672: "O that inferiour Schools were every where so setted and encouraged as that the College . . . might not now languish for want of a sufficient supply of young ones from thence!" He proposed that a foundation be laid for free schools where poor scholars might be educated by some "Publick Stock." "Let the Schools flourish: This is one means whereby we have been, and may be still preserved from a wilde Wilderness-state." The following year, Urian Oakes repeated the "general, sad Complaint, that the Schools languish."[68]

The narrower career expectations prevailing for girls, all of whom were assumed to be destined for housewifery, meant they received even less schooling than the boys. Most of them probably learned their letters at home, but how many went on to attend dame schools for more advanced reading instruction is unknown. The scarcity of female signatures on documents indicates that a much smaller share than boys stayed in school long enough to learn how to write their own names. Among rural children in Suffolk County guardianship accounts who were born from 1673 through 1694, only 13 percent of the girls could write their names, compared to 70 percent of the boys. Both proportions rose among those born in 1695–1710, to 42 and 85 percent, respectively, representing a spectacular increase for the girls in what appears to have constituted a major turnaround in Massachusetts public education.[69]

Letters of guardianship undoubtedly overstate levels of literacy in the general population, since their purpose was to facilitate the distribution of inherited estates. An alternative set of evidence from 1690 to 1772 derives from accounts of administration in Suffolk County probate records by rural widows of the estates of their deceased husbands. Although these records deal with adults, their accomplishments reflect the levels of opportunity available to them earlier. The value of the accounts lies in the estate value one can attach to signing versus marking. Thus from the accounts one can calculate the rate of signing among widows at various levels of wealth. As one would expect, the richest widows were more likely to sign than those merely well off, but by the end of the period a clear majority of every class except the poorest were capable of writing their own names. Female literacy was reaching further down the wealth ladder as the eighteenth century progressed, and the spread of public schooling in the rural interior of New England surely accounts for much of that increase.[70]

Despite the good intentions of the founders, the drive for universal literacy in the seventeenth century had stalled on the twin rocks of high costs and popular resistance, the latter arising out of the conviction that the curriculum was designed primarily to benefit the children of the privileged classes. The education of New England's children had not come to a total halt, but the experience of going to school was, for most, only a sometime thing.

Until relatively recently, all societies believed that children of nonelite status should contribute to household production. Indeed, the heavier the subsistence work load of the mother, the more dependent she is on the contributions of her children. She therefore will teach them what to do and encourage them to cooperate. In early New England, even quite young children could be useful, looking after younger siblings, gathering berries and nuts, killing insect pests, or scaring birds off ripening crops. There is a deeply satisfying, wholesome dimension to such work. Children who cooperate in the household routine feel needed and respected by their parents and siblings. Sibs too young to do adult work can take over much of the childcare in the family. Boys as well as girls do so today in many pre-industrial societies, although girls do it more often than boys because they identify with women as the gender group for whom childcare is specialized. Both are expected to interact with younger children in a responsible and caring way. Doing so also shores up their *right* as older sibs to exert authority over younger sibs. Parents reinforce that authority by giving greater responsibility to the older sibs. They see birth order, experience, and responsibility as going together.[71]

In societies in which boys as well as girls babysit their younger siblings, males gain experience as nurturers. As in early New England, they learn empathy and responsibility in their interactions with babies and toddlers, which carry over into their adult lives. When, as men, they are not continually burdened with life-sustaining tasks or away from home for long periods, they can be attentive and responsive to their own children. In societies in which the masculine honor of even young boys is considered to be compromised by such contacts, however, males grow up to be uncomfortable when left alone with children. For an English gentleman of the seventeenth century to appear in public with an infant in his arms would have caused great amazement and some repugnance. Robert Burton, for instance, remarked in 1623 that it was "odd" and "effeminate" for men to play with their children.[72]

Some of the most revealing sources on children's daily activities in early England are late-medieval coroners' records. They identify victims and witnesses by age and gender and describe accident scenes. Fatal accidents most often befell children between the ages of eight and twelve who had been sent on errands, a common task in pre-industrial times. Another frequent assignment concerned animals. Depending on the region, children of both sexes might have the care of sheep, geese, or cows. Where farmers kept large flocks of sheep to manure the soil, the children helped herd the flocks back and forth between pastures during the day and fields at night. Children were useful in scaring away birds after sowing or before harvesting, in weeding and plucking insect larvae and snails, in picking fruit and gathering nuts.

They carried food to workers in the fields, helped to bind cut grain into sheaves, and gleaned the fields after harvest. Even in winter, children could assist in threshing and in mucking out stalls. They worked alongside women at many outdoor chores, such as spreading dung, and they were invaluable in fetching water and gathering kindling.[73]

Putting children to work at an early age prepared them for more demanding tasks later. Not until they were at least ten, however, were English children given "more than simple" tasks, and this was the age when firm distinctions regarding work suitable to each sex emerged clearly. When John Clare turned ten, his father began taking him into the fields with him, and Josiah Langdale started as a plowboy when he was only nine. By age thirteen, he could handle four horses and a plow by himself.[74]

The incessant routine of daily chores in farm life formed deeply ingrained habits that shaped personality, and the association of particular tasks with particular age and gender groups fortified their distinctive social roles. In this way, work shaped both personality *and* identity. The more distinctive the work assignments among age groups, the more hierarchical the ordering tended to be, and the more children were motivated to move up the ladder of responsibility because of the increased respect they could earn. Whether the division of labor between the sexes was also hierarchical depended on the distribution of power between them in the adult world. If women were seen as incompetent in key areas, as they were in England and New England, men's status clearly exceeded theirs. Men had to be careful in respecting women's sphere, nevertheless, or the boys would come to believe that women were "stupid" and perceive their mothers, aunts, and sisters as performing less valued work. They might then become resentful if asked to do "women's work." Compliance with women's commands then became unpleasant and unmanly. In such circumstances, obedience degenerated into the mere granting of a favor, of humoring the "old lady"; otherwise, it was a source of shame. Yet much of men's work was physically unsuitable for preadolescent boys, so there was a range of years when boys tried to evade their mother's commands but would have been eager to follow their father's. In New England, hunting, trapping, and fishing kept them out of trouble and made them consequential contributors to household income. The tension between prepubescent boys and everybody else must often have induced adults to "look the other way" when such boys "disappeared," letting them go off on adventures of their own or with bands of peers.[75] An alternative in New England was to send them away to work under the nonindulgent command of a tutor or master, but many men began performing some sort of home manufacture during the off-season, and this served to keep their sons busy.

In societies like the Ninnimissinouk, women performed most or all of the primary subsistence work, and boys may well have resented helping their mothers in the fields. Where men also do field work, as among the English, no such stigma attaches.[76] How work was organized and distributed, therefore, made a major difference in relations between children and adults.

The division of work in the pre-industrial world, then, wielded a particularly formative force on family relations and on the individual psyche, beginning early in childhood and growing stronger with each passing year. This was true of New England as it was of old England, although the lines between men and women in the colonies blurred in meeting common challenges of pioneering. Carving farms out of the forests with nothing but hand tools and a few oxen was arduous, mind-numbing work, and there was no question that everyone had to work to eat, if not by farming then by lumbering, fishing, or seafaring. In this frontier society, without a hereditary aristocracy and lacking a permanent class of servants, only a handful of the most privileged elite entirely escaped heavy labor. Given the reality of their lives, it is no surprise that the Puritans believed that hard work was good for children, that it built good habits and strong bodies while also keeping them out of mischief.[77] In such circumstances, the children themselves felt needed and useful and had no question about their obligations. Ministers, meanwhile, urged parents and masters to inculcate sound moral values as part of the work regimen: honesty, reliability, respect for persons and property, thrift, pride in workmanship, and willingness to accept responsibility.

Since everyone but the sick was expected to work, it is not surprising that the colonies early established laws to that effect. They were drawing on long-standing English institutions of apprenticeship and contract service. A majority of the young people in seventeenth-century England worked as servants in husbandry, often on farms many miles from home. Plymouth Colony passed the first colonial version of the English Poor Law: "It is enacted that those that have releefe from the townes & have children and doe not ymploy them that then it shalbe lawfull for the Towneship to take order that those children shalbe put to worke in fitting ymployment according to their strength and abilities, or placed out by the townes." The lawmakers saw young children as a cost to whoever had their care, so as soon as they were able, they should be put to work to reduce that burden. Poor parents could also turn to their town governments for helping their children acquire the means for earning their living (and staying off welfare). Henry Flood, for instance, petitioned the town of Amesbury in 1735 to pay for the training of his son, "a creppel, and is not likely ever for to get a living in ye world without a tylors trade ye wch ye sd Henry Flood cannot procure . . . by reason of his poverty."[78]

Children who lost a parent also risked being put out to service, although the risk was far greater in old England because of the poverty and unemployment there. One out of four children born to first marriages in a large sample of genealogies lost one or both parents before reaching age twenty-one. Most widowed households with young children could not function for long with only one parent, and if an appropriate partner did not soon materialize, the children were put out to service to another couple. Bereaved fathers could pay a neighbor to come in or hire a servant girl, but such strategies were makeshift and unstable. According to genealogies, most widowers remarried within a year, thereby enabling their motherless children to stay together and possibly be joined by the new wife's children from her own previous marriage. Children without fathers were much more likely to be bound out to service, because poor widows were less likely to remarry, especially after the sex ratio equalized.[79]

Wills expressed the expectation that children would be put into service. Thomas Scot of Hartford, for instance, directed that his three daughters "be disposed of both in service and mariedge by my wife and overseers." In 1654 Jeffrey Turner, husbandman, instructed his wife in his will to put out to trade his fourteen-year-old son, Praisever, and to abate his portion for the cost of his apparel and his forgone labor at home. A New Hampshire testator, Thomas Peverly, instructed his three older sons to support their younger brother until he was ten years of age, at which point the boy was to work for them, and they were to pay him his portion when he turned twenty-two. In July 1674 William Austin, weaver and dyer of Rhode Island, took young Moses Lippett as apprentice at the age of six, to serve until he was twenty-one to learn the trade of weaver. A couple in Plymouth Colony who had too many children for their means gave their nine-year-old son to a man as a servant until age twenty-one, the man agreeing never to sell him or his time without his consent.[80]

Eldest sons could assume the father's duties and responsibilities even when their mothers were still alive. When George Manning of Boston died in 1677, he left his family and goods to his son, George Jr., who died only two years later. The younger George's will made his mother, Hannah, executor and he gave her the whole estate his father had given him for her to distribute among his siblings, his brother James to have a double portion "if he carry it dutifully to his mother." "I also assign over my Brother James to serve out his time with my Grandfather." Although language such as this treats children as a species of property, law and government set limits to those rights. A case in New Haven in 1651 spotlights those limits. William Bunell had gone to England, leaving his wife with no means of maintaining herself or their "divers small children," nor could her father provide for them. So together they apprenticed a son to one man and a daughter to another. When Bunell came back, he complained to the court, saying he "disallowed it" and demanded "them again for his help." Bunell was told by the court that people did not take small children and then return them without recompense for the keeping, and since he was not in a position to pay the fair charges, the court reaffirmed the outplacement of the children.[81]

Masters stood *in loco parentis* to their wards, exercising similar property rights and responsibilities toward them. One boy servant in New Haven was so badly treated by his master that neighbors complained to the town, accusing the master of beating him, failing to treat his skin sores, and giving him insufficient food and clothing. His master called the boy "nasty," because he could not control his bladder and stole food out of the pot with his dirty hands. In this case, the court assessed damages against the master and placed the boy with another family. But in the absence of such extreme physical abuse, judges and neighbors preferred to stay out of domestic matters rather than trespass on the rights of fathers and masters.[82]

Diarists frequently complained of their need for servants. When John Hull went to England in 1662, he found it profitable to bring back several children to sell in Boston as servants. Samuel Sewall needed "a Maid very much, courted Goodwife Fellows Daughter: she could not come till spring. hard to find a good one." So when his brother brought their sister, Jane, at age seventeen to live with Mrs. Usher, and Mrs. Usher had already secured someone else, Sewall thankfully hired his own sister. Peter Thacher, minister of the church at Milton, wrote in his diary October 21, 1681: "I went to goodman Tiffenys for one of his sons to live with me & I was to perfect him in reading & teach him to write." Young James arrived a few days later, but he did not stay long. Thomas Swift, probably the son of the deacon, came in November and stayed for a year, but Thacher had to pay for him. "I was to give L12, four in money and 8 at ye store." Lawrence Hammond of Charlestown summarized a verbal agreement between his wife and the mother of Betty Newinson, who was four months shy of age thirteen, in which both sides agreed that she was to live with the Hammonds as a servant for six years, "to be taught, instructed, provided for as shall be meet & that she shall not depart from our family . . . without my wive's consent." Note that it was Hammond's wife rather than Hammond himself who conducted the negotiations with Betty's mother. In 1708, when the Reverend Joseph Green of Salem Village already had four children and his wife was delivered of their fifth in May, he lamented: "We have this winter lived mostly without any boy or maid because we could not procure any."[83]

This shortage of the cheapest sort of labor was partially met by the importation of African boys, a practice that peaked in the period 1690–1730. Boys were more tractable than men and could be more readily socialized to a life of obedient, loyal service.[84]

The account book kept by the Graves family of Guilford, Connecticut, is particularly useful for analyzing the economic uses of children, hired laborers, and slaves. John Graves III, who married Elizabeth Steven in 1714, was keeping the accounts during the 1730s when a young slave, Stepney, makes his first appearance. John and Elizabeth had four children at the time: Anna (born 1715), John (born 1719), Ezra (born 1722), and Simeon (born 1729). Elias was born in 1733 and Timothy in 1740. All the children except Timothy appear in the accounts when their father hired out their services to neighbors. Stepney and Ezra were paired repeatedly in the account book beginning in 1733, perhaps an indication that they were of an age. If so, Stepney was ten when he was first recorded the year before for "driving plow." His chores were no different from those of Graves's sons: spreading flax and taking up stalks when Ezra was eleven, day work and hoeing when he was twelve, filling dung at age thirteen, digging stones at age fourteen, helping John with sawing at night when they were seventeen, managing a team of oxen together at age nineteen. Stepney assisted a mason in 1742 and was doing the full range of men's farm tasks by that year. He continued in these tasks long after Ezra's place was taken by Simeon, then by Elias. The last entry for Stepney was "mowing, 2s6d" in 1757, when the account book was petering out.[85]

By their very nature, court records give emphasis to violence and abuse, but servitude was not a purely exploitative institution. Masters had obligations to their charges, and not all masters were unkind. Some even went to bat for their young wards when they got into trouble. Isaac Gleason, the master of young Josias Miller, complained to the court that his neighbor Isaac Morgan had confiscated the boy's gun and knife and beaten him for eating his "water million." Stealing watermelons was a common problem, but it is interesting that this young servant went about so well equipped.[86]

In New England, masters could not sell their young servants without their consent or the consent of their parents, a very different situation from that in the tobacco colonies. A dissatisfied master would try to return the child and receive compensation for his costs. When Joshua Hempstead's own children grew up and moved away, he turned to neighbor children to help him during the summer season. In June 1746 he hired young Ben Want for three months at twenty shillings a month (Connecticut currency, then worth about fifty cents in hard money). The boy played truant nine days over the next two months, so the exasperated Hempstead sent him home without pay at the beginning of the third month. Ben must have learned his lesson, because Hempstead became dependent on his help in later years.[87]

Parents with older children who were employable could send them off for shorter or longer terms to live and work for someone who offered them clothes and money in addition to room and board. Their motive for doing so might be simply economic, but parents also made such arrangements in the absence of compelling economic circumstances. Thomas Minor's oldest son left home at the age of nineteen to work for a minister in Hartford in exchange for missionary training. This arrangement did not work out as planned, and a year later he went to work for another man in the town of Stratford, about seventy miles away. He never returned home thereafter except for visits, nor did he marry until three years had passed. Minor's diary contains no explanation for his son's departure, but reports many welcome visits with this son and his family over the years. Minor also reports transactions involving paid work performed by his other children for kin and neighbors. On only one occasion, however—his son Mannasah's indenture with Thomas Beld for six months in 1664—does he note the terms and wages of the agreement.[88]

The Minors were in the midst of pioneering a new farm in a new town, far from neighbors. They unquestionably could have used their children's services at home, yet they willingly sent them off to live and work for other families.

Minor's silence on their reasons is provocative, to say the least, but it is worth noting that in 1694 Samuel Sewall of Boston dragged his thirteen-year-old daughter, Hannah, up to Rowley against her will, apparently to live with Sewall's sister there. Sewall was wealthy enough to build a big brick mansion, so he had enough room for her and he did not need her wages. On the other hand, he and his wife probably could not keep a city teenager sufficiently busy with chores at home. His younger daughter, Betty, remained behind to help her mother with her little sister, Mary. Sewall's sister Dorothy had only one small child at this point, so it seems a reasonable guess that the motive for sending Hannah away was to keep her out of trouble in Boston by giving her something constructive to do: babysit her one-year-old cousin.[89]

Servitude and apprenticeship were the common lot of older children in old England, and it is clear that economics was the major reason but not the only reason. The argument for sending off one's children, whether they could be useful at home or not, whether they had lost a parent or not, boiled down to a conviction that the children would benefit from the experience. Edmund Morgan speculates that Puritan parents did not trust themselves to be sufficient disciplinarians with their children. Some of these offspring may have become obnoxious at home, to their siblings or to their parents, and shipping them off would provide relief all around. Sometimes removing a troubled child or one that is being victimized is a sensible solution to problems within the household. Sending the child away from bad company in the neighborhood might break an escalating pattern of antisocial behavior. In the meantime, there were always young parents like ministers Peter Thacher of Milton or Joseph Green of Salem Village or Ebenezer Parkman of Westborough, who desperately needed help around the house and on the farm while their own children were still too young to be useful.[90]

Putting children to work, at home and away, was good for them and for society, everyone seems to have agreed, because it broadened and hardened them, and equipped them with skills they needed as adults.[91] There was the danger of abuse, however, as we have seen. English institutions and customs gave parents and employers remarkable authority over their wards, sanctioning physical and mental punishment "for the good of the child."

A life of unremitting labor would be soul-destroying, and play comes naturally to children. In agricultural societies observed by modern anthropologists in the Yucatán and in Kenya, parents do not visibly encourage their children to play or provide any special means or structures for the purpose, yet neither do they forbid them. On the other hand, children are not at liberty to do just as they please. They know they may be called upon at any minute to run an errand or carry out a task. They are supposed to remain within earshot of their mother's call. In such circumstances, children readily mix work and play. Many carry lap babies on their backs. They come together in small, mixed-age groups that are free-form and unstable, as are their helter-skelter patterns of play. Games form and proceed with few fixed rules and consist mainly in "let's pretend" mixed with a good deal of boisterous roughhousing.[92]

This may well be what daily life was for the children of the English in rural New England. It is true that winter weather would have kept them indoors and underfoot a good deal of the time. On such days, parents would have been particularly anxious to make them busy in order to keep them out of mischief and from getting on one another's nerves. Hand work would help to fill this need: carding and spinning, sewing, embroidery, weaving twine, making hats and brooms of straw, carving spoons and handles for all kinds of things. Devout parents would have led the children in daily prayers and taught them to sing psalms. Family members could take turns reading aloud as others worked. The Bible is a mammoth compendium of great stories, and most families owned one.[93]

Even in winter, days of brilliant sunshine with snow on the ground or ice on the pond invited families outside for sliding and sledding on makeshift gear. (Probate inventories indicate that they had no skates or skis or even snowshoes until the end of the seventeenth century.) It was in the summer and fall that the woods, ponds, and seashore supplied the most opportunities for fun. Ninnimissinouk boys "played" all day long with their bows and arrows, spears, and fishing gear. They trapped small animals, swam and canoed, fished, and built forts. They also joined large parties to gather berries in June, nuts in October, with edible roots and fungi all the time in between. When bands came together for the Green Corn Festival in August or the harvest celebrations six weeks later, they also played organized team sports like lacrosse and a form of soccer, and danced and sang with the grown-ups at night.[94]

English boys, too, could fish, shoot, and trap, and they certainly wrestled and raced each other, but they had far less opportunity for free, unsupervised activity than did their Ninnimissinouk neighbors. Moreover, their chances of participating in large festive gatherings such as the Green Corn Festival were close to nil. New England townships were as big as small counties, and farm families were often isolated. Occasions such as weddings could bring cousins and neighbors together for a bit of merriment, unlike the sober Sunday meetings. Work routines could be greatly enlivened by the presence of outsiders. Haying and harvesting grains particularly benefited from team work, with the strongest men handling the long scythes, each at the head of his own lane. Behind them came the other men and boys to rake up the straw, after which came the women and older girls to bundle the grain into sheaves.[95] Communal work during harvest time became occasions for frolics, when the host whose crop was brought in provided grand feasts to the workers.

Playmates for most farm children in New England probably consisted only of their own sisters and brothers, plus live-in cousins and servants, of assorted ages but few in number. Children would have had little opportunity to play with others of their own age and sex, a circumstance that ruled out team sports. Their games would have been of the informal hide-and-seek and follow-the-leader variety, with fluid rules and minimum competition. Although rivalries and disputes must naturally have erupted, the children would normally have settled them among themselves, with the eldest and strongest lording it over the younger and weaker. Adults understood young children's need for play and tolerated a surprising amount. Even John Cotton, the most famous of New England's first generation of ministers, could affirm that it was quite all right for them to "spend much time in pastime and play, for their bodyes are too weak to labour, and their minds to study are too shallow . . . the first seven years are spent in pastime, and God looks not much at it." Joshua Hempstead noted in his diary that his grandchildren had played awhile in his room while he was gone. They "kindled a fire up and roasted potatoes." Hempstead says nothing about being upset or angry over this intrusion.[96]

The Puritans banished Christmas and eschewed many of the traditional English modes of public recreation such as maypoles and morris dancing. They sought to avoid public ceremonies and celebrations that could not be justified in terms of responsibility toward God or country. Public executions in the capital cities and Harvard graduations provided two such publicly sanctioned occasions for large outdoor gatherings and were eagerly attended as sources of entertainment. Elsewhere, militia training days provided virtually the only public occasions for children to assemble in groups without supervision as well as to observe men doing uniquely men's work. These were gala affairs, not only for their parades and displays of martial arts, but because company captains "treated" their men afterward with food and drinks. It was not exactly Carnival, given the austerity of Puritan public culture, but there was plenty of merrymaking.[97]

Daily life for children in colonial New England, then, was filled with the

round of chores, never solitary and seldom exciting, although accidents and
adventures might introduce occasional drama into their lives. Josiah Cotton,
writing his memoirs in the eighteenth century, transcribed a letter he had
received from his mother when he was a college preparatory student living
with his minister-tutor at Barnstable. In the letter she speaks of God's many
mercies to him and recites, presumably in chronological order, a remarkable
series of near-fatal accidents and illness he had suffered as a child: he had
been lamed in one leg but recovered fully; he had fallen into a tub of water
and been brought in for dead; he had been blind for thirty hours but re-
gained his sight; he had fallen into the wellhead but lived; he had been run
over by a loaded cart with iron-shod wheels, but not a bone had been bro-
ken; he had had a violent burning fever from which he nearly died; he had
had another serious sickness; he had had a "bladder" in the throat (diphtheria?) that had killed his brother and scores of other children; he had fallen
out of a tree and nearly died; and he had only recently been saved from
drowning at Barnstable.[98]

Josiah may have been unusually accident-prone, but this list illustrates
the dangers of rural life in the pre-industrial era. Josiah came from a line of
notable ministers and would himself be trained for that profession, so his
childhood should have been safer than most, but as the youngest of many
children he perhaps received less supervision than usual.

Colonists' views on children and childrearing accorded with the long Eng-
lish/European tradition of activist parenting, an interventionist style of raising children that did not hesitate to use corporal punishment to make children "behave." A "good" child was one who was respectful, compliant, and
obedient, but also one who performed tasks willingly, promptly, and well.
Adults tolerated play, calibrating their demands to the age of the child, but
no one was completely free of work demands in the frontier environment.
Puritan parents were anxious to inculcate a work ethic early, not only to
prepare children for adult responsibilities but also because the devil preyed
on children who had too much free time. Without adult oversight, children
would fall into slothful ways, inviting trouble.

Despite the importance of Bible-reading in reformed Protestantism and
the good intentions of the founders, colonists in the seventeenth century
struggled but failed to erect a school system that would teach reading competence to every child, and their college struggled to attract students. The
demands of building a new society and creating farms took precedence over

schooling, and levels of literacy gradually slid backward, particularly among females. Meanwhile the passing generations were less and less enamored of diverting tax monies to support curriculums that they saw as benefiting only a privileged few. The end of the century witnessed a renewed initiative at the provincial level that soon drew majorities of children into the schools, raising literacy levels most spectacularly among girls. By the end of the colonial period public schooling became nearly universal in Massachusetts and Connecticut, although Rhode Island continued to lag behind.[99]

Despite romanticized notions of New England towns as compact communities arranged around white-spired churches on village greens, most of the rural population lived on separate farms, not in urban centers. Going to school in the seventeenth century was not as common as it came to be later. Children grew up in households consisting principally of nuclear families, and because their neighbors were not right next door, young children played with their brothers and sisters. Devoted sibling relationships often endured long into adulthood; there is an abundance of wills predicated on brotherly or sisterly cooperation. Sewall was not alone among New Englanders in sentimentalizing such bonds: he noted in his diary that two brothers, the mate and the purser of a recently arrived ship, had died in one bed of a malignant fever. They were buried together.[100]

7

Youth and Old Age

Like apes we are sporting till twenty & one
As fierce as a Lion til forty be gone
As subtil as foxes till fifty & three
And after for a . . . s accounted we be.

—Josiah Cotton, "Memoirs"

In Cambridge, Massachusetts, on January 9, 1677, four girls in their teens and early twenties and nine youths were admonished by Judge Thomas Danforth and fined court costs for "being from out of the house of their parents and meeting at unseasonable times, and of night walking, and companying together contrary to civility and good nurture." Two other young men, part of the same company, were given heavier fines. If they couldn't pay their fines, they would receive a public whipping.

Abraham Arrington, aged fifty-five and presumably unrelated to any of the miscreants, was described as commenting on the matter in a public shop to others present:

> it was a sad thing young persons could not meet together wn they were
> come home from the warr but they must be thus requited, and he did
> beleuiv if the young men of watertown should be dealt with in the man-
> ner[,] they would go negh to burne the towne over their eares that should
> so sere them, and it was a pitfull thing that a young man and mayd could
> not be together but such reports must come of it, and he did beleuiv ere
> long the young must pass by the mayds like quakers and take no notice of
> them [or else they would get into trouble with the law] . . . and if there
> were any Service to be done for the Country it must be the young men that
> must do it, and let them do all they could a young man could neuer be
> made an old man.[1]

Here is a sympathetic apology for youthful hijinks and an argument that men who have fought in the service of their country deserve better of their elders. That a man in late middle age should air these thoughts in public suggests that the common people of Puritan New England may have become more forgiving of youthful frivolities than their magistrates were. Moreover, it was this man's belief that justices in the neighboring farm town would not have dared to act in so heavy-handed a fashion as Danforth had in the college town of Cambridge.

Arrington was arrested and bound over to the next county court "to answer for uttering seditious and naughty words . . . tending to breaking down the pales of government."[2] The large number of young people involved in the incident, a citizen's fearless criticism of the judge's handling of it, and the judge's prompt use of his power to retaliate, all make this case a useful starting place for an inquiry into age relations in Puritan New England.

The young people scolded by Judge Danforth had sneaked out of their parents' houses at night to "company together." According to this magistrate, single adults did not have the right to come and go freely but should stay home under the supervision and direction of their parents or masters. That such attitudes were highly repressive goes without saying. The English had long been anxious about youthful sexuality and feared their overflowing energies. All the advice about raising children and the necessity of inculcating discipline and obedience was aimed at this most dangerous stage in the life-cycle, when young people with fully functioning gonads were not yet safely married. The message warned parents that if they failed in training them early, their children would grow up to become "perverse and headstrong" in their teens.[3]

Unlovely images still persist in our minds of austere Puritans solemnly marching their children to church, vigorously applying the rod for discipline's sake, and whipping women in public for crimes against patriarchy. These images are not without truth, although one should mentally add male partners alongside those women tied to the whipping post. But contemporary diaries show that parents on both sides of the Atlantic varied widely in their use of physical punishment, and most of them loved their children as dearly as did the Ninnimissinouk. Love, concern for socially responsible behavior, and the use of physical punishment were not, after all, mutually exclusive components of parent-child relationships.

Was the atmosphere in New England more repressive toward youth than in old England? Perhaps not. In the old country, most town fathers appear to have been more cautious in fiscal than in ideological matters in their dealings with youth, but their apprehensions were the same. Young men and women were dangerous to good order precisely because they were so attractive to each other. A young woman who got careless might bear a child out of wedlock who would then require public support. For example, a petition by men of a town in Wiltshire, England, in 1607 beseeched the court to prosecute a young woman there for her "filthy act of whoredom, by the which licentious life of hers not only Gods wrath may be powred down uppon us inhabitants of the town but also her evill example may so greately corrupt others that greate and extraordinary charge for the maintenance of baseborn children may be imposed uppon us."[4] There are several arguments here. The first is that a single woman who engaged in sex was a filthy whore and a dangerous person who, *if not punished,* would call down God's angry retribution on the entire community. She might also inveigle other women into similar sins, thereby launching a burdensome tide of illegitimate children who would have to be supported at public expense. Of the two sets of concerns about the woman expressed in the petition, the second is a straightforward pocketbook issue: prevent a tax increase due to illegitimate births by making a public example of a woman who has borne a child out of wedlock. The first, less mundane concern was that God would punish the entire community for the private sins of a single individual. Whether the men of Wiltshire actually feared that God would do so is unknown, but they perhaps expected that the magistrates would be more likely to attend to their petition if they invoked the imminent threat of divine wrath.

Besides their dangerous tendencies to deflower maidens and sire bastards, young men posed other kinds of challenges to authority and good order. Then as now, males between the ages of fifteen and twenty-five committed most of the acts of violence and aggression that appear in court records.[5] Proportionately this threatening age group was far larger then than it is now, yet no trained, full-time police force stood poised to protect the citizenry from the multitude of crimes then plaguing old England. It was up to the citizens to defend themselves, to respond to the hue and cry, and to assist the constables in doing their duty. Given the violence of daily life, it is not too difficult to understand why the English sought to keep young people dispersed through the population and isolated from one another, under the eye of parents or employers.[6]

Young people in rural New England were even more physically scattered and segregated than in the old country; hence they had even less opportunity to gather in large groups and foment trouble. When they did get into difficulty with the law, they did so singly or in pairs only, seldom in groups or gangs.[7] Militia training days offered one important exception to their usual isolation, and many of the cases of illegitimacy investigated by the courts can in fact be traced back to the time of holiday frolicking that accompanied these martial exercises. The collegiate setting of Harvard in Cambridge, however, was unique in providing a critical mass of young people living in propinquity, creating abundant opportunities for youthful escapades, with which eighteenth-century student diaries are replete.[8]

Despite the farmbound lives of most young people in colonial New England, local circumstances encouraged their willing cooperation with adult demands. Young people there were even more numerous, proportionately, than in old England, but the abundance of raw land in North America made their labor far more valuable, with powerful social ramifications. The first concerns the amount of time spent as servants. As we saw in Chapter 6, service in husbandry was the characteristic experience of plebeian youth in England, where servants composed the largest single group in the work force. The reasons for this were principally economic: most parents lacked the capital to keep their children usefully employed at home. They therefore sent them off to earn their keep.[9] In New England a sizable portion of young people likewise experienced service, but seldom on so extended a basis. The majority of families operated independent farms where children's labor could be profitably exploited. Wages were so high and land so cheap by comparison with England that, once free, most young men could quickly accumulate a stake and, if necessary, move to some new settlement where they could acquire raw land and begin the long, arduous task of developing it into a farm capable of supporting a family.[10] Under such circumstances, free adult males could not be readily tempted to work for others on a more than short-term basis. Service, after all, implied the surrender of identity. When one entered service, one became the master's creature; one's loyalties were to be to him, superseding even those to parents and kin. Servants were not allowed to marry, because marriage vows would compromise that loyalty. The nature of the customary relationship between servant and master was fundamental and sacred in English culture, but it came at a personal cost to the servant that sons of New England freeholders found intolerable: because apprentices and servants were dependents, they could not be real men. Only heads of households held that honor, because they held mastery over those under their care. Dominion, especially over a woman, validated a man as a man.[11]

The experience of service in England was more widespread, longer-lasting, and probably more psychologically stressful to youth than in New England. The legal age of adulthood was the same in both places—eighteen for women and twenty-one for men—but despite these statutory definitions of adulthood, even free young men and women on both sides of the water had scant more independence or rights than their younger peers.[12] Until they married, they were to "live under family government" and be "pliable to the orders of" the masters in whose households they resided. They should oppose "all vice and vanity," "walk inoffensive to all men," and have "Christian conversation."[13] "Good conversation" meant avoiding offense, that is, not lying nor speaking ill of others, especially of those in authority, and avoiding bad language and swearing. What it boiled down to in practice was behaving in such a consistently wholesome and ingratiating way that people would speak well of you and testify in court on your behalf should you get in trouble.

Sexuality simply compounded the trials and temptations of youth's prolonged apprenticeship in the societies of old and New England. There was broad agreement across the religious spectrum about the need for controlling that sexuality in order to prevent the births of illegitimate children. Even when not bound by contract of servitude, single men and women of lawful age were in need of close supervision, because they were legally free to make binding contracts and to inherit property. They were not to make important decisions concerning marriage or property without consulting their "friends." "Friends" included parents and other "weighty" kin, as well as nonkin. This term reveals that parental control of grownup children was in fact no longer absolute, but was at least theoretically subject to modification by unofficial advisers. The role of "friends" is nowhere clearly spelled out in the secondary literature, nor could the opinions of either parents or friends concerning marriage choice or the disposal of property have stood a test in courts of law. Indeed, it is a telling characteristic of English society that its courts on both sides of the Atlantic enforced the rights and liberties of free, single adults with respect to property and marriage, but countenanced the physical incarceration of their bodies by their parents.

The transition to marriage and parenthood conferred full adult status on young people. The troublesome youth was at once transformed by his vows into the master of a household, a magistrate and teacher set by God over his wife, his servants, and his children.[14] For women, who played little role in the public sphere, the transition became visible in where they sat in church. Instead of being addressed by her first name, a woman became "Goodwife," a title of respect signifying her new importance in the community.

Efforts to control youth's liberty and sexuality in the two Englands were undermined by the inability of parents to keep their offspring financially dependent once these legally became adults. Although the earnings of minors legally belonged to their parents, grown children who remained with their parents after becoming adults "owned" their earnings, in New England at least. When a son turned twenty-one, he and his parents began a business relationship in which the parents credited the son for his work but the son owed them for his room and board. He became responsible for all his expenses, although his parents or uncles might advance him cash or other kinds of aid. These were the arrangements recorded in their diaries by John May of Roxbury, Massachusetts, in 1707, Samuel Lane of Stratham, New Hampshire, in 1739, and Jabez Fitch of Norwich, Connecticut, in 1752. Any work that young men performed for their parents beyond the cost of their keep became a debt owed by the parents that probate courts would recognize as legitimate and enforce.[15]

Wills drawn up by parents sometimes make this unwritten contract with sons explicit, as in Thomas Minor's second will, where he acknowledged that his son Samuel had kept up their common fences at his own cost, and drew up his bequest to Samuel with this in mind. Accounts of administration of probated estates placed a money value on such work and treated it as a debt owed to the child by the parent, and the court would direct the payment of the debt out of the parental estate prior to the distribution of the remaining assets among all the heirs. For example, Samuel Ruggles, son of Widow Elizabeth Ruggles, claimed in 1679 that his deceased mother's estate owed him for the three years and seven months in which "he wrought for her at the trade of a weaver," which he valued at seventeen pounds per year. Similarly, Samuel Bullen of Medfield submitted a claim to the probate court in 1696 for seven years' service before his father's death. His brother Joseph attested to this service and its value, "by mutual agreement of all the children and heirs." The sons of John Beal, yeoman of Hingham, detailed exactly what their father's estate owed them in 1715: five pounds per annum, John "for his service to his father 3 yrs 9 mos after he was of full age," and

Thomas for "1 yr 6 mos." Daniel Whiton's son, also named Daniel, acted as executor of his father's estate and charged sixteen pounds for one year's labor in his account dated 1772.[16]

Even after marriage, sons might remain tied economically to their parents. In a study of Essex County land transfers between parents and children, Daniel Vickers discovered that parents often did not transfer the deeds to land they had "given" sons until the father's death. Without a deed, of course, the son could not sell out and take his assets with him. He was therefore far more likely to remain where he was, a source of labor and support to his parents.[17] But this ploy worked only for the father who had enough good, attractive land for all his sons. Otherwise the younger sons would call his bluff and leave for high wages and cheap land elsewhere, an option that remained open until King Philip's War in 1675 and reopened again in the eighteenth century.[18]

All the evidence points in the same direction: adult sons who lived and worked at home or on their parents' land expected satisfactory recompense at some future time, even if they had to wait for the parents to die, and the courts would back them up. Sons' labor could not be legally appropriated by the parents, although it is not difficult to imagine that they tried to keep their sons home and unmarried as long as possible in order to benefit from their labor services.

Since men came of age at twenty-one but did not usually marry until age twenty-five or later, the situation was a common one in colonial New England, especially in newer communities, where land was plentiful and marriageable young women scarce.[19] In contrast, there was no end to daughters' obligations. Most women in colonial New England lived with their parents until marriage, although they may have spent time working as maids or nannies in others' households. Yet accounts of administration never list the earnings of grown daughters as legal obligations of the estate of the deceased parent except for nursing in the deceased's final illness. This lacuna cannot be explained on the grounds that women's work had no market value. There is ample evidence that young women could earn wages over and above room and board by working as maids. Moreover, there were opportunities for them to make money while still living at home. Entries in a Wethersfield account book, for instance, show women selling onions to a storekeeper who credited their accounts at a price per unit of weight or by the bunch and then shipped the onions for profit to the West Indies. Women could also sell their spun yarn by weight, although such earnings were more often subsumed in their fathers' accounts. Furthermore, account books and accounts of administration in the probate records show married women and widows credited for doing laundry, cleaning house, doing maid's work, nursing the sick, and selling butter, so women were capable of "earnings" that the courts recognized as legal obligations of those employing them.[20]

To judge from market rates for wages, then, the labor services of daughters living at home would more than cover the cost of their room and board, clothing, and so forth. A second possibility why these net earnings did not accumulate as legal obligations of their parents' estates is that the parents rewarded their more useful daughters by giving them larger portions or shares in their estates at death. For instance, in 1650 John Greeneaway made out a deed of gift of part of his house to his spinster daughter, Ursula, in gratitude for her service to himself and wife Mary. After their deaths Ursula was to get all the real estate for life, and then it was to go to his "kinsman & servant." Andrew Sanford, widower of Milford, Connecticut, had two sons and five daughters. To the sons and four of his daughters he left lesser sums than the forty pounds he gave his daughter Hannah, "because she has carried on my business for me."[21] Most wills, however, say nothing about repaying daughters except in cases of extended nursing care.

Given the lack of evidence that daughters received fair compensation for services to their parents, the conclusion emerges that in this society, unmarried daughters owed their parents a debt that could never be repaid except by full-time nursing. Even when parents gave unequal portions as dowries, they did try to make "all even" at their death. Doing so, however, denied or ignored daughters' uneven contributions to parental income, and there was no acknowledged legal recourse open to young women to recover the difference. Court-directed distributions in cases of intestacy also tried to equalize the apportionment of parental estates by inquiring into gifts and loans made to children before the parent's death and deducting these from their final shares. Yet, as we have seen, sons, but not daughters, were compensated by parents and by the courts for their services as adults, in addition to their full shares in the estate.

This gender-based inequality in parental expectation parallels the legal inequality that prevailed between spouses. Husbands became full owners of their wives' personal property upon marriage, owed nothing to their wives beyond maintenance and dower rights, and were legally free to appropriate any and all of their labor and earnings. Wives and unmarried adult daughters were not chattels, but neither were they free. Freedom for women, if not full civil rights, came only with widowhood, an irony of sorts, since the loss of one's life-mate could exact a steep price, if not in grief, then perhaps in penury.

Growing Up and Growing Old: The Life-Cycle of New England Farm Families

It was on the occasion of his fifty-third birthday in 1733 that Josiah Cotton of Plymouth County in Massachusetts inscribed in his journal the rhyme about the ages of man that appears as the epigraph to this chapter: "As subtil as foxes till fifty & three, And after for a . . . s accounted we be."[22] Cotton, it seems, was not garnering the respect he wanted, and his resentment was not just a passing mood. As an educated man of substance, of distinguished lineage and connected to major families in the region, living in a society that esteemed learning, he should have been awash in public esteem.[23] Cotton does not explain his bitterness, but his memoirs provide several possibilities. They are filled with a sense of failure. He came from a line of well-known ministers. His parents were strong personalities and had expressed high expectations of him. His brothers and cousins were successful ministers, magistrates, and merchants. He himself had failed early as a minister and had trouble making enough to support a gentleman's household. Just the year before this birthday lament, he had quit twenty-seven years as a paid missionary to the Indians. He acknowledges that he is not particularly good as a judge and is unable to hold up his end against his political rivals; and he continues to mourn the death in 1732 of his favorite daughter, Hannah Phillips Dyer, at the age of twenty-two. "The other six Children that I have lost made some impression on me, but nothing like this."[24]

Later in his memoirs Cotton wrote that his wife never really recovered from the birth of their last child, born while Josiah was away on business to Connecticut.[25] That he was not there at the time may have opened or widened a gulf between them. The journal is silent on their relationship. Indeed, he seldom mentions her in his journal, even less often than Thomas Minor, and far less than Peter Thacher or Samuel Sewall, but he speaks frequently of the children, individually as persons in their own right and collectively as wards in need of guidance and instruction. Like most educated men of his time and place, he expected to use his well-honed powers of reason to impose wholesome discipline on himself, his wife, and his children. To resist rational arguments about what to do and how to behave was not only foolish and shortsighted but also sinful, because of the disobedience it implied toward God.

Cotton at age fifty-three had had fifteen children born to himself and his wife. In 1733 the survivors ranged in age from twenty-three to one. Nine of the fifteen had died, including two daughters in their early adulthood and seven sons in infancy. His oldest son, John, twenty-three, had taken his A.B. at Harvard two years before (but did not marry until 1746). Daughter Mary had married John Cushing of Scituate at age nineteen. Still at home were Theophilus, seventeen, who did not go to Harvard; Lucie Lightsom (or Delightsom), age fifteen; Josiah, age nine, who would enter Harvard with the class of 1740 but did not graduate and was lost at sea in 1745; Margaret, age three; and Roland, age one, who would die within the year. Lucy and Margaret both survived and married.[26]

Hence, Cotton was "going through a stage," just as were some of his children. The English nuclear family model tends to isolate parents from their kin, and they usually must raise their children by themselves. Colonial houses held many people. When the children were all young together, the four walls must have rung with their cacophony and chaos have reigned. The wife was constantly nursing or pregnant and got little uninterrupted sleep; she desperately needed help with all the work of a busy household, fetching water, tending the fire, washing the dishes, the clothes, the linens, and the diapers, and keeping small children out of danger. Hiring temporary help was not difficult, but keeping good help for very long was another matter.[27] The husband, meanwhile, had his own responsibilities and did not normally help with domestic duties. That was his wife's concern. It is small wonder that Josiah's wife never really recovered from the birth of their fifteenth child.

The Cotton family lived on the farm she had inherited outside Plymouth, despite Josiah's multiple public offices in town. They operated it with what help he could arrange. Despite their middle-class status and the educational opportunities their boys enjoyed, their daily lives were little different from those of common farm families. Such households moved through phases of a family life-cycle: as the eldest children pass into their nines and tens, they take on the care of the new babies and toddlers continuing to come along. Both parents are still in desperate need of help, but as the big boys put on height and strength, they join their father full-time in the yard and field, and the big girls begin to work closely together, no longer needing minute-by-minute instruction from their mother. When the last baby is born, it and the other small children become the darlings of their now highly competent big sisters. By the time the oldest girl is capable of running the household herself, the rhythms of the household and farm have become predictable and are under control. If nothing serious has impeded its progress, if illnesses have not been more than common, the healthy, intact Anglo-American farm family will have reached at this point its economically most productive stage. But it cannot last. Life and time march on, the sons and daughters marry and move away, leaving the parents to make do and grow old.

Although the duration of the stages of this cycle necessarily varies from family to family, they follow generally predictable outlines. Certain "firsts" mark its passages: the birth of the first child, then its first fever, its first tooth, its first steps and words, its first recitation of the alphabet and the Lord's Prayer, its first halting reading of a Bible verse. Other major firsts of the oldest son are his first time in breeches, his first solo ride on a horse, his first errand alone away from home, his first knife, his first gun, his first kill. The other boys recall their own like occasions, especially as they feel its significance manifested in their parents' proud gaze. Daughters' firsts are no less meaningful if less dramatic: sewing their first hem, changing their first diaper, rolling out the pie crust the first time, baking their first loaves of bread, making butter by themselves.

Relationships within the Anglo-American farm family must have been complex in their many dimensions, each combining age and gender in different ways, but they were ordered hierarchically, in accordance with those same two determinant categories: father, mother, eldest son, eldest daughter, and the rest in order of birth. Parents saved themselves a lot of grief by siding with the elder over the younger when children quarreled. Continuous close contact and frequently shared tasks provided ample testing grounds for contending egos. The arrival of a stepparent and stepsiblings would pose new challenges. They might exacerbate problems in an already unhappy situation or simplify them by aligning one set of children against the other. Much depended on the combination of temperaments and ages and how the parents handled things. Perhaps individuals in these circumstances were more likely to establish crosscutting alliances. Diaries and memoirs say little regarding these relationships, but genealogies occasionally identify marriages between stepsiblings. Frictions and jealousies between boys and girls in middle childhood, on the other hand, probably evolved into more-or-less amiable teasing relationships as their worlds separated ever more sharply with advancing age.

Babies cry, children quarrel, adolescents sulk: raising children is never easy, but in colonial New England, healthy, sexually active couples could hardly avoid having them. As parents, they benefited from their children's contribution to family income, and when the time came to send them out into the world, they would do the best they could for each in turn. Whether they did it for love, for genes, or for security in their old age is moot. For each parent, for each child, the reasons came together in unique ways. But because children also represented investments by the parents in the future, each one who survived moved through an age-related cycle that was constrained by those of the others.

In a society composed principally of farm families raising most of what they needed, the majority of households were more or less equal in terms of economic opportunity if not of wealth or prestige. Variations in life experience, therefore, were essentially matters of luck and temperament. Birth order was important only to the oldest, in their peculiarly intense relationships with their parents, and perhaps to the youngest, who faced more relaxed expectations, and who may even have reigned in solitary glory as the last and best-loved. Wherever in that order they came, the passage of years for almost every colonial child eventually brought marriage and children, and for the men, this was normally followed by growing participation in community affairs and rising income for the household as the children become valuable workers. Then came the time when the children in turn wished to marry and strike out on their own. Fortunate parents helped them build up a stock with which to do it, child after child, striving to make each portion as nearly equal as possible to those given previously. If they were like most married people of English descent in early New England, they had turned sixty or more before the last one flew the nest. The odds were such that the last might have to postpone departure in order to take up full-time parent care.[28]

Aging and Retirement

People did not officially "retire" in early New England. They worked until they could do so no longer, but they slowed down long before they finally ceased work altogether. As their children grew up, farm parents shifted more and more of the burden onto their shoulders. When they could, these parents gradually redirected their energies into specialized forms of production and services. For instance, older men who had earlier put by a craft while they devoted themselves to developing their land holdings might resume craft work during less busy times of the agricultural year as their sons took up the heavy work. Women past childbearing who had daughters still in the household could let them take over the daily chores of running the house, doing the laundry, cleaning, and getting the meals while Mother taught young children how to read or did fine sewing or developed her herbal and distilling business, or served her community as a physician or midwife. In the eighteenth century, women took up tailoring and weaving, and the opening of markets in nearby urban centers encouraged many others to specialize in truck farming or dairying. By such means, older people could reduce the stress on their aging bodies without suffering a catastrophic loss of income.

The age structure of local populations in New England must have gradually shifted to include more and more older people, but clear quantitative evidence is lacking. The initial generation of immigrants, composed principally of families and young single persons, would have given way to a more "normal" distribution of ages as the second generation moved into their middle years. Then, as towns founded during the years of the migration stabilized in terms of resident households, and as the children grew up, married, and set up their own farms, the pressure on the local supply of undeveloped land would encourage young people to move to new towns. This trend reduced the relative numbers of young adults in the older towns and increased those of the older people. In succeeding generations, whole families began moving out, but the development of new towns was preponderantly a young person's job.

The aging of the population in older communities proceeded apace with each successive generation. Some towns continued to develop economically as their populations grew, with greater specialization in all forms of labor, so that jobs opened up for the unskilled. Such towns would continue to attract an influx of young workers, shifting the local balance between younger and older adults. Most of the new towns founded in the eighteenth century, however, were established on sites that were less promising for this kind of long-term development, and their available economic niches for farmers and artisans were quickly filled. As a consequence, these towns exported their young on a continuing basis, with the result that their residents included a much greater proportion of older people than was true elsewhere.

The proportion of aged in rural New England also grew as a result of another demographic factor: longer life expectancy among adults. The average

age at death of ever-married men and women in sample genealogies rose persistently if unspectacularly over the colonial period, from sixty-three to sixty-four for men and from sixty to sixty-five for women.[29] Because of the outmigration of the young and the longer life expectancies of the old, rural communities throughout southern New England housed more and more older people. Sociologists believe that public attitudes toward the retired elderly are heavily affected by their relative numbers in the local population: the fewer of them there are, the greater their esteem. Rarity lends a special status: having lived so long, elders remember important events in the past. As survivors, they come to embody those events. Long lives and much experience, moreover, ought to lead to the accumulation of practical knowledge and perhaps the growth of wisdom. Old age, therefore, should be honored, and if some prove not so wise, they have at least earned an honorable retirement.[30] But in New England, as the numbers of elderly in old communities began to balloon during the expansionary years of 1725–1750, local attitudes may have moved toward less friendly assessments.

Among the English, being an older person, in and of itself, had never meant much in terms of prestige. To be rich as well as old, on the other hand, was to be in the enviable position of one who has been successful and must, therefore, be smart. To be poor, of whatever age or sex, was to be a loser, an object of pity or contempt.[31] By contrast, in many Native American groups, the elders were revered founts of wisdom, or at least so informants told Europeans. They exercised little real authority unless they were clan mothers, medicine men/women, or sachems, but they were probably well taken care of in those groups that were truly sedentary, such as the Iroquois nations.[32]

Among the mobile Ninnimissinouk, however, commoners who succeeded in living beyond their most productive years faced the same problem as the English of how to go on earning their living. Ninnimissinouk men who could no longer tend miles of traps or keep up with their younger comrades on the warpath or pull their weight in the fishing boats could still participate in the dances, the group hunts, and the frequent council meetings. Indeed, retired warriors with great reputations would have been among the most influential men present, their experience and recollections making them veritable libraries of pertinent knowledge. It was principally the older men, also, who fashioned the tools and weapons, wove the fishing nets, and made the ceremonial objects. They practiced the old rituals and retold the stories heard in their youth. These were all useful and honorable activities for men, earning them prestige and rich gifts. Many were also expected to help the women in the fields, however, an activity that may have challenged their masculine identity.[33] There are no clues to their thoughts and feelings as they stood among the corn hills and watched the younger men coming and going on vital missions or bringing home a meaty deer across their shoulders or racing up and down the lacrosse field in the fullness of their strength and agility. Did these older men find working with women a gall to their pride? Did they feel themselves polluted by such contact? Perhaps this work was strictly voluntary and gratefully received, so that they were not bossed by women as they worked. Yet, as they aged, the relationships between them and women must surely have altered.[34]

There seems little doubt that women of the Ninnimissinouk grew in prestige as they aged. Once they passed childbearing, they faced fewer watershed transitions than men. Their usual tasks continued with little alteration, because these did not require speed or quick reactions. Skill and pertinacity accomplished most of what women normally needed to do. Nevertheless, there were significant shifts in how they spent their time as the need for tending children diminished. They could give more attention to collecting herbs and learning more about their uses as natural remedies from the old ones among them. After the last baby and before the onset of serious physical debility, women probably reached their pinnacle in terms of prestige, serving their neighbors and kin as healers and midwives and exercising whatever political power women possessed. The medicine men who invoked spirits and used magic—the shamans—were more often male, although there were women among them, too. Yet women of this stage in the life-cycle could use their time to focus on those other dimensions of living that younger people were too busy to appreciate. This period in their lives was, above all, the season for study and meditation.[35]

The life stages of women in Ninnimissinouk society had a seamless, slowly evolving quality, whereas males negotiated life careers in more clearly defined steps, first by joining the company of men, and then by reentering the world of women as they became "old." Probably few people among the Ninnimissinouk ever reached true old age, however.[36] Despite the decrease in mobility associated with the pursuit of more intensive farming in the seventeenth century, their seasonal movements continued and were physically very demanding.

The life passages for English women in early New England probably bore greater similarities to those of their Ninnimissinouk counterparts than was true for English men. Although this is only speculation, women in both societies may have particularly enjoyed their postmenopausal years, at least so long as they remained reasonably healthy and avoided poverty. One old woman, "Widow Wyat," who died in Dorchester, Massachusetts, in 1705 at the age of ninety-four, had long been a notable midwife, assisting at the birth of some "1110 and odd children."[37] Nevertheless, older women among the English were usually far more dependent on their husbands' and sons' economic contributions than were their native counterparts, as will become clear below.

Despite flattering self-images among traditional societies about respecting the elderly, there seems to be, in reality, a near-universal pattern of dissonant tensions between cultural precepts concerning the obligations of the young to the old and how the young actually treat them. From the viewpoint of the younger generation, the aged pose problems. They no longer produce as much as they consume; they may stand in the way of young adults' advancement; and their decrepit appearance offends them. Much like today, therefore, the effective status of older individuals depended on their control over valuable resources or special knowledge. These could be traded for gifts or pay. Those having neither fell into dependency on others. For the elderly among the English, if not for the Ninnimissinouk, dependency brought a steep decline in status and seems generally to have bred contempt. Continuing to live in one's own domicile as its head, on the other hand, signified one's continuing competency as an adult and a citizen. This held just as true for wives as for husbands, because the customary English division of labor between the sexes gave married women almost absolute rule within the house and its immediate grounds. For a woman to give up her kitchen and dairy, or control over those working for her there, was to lose her identity.

Running your own home, then, signified independence and honor among the English and was not a situation to be surrendered lightly. In New England, however, older people needing help in running a house or a farm ran up against the problem of labor scarcity. Although farming brought many psychic satisfactions, the primitive technology of the times imposed a wearying round of work that took a great toll on human bodies. At some point, everybody faced the necessity of cutting back on the most demanding chores.[38] Most strove to retain their hold on the reins as long as possible, but as their vitality flagged, they faced the momentous question of turning over the farm to someone else. In the early New England economy, where access to cheap, undeveloped land was almost wide open, it was nearly impossible to find a tenant to lease an entire farm.[39] Young men in their physical prime found it more profitable to put their labor into their own holding, turning cheap, raw land into a valuable working farm. So, for aging farmholders, a more common, and generally more desirable, solution to their labor problem was to ask a young unmarried son to stay on in return for a deed of gift later. If such an arrangement was not possible, they might invite a married son or a daughter and her husband to move in on similar terms, but this was never a popular solution in New England.[40] Elderly couples proved extremely reluctant to share their home with another married couple, even when one of the pair was their own child. The reason for this aversion seems to be that among the English only one male could be boss at a time.[41] Since the older couple owned the property and were presumably more skilled, they naturally expected deference from the younger couple. Although the younger man would know that he ought to defer to the elder, he might regard himself as more competent and productive, and his private opinion, of course, could breed tension between them as they discussed the multitude of decisions relating to running the farm on a daily basis. Sons-in-law might be inclined to be more deferential than sons, but building sufficient trust between the two men to make a true working partnership required patience and goodwill on both sides. Mothers and daughters, on the other hand, might get along fine because of long practice together, although that alone, of course, was no guarantee of a tranquil relationship. One suspects that they would not even attempt the arrangement, however, unless they thought they would get along well. If quarrels erupted between the men, however, the daughter's loyalties would be sorely challenged. A daughter-in-law, on the other hand, had to please her mother-in-law on the latter's own ground. Relations between the women might become tense, and it would be the son of the family who got caught in the middle.

It is not surprising, then, that records of such arrangements are uncommon. They placed an unreasonable burden of conciliatory behavior on the young while challenging the moral position of the older. Another alternative for the aging parents was to make a contract with a son, son-in-law, or acquaintance in which the older couple deeded over the farm at the outset and surrendered all control in exchange for guaranteed support. Such contracts appear in the records but are understandably rare.[42] As the following story of one canny old man emphasizes, signing over one's property was risky because there was no effective recourse available should the recipient give back less than had been bargained for.

This amusing but probably apocryphal story comes from Vermont and dates to the early nineteenth century. An old man,

after his wife's death, concluded to deed his property to his children on condition that they should take care of him. He retained only an old chest in which he stored his clothing and keepsakes. He soon found his children considered him a burden. A little strategy on his part changed their opinion. He went to an old friend and borrowed a hundred dollars which he locked up in his chest. His friend, as arranged, called in a few days and, on some pretext, wished to borrow one hundred dollars. He was at once accommodated, and the children's regard for their father changed at once. That old chest, they imagined, had more money in it. Soon the old man died. The children, with anxious curiosity, unlocked the chest. They found nicely wrapped up a wooden mallet with this couplet attached: "When a man gives away his property before he is dead, take this mallet and knock him in the head."[43]

Warnings about children's lack of gratitude toward aging parents go back millennia. In an English marriage manual published in 1642, Daniel Rogers argued that no prison could be more irksome than a son's or a daughter's house and urged parents not to trust their children: "Love must descend, not ascend: its not naturall (saith *Paul*) for children to provide for parents, but for parents to provide for them, therefore invert not providence . . . be sure to hold stroake sufficient in your hand, for the securing of love and duty from your children."[44]

"Holding stroake sufficient in your hand" meant retaining control over the means of subsistence. The ideal solution was to have a grown child, still unmarried, live under the same roof and act as a trusty servant and caretaker. It was the most common solution where feasible.[45] As mentioned earlier, John Greeneaway in 1650 gave his spinster daughter, Ursula, a part of his house in gratitude for her service to himself and wife Mary. After their deaths, she was to get all the real estate for life, after which it was to go to "my kinsman & servant Thomas Millett the sonne of Thomas & Mary Millett my sonne in lawe & daughter." This wording suggests that his grandson was already living with him and his wife, as was his daughter.[46] Lieutenant Joseph Rogers of Eastham, in Plymouth Colony, worked out a similar arrangement. In his will he stated that if his grandchild, Beriah, continued "to live with me until I die," he would get land, plus a cow, his best suit, and the bed "daughter Hannah lyes on."[47] Rogers also directed that his wife, Hannah, presumably the mother of daughter Hannah and grandmother of Beriah, should continue to live in "my" house and was "to be comfortably maintained." These instructions placed the well-being of both women in the discretionary care of the grandson, denying them any means of enforcing that promise of "comfortable" maintenance.

Grandparents, of course, also took in grandchildren for reasons other than their own needs, such as to provide them with a home that they might not otherwise obtain. John Gill, yeoman, directed in his will that his grandchild, "who now liveth with me," be maintained at school until age fourteen and then put out as an apprentice. The will of John Davis of Oyster River, New Hampshire, states that he had kept and brought up his grandchild John Hearth since the latter was two. If John stayed with wife Jane and son James until he turned twenty-one, he would then receive twenty pounds from Davis' estate. (He gave his three younger daughters only fifteen pounds apiece.)[48]

Clearly, if one's physical disabilities were not such as required muscular strength in the helper, a grandchild who was not too young could provide many small services and run errands.[49] And an older grandchild who had loyally served until adulthood was deserving of a substantial inheritance.

When one elderly spouse died before the other, the survivor might then give up independent living and move in with a married child, as happened in the Vermont story above. Surprisingly, this seems not to have been a common arrangement for widowers in the seventeenth century. A close reading of Hartford district wills probated before 1700 reveals that very few were actually forced to move in with a son or daughter.[50] Widowed men of property retained control of the full estate after their wives died, enabling many to offer an enticing deal to a vigorous new wife. She then moved in, and life for him could go on much as it had before. A widow, on the other hand, could claim only a third part of the estate after her husband died, and the share in real estate was hers for life only. An older woman in reduced circumstances attracted few suitors.

Although "widow's thirds" has taken on near-mythic importance as a woman's right under English coverture, the actual history of widows' property rights in both the old country and the colonies proves rather complicated. New governments in the colonies wanted to streamline the cumbersome old probate system, on the one hand, but favored giving magistrates discretionary power in settling intestate estates, on the other. There was a firm sense among Englishmen that widows who had borne children, worked hard, and contributed to the family's well-being were deserving of a comfortable retirement, if the estate could support it. How to achieve this outcome varied with the circumstances, although there was no question in most men's minds about husbands' property obligations toward widows. The real issue, then, was how much autonomy they chose to give them. To what extent wives and widows should be permitted to exercise control over family resources, particularly land, became a central policy issue for colonial legislatures as soon as a market in real estate appeared. The earliest drift in probate practice sought to curtail the right of wives to veto their husbands' sales of land and to make widows' shares in estates contingent on circumstances. New Haven leaders were alone in championing liberal probate practices on the London model, but elsewhere, magistrates made some novel and arbitrary decisions, according to the records. Massachusetts and Plymouth Colony soon retreated from tinkering with common-law dower, and Rhode Island never mustered sufficient authority to overrule widows determined to manage family property. Connecticut swallowed New Haven in 1661 but only slightly modified its own paternalistic policies toward widows' dower rights as a result.[51]

Before King Philip's War, male testators who were still married to their original wives usually awarded them in their wills with more than their legal and customary dower rights, which were one-third of the personal estate net of debts and probate costs, and one-third of the real estate for life. The real estate might be title for life to actual parcels of land and buildings (more common in the seventeenth century), or it might be one-third of the income or produce generated by productive land, paid semiannually by the heirs utilizing it. This latter option was more commonly adopted in the eighteenth century, when most farms were fully developed and constituted a preponderant share of the estate's value. This option removed the widow from control over the real estate but assured her an annuity based on its income. In cases of intestacy, the distribution of the estate was supervised by the court and frequently reflected variations on this scheme. One out of five testators wrote highly detailed wills after first bequeathing full title to the family home and farm to a son or sons. These instructed the heirs to provide their mother with various kinds and quantities of farm produce and to set aside for her benefit specific parts of the house, yard, barn, and orchard. Such a will often enumerated the actual number of bushels of various kinds of grains and legumes, in addition to cords of firewood "cut and stacked at her door," and might even include the requirement that a horse be available for her use every sabbath day, ready saddled at the front door to take her to meeting. Wills of this sort often identify precisely which room or rooms were to be hers, even indicating which part of the cellar was for her use. They might specify that she be given access to the kitchen, the bake oven, the well, the yard, and part of the barn for her hay or her cows.[52]

Such wills were clearly intended to give Mother her own space, separate from her daughter-in-law's, which was probably very welcome to both, given the circumstances. In wills of this type, the testator never explains why he has made these particular arrangements, nor does he give any indication that he has ever consulted with his wife to hear her preferences in the matter. Since wills became public documents once they passed through probate, men who sought their wives' opinions in these matters might not have wished to reveal this fact. But if one of the women whose lives were directly affected by his arrangement became unhappy with it or overstepped her bounds, then what? Deacons of the church might have tried to arbitrate disagreements, but there were no practical means of enforcing the terms of such wills, despite their specificity. Indeed, who outside the household would want to meddle? Worse, what male judge would listen for long to a woman whining about her daughter-in-law? At most, the judge would urge the son to quiet his household.

Widows might prefer to be given the property outright so that they could make their own arrangements with the heirs. This is what Margery Scruggs did in 1654, when she made an agreement with her son-in-law in which he paid her five pounds immediately and twenty pounds per year, paid quarterly, and the "use of necessary household effects." He also promised to give her five pounds "at the hour of her death to be freely at her disposal."[53]

Although widows had the legal right to go to court to challenge a will, the best they could hope for after 1691, under the laws adopted under the new Massachusetts and New Hampshire charters, was only one-third of the income of the real estate, for which they would have to surrender all personal estate, such as livestock, tools, furniture, and monies owed. Connecticut and Rhode Island had never treated widows as potentially independent decisionmakers and saw no reason to change their stance. Thus in most cases in the eighteenth century, aggrieved widows would be worse off going to court, and few did so.[54]

As we saw in Chapter 4, men and women who had children from a first marriage, and who were contemplating marrying again, usually made a contract (a prenuptial agreement) guaranteeing an agreed-upon limited settlement to the surviving spouse in order to forestall distribution of assets by the court in accord with the laws of intestacy. The usual purpose for making such contracts was to guard the portions of their children against dower claims on the estate in the event of their own premature death. Older men with grown children were particularly apt to make such arrangements. They generally crafted the document specifically for the purpose of bringing the prenuptial agreement to the attention of the probate court in order to bar their second wives from claiming dower rights. They probably did so not because they loved their second wife less than the first but to assure to their children the same shares in the estates they would otherwise have received had they not remarried. Their behavior suggests that the claims of children on their accumulated assets took moral precedence over their own personal desires for a companion, bedmate, housekeeper, and/or nursemaid.

Widows past childbearing age were unlikely to remarry unless they were well-off. If they stayed single, headed their household, and owned land in their own right, they wielded an unusual degree of power for women in rural English society.[55] As a consequence, they had to mind their behavior in public so as not to cause "talk." In particular, they were expected to extinguish all lingering flames of carnal desire, not only because sex outside marriage was sinful, but also because God intended sexual relations for reproductive purposes. Since it was supposedly women's generative organs that drove their sexual appetites, the decline and disappearance of menstrual flow should have diminished such desires. Hence for an "old" widow to sleep with a man was not only sinful but unnatural. There was a widow in Salem Village who had, years before the outbreak of witchcraft hysteria there, shared her bed with, and then married, the young Irish manservant whose contract she had purchased to help her run the farm after her husband died. So far as the community was concerned, her character had been irredeemably destroyed by that relationship, and she fell target to accusers early in the 1692 witch-hunt, even though she was bedridden at the time.[56]

Since males remained capable of fathering children long after females lost their fecundity, it was considered altogether seemly for a healthy widower to seek a second wife. When, however, an older widower of substantial property courted a woman young enough to bear him children, issues of inheritance, dower rights, and sexuality at once came to the fore. Not only would such a union pose an even greater financial threat to his children from the first marriage; it might also hint at a degree of lust inappropriate in older men. The disparity in age must not be too great. Christian advice manuals had always urged people to marry others in like circumstances, with respect to age and estate, as being more conducive to happiness in the relationship. People seemed less worried about the potential in May-and-September marriages for exploiting poor young women than the possibility that such a one would manipulate a besotted old man and swindle the estate away from the "rightful" heirs. Although sexuality was taken for granted among young people, the culture deemed sexual relations between older couples as mildly salacious and regarded as downright disgusting an "old" man's pursuit of a young woman. Cotton Mather at age twenty-seven wrote a highly charged attack on dirty old men. "Unchastity in any man renders him the Abhorred of the Lord, But in an Old Man it is more peculiarly fulsome, nasty, and that which renders him the abhorred of the Neighborhood . . . Nothing is more Nauseous and Odrous in an Old Man than the Levity of Lasciviousness."[57]

A secure and independent retirement was the dream of every elderly person in seventeenth-century New England just as it is today. But achieving their goal was made difficult by the absence of safe forms of investing for income. Land was the only low-risk choice. But how were those who were past their prime physically to convert a tract of land into a reliable stream of current income? Putting up the property for rent or lease brought few worthy prospects so long as the returns to labor invested in raw land were greater than the returns to labor expended in running an established farm. This was the situation for much of the colonial period. The introduction of paper money as a medium of exchange in the 1690s sped up debt collection and led to far greater use in the eighteenth century of instruments of credit, such as mortgages, that could be bought and sold. These gave men and women in their declining years ways of converting fixed, material forms of capital into investments that returned income in the form of interest or dividends. Doing so eliminated the need to employ their own labor or that of others. These pieces of paper worked only if the promises to pay which they embodied could be cheaply and promptly enforced by disinterested agents of the state, in the form of civil courts. The English system of local county courts, installed by New England settlers in the 1650s, had traditionally acted as guarantors of property rights and enforcement agencies for private contracts. Once transplanted to the colonies, they rapidly evolved everywhere in response to the needs of the developing economy. With the growth in the supply of money in the eighteenth century, these courts were able to provide creditors with prompt and low-cost recourse against debtors.

Mortgages, for instance, became common in the Boston area well before the end of the seventeenth century, and their use spread to other parts of the region in the eighteenth century. They benefited the young as well as the old, because they enabled the young to acquire their own farm or shop much sooner than they would have otherwise. Instead of working for wages on year-to-year contracts and slowly accumulating all the savings necessary to pay up-front for a farm, they could now borrow the funds necessary to acquire land and repay the loan out of the income generated by their growing capital. These instruments of credit were liberating devices for widows and the elderly. Widows no longer had to remarry just to get someone to help run the farm. And widows could lend assistance to other widows: Prudence Thompson of Roxbury, Massachusetts, mortgaged her house, meadow, and orchard for fifty pounds to Mary Greenhill of Boston, widow, in November 1720. The mortgage was canceled on February 1, 1722, meaning that Thompson had repaid the fifty pounds, probably with interest.[58]

There were drawbacks to this new monetary and financial system, as there so often are with technological changes. Manipulating figures of debits, credits, and interest requires a level of arithmetic skills that country people had not needed before. The invention of paper money in 1690, the proliferation of separate colonial currencies, and the uneven erosion of their values stimulated ordinary farmers to teach themselves and their children how to write down and calculate such things. They could be serious losers if they did not keep track of the exchange values between currencies. They also needed to watch shifting structures of prices as well as individual prices of the things they sold or exchanged. They quickly learned what their paper money was worth in British sterling when they bought imported goods such as new metal tools, salt, and later sugar and tea, plus nice cloth for their Sunday best. The spread of storekeeping and financial instruments in the eighteenth century spurred their engagement in these new kinds of transactions, especially after they discovered how directly inflation affected the real rate of return from interest. For all these reasons, they needed to master multiplication and division in order to avoid paying too much as borrowers or charging too little when making loans to others.[59]

Although the commercializing economy of the eighteenth century created more options for elders and youth, it put the less well educated at a disadvantage. At first the increasing need for arithmetic skills seemed to be a matter for male concern only, and it certainly fueled men's demands that tax-supported schools supply such training. As we saw in Chapter 6, girls traditionally learned only to read, not to write. Their reading ability, therefore, was probably limited to perusing printed materials such as the Bible or legal forms such as deeds. Only daughters of more affluent or ambitious men actually learned to write for themselves (the first step toward reading the handwriting of others). Fewer still acquired even a rudimentary knowledge of arithmetic. Hence what amounted to a revolution in financial transactions between 1690 and 1740 initially handicapped girls because so many country men were reluctant to provide this instruction to females. Farm women of the early eighteenth century, who were born before the spread of schools, were worst off.

The poorly educated always suffer the most in a changing economy, and in the English colonies for a few decades in the eighteenth century, the playing field became yet more uneven. Unless women took the initiative themselves to acquire these necessary new skills, they would find themselves even more dependent on their husbands and, when widowed, on their adult sons. Prolonged widowhood in a commercializing society such as eighteenth-century New England's only worsened their dependency. But for those able to put their assets to work in these new ways, investing in mortgages and other loans provided the means to a more secure, more independent retirement.

Sickness and Death

Sickness and death hit hardest at the very young and the very old, but accidents, childbearing, warfare, and epidemics also took their toll of young adults. For Ninnimissinouk men, occasional war parties probably took the lives of only a few on an intermittent basis, in contrast to the enormous casualties suffered on both sides during King Philip's War, in 1675–76. Smallpox was the most feared disease of the times and killed as many as one out of six of its victims—one out of three or worse if there was no one to supply nursing care. This is what happened whenever it struck down many adults simultaneously, as it did the "virgin" populations of previously unexposed Native Americans. So-called childhood diseases did not become endemic in New England until populations reached sufficient densities to keep the infectious agents viable. Measles, for instance, ranks with smallpox as one of the most contagious of epidemic diseases and often follows in its wake. To keep the propagation going, however, measles requires a large minimum number of susceptible individuals perpetually available, at least 7,000 according to calculations by modern epidemiologists. Hence when the virus is freshly introduced into a smaller population after a period of some absence, it will spread like wildfire and then "burn itself out." Not only was measles often fatal on its own, but it proved a serious secondary source of danger because of the complications that often followed. It and other diseases such as chicken pox, whooping cough, and mumps made rare but painful visitations in southern New England until there were sufficient numbers of children present, mixing with one another at school, to provide a constant pool of vulnerable victims. These are the conditions that came to prevail in the older settled areas by the 1730s.[60]

Diphtheria and scarlet fever have somewhat similar symptoms but in the seventeenth and eighteenth centuries were both in the process of evolution, and reports of their appearances are confusing to modern diagnosticians. Diphtheria, however, produces the "bladder" in the throat described by many writers reporting the epidemics of "throat distemper" in the middle decades of the eighteenth century. This false membrane thickens and spreads down the larynx and trachea, blocking the air passages, often suffocating its young victims.[61]

Influenza, colds, and other respiratory diseases afflicted both natives and newcomers in New England every winter, and tuberculosis proved especially troublesome to the Ninnimissinouk, according to skeletal evidence. Among the many scourges brought by the English was malaria, probably carried over in the bloodstreams of people emigrating from the fen country, and then picked up by local anopheles mosquitoes in coastal New England marshes. Calculations based on data from the town genealogies of Rowley, which borders the extensive Ipswich marshes in eastern Essex County, Massachusetts, reveal sharply higher childhood death rates there than appear in other town genealogies. These extra deaths may have been due to water-related diseases such as malaria, dysentery, typhus, or typhoid fever.[62]

Physicians, healers, and herbalists among the immigrants purveyed a broad range of natural medicines and chemical compounds, some benign, others simply ineffective, and many just plain poisonous. Native herbal remedies, as described by observers such as William Wood, Roger Williams, and John Josselyn, were highly efficacious for the treatment of sprains, wounds, and scurvy and for the bites and stings of poisonous snakes, spiders, and insects. Ministers such as Peter Thacher and Michael Wigglesworth often dispensed advice and medicines when visiting sick parishioners. Toward the end of his life the indefatigable Cotton Mather compiled an encyclopedia of common maladies and remedies. Some colonial doctors pursued an aggressively interventionist regime, such as bleeding, vomiting, and purging, which deprived the patient's body of vital fluids. College-trained physicians were very expensive and so were usually called in only when all other remedies had failed, often when the patient was already dying.[63]

Victims of infectious diseases might die in a matter of days, but other illnesses might last many months before death came or health returned. In the meantime, someone had to empty the bedpans, wash the sheets, bathe and feed the patient. Servants and hired nurses helped to supply these services to the well-to-do, but in more ordinary households female members of the family bore the brunt of practical nursing. Women who witnessed the wills of the dying were very often those involved in the active care of the testator, who occasionally expressed gratitude in the form of a bequest.

Despite the ubiquity of death, the ending of a human life is usually freighted with deep spiritual meaning for all concerned. This was as true for the Ninnimissinouk as it was for the English newcomers to New England, although the surviving evidence on native beliefs is slight. Roger Williams describes the highly expressive displays of Narragansett parents over the death of their children, and he reports that the death of a sachem plunged an entire tribe into deep mourning for a year. In some puzzlement he also described the strange behavior of the old sachem Canonicus, who burned down his chief's house and all its treasures in his grief over the loss of his son, a young man of promise. After reviewing the anthropological literature on burial practices of the Ninnimissinouk and other northeastern Algonquian speakers, Kathleen Bragdon concludes that goods buried with the dead did not represent sacrifices intended to appease or court a personal god. Rather, the outlay and choice of goods served as an investment of sorts, as gifts made to the supernatural realm in the same spirit of coercive reciprocity that informed relations between people and their leaders. The greater the gift, the greater the compensation expected. The destruction of the individual who died was a loss not only to the parents and other kin, but to the people as a whole. That loss could be used to bargain with the spiritual realm, and the loss could be further enhanced by a material sacrifice in order to coerce from the spiritual world a renewal among themselves of even greater strength and efficacy. After the English arrived, bringing diseases and social upheavals in their wake as well as desirable and prestigious trade goods, the Ninnimissinouk, according to Bragdon, sought to make use of their burials to advance the general good. The sharp increase in trade goods buried with the Narragansett dead, so visible in postencounter graves, perhaps do not so much represent greater inequality among them as ever-bigger investments intended to counteract the diminution of their spiritual energy.[64]

In contrast to what Bragdon characterizes as the coercive intentions of the Ninnimissinouk in their interactions with the spiritual world, the relationship between Puritans and their great spirit might be described as one of appeasement and self-abasement. When God took away a loved one, the proper response was "Thy will be done, O Lord."[65]

Colonial New Englanders believed that when the body of a true believer died, his or her spirit/soul was released for angels to guide to heaven. When Mary Cooper of Oyster Bay, Long Island, was told of the impending deaths of her elderly aunt and uncle, she wrote in her diary: "I felt heavy harted and so distrest that I could hardely set up . . . about five a'clok this afternoon the Lord met with my soul in mercy and told me that thier departed souls should mount on the wings of saraphs to the relms of etarnal day, and that thier weathered limbs should leave thier dusty bed like the bounding robe [winding-sheet?] and made parfet in their Savour's righteousness. Immortal youth and beauty mount to meet thier redeemer in the clouds of heaven."[66]

The poetry of Edward Taylor, minister of the remote country town of Westfield, Massachusetts, beautifully expresses the Christian idea of death as both ending and beginning:

> Heavens brightsom Light shines out in Death's Dark Cave.
> The Golden Dore of Glory is the Grave.[67]

In the bleak skull-face of death, Puritans imagined a glorious millennial future. The epitaphs and images carved on their gravestones reflect these beliefs, transfiguring emblems of death into symbols of spiritual triumph. When Jesus returned on Judgment Day, the souls of the believers in heaven would joyfully accompany him to earth to rejoin their buried remains, each to be resurrected into a glorious, new, and immortal body. For this reason, New Englanders buried their dead on their backs with their heads to the west, so that when they sat up on Resurrection Day, they would be facing east, the direction from which Jesus and the heavenly host would come. But Puritan Calvinism also emphasized that salvation was not guaranteed to all, or even to all good people. It was a free gift of God and, as such, could not be earned by any human act, no matter how selfless or saintly. For Puritans there was no sure way to know God's mind; they might spend their lifetimes prayerfully seeking after God, but they could never be sure of their own sal vation, much less the spiritual state of others. When people died, therefore, those in mourning could never be fully reassured concerning the fate of their souls, nor was there anything further to be done on their behalf.

Because death closes off all avenues of appeal, the devout did not fear death itself so much as the possibility of dying too quickly, before they had the chance to repent the harder, to plead their case one last time. So long as one lived, one could hope. When someone lay dying, it was with a profound sense of urgency that people gathered round to pray for the endangered soul and to exhort the invalid to examine his or her conscience and to pray earnestly for forgiveness. A good death was one to which the dying came fully prepared, at peace with God and the world. Such a death edified those watching and praying, who, when their own time came, would strive for just such a closure.[68]

When a Christian died, the family or the town hired women to wash the body, shave the face if he were a man, wind the body in a sheet, and place it in a made-to-measure wooden coffin as soon as it was ready. In the meanwhile the family or friends sent messengers to carry the news and bid people to attend the funeral. If the meeting house had a bell, somebody would toll it to let the community know of the death and the pending burial. Watchers stayed by the body until the funeral party assembled. The assembled guests might share refreshments and speak respectfully of the dead as they waited for the signal to move. Members of the funeral party then walked in a solemn procession behind the covered coffin and its attendants to a nearby burial ground and lowered it into a grave, freshly dug by men hired for the purpose. After speaking a few words of remembrance and consolation, each threw in clods of earth, and the closest family members then distributed thank-you gifts, such as gloves or rings, to those who had carried the coffin or walked with it holding the cloth covering, called a pall. In late seventeenth-century Boston, friends pinned funeral elegies to the pall. Everyone then returned to the deceased's home to eat cakes and drink well-spiked punch. Meanwhile the grave diggers filled in the grave and placed fence rails around it to mark it off from the other sites. If the deceased was a church member, the minister preached a funeral sermon the following Sunday. In cases in which the deceased had no family and no money, town officials ensured a "decent Christian burial" and sold what effects they could to help cover the costs.[69]

Accounts of administration of probated estates show that the minimal requirements for Christian burial in New England included a winding-sheet, a coffin, and a grave. These costs would be paid out of the deceased's estate ahead of all others, and if there were insufficient assets, the town would pay them. The purpose of the coffin and sheet or shroud was to help keep the body together as it decomposed, so that when Christ came again, the body could instantaneously reassemble itself to rise and meet him.[70] After these three requirements, the most frequent additional funeral expenses were those contracted by furnishing drinks to the guests. When a homeless man named Titus Waymouth died in Plymouth in 1656, the charges for his burial included the sheet, the coffin, and the grave, totaling nineteen shillings five pence, plus twelve shillings for the "charges of the ordinary," where everyone went after the funeral, presumably to drink farewell toasts to the newly departed. After Samuel Cutbert, of Middleborough, Massachusetts, passed on to his reward in 1698, the administrator of his minuscule estate spent eighteen shillings on his burial and close to six shillings on rum and sugar.

Ceremony and show were generally eschewed in Puritan burials, out of a sense of propriety. The Bible, after all, did not condone status-seeking display or popish ritual. On the other hand, there was a kind of inevitable force at work to expand funeral expenditures. The more people who showed up to mourn, clearly the higher the public regard for the deceased. The honor of the family, therefore, came to be at stake as they made plans for the public ceremony.[71]

Despite the social bonding that funerals promoted and the well-intentioned hope that the deceased would have a better life in the afterworld, death was a somber occasion for the colonists as it is for most peoples. Puritans were expected to mourn the passing of their loved ones, even to cry, but they must not grieve too much or too long. They must try to accept the death as God's will and to resign themselves through prayer, a difficult process through which ministers and church officers endeavored to assist the bereaved. Diaries of parents who lost a child are particularly poignant in revealing their struggles to forbear questioning God's decision. Later, grief might suddenly rise to consciousness and overwhelm the mourner, taken suddenly unawares.[72]

Inscribed and decorated gravestones came into use among the English on both sides of the Atlantic at about the same time: the 1670s and 1680s. They were purchased after the funeral only if there were sufficient means remaining after all the debts were settled and the family taken care of. Depending on the size of the community and the proximity of a quarry, there might be men locally available who worked part-time as stone cutters on commissions. Otherwise, pairs of stones might be ordered from professionals living in a major urban center, such as Boston, and shipped by water before being carted to the burial ground. Years might elapse before stones were finally erected. Indeed, the earliest dated gravestones were probably placed years after the deceased was buried. Here is the epitaph appearing on the earliest dated stone, erected sometime later in the century, on the grave of Joseph Drake of Windsor, Connecticut, who died in 1657:

> My body sleeps
> My soul is blest
> In arms of Christ
> Where I do rest

Another early one is that of William Paddy of Boston, who died about 1658, and whose stone at King's Chapel, Boston, was probably placed there in 1674 (slightly modernized here to make the meaning clear):

> Here sleeps that
> Blessed one whose life
> God help us all to live
> That so when time shall be
> That we this world must leave
> We ever may be happy
> With blessed William Paddy

Sleep and awakening were popular metaphors for the body's death and resurrection, and their symbolism was ubiquitous in New England grave-yards. The very shape of the gravestone resembled the headboard of a bed, for instance. In the two cases above, the epitaphs speak with surprising as-surance about the spiritual status of the deceased. The headstone of Thomas Clarke of Plymouth, dated 1727, registers a bit more caution in this regard:

> Many that now are
> Fast asleep in dust
> of earth remain.
> Some shall to everlasting life
> Awake from thence again

Similarly, of Festus Colton's fate, his stone of 1768 reads:

> When Saints shall rise
> that day will show
> the part he acted
> here below[73]

With the passage of time, especially in the later eighteenth century, New England epitaphs sounded notes of greater assurance, such as this epitaph of Betty Lane and her children from 1791:

> Our Flesh shall slumber in the ground,
> 'Til the Last Trumpets' joyful sound:
> Then burst the chains with sweet surprize
> And in our Saviour's image rise[74]

In seventeenth-century New England, death might strike anyone, at any time in the life-cycle. Both natives and newcomers feared death, but both cultures put it to work for the benefit of the living. The Ninnimissinouk used the loss of life as a bargaining chip with the spirit world to obtain replenishment of their vital energies. Gravestones in English burial grounds reminded the casual passerby that all must die and go to meet their judgment. If they are ready, they too can make their peace with God and welcome death as the doorway to paradise.

8

Transitions: The Narragansetts

Boast not proud English, of thy birth & blood,
Thy brother Indian is by birth as Good.
Of one blood God mad Him, and Thee & All,
As wise, as faire, as strong, as personall.
By nature wrath's his portion, thine no more
Till Grace his soule and thine in Christ restore,
Make sure thy second birth, else thou shalt see,
Heaven ope to Indians wild, but shut to thee.

—Roger Williams, *A Key into the Language of America*

The English colonists had spread over the land like the incoming tide, gradual but inexorable as their numbers multiplied. For more than a decade, the English had poured forth off the ships, onto the beaches, moving up every waterway and along every coast. When the ships ceased coming in the early 1640s, the force of their increase scarcely faltered, as their children matured and themselves had children. The intruder population burgeoned and swelled in great generational pulses, surging relentlessly, lapping further into the interior in ever-widening half-circles, rising like the flooding sea to sweep over the land, engulfing native cornfields and beaver meadows, clearing the lowlands and toppling the trees.

After Dedham came Deerfield; after New London, Stonington; after Roxbury, Woodstock. Immigrants' grandchildren and their grandchildren's grandchildren grew up to found new Stoningtons and new Woodstocks, each generation avid for the land, to take it, tame it, fence it off and make it theirs. Families and their farms are the means by which the English took New England—and how their descendants would take upstate New York, the old Northwest, and the Oregon Territory.

The English had brought their children, their livestock, and their technology into a very different ecological environment from that whence they had come, one that was comparatively empty of human and faunal rivals. The firstcomers, the Ninnimissinouk, had used the land and its resources extensively rather than intensively, grazing in seasonal turns upon varied communities of plants, marine life, birds, and other animals. Into this species-rich, complex landscape entered the foreigners, primed to exploit what they viewed as an underutilized world.[1] The English saw their new surroundings as raw and disorderly but awash with possibility. Hard work and discipline, they thought, would make New England into old England, only better. Armed with a reproductively superior family system and an arsenal of infectious diseases, they and their descendants swarmed and hived, colonizing the region, and the Ninnimissinouk, by biological force. And in the process, what they, their hosts, and the land made together was not a reformed version of England at all; it was a *new* New England, an American society.

The immigrants, with the help of their animal retinue, reproduced at long-term rates substantially higher than could ever have been possible for the Ninnimissinouk living in traditional ways, even before the arrival of epidemic diseases. Domesticated livestock provided their keepers with several major advantages in the competition for biological space. Cows' milk not only supplied fresh protein for more than six months out of the year; it also allowed women to wean their babies earlier and to shorten the interval between births. Steers and hogs raised at home provided meat that the men would otherwise have had to spend time hunting and trapping, and oxen powered the heavy-duty tasks. The division of labor between the sexes encouraged by this agricultural system afforded English women a more sedentary lifestyle than was possible for the women of the Ninnimissinouk. Although it is impossible to know with certainty, the physical costs imposed on native mothers during their seasonal moves and in carrying heavy burdens as well as farming may have hindered fetal and infant survival.[2]

The reproductive success of the English in New England was not unique to them, nor was it due to their Puritan ideology. The Catholic *habitants* in New France experienced comparable rates of birth, death, and marriage formation. Good systematic data on their population history have been intensively analyzed by demographers. Their calculations make it clear that Anglo-Americans were neither unnaturally fecund nor uniquely long-lived. Indeed, French women born in Canada married even younger and bore more children as a result. French Catholics and English Protestants shared key values with respect to the family. Both prized female virginity before marriage, practiced serial monogamy, married fairly young, bore their children at roughly two-year intervals, and apparently weaned their babies at about the same time, when the contraceptive effect of breast-feeding had begun to wear off. Both peoples fit James Wood's model profile of colonizing populations, as do the Dutch Boers in eighteenth-century South Africa and the Latter-Day Saints who moved to Utah in the nineteenth century. French and English, together, heighten the contrast between European and Algonquian.[3]

Wood and others have observed that when colonists move into regions they perceive as "empty," they marry younger and produce more children, as though they were subconsciously seeking to fill the void. Authors of the Utah study stress the importance of a pronatalist theology that was reinforced by pronatalist behavior of church leaders. This emphasis on building numerical strength, they argue, derived from defensive psychological attitudes often found among persecuted minorities. One could argue the same case for Puritans and point to the example set by John Winthrop, the most famous leader of the "Great Migration" to New England and repeatedly elected governor of Massachusetts Bay. He provided his constituents with an exceptional role model, marrying at age seventeen and having a series of four wives and sixteen children. His last was born when he was just shy of sixty-one years of age and only three and a half months before his death.[4]

Post-hoc arguments based on the psychology of persecuted minorities cannot account for the fertility of the habitants of New France, however. They were Catholics living under a Catholic king and led by priests vowed to celibacy. Perhaps Wood's guess is closer for the French: family-building as a response to feeling alone in a vast landscape devoid of permanent human settlements. The St. Lawrence Valley in 1619 was far emptier of native rivals than was New England before the *Mayflower.*[5]

Yet the English experience was initially not so dissimilar from that of the French in Canada. They began their invasion by establishing beachheads in territories where epidemics had already reduced inhabitants to a small fraction of their former numbers. From these initial encampments, colonists and their cattle then moved out, taking more land as it was vacated by the scything effects of disease. Over the next few decades they negotiated dozens, perhaps hundreds, of separate land deals with surviving native bands, fragmenting the Wampanoag confederacy in the southeast by physically isolating its remnant groups. Puritan missionaries, moreover, created dissension within bands of Nipmucks and Wampanoags, as their converts contended with traditionalists for political control.[6]

The rapid extension of English settlement in its earliest phases was fueled by the need for grazing land for livestock. When prices of livestock dropped by half after the end of immigration and then continued to decline, colonists switched their energies away from cattle to raising wheat for export. This effort required enlargement of the arable part of their holdings in the older settlements or the colonization of more promising areas elsewhere.[7] Once they had appropriated all the native fields within their townships, they turned to clearing new land, an arduous, time-consuming process when practiced in the English style. Settlers with poor land scouted the new towns in hopes of obtaining land more rewarding to their time and effort. By the 1660s, the generation of children born to the immigrants of the 1630s began coming of age in large numbers and demanding land of their own. As we saw in Chapter 7, a son was legally free to leave when he turned twenty-one, but he would stay on to work for the family if the parents agreed to help him attract a good partner and launch his own enterprise. With many sons to endow, parents felt constant pressure to accumulate land for the future.

Ninnimissinouk resistance to this process took a long time to jell. Their old rivalries and enmities continued to divide them, and many were able to make a good thing out of trade with the settlers.[8] Moreover, the various colonial legislatures freely acknowledged native titles and regulated purchases to prevent fraud, but petitions for adding more land to existing towns and to create new ones became harder for local legislators to resist. Indeed, from the newcomers' point of view, where was the compelling argument to refrain from acquiring land for town expansion? Instead of hanging on to their land, compliant local sachems repeatedly sold off tracts that brought colonists and their free-roaming animals directly into the territories of confederated allies.

The process of English expansion was orchestrated by developers who had the capital to make purchases from the sachems and the expertise to win votes from legislators. Engrossment of land by individuals had occurred since the very beginnings of settlement at Massachusetts Bay, and although legislators sought to control and curtail the acquisition of large chunks of territory by entrepreneurs, their own actions propelled the process. In lieu of covering his expenses and paying a good salary to Governor John Winthrop, for instance, grateful legislators awarded him a 1,000-acre farm in Medford in 1630. His son John Jr. received a 300-acre farm in Ipswich as an inducement to undertake the development of that town on what was then the northern edge of Massachusetts Bay settlement.[9]

Indeed, the younger Winthrop provides an excellent portrait of the Puritan as simultaneously a public servant and a land developer. Before 1657, when he was first elected governor of Connecticut, he had helped to found Ipswich, Massachusetts, Saybrook, Connecticut, and New London, Connecticut. He and many others had long been interested in the land of the Narragansetts, a people who obstinately refused to cooperate with their own subjection. Then, in 1659, he joined Massachusetts business acquaintances in acquiring a mortgage on two enormous tracts of land from the Narragansetts in Rhode Island in return for paying a penalty levied against them by the Commissioners of the United Colonies, of whom he himself was a member. Title to this land, referred to as the "Narragansett Country," was the principal asset of what came to be known as the Atherton Company. When Winthrop died in 1676, his estate included land in four colonies. Tenants operated farms for him in the Narragansett Country, in New London, on Fisher's Island, and in Charlestown, Massachusetts. No complete inventory of his wealth survives, but a Suffolk County inventory valued the Charlestown farm alone at close to two thousand pounds in money.[10]

Rhode Island, close neighbor of the Narragansett people, was the site of several contests over land in seventeenth-century New England, the target of hungry speculators from all three of its neighbors as well as its own residents. Rhode Island's legislature had passed a law forbidding private purchases of land from the Indians without its permission, so outside developers could not expect to get their Indian titles validated by Rhode Island without cutting legislators into the deal. Roger Williams' charter from the restored royal government in 1661 dealt a great blow to the outsiders' cause when it awarded the colony boundaries that conflicted with Connecticut's, despite the spirited efforts by John Winthrop Jr. and the Atherton Company shareholders to get the Narragansett land transferred to Connecticut. The whole tawdry tale, uncovered by Richard S. Dunn, demonstrates that by the 1660s real estate schemes had superseded whatever communal impulse may still have survived.[11]

Roger Williams found his own neighbors engaged in outrageous legal shenanigans designed to steal land not only from Indians but from fellow Christians. Whereas Williams had intended a peaceful haven for religious refugees who would share more or less equally in the land given him by Canonicus and Miantonomi, William Harris and others had pooled their voting rights against Williams in order to restrict access to newcomers and to grab a large, choice tract for the sole benefit of themselves. Now, in the

1660s, Harris wanted to increase the value of his stake in Providence land by winning the support of powerful friends in England for his court suit claiming far greater boundaries for Providence than Roger Williams and Canonicus had ever envisioned.[12]

Notwithstanding his preoccupation in fighting Harris, however, Williams reserved his strongest censure for the imperialists of Massachusetts, denouncing their "depraved appetite after the great vanities, dreams and shows of this vanishing life, great portions of land, land in this wilderness, as if men were in as great necessity and danger for want of great portions of land, as poor, hungry, thirsty seamen have, after a sick and stormy, a long and starving passage. This is one of the gods of New England, which the living and most high Eternal will destroy and famish." The irony behind this ringing denunciation of Puritan perfidy was his continuing epistolary professions of esteem for Winthrop. One wonders: was he really so naive, or was he using flattery as a gambit in some subtle game?[13]

The engrossment of Native American land for personal gain was not solely the prerogative of the rich and famous. The number of unimproved acres catalogued in the probate inventories of ordinary farmers continued to grow.[14] Some of these acres were dividends from residents' own towns, but the rest were claims or shares in the undivided lands of new towns. These were tax-free investments. As we saw in Chapter 3, the founding of new towns such as Deerfield had gone on apace, right up to the onset of King Philip's War, attracting both well-to-do investors who stayed at home and poor, landless families who actually undertook the move and did the work.

Hunger for land permeated New England culture. After King Philip's War, Massachusetts' Reforming Synod of 1679–80 met to consider the sins that had brought about that terrible conflagration. The synod condemned residents' "insatiable desire after Land and Worldly Accomodation, yea, so as to forsake Churches and Ordinances, and live like Heathen, only that so they might have Elbow-room enough in the world. Farms and merchandising have been preferred before the things of God."[15]

King Philip's War put the brakes on this internal expansion in 1675, when Wampanoags and Nipmucks staged lightning raids first along the perimeters of settlement and then against older towns nearer the coast. Although English aggression finally drove the Narragansetts into the coalition led by the Pokanoket sachem Metacom (known as King Philip to the English), their fragile alliance ultimately crumbled under the blows administered by the Mohawks, who had entered the war on the English side.[16] Despite their victory, English resettlement of interior New England would not resume until peace had fully returned, decades later.[17]

King Philip's War destroyed not only lives and homes but all hope for peaceful coexistence between the Ninnimissinouk and the outsiders. References to enemy Indians by Englishmen thereafter took on more clearly racist overtones, as in the will written by young Benjamin Ludden of Weymouth before he joined the disastrous Canada expedition in 1691: "called forth as a souldier in this time of great distress for to fight the Lords Battells against . . . those Bloody Martherous & Salvage Indians." Neal Salisbury has estimated that five thousand Indians and half that number of English perished in the conflagration. Plymouth alone lost nearly a tenth of its adult males and saw three of its fourteen towns demolished by fire and five more damaged. To pay for the war's costs, the taxes of survivors rose sixfold, and Plymouth's government soon lost all credibility as its collections fell further and further into arrears. Altogether, enemy Ninnimissinouk wiped out thirteen English towns in the war, and it was not until 1713 that colonists could safely reoccupy all the sites they had held in 1675.[18]

Far worse, however, was the fate of their onetime hosts and neighbors. Of the nearly 12,000 Ninnimissinouk estimated to have entered the war against the English, 1,250 were killed in battle, 625 died of wounds, and perhaps an additional 3,000 died of exposure and disease. Another 1,000 were sold as slaves—all males age ten and above were to be shipped to the West Indies—and something like 2,000 fled the region entirely, some to join the Mahicans of the Hudson Valley, others to find refuge with bands of the Eastern and Western Abenaki of Canada and northern New England, all allied with the French and all now imbued with an inextinguishable hatred of the English. Thus, with the timely assistance of the Mohawks, the militiamen of southern New England had won a decisive war against their Algonquian neighbors, but would face ninety years of relentless retaliation.[19]

Not all the Ninnimissinouk had joined Metacom's alliance. Those in the praying towns in Massachusetts were rounded up and incarcerated on an island in Boston Harbor, where scores died of exposure, disease, and hunger. Many Mohegans, Pequots, and Nipmuck fought on the English side. Others, like the Eastern Niantics and groups of Wampanoags on Cape Cod and in eastern Plymouth Colony, maintained strict neutrality and were left in peace by the English. In 1684 the governor of Plymouth Colony reported 1,439 Indians still living there, "besides boys and girls under twelve years old, which are supposed to be . . . three times so many," or roughly 5,500 altogether. Of the original fourteen Christian Indian towns in eastern and southeastern New England, only four survived into the eighteenth century. Many of their inhabitants had died in the roundup instigated by English hysteria. Natick, eighteen miles west of Boston, became a center for Christian Ninnimissinouk remaining in Massachusetts after the war. They were all but forgotten by the colonists, whose retreat to settlements closer to the coast left the town isolated and exposed to raids by Abenaki from the north. In the ensuing half-century of virtual autonomy, the town's heterogeneous inhabitants resumed many of their old aboriginal ways. The scramble to survive had abridged their commitment to Christian patterns of work and worship, opening the way for the reassertion of traditional female autonomy in the domestic sphere.[20]

Cotton Mather estimated that there were only 2,605 Indians still living in Massachusetts in 1695, including those in the former Plymouth Colony, but this surely understates the actual total. There were perhaps 2,000 living in Connecticut in 1680, mostly Mohegans and Pequots who had fought on the English side in the war. In the census of 1756, they were all in New London County—some near Norwich but three-fifths in the Stonington area. Stonington was only fifteen miles west of the area occupied by the Eastern Niantics. Though long affiliated with the Narragansetts, the Eastern Niantics had stayed strictly neutral in the war and so were left alone by the English and their native allies. It was with these people that a group of surviving Narragansetts found refuge. The Niantic sachem Ninigret welcomed them and gave them land on which to settle.[21]

Despite the scattering of Ninnimissinouk survivors, whether classed as enemy and therefore sold into servitude or deemed friendly and not enslaved, significant numbers remained in southern New England after King Philip's War. They were able to maintain their native identity, establish or continue families, and get on with their lives. Like ghosts only fleetingly glimpsed, their names haunt scattered pages of surviving records. Indians Francis and Josiah sold meadow land to Lieutenant Joseph Rogers in Eastham sometime before he wrote his will in 1678, bequeathing that land to his sons. John George, Indian, died in Roxbury in 1695 with sufficient property that the probate court appointed two Englishmen to administer his estate. Jonas Jones, "Indian Man, Saylor," died in 1704 leaving apparel, cash, and six pounds' worth of shop goods. "Indian squaw" Nan Allbro of Portsmouth filed an action for debt in 1710 against Samson Baily, an "Indian man" of that place. At his death in Boston in 1718, Anthony Ellis, "Indian, Lighterman," owned wearing clothes, a gun, and a boat, altogether valued at more than twenty-six pounds.[22]

Then there is the case of Apenamucsuck, who, being drunk, was brought before Richard Bushnell, justice of the peace in Norwich, Connecticut. He sentenced Apenamucsuck for his transgression to pay a fine of ten shillings or be whipped ten lashes and to pay court costs of six shillings six pence. John Waterman offered to pay the court costs, but unless Apenamucsuck paid the ten-shilling fine, he would have to take his whipping. Apenamucsuck thereupon accused Samuel Bliss of selling him the offending two pots of cider. When Bliss admitted it, Bushnell sentenced him to pay twenty shillings as a fine, half to the town and half to the complainant, Apenamucsuck, who thereupon paid his own fine and departed the court a free man.[23]

Children of Indians appear in guardianship records. In 1702 David, son of "Sagamore" John Totouhe of Martha's Vineyard, now resident in Roxbury, chose as his guardian Master Samuel Williams of Roxbury, yeoman, signing his petition with a mark. Benjamin Larnell, "Indian," aged eighteen, the son of Solomon Pesacus, deceased native of Woodstock, chose Samuel Sewall Esquire in 1711 as his guardian and tutor, signing his name to the petition.[24]

An estimated 1,000 enemy Indians were bound into service for lengthy terms. The inventory of Lieutenant George Gardner of Salem, dated 1679, included an Indian servant valued at ten pounds. Minister Peter Thacher purchased an Indian girl named Margaret in 1679 for ten pounds, whom he beat two months later with a "good walnut stick" for carelessly dropping his young daughter on her head. While he was preaching at Barnstable, he twice mentioned in his diary hiring Indian servants from his neighbors: on the first occasion to sweep the chimneys and on the second to mend fencing. An Indian woman named Mercy, servant to Thomas Olney of Providence, Rhode Island, gave birth in 1695 to a baby boy identified by Olney as the son of the intriguingly named "Richard Virgin a wandring person who to avoyd the charge of maintaining of the Said Child runn away." When John Marsh of Hadley died in 1725, his inventory included a little Indian boy only four years of age. Joshua Hempstead commemorated the passing of "Old Rachel" in 1746: "She was a Captive taken in the Narhaganset war in 1675 . . . She always lived in the family [of Captain John Prenttis to whom she was servant] & had many Children by her Husband [York, servant in another famiiy]. She was an Honest faithfull Creture & I hope a good Christian. She was one of our Church for many years past."[25]

Although individual Indians appear almost fortuitously in Englishmen's records, there were also whole families and entire communities still sustaining themselves, however obscurely. Josiah Cotton, son of the second John Cotton, took up his father's mission to the Wampanoags in the early eighteenth century, and for twenty-seven years preached to communities of Christian Indians scattered across Plymouth County. Besides these and the remaining praying towns in Massachusetts Bay, there were collections of Wampanoags at Herring Pond, Mannemet, and Mashpee, in the western part of Cape Cod; Acushnet, on Buzzard's Bay; and three on Block Island Sound. Both Martha's Vineyard and Nantucket had Indian enclaves, of which Gay Head on the Vineyard was the most sizable and longest enduring.[26]

Among "friendly" Indians, the men had not been subjected to exportation as slaves, and their numbers should have continued to be sufficient, or nearly so, to maintain customary family relations. This was not the case with enemy Indians, whose men were shipped off. Among survivors, therefore, females predominated. Children grew up without fathers; women struggled without husbands. For sons coming into manhood, the challenge was to adapt to new economic conditions. If there was insufficient land for hunting, and this was more and more often the case, the choices were helping women with the farming, going to work as wage laborers for English neighbors, or becoming mariners. Men adept with huge canoes readily took to life at sea. The expansion of whaling out of Rhode Island ports made good use of their skills. Moreover, in time of war they were eagerly courted by the various colonial governments for military service.[27] As a consequence, Ninnimissinouk men were away for long periods, and many never returned. The sex ratio among adults in many native communities was therefore lopsidedly female, and lonely women gladly took husbands from outside. Although Englishmen did not often choose to marry the independent-minded women of the Ninnimissinouk, men of African descent were eager to do so. They were perennially short of women, as a result of the sexual imbalance created by the slave trade and the geographical concentration of female slaves in urban households. Indian women who owned rights to reserve lands made great catches because they were freeborn, because any children born to them were also free, and because they were in possession of a resource that would support their families. From these women's point of view, Africans made good husbands because they did not have a culturally bred distaste for tasks associated with women's work and were far more helpful to their wives.[28]

Eighteenth-century colonial censuses are very misleading about the numbers of Native Americans present. They counted "Negroes" but often made no mention of "Indians." That the latter were there is clear from other sources, including other censuses, revealing the inconsistency of enumerators. Their confusion underlines the ambiguity of Indian status everywhere in southern New England. Ninnimissinouk on and off reservations were clearly not English, did not vote, and often did not pay taxes. They were anomalies, neither citizens nor slaves.[29] Even their native heritage came into question if they did not "look" Indian. Children with African features born to Indian mothers and raised as Indians were usually classified by white Rhode Islanders as "black" rather than Indian.[30] That the English were denying cultural identity on the grounds of racial admixture posed major problems for Indian communities in their dealings with outside authorities, even as their new racial classification narrowed individual career options by tainting them with slavery.

For communities wishing to maintain their separate native identity, the disinclination of the English to marry in brought a welcome freedom from outside interference. But such freedom was enjoyable only so long as Native Americans had a viable economy with which to support themselves. They needed sufficient numbers to maintain a critical population mass and ample stretches of contiguous territory to support seasonal foraging. The challenge they faced was an ecological one, and sooner or later they would find themselves in competition with the more rapidly reproducing English for the same resources. As their territories shrank, they had to adapt by developing and honoring new occupations for their members.

The Niantics, together with the Narragansett families who had joined them, lived in the area near present-day Charlestown, Rhode Island, where there were, in 1676, few English or other Indians to contend with for access to a still vast territory. They had it pretty much to themselves for awhile. The beach, marshes, islands, and coastal waters formed integral parts of their ecology, as did the woods to the north and the dispersed patches of good soil suitable for raising crops. The men could continue their annual rounds as fishermen and hunters, and the women went on maintaining their fields and crafts. They gathered greens in the spring, berries in summer, nuts in the fall, and shellfish in the winter. They continued to weave mats and baskets from native grasses and to string wampum beads from the whelk shells gathered nearby.

Peaceful isolation in the far western corner of Rhode Island came to an end in 1709, when the legislature designated the Niantic sachem Ninigret II as the legal proprietor of the community's land in return for four-fifths of Niantic territory. They made the territory around Charlestown into a reservation, with Ninigret as sole owner in exchange for his quitclaim to the other 135,000 acres.[31] This action was a double calamity for his people. First, it took away most of their land and put it at the disposal of English developers. Second, it vested absolute title to the remainder in a single individual who was to betray his heritage and treat it as personal property for the benefit of his own family. This deal between Ninigret II and colony leaders turned a formerly free people into Ninigret's tenants-at-will.

Despite this expropriation of their land and the state-directed detribalization in the nineteenth century that resulted in the loss of their reservation, the Niantic-Narragansett community at Charlestown continues in existence to this day and retains its native identity. The community's church made this possible.[32]

The Narragansetts had rebuffed all offers of missionaries before King Philip's War, and the Niantic country to which they later removed was far distant from the homes of Christian ministers. Isolation gave their culture a breathing spell, as is clear in the following story from the diary of Ezra Stiles, written down in 1773 but relating events of an earlier period:

> Some 40 or 50 years ago, there was a great Drought and the Indians of Narragansett held a great Powaw for sundry Days. One Babcok or Stanton at length, being well known to the Indians, went among them and rebuked them as serving and worshipping the Devil; an old Powaw Indian readily owned and justified it—saying all the Corn would die without rain and Chepi the Evil Power withheld that—now said he, If I was to beat you, who would you pray to? To me, or to your Father ten Miles off? You would pray me to leave off and not beat you any more: so we pray to the Devil to leave off affecting us with Evil.[33]

The first Christian missionaries to attempt to convert the Narragansetts were themselves Indian: Japhet, of Martha's Vineyard, and William Simons, of Dartmouth, visited them in the early eighteenth century without visible success. Experience Mayhew called on them in 1713 and likewise failed. Ninigret II pointed out to him that their English neighbors followed many different faiths. For Indians to choose one faith among several, he explained, would create uncomfortable tensions with their English patrons and employers.[34]

The Reverend James MacSparran, who served as minister of Saint Paul's Anglican Church in the English town of Narragansett, located to the east on

Narragansett Bay, aggressively sought out Indians and black slaves in his own parish and made preaching forays onto the Narragansett reservation, but he, too, failed. Over the thirty-seven years of his ministry, he managed to convert only fourteen souls of full or mixed Indian ancestry, none of whom lived on the reservation at Charlestown.

The old dream of converting the Indians revived afresh in the 1730s and 1740s. A "Letter to Mr. Serjeant at Housatunnuck" appeared in the *Boston Gazette* in 1735, relating a fable about a wounded man, Evangelistes by name, confined to his study. Given a magic glass, he could see in the far distance a wild, inhospitable desert on the near edge of which lived a people of "sallow brown complexion, fierce and intractable, under the Government of their Passions, and Slave to every Sense, to Vice and Wickedness." But our hero saw them change in his magic glass and saw, beyond the river, heaven filled with immortality and love, and God's throne in its midst. Thus, it became the hero's task to convert the Indians and turn the wilderness into a fair heaven that would be their, and his, reward.[35]

It was George Whitefield's visit to New England in 1741 that put into motion the events that led to the conversion of the Narragansetts. Whitefield's successes electrified many ministers and college students as well as lay hearers and transformed their preaching styles. The Reverend James Davenport was among them. Joshua Hempstead noted in his diary: "Mr Davenport preached at Groton 4 or 5 days and mighty works followed, near 1000 hearers . . . held the meeting till 2 Clock at night (Some Stayed all night under the oak tree & in the meeting house). About 60 Wounded [deeply moved], many Strong men as well as others." Davenport came to Stonington, where he again preached out-of-doors, "on the Rocks," where hundreds "Cryed out." The Reverend Joseph Park of the Congregational mission in Charlestown went to hear him at the church and reported to Thomas Prince in Boston: "He preach'd a plain and awakening Sermon . . . when to my Surprize their was a Cry all over the Meeting-House."[36]

Although James Davenport was soon to fall afoul of Connecticut authorities, Reverend Park took back with him a new way of reaching his audience. He preached aggressively and by the spring of 1742 had gathered many new English converts at Westerly and Charlestown, who then founded a church and ordained him their pastor. The turning point for the Ninnimissinouk in his area, however, came almost a year later, when a group of Christian Indians from Stonington came to visit the Narragansetts and invited Park to preach to them. He was successful beyond all expectations, for after prayer and a hymn, "I attempted to preach . . . but was unable to continue my Discourse by Reason of the Outcry." After this wondrous experience, about a hundred from the reservation began attending services regularly. Within a few months he had baptized a majority of these, and they were admitted to full membership in the church, at which point they outnumbered the English. They changed their habits, dressing more "decent and cleanly, provide better for their Households, and get clearer of Debt." They ceased drinking and quarreling, and sought education for their children. Less than a year later, "an Indian Woman [was keeping] School in a Wigwam."[37]

This was a startling transformation of what had been a despised and presumably demoralized people. Passionate, extemporaneous preaching delivered what was perhaps the first message of hope heard by these children and grandchildren of refugees. Park was impressed with their great zeal, their seriousness, and their efforts to win over others who continued to adhere to the old ways. There is a story about an Indian woman told by the historian of Westerly, a bit of folklore that perhaps sheds light on Narragansett experience during this exciting period. As Reverend Frederic Denison tells the story, the Indian woman thought that God would not hear her because she could not speak English.

> She . . . had learned to pronounce but one word,—the word "broom." Her anxiety became intense. Her Christian countrymen exhorted her to pray. She felt a deep desire to pray, but knew not how to pray as she supposed she ought, since she could not employ the acceptable tongue. At last the demands of her soul and the strivings of the Divine Spirit so far overcame her, that throwing herself into the attitude of a suppliant, she cried aloud, "Broom! Broom! Broom!" God answered her heart instead of her lips, and instantly filled her soul with light and love and the joys of His salvation.[38]

"Broom" probably refers to her sole link to the English, the brooms she made and sold to them. In any case, the story illustrates the continuing separation between reservation Indians and their English neighbors. They were Narragansett still.

The Narragansetts formed their own church, which, Stiles reported, was in communion with Separatist Indian congregations in Groton and Mohegan in Connecticut as well as with members of the Western Niantic, Pequot, and Montauk (Long Island). A common Indian identity came into being as Separatist Christian beliefs created a new, enduring, and overarching bond among them. A movement began, inspired by the Mohegan missionary-preacher Samson Occum to emigrate west to Oneida lands in northern New York in order to create a new Christian Indian community, self-supporting and self-governing, living apart from a corrupt world. The Oneidas granted them a large tract for this purpose in 1774, but with the startling stipulation "that the same shall not be possessed by any persons deemed of the said Tribes who are descended from or have intermixed with negros and mulattoes." Even before the American Revolution, then, religious and racial purity had come together as defining goals for reform-minded Native Americans in the Northeast.[39]

Occum's followers attempted to create their settlement in New York in 1775, but the outbreak of war quickly drove them back to the safety of Stockbridge, the Mahican mission-fort in far-western Massachusetts, where they sat out the hostilities. They recommenced their settlement soon after the war was over, naming it Brothertown to signify pan-Indian brotherhood. A half-century later, they moved again, with many other New Englanders, to a new frontier in Wisconsin.

How many Narragansetts from the reservation participated in these moves is unknown. Presumably they attracted only the most serious Christians and the least mixed racially. When the last hereditary sachem died sometime in the 1780s, the tribe became self-governing, electing a governor and council on an annual basis. Inevitably disputes arose over who was entitled to vote in the elections. They were finally resolved by "An Act Regulating the Affairs of the Narragansett Tribe of Indians," passed in 1792. The act stated that "every male person of twenty-one years, born of an Indian woman belonging to said tribe, or begotten by an Indian man belonging thereto, of any other than a negro woman, shall be entitled to vote." Native women were still free to marry whom they wished and to pass along their tribal membership to their children. In effect, the power of defining who was Narragansett continued to lie with the women of the tribe.[40]

Despite the departure of Occum's disciples in 1775, the Narragansetts' church continued to serve as their meeting center. Through it they remade their cultural heritage, appropriating and adapting English-sanctioned forms and customs to gain respectability with their English patrons and neighbors, but also performing ceremonies that resonated particularly for them. The best known and most enduring of these is the August Meeting, which continues to be held every August as part of the New England Powwow circuit.[41]

9

Transitions: The English

My heart is burnt with anger and discontent.

—Mary Cooper, *Diary*

After King Philip's War, some groups of Ninnimissinouk took refuge among the Abenaki of Canada, who had allied with the French and welcomed their missionaries. Abenaki war parties penetrated deep into Massachusetts, and one of their favorite targets was Woodstock, located in what had formerly been Nipmuck territory, not far from northwestern Rhode Island. Woodstock is in a beautiful river valley with broad natural meadows lying on either side. Its farm produce found easy transport to Providence, and from there to the West Indies. Settled and abandoned twice, the town became a coveted site for reclamation when peace returned. The Treaty of Utrecht in 1713 inaugurated a long era of recovery, permitting town settlement in New England's interior to resume in earnest.

The eighteenth century brought significant changes in the region's legal structure, economic organization, standard and style of living, religious sensibilities, and gender perspectives, all affecting family ideology and power relations in interesting ways. Most important, opportunity still prevailed in the region's farm sector until at least midcentury. For a poor but honest young man with good health, good fortune, and good connections, the sky was the limit, especially if he got in on the ground floor at a place like Woodstock. The diary of John May shows how it was done.

John May was the first surviving son of Deacon John May and his wife, Prudence Bridge, of Roxbury, Massachusetts, where the younger John was born in 1686. He began keeping an account of his employment by others in June of 1707, the year he attained his majority. In that month he worked eight days digging stones and making walls; in September he mowed oats and cleared swamp; in October he carried apples to the cider mill; he cut cord wood and fence rails in December. There are many entries for 1708 and 1709 for cutting wood and unspecified work for which he received two shillings per diem and, for ditching, three shillings. All accounts were kept in money, but his pay might have been in country produce or paper currency. He received pay the same day he worked or later in a "reckoning," but no employer kept him waiting for long.[1]

In 1710 John began steady work for his maternal uncle, Lieutenant Bridge, doing a wide variety of farming and carpentry chores of the types familiar from Thomas Minor's diary, including work on Bridge's newly raised house. The listing of paid employment and wages gradually evolved into a daily record of his activities, but like Thomas Minor, May did not use the diary to confide his thoughts or feelings. He says nothing about church matters or prayer. Although he records visits with family and occasional family news, the diary's main purpose was to keep track of his business affairs. Because he worked for divers employers and exchanged work with his cousins, the diary is much fuller than Minor's in its daily details. Occasional brief passages are in code or shorthand, but the bulk of the diary is fully legible.[2]

When, late in 1710, he and his uncle Bridge settled their accounts, there "remained due to me" some seventeen pounds. Within a few days John had moved to Woodstock with a yoke of oxen and purchased a lot. He moved in as a paying boarder with "Mr. Child" (note the careful use of honorific titles), to whom he was related, and called his landlord's sons, Joseph and Benjamin, "cousin." May at once began to chop down pine trees on his lot—soon breaking his ax—and then dug a cellar. Over the next few days, he cut and trimmed pine logs and quarried stones to line his cellar. Another cousin, Joseph Lyon, carted at least four loads of additional stones from Quinebaug for him. With the help of Ben Child and Joseph, he continued work on the cellar, finishing it on January 12. During these two weeks of backbreaking labor he was aided immensely by the two young kinsmen and his pair of oxen. Over the next month he cut more timber, this time for his house. By the end of February he had also dug stones for his chimney and cleared swamp.

When May wasn't working on his lot, he dressed flax or made fence for his landlord. He recorded the birth of a daughter to Joseph toward the end of February, shortly after which he went home to Roxbury for a round of visiting, cutting wood for hire, attending a town meeting and lectures, returning in mid-March to Woodstock, where he spent most of his time cutting and hauling wood for a log fence, built with the help of two borrowed yokes of oxen. On April 4 he sorted nails and began hewing timber to frame his house: squaring the logs (probably the three trees he had selected and cut in January) for beams and joists. He took time off the afternoon of April 28 to kill rattlesnakes before helping Ephraim Child "cover" corn. In May he "rolled over my logs at the mill," presumably to have them sawed into clapboard siding for his house, and he purchased a cow for three pounds six shillings.

John and his neighbors and cousins continued helping one another with fencing and farming chores, everybody keeping careful track of his work to avoid disputes. "Reck'nd with Benjamin Child about work done by each of us. I remain debtor to him 4 days work; on the same day reckoned with Ephraim Child about work done between us at fencing and plowing and building and I remain debtor to him one day likewise he one day to me." The circle of his manifold dealings included the wife of Joseph Lyon, with whom he also "reckoned."[3] He began digging and carting more stones for his cellar, exchanging work with Lieutenant Morris, ditching for him in return for the expert stonework Morris would do on his cellar.

He brought down two thousand boards, probably the clapboards for siding his house after the frame was raised. He then "went down to the Bay," where he worked for his father, visited, attended lectures, then returned to Woodstock in June and began hoeing and plowing. In late June he hilled corn, hoed, plowed, and carted timber. Mowing got underway in mid-July, when he got home three "jags" of hay. He continued to mow for himself and others, sometimes exchanging help as on July 23, "Ichabod [Child] helpt me in the forenoon and I helpt him in the afternoon." Mowing continued until August 24, when he wrote, "We finisht our stacks."

On August 27, Lieutenant Morris began stoning May's cellar while other men helped John build the frame of his house, which they finished on September 12 and raised the next day. They began work on the roof on September 22 and started to "do" the windows a week later. Morris "underjoined" and underpinned the house and helped build the chimney. On September 23 "I hewed my last mantletree, Ben and I got them home." ("Last mantletree" suggests at least three in number, so his new house would have had multiple fireplaces with flues serviced by a single chimney stack.)

After several days of cutting wood, dressing flax, and working at the schoolhouse, probably as part payment of his tax obligations, he returned to boarding his house in early November and finished enclosing it on the ninth. With the help of others, he laid floors over the next four days, then made latches and catches for his doors. On November 19 he "fetcht home" his oxen, reckoned with his landlady—he owed her two shillings—and spent the rest of the day "filling walls."[4] While waiting for expert help with the chimney, he made a bedstead. This is the first entry about making bedsteads, a practice he would continue over the next dozen years as a way to make money.

On November 24 Lieutenant Morris laid the (last?) hearth, and John bought a mare, which he rode back to Roxbury, arriving three days later. Thanksgiving Day (at this time only a sporadically proclaimed celebration, along with "days of repentance"; the formal holiday was instituted by President Lincoln) was November 29, and he spent the next two weeks on sundry chores for his father and neighbors. On December 18 he wrote in his diary: "A Great Days Work." It was his wedding day.

John May's new bride was his cousin, Elizabeth Child, born in 1691 in Brookline, Massachusetts, the daughter of his Woodstock landlord and sister of his frequent sidekick, Ben. Elizabeth and John were to have ten children together, of whom six would survive. He and his bride went visiting for the next week, including a day in Boston. They set out for their new house in Woodstock on December 27, arriving the next day.

John then made several trips to "the French town," with one or the other of his cousins along to help, getting "our goods," which included a chest of drawers. They began "setting our house in order," because soon "Young and old came to see us."[5] Besides clearing new ground and pursuing the usual round of seasonal chores, John made a variety of tools and utensils out of wood for himself and for his wife, including a shovel, a new handle for his pitchfork, two troughs, a hand reel (for spinning yarn), and a peel (a long-handled, flat-bladed tool something like a short oar for reaching into places such as ovens to retrieve loaves of bread). He also continued to exchange work with his cousins and neighbors.[6]

That summer he followed a calendar of tasks little different from Thomas Minor's in the 1660s. After the harvest was in, he turned to his wood-working. He "finisht my trundle bed," began work on another bedstead, and then made a cradle.

Finishing the new house took a while, because the demand for his bedsteads and other woodwork kept him sufficiently busy to justify purchasing additional "tools at Rices'" in December. After a typical January in which he hewed pine logs, cleared swamp, split posts, dressed flax, cut steps, and sledded wood, "we went avisiting." On January 25 he "fetched wife home."

This is about the time their first daughter, Elizabeth, was born. The diary omits this momentous occasion: the separation of John's world from his wife's at this point in their lives was even more complete than it had been for the Minors.

Notable events that he did put on record included his attendance at "Indian" lectures, perhaps intended for a nearby community of Ninnimissinouk but open to the public. His parents paid them a visit in October 1713. He came down with the measles after a visit to his brother in Boston. A son, John, was born a year after Elizabeth, and son Joshua two years later. Neither birth appears in the diary. (Note that the firstborn of each sex was given the name of the parent of that sex, a common New England pattern.)

From 1713 through 1718 the diary recounts an annual round of farm work familiar from the Minor diary, but the great value of May's book is that it describes the process of building a farm from the very beginning, when he had nothing but his hands, a lot, a few tools, and his faithful yoke of oxen—no house, no wife, and no other animals.[7] Then, in 1714, he began scouting new towns: Ashford, then Pomfret. At Pomfret, "My father went with me to look of land." While there, he took a good look at the community coming together: he went to a raising, trained with the militia, heard the new minister preach, and attended his ordination. Nothing came of this patch of restlessness, and he continued to "improve" his Woodstock place.

By 1721 the diary had become an account book, with a page or half-page per person (customer/client/patron/cousin), replete with wages and prices of goods exchanged: butter, cheese, pork, beef and veal by the pound; corn, rye, wheat, oats, and turnips by the bushel; occasional hens; milk and rum by the quart; hemp and tobacco by the pound. Reckonings took place annually or biannually. This new phase of the diary marks a graduation from May's status as beginning propertyholder—one who exchanged labor with age peers among his kin—to the mature household head whose transactions were more complex and included a far wider range of people. At this point his family affairs enter the diary more prominently. He notes the birth of son Steven and the comings and goings of a maid named "Prush." By 1731 he is recording "work done by Boys, 2 days," valued at seven shillings. This is roughly at the same point in Thomas Minor's career that Minor began his diary, but May's activities are far more commercially oriented. The sixty years between the two had seen a lot of change in the New England economy.

The growth of population in the Woodstock area—human, equine, and bovine—created openings for entrepreneurial energies, and May pursued new lines of work: making and selling halters and ropes.[8] From ropemaking, May graduated to tanning, and within a few years had built a dam to divert water to pits for tanning leather. He had progressed from propertyless day laborer to prosperous farmer-artisan in the space of little more than a dozen years.

John May could not have advanced so far so fast without his family connections and a bit of capital: the money he had saved from his earnings supplemented by the five pounds lent him by two uncles and three cousins. That his father was a deacon helped his reputation in the community, but John says nothing about receiving more substantial parental assistance.[9] After arriving in Woodstock, John was able to call on his cousins and neighbors for help. They exchanged their own work and that of their oxen and horses when they acquired them, and in their dealings with each other they always came out equal.

John May began his diary when he turned twenty-one and was on the lowest rung of the economic ladder: first he worked for others, but soon others were trading work with him. Their relationship was that of equals in age and resources. Then his own sons grew up to work for *him* and at his behest. They increased his income and gave him the free time to serve in public office and become a weighty member of his community.

There were thousands of John Mays at work in New England's interior, and they were gradually transforming its landscape into a world of fields and fences.[10] As the mix of land uses evolved, so did the composition of farm animals. Oxen were the heavy-duty Mack trucks of their day, and John May could not have got very far without them. Once the best land for cereal crops had been brought into cultivation and its soils pulverized, a horse could generally do the annual plowing and do it much faster than oxen. And once there were roads, the far speedier horses could draw the two-wheeled carts that farmers used for hauling.[11] As the local need for oxen declined, fewer farmers bothered to keep them, so entrepreneurs who were usually large landowners often made a business of hiring them out, U-Haul fashion. This process of pioneering with oxen and then shifting to horses repeated itself in new towns as the waves of settlement pressed deeper into the interior. By the closing decade of the colonial period, only in the newest towns did a near majority of farmers have them. The number and distribution of horses likewise altered with time, as fewer households needed the full-time services of a horse. Stables specializing in the renting of riding and coach horses made their appearance in the largest towns.[12] This pattern of more selective horse ownership, like that of oxen, was the product of increasing specialization among rural households, making for greater efficiency in the production and exchange of goods and services in the community at large. The growth of markets for these and the positive response of rural households to their opportunities translated into growing income per capita.

As the need for raw muscle power receded in the evolving community, specialized skills became more important. The greater the local density of population, the greater the varieties of work that became possible: stoning cellars, plastering interior walls, building sophisticated chimneys, caning chairs, turning table legs, cabinetmaking, throwing pots, making saddles and shoes, tinsmithing, fancy weaving, elaborate sewing, midwifery, nursing, doctoring, and teaching, to name the most common. Probate inventories and accounts show a broad array of trades emerging in the older towns by the end of the seventeenth century and becoming more common throughout the region as the colonial period drew to a close. Mature farm communities were tied together as much by networks of transactions as by expanding generations of kin.

This increasing differentiation of work also opened opportunities for women and children. Most tailors and weavers, for instance, had been male until women began taking up these trades. The process accelerated during the Seven Years' War, when provisioning demands of military forces diverted men to more lucrative lines of work.[13] As diaries and account books make clear, children and young adults continued to form the backbone of New England's labor force throughout the colonial period. There were only scanty supplies of cheap labor outside the family. Despite a high standard of living by comparison with Europe, New England failed to attract new immigrants, because its farms did not produce a cash staple. Markets for farm produce were small in scale and local. Jobs were intermittent and often kinship based. Newcomers would have to marry in or set up their own exchange communities. Except for small numbers of Africans and Native Americans, no underclass of permanently landless men emerged until the final two decades of the colonial period, although there were failures, misfits, and hard-luck cases in every generation, as there are in most societies. Ninnimissinouk supplied occasional labor in those parts where they were still numerous, but Indian slaves appear only rarely in the records. As for "Negro" slaves, only a handful had arrived in New England prior to the 1690s, and there concentrated in port towns, not in farm communities.[14] Although a vast expansion in the Atlantic slave trade brought in numerous Africans after the 1680s, blacks made an impact on the farm labor market only along the coasts of Connecticut and Rhode Island.[15]

Hence, unlike in England or the colonies to the south, there was no large pool of legally entrapped laborers that the yeomen of New England could call upon at their convenience. Their primary source of labor remained their children, whom they continued to produce in bumper crops. At some point, theoretically, this multiplying number of mouths should have exceeded the available resources to feed them. Southern New England was a finite place, after all, with a finite number of acres, most of them unsuited to farming. At some point, population increase would push land prices out of reach of all but those already endowed. Agricultural productivity and wages would then have to fall, dragging down the standard. In such depressed circumstances, fewer young people could afford to marry, the age at marriage would rise, and families would curtail childbearing because the cost of raising children would exceed their potential earnings. Did this very plausible scenario actually unfold in pre-Revolutionary New England? The price of developed land certainly rose and continued to rise, but the proportion of landless among young married men aged 25–44 did not increase until the late 1750s. The median age at marriage for men remained stable at 25 from 1640 to 1740, when it *dropped* temporarily to 24 during the wartime boom. Women married at the median age of 22, although this index likewise fell by a year during the 1740s and 1750s. The proportion never married rose by some indeterminate amount for both sexes throughout the eighteenth and early nineteenth centuries, but the average number of children born to first marriages formed before to 1776 remained at six. If there was a painful economic squeeze in the New England countryside on the eve of the Revolution, it is not apparent in these statistics.[16]

The colonial farm economy proved remarkably resilient, then, absorbing the losses inflicted by numerous wars, while expanding household investment in capital improvements. These raised the estate values of even the poorest third of probated decedents (weighted by region and age to mimic the living population) by some 60 percent in real terms in the years 1635–1774. (See Figure 2.) The rich got a good deal richer, but the poor of rural New England were not becoming poorer. The growing economy, like the incoming tide, was lifting all boats.[17]

How did this region, underblessed with good soil as it was, manage this modest miracle? Part of the answer derives from the greater efficiencies in farm production mentioned above, but perhaps just as important was the availability of new consumer goods that encouraged families to expand their indoor tasks and work "smarter."[18] The continuing strong growth of the rural economy made bootstrapping such as John May's possible for subsequent generations. The career of Samuel Lane, of Stratham, New Hampshire, for instance, shows how it was done at midcentury. Lane left behind a journal and memoir when he died in 1804 in which he describes how he was able to set up on his own as a tanner with a tiny bit of capital in the early 1740s.[19] Let him tell his own story (I have modernized the syntax, not the spelling, and patched together selections from the journal with parts of the memoir):

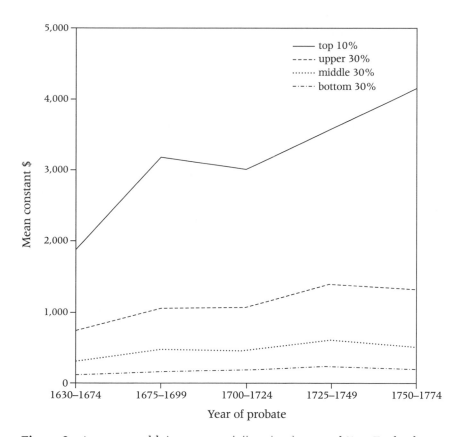

Figure 2. Average wealth in constant dollars, by class, rural New England, 1630–1774 (Source: County probate records listed in Gloria L. Main and Jackson T. Main, "The Red Queen in New England?" *William and Mary Quarterly* 56 [1999]: 148)

When my time was first out [in 1739, when he was twenty-one], my Father [Deacon Joshua Lane of Hampton, New Hampshire] gave me near 20£ old Tenr worth of Lether to begin with. He also gave me my Board the first year; after that, I Boarded my Self. Money being Scarce, it was Difficult to get Money for my work: and the best Method I could think of was, to make Shoes & Some fishing Boots, for the Shoals [fishermen at Isle of Shoals]; and my practice was when I had got a little Cargo made, to carry them over to the Shoals; and when I could not get money for them, I would Sell them for oyl, Blubber, & Fish &c. . . . [even] Sold it for Corn; then I would Endeavour to turn the Corn into Money; Sometimes get it ground, & hire a Horse, and Carry the Meal to Portsmo, and the Cost of that Eat up all my gain; only I turned my work into Money; and at the years End I found I had got Something to help Set me up. Sometime I took Boards & Shingles & Nails for my work wh I Expected to [use]. I also work'd Some Lether of other Peoples; & did any Business that I tho't would turn to any Account . . . and took any Sort of pay that I tho't would turn to any Account. Note. I work'd in a little Shop I parted off for that use, in one Corner of my fathers Shop.

This Method I followed a year or More, & found I had Acquired Something as aforesaid to help Set me up; and thinking it might be better for me to Settle (as I had Courted Some time) I try'd verry hard to purchase a House Lott (for I had Not Money to purchase much Land) I tryed in Several Towns, as Hampton, Northill, Kensington &c but could not obtain a Suitable place for a Tanyard, which caused me much trouble & perplexity; before I obtained one to my mind, So well as I did.

He had been invited by customers of his father to settle in Stratham.

He went out there several times to find a suitable place, explaining that he was "Uneasie in my present Circumstances; my Father had a great Family, and I knew I was Burthensome to them, tho' I paid for Dressing my Victuals, which I provided for my Self, after the first year; yet as I wanted to Settle, they Also wanted I Should; and I took all possible pains to get a House Lott to Sit down upon." He finally chose his spot on the north side of a mill pond, two acres, for which he paid £26 Old Tenor (depreciated currency of the province) on February 19, 1741. He bargained for "a House Frame 26 feet long 29 wide to be raised for 30£, 18£ of it to be pd in mens shoes, 18/ a pair, womens 13/6, & 12£, in money." He also bargained for the bark house frame. He bought an acre on the south side of the mill pond in order to prevent anyone else from settling there. On April 20 he began digging a foundation on the north side for his house and discovered water almost right away, so he bought another acre on the south side, adjoining the first, which had a brook running through it suitable for his tanning yard. He had to pay twice as much for this acre, but the investment paid off.

"On May 28 I drove my cow [from Hampton, about seven miles] to Stratham to Jno Thirstons where I had Agree'd for my Board. Note. before I was 21 years old, I Bo't a Calf & hired it kept, and it is now a Cow (as above) which is of great service toward my Support, for Milk, Butter & Cheese: I also have a heifer, & Eight Sheep. Note. all these Creatures (but my Cow) I was obliged to Sell to help Build my House." He moved to his new lodgings in June and lived there until the following January, when he moved into his own house. "I gave mrs Thirston 3s a Week for Dressing my Victuals and I had Milk Butter & Cheese from my own Cow of her Make." The frame of his house was raised two weeks later, and his bark-house frame was raised July 1. "I Bro't Some Boards & Nails from Hampton wh I had Bo't there, and Clam Shells for Lime, Shingles &c to help build my House withal." He next hired one man to dig and stone his cellar and "lett out" the boarding of the sides to a second and the shingling of the roof to another, the brick and tile work to a fourth, and the chimneys to the man who was to do the shingling. "A common Labourer had now 6s a Day and I gave them 7s a Day & they found themselves [supplied their own meals] to make Morter." The man who did the ceiling and finishing of the "great room" did it in exchange for his heifer; another did the lathing, plastering, and setting of glass. On September 14, 1741, he "Laid the foundation of my Chimneys, and begun to Board my House." Ten days later "I was Published at Hamptn & Stratham." (That is, notification of his intention to marry was posted in both churches.) On October 5, "my Chimneys were finished." The next day was his twenty-third birthday. Other men made his window frames and sashes and built the chamber stairs. He finished his northeast corner bedroom, "so as to Make a Shop of it, where I work'd at my Trade till I built me a Shop, in Oct. 1742. Note: my Purchasing my Land (tho' but Little) and Building my House & Setling so Exhausted my Little Substance, that I was obliged to part with all I Co'd Spare, to pay for it."

He finished two rooms in his house "as fast as I could, in order to Settle. But having no Barn I hired my Cow Winter'd by Jno Thirston in part and Neighbour Mason in part, for which I paid [five pounds]. I painted the foreside and East end of my House Red." "Dec 24th 1741. I Married my Wife

[Mary James of Hampton, aged nineteen]. Note: the Anniversary of our Marriage comes on Jan. 4th New Stile. Jan 6th 1742. I Mov'd my Wife and her goods to my own House . . . Jan 26, 1742 our Fathers and Mothers come first time to See us . . . Feb 24. I carried my wife to See her Friends 1st time after She removed to Stratham." Later in the spring, he drove her heifer and calf home from Hampton. "And now having to my great Joy & Satisfaction, got comfortably Setled in my own House; with an Agreable Wife; I began to look over my Accounts, to see what I was in Debt toward my Building &c and found that I ow'd toward my House &c about . . . Dollers:—and having no Creatures to look after this Winter but a Pig; I went to work night and Day to pay my Debts; and by the last of the Spring, I believe I was pritty near out of Debt."

There was much more to be done, of course. He needed a real shop, a barn, and the covering for his bark house. The well "did not answer," and they had to dig another one. To save on fuel wood, the young couple moved into the shop when it was finished. "This Shop Stood Against the West End of my House, at a Chimney of my House. Note. This Winter I having no Barn kept my Cows in my Bark-House."

Lane had started with the small stake of leather given him by his father and parlayed it into a shoemaking business and tannery, thanks to the skills he had learned in his apprenticeship, to all of which he added his own excellent business sense. He had quickly achieved financial independence, marriage, and his own home, albeit only a partly finished skeleton of a house, but he painted it red. That house is a measure of his confidence in himself and in the local economy, because he chose to erect at the outset a two-story frame with sufficient space for four rooms on each floor. This was the quintessential New England/American way: work hard, borrow when you have to, pay it back promptly, live frugally, put what you don't spend into something productive, and think big.

Samuel diligently plied his trade while continuing to work on the house. He put up a new shop on the east side, dug a second well in 1750, "very costly in digging & blowing 8 feet in a rock," and raised an addition in 1752. This came to be a very large house for the times, with chimneys at either side of the original structure, rather than a single one in the middle as was customary. It had grown along with the family and the business. Samuel and Mary had six surviving children born between 1744 and 1760, and over the years he took in occasional apprentices, including at one point his own younger brother.

The burgeoning economy helped Samuel Lane's business to flourish, as his memoir makes clear, but it is his house that tells us about his other aspirations. Its form embodied his ideas about how a family domain should be structured. Two stories, four rooms to a floor with central stairs and hallways, two chimneys, workshop wings on either side to tap into the chimneys, and a stone cellar beneath—this is a "Georgian" floor plan.[20] Although analyzing the architecture of houses does not provide us with detailed roadmaps of the New England mind, their layouts and contents tell us a surprising amount about family dynamics in the eighteenth century and the evolving politics of family life.

At the time that Samuel was building his dream house, prosperous members of farm communities in New England could choose between two basic floor plans, as seen in Figures 3 and 4: the old hall-and-parlor plan, which had evolved around a central chimney in the seventeenth century; and the newer Georgian style, which was two rooms deep and replaced the central chimney with a staircase and hallway, placing chimneys to either side. The distinguishing marks of the new floor plan were its geometrical symmetry and central hall. The installation of a hallway obviated the need for people to pass through one room to reach another, allowing family members to close their doors to one another as well as to servants and outsiders. Photo-

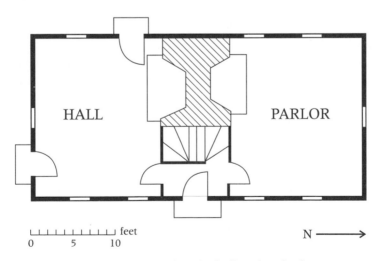

HALL   PARLOR

⌐ ⌐ ⌐ ⌐ ⌐ ⌐ ⌐ ⌐ feet
0   5   10

N ———→

Figure 3. Plan of a typical central-chimney hall-and-parlor house (Drawing by Kevin M. Sweeney)

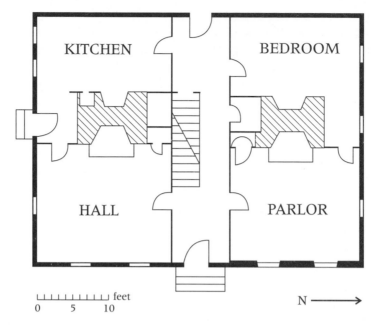

Figure 4. Plan of Seth Wetmore house, Middletown, Connecticut, built ca. 1750. Later modifications make it impossible to determine the original location of doors and windows on the rear (west) wall. (Source: adapted from Bertha Chadwick Trowbridge, ed., *Old Houses of Connecticut* [New Haven: Yale University Press, 1923], p. 222) (Drawing by Kevin M. Sweeney)

graphs of two Connecticut houses illustrate the contrasts between the two housing styles. The old hall-and-parlor plan is represented in Figure 5 by a two-story version, the Buttolph-Williams house in Wethersfield, built around 1720. The Eliphalet Williams house in East Hartford (Figure 6) exemplifies the Georgian ideal. It was built in 1751 but is no longer standing. Whereas in the old two-rooms-to-a-floor, hall-and-parlor arrangement the visitor entered directly through the front (or side) door into the family's all-purpose, work-and-eat room with its big fireplace, in a Georgian home the front door admitted the visitor into a hallway lined with doors and a handsome staircase directly ahead. The stairs provided a stage entrance for the hostess as she descended to greet her guests, while the doors stood mutely shut unless she invited the visitors in. The Georgian house was designed for "gracious" living. It embodied an entire package of emerging Anglo-American ideas about asserting social rank, employing good manners, acting out approved gender roles, expressing virtue, and maintaining ideal family relationships.[21]

Although Georgian houses in the colonies varied by locale in the details of their decorative elements, all conformed to a general model, one that stressed symmetry and balance on the outside—centered on the front door —and specialized, socially ranked spaces within. How far down, and into, New England's rural society had the Georgian-Enlightenment sensibility penetrated by the time of the American Revolution? Geographer Michael Steinitz has located and analyzed all existing houses built before the Revolution in present-day Worcester County, Massachusetts, a total of ninety dating to the years before 1750 and eighty-eight from the period 1750–1775.[22] Having endured for some 250 years, these homes are undoubtedly larger and better built than were the common run of the times. Their original owners were probably among the most affluent in the county, because in the 1798 federal housing census, the vast majority of country people lived in smaller, older quarters built in the cheapest fashion.[23] For Massachusetts'

Figure 5. Buttolph-Williams house, Wethersfield, Connecticut, built ca. 1720 (Photo by Kevin M. Sweeney)

Figure 6. Eliphalet Williams house, East Hartford, Connecticut, built 1751
(Photo courtesy of the Connecticut Historical Society, Hartford)

rural elite, however, Steinitz' survey offers an excellent review of their architectural choices—and an opportunity to gauge the nature and direction
of change in New Englanders' ideas about the allocation and use of family
space.

The first point worthy of notice is that later-built houses in Worcester
were considerably bigger, on average, than those erected earlier. Fifty-one of
the eighty-eight structures in the Steinitz survey from the period 1750–1775
were two rooms deep, in contrast to the one-room depth that prevailed in
earlier houses. Thirty-four were single-story, and fifty-four had two stories.
Most had pitched roofs, and the frequent addition of lean-tos to hall-and-
parlor houses created the familiar saltbox outline typical of so many colonial
New England houses. Meanwhile many older house were remodeled and
expanded, reflecting the rural county's increasing affluence. The Willard
house, on a farmstead in northwestern Grafton, for instance, began as a
one-room structure that was first enlarged to a hall-and-parlor plan and
then converted to two stories in the 1760s.[24]

Despite the trend toward increasing size, very few houses built in Worcester County between 1750 and 1775 and surviving today can be classified as

truly Georgian in design. Of the fifty-four in the survey with two stories, only twenty-eight are two rooms deep in both stories, and only six of these have a central hall, the key feature of the Georgian style. Without a hallway, there can be no real privacy.[25] The Worcester houses nonetheless feature certain amenities that had been lacking earlier: higher ceilings, larger and more numerous windows, plaster walls and painted surfaces. There was also much greater use of stairs instead of ladders, usually boxed in next to the central chimney stack. Deliberate placement of doors and windows, meanwhile, created a more balanced public facade. All in all, the modifications made houses that were nicer to live in and to look at, but they stop short of employing the full Georgian panoply.[26]

Since the well-to-do of Worcester County had a choice in what they built–and even the not so well-to-do, if we recall Samuel Lane's determination—what was holding them back? The experience of Reverend Ebenezer Parkman when he was building a new home in Westborough, in Worcester County, in 1751, is informative. He noted without comment in his diary that "Lieutenant Taintor was very Sharp upon me about the pride of Ministers, when he saw the Window Frames."[27] Parkman had ordered thirteen windows installed, each with twenty-four squares of glass, seven by nine inches in size. These numbers suggest that the windows were three feet across, plus framing, and three-and-a-half feet in height, which were indeed ample, but thirteen in number implies that there would be only four windows in front and four in back, with two on each side, and one for the garret. Whether Taintor's objection was to the size of the windows or their number is unclear, but whichever was the case, they apparently exceeded what Taintor thought appropriate for a man of God, especially one whose salary came out of the pockets of himself and his neighbors. To at least one weighty member of Parkman's congregation, therefore, architectural features such as these could be viewed as extravagant, exemplifying the sin of "pride." Envy mixed with self-righteous disapproval may likewise have characterized the common reaction to the handsome Georgian houses we so admire today.

Although most of Worcester County's middling and better sort sought to avoid prideful display in their new homes, their emerging concern for balance and symmetry in housing facades shows that they had come to think about houses as important moral or aesthetic statements of who they were or hoped to be. Since even those who presumably could afford to build the largest houses overwhelmingly rejected the central-hall, two-chimney Georgian design, it seems clear that they wanted their homes to represent themselves as modest and unpretentious, yet also highly respectable and of solid worth. Apparently few desired a degree of distinction that would create a gulf between themselves and their neighbors.[28] The 7 percent of the Worcester sample who erected Georgian houses must therefore have been quite self-conscious about what they were doing. They were, in effect, declaring allegiance to the cosmopolitan, Anglicizing world of fashion and secular ideas, but running the risk of cutting themselves off ideologically and politically from their community.[29]

If this group of Worcester County houses is not aberrant in some way, it demonstrates that the better sort of New England's rural interior either did not *want* houses like Samuel Lane's or were simply unwilling to pay for the second chimney and additional square feet needed for the "waste" space of the hall. When we recall that Samuel Lane, who could ill afford his two-chimneyed double-decker, went ahead and began it anyway, we understand that choosing or not choosing a house with a hallway was as much a matter of desire as it was of cost. By failing to adopt key parts of the Georgian style, however, New England's yeomanry were not thereby rejecting Georgian sensibility *in toto*. Inventories of their houses in probated estates reveal that they happily acquired many of its material aspects.

Although probate inventories provide only imprecise glimpses of material culture—one can never be sure that what was not mentioned in the inventory was truly not there in fact—it seems fair to assume that if inventories of middling farmers aged forty-five to sixty-four show more chairs or more glassware over time, they reflect a real increase in the standard of living.[30] There are plenty of useful inventories available from all but the lowest ranks of society with which to build a profile of domestic life in early New England. One fact that quickly emerges is that assemblages of furniture and tools in early homes tended to be sparse yet eclectic, indicating that varied activities involving both sexes and all ages went on in common spaces.[31] Over the course of a century these furnishings not only increased in number but came to be differentiated into more specialized ensembles located in specific activity areas. As early as the 1660s, prospering families began turning all-purpose halls into kitchens with service areas, although they continued to use them for other kinds of work as well. By adding a lean-to along the back, they could push the kitchen to the rear of the house, where it became a segregated domain of women and servants. The parlor, which had always served as the "better" room for the parents as well as a bedroom, became the favored site for selective hospitality. The best seating and display items were here. Even as late as the 1750s, however, the parlor continued to retain the best bed, although ceilinged chambers upstairs in larger houses also became personal realms as well as places for sleeping.

Small, crowded, one-story houses that had provided little space and no privacy in the seventeenth century thus gradually gave way among the middling and wealthier sort to larger and more comfortable two-story homes that organized activities in areas specifically equipped for them. Whereas spinning wheels were earlier stored in lofts to get them out of the way, they could now be left out indefinitely in a room situated to take advantage of natural light. Previously itinerant weavers now had shops attached to their houses where they could set up more elaborate looms. Given the division of labor within the household, this specialization of room use meant that the sexes were now spending more of their indoors time working apart. Dining together therefore became a more significant occasion, although the majority of families continued to eat in the kitchen, where most housewives participated in the serving as well as the cooking.

The setting aside of a specific room for dining marked a key boundary between yeoman families and the truly genteel. In Georgian households, family members not only dined away from the kitchen but were waited upon by nonkin of inferior rank. Ideally, family members and guests sat on matching chairs and ate from matching plates, creating a symmetry and sense of completeness that echoed the facade of a Georgian house.[32] Meals were marked by greater or lesser degrees of formality, depending on the social pretensions of the family head. When, in 1700, the young minister of Salem Village dined at Major Vaughan's in Portsmouth, New Hampshire, he later declared excitedly in his diary that he "had ye most Genteel dinner & attendance that ever I saw."[33]

As household furniture became more abundant and comfortable in ordinary homes, greater democratization came to characterize its use by members of the family. Almost every house now had at least one featherbed, a mattress tick stuffed with feathers preferably plucked from live birds in just the right season to obtain their maximum loft. Such mattresses had been a true luxury a hundred years earlier, and to some extent still were. Samuel Lane, for instance, purchased "flocks" (shavings from woolen cloth after it has been taken from the loom and fulled) from a clothier in 1743 to stuff a mattress tick. Flocks were a common choice for colonial mattresses, but sleeping on a feather mattress with curtains hanging around it had become a coveted symbol of respectability for married couples. Such a bed had its practical side: the curtains shut out drafts as well as prying eyes, so they supplied comfort and warmth as well as sexual privacy. What is striking about the inventories from late in the colonial period is their frequent listing of *more than one* of these quintessential objects of desire, evidence that the heads of these households were no longer reserving these luxuries for themselves.[34] Separate bedrooms, separate beds, even bedsteads with curtains—these were still luxuries reserved for favored adults such as a widowed mother or sister-in-law, and were not yet the prerogative of farm children.

Other upgrades in New England furnishings included many more cushions and chairs for comfortable seating. The latter often had turned frames and woven rush seats, products of local craftsmen appearing in rural inventories as early as the 1690s. The cushions were stuffed with feathers and finely sewn. Some bore home-embroidered flowers and homilies. Both chair and cushion embodied traditional folk art while also signaling the family's affluence. Needlework for display provided a satisfying medium for daughters' artistic efforts, but it did not involve any redefinition of traditional gender roles.

The kitchen likewise saw improvements. Basic equipment for cooking over an open fire consisted of a pair of andirons or an iron grate to hold the hot coals, a frying pan, plus a rod inserted into the chimney walls from which to hang the large, all-purpose cast-iron pot. A larger budget would permit adding more items of wrought iron, but they were heavy and cumbersome. Brass utensils were lighter and easier to handle though more than twice as expensive as cast iron, pound for pound. Ordinary households acquired them if cash permitted because they provided the flexibility necessary for preparing a variety of dishes. To judge from their kitchen utensils, people were eating better in the eighteenth century, but no innovation had yet transformed the farm kitchen as would the adoption of iron cooking stoves in the 1830s.[35]

Inventories also disclose items new to the times that represented a refinement of ordinary life styles. Figure 7 shows that knives, forks, and "groceries" (sugar, molasses, tea, coffee, chocolate, spices, or the paraphernalia for storing and serving them) had become highly popular by 1750, appearing in nearly half of the estates of middling householders. In contrast to these, only 5 percent mention a watch or a clock, or list pictures, prints, or wall maps. Wigs, secular books, and timepieces most often belonged to men in public life, those who strove to project an image of education, taste, and good breeding, personal equivalents of the Georgian house. Samuel Lane acquired his first clock in 1745 when he was only twenty-seven, a precocious act for his age and the times. But then, Lane was no ordinary yeoman.[36]

The advent of knives and forks, tea and sugar denoted a broad shift in dining habits that appears to have penetrated about halfway down rural New England's social ladder by the time of the Revolution. Previously people had eaten from shared wooden dishes and drank from a common mug, each taking a turn from his or her customary "place" on the rim. They had used

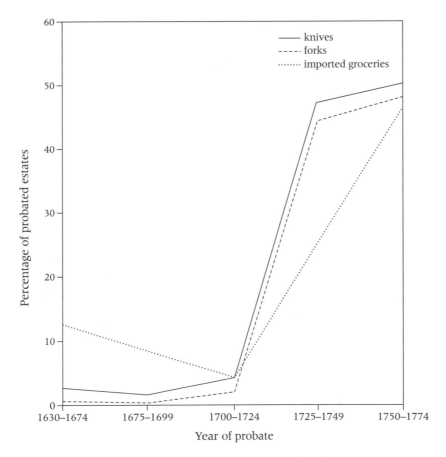

Figure 7. Knives, forks, and imported groceries: middle 60 percent of men's probated estates, 1630–1774 (Source: Sample probate records reported in Gloria L. Main and Jackson T. Main, "The Red Queen in New England?" *William and Mary Quarterly* 56 [1999]: 148)

carved or horn spoons to scoop up thick porridges and stews, such as pork and beans, cooked in the ubiquitous cast-iron pot. People of means replaced wooden dishes with pewterware, and by the late colonial period some were switching to glazed ceramic wares mass-produced by the Wedgwood factories in England.

In the most up-to-date yeoman households at midcentury, then, everybody at the table had a knife and fork flanking his or her own plate. The use of individual settings promoted the idea that it was not "nice" to eat or drink from something someone else had used unless it was first washed with soap and hot water. Indeed, inventories show much higher frequencies in the eighteenth century of soap and soap-related items such as washpans, pot ashes for making soap, and soap boilers. Keeping the house neat and clean helped to make a family respectable, but it had probably not acquired the high moral and religious character in eighteenth-century New England that it had among the Dutch.[37]

The growing demand for cleaner houses and utensils extended to bodies and clothing, too, but not in that order. People of the seventeenth and early eighteenth centuries thought it neither necessary nor wise to bathe all over. Polite people washed their hands and faces in the mornings, cleaned their teeth, and combed their hair. They were careful to wash their hands before and after eating, because dirty hands and faces were "beastly" and repellent. Yet people did not wash their bodies or their heads. They combed their hair and kept it covered with a kerchief or cap, but everyone suffered from lice, and some doused their hair in powder to suffocate the pests. Late in the seventeenth century, gentlemen began having their heads shaved and wore wigs or scarves—called "turbans"—instead. One kept clean by changing clothes: the more changes one made, the cleaner and more elegant one was thought to be. Cotton garments were much lighter in weight and far more washable than wool, so, as cotton became more common, frequent changes of shirts, collars, and cuffs became more practical.

Washing the body was quite another matter. Immersing one's naked self in water had been regarded as perverted or fanatical and dangerous to the health, but attitudes were changing. Warm baths were still regarded as effete, but some doctors in the eighteenth century began advocating regular cold baths to harden the body. Because the emerging standard of civility among the "better sort" stressed behavior that avoided giving offense to others, cleanliness became an important way to make oneself agreeable to one's fellows. This theme had appeared in English manuals on manners as early as the sixteenth century, but it was also associated with ideas of preventing pollution and the spread of infection. The medically approved response to epidemics and death was to clean indoors and out with liberal applications of vinegar water, and to make everything smell fresh.[38]

The heightened interest in cleanliness and avoiding contagion improved sanitary conditions for families and probably contributed to longer life expectancy for adults but reflected no breakthrough in medical knowledge.[39] Cleaner dishes, houses, and clothes also imposed heavier work loads on already overworked housewives. Mary Cooper, a farm wife of Oyster Bay, Long Island, left a diary from the late colonial period filled with complaints of tiredness from her never-ending round of cooking, cleaning, washing, and ironing. She often had to miss "meeten" on the sabbath because she had been unable to complete the week's laundry and had no clean, pressed clothes to wear.[40]

Tea and glazed earthenware constituted two significant innovations in New England domestic life. Traditionally, silver candlesticks, bowls, and so forth had provided an excellent means of storing savings in the absence of banks, and their presence on parlor shelves projected a sense of solid, enduring worth. Colorful patterns on comparatively fragile potteryware, in contrast, were merely decorative. Whereas men of substance often bestowed pieces of silver plate on churches, one never reads of a woman donating a china bowl. Farm people had generally avoided such fripperies, so the acquisition of even one pretty or colorful item represented a new willingness among a deliberately "plain" people to indulge their senses a little. There were always those critics who deplored such extravagances, especially if the family was poor. When Dr. Alexander Hamilton was touring New York's Hudson Valley by boat in 1744, he and his companion stopped at a lonely stretch along the west shore to take on water and visited the nearby house of a poor family, which was neatly kept. Hamilton's associate noticed the presence, however, of such "unnecessary" luxuries as a mirror and a set of tea dishes and complained of them later to Hamilton as unsuitable to their "station." They should have sold them and invested the proceeds in raw wool, he asserted, which the woman and her children could then have worked up into yarn and sold at a profit.[41]

Clearly, there was a moral economy at work. Purchases of goods unrelated to the practical necessities of life required justification. Although New Englanders might have denied themselves a pretty dish because it was frivolous, they could justify giving such things to others. Each step in the process of making and serving tea provided opportunities for gifts: a kettle to bring the water to a fast boil, a covered pot in which to steep the leaves and a slop bowl in which to discard them afterward, containers for the sugar and cream, silver spoons to stir them, cups with handles from which to sip the hot liquid, and saucers under the cups to catch the drips. A nice tray to bring in and remove the crockery rounded out the list. Tea-drinking even among plain people not only required imported groceries and dishes for which one had to pay scarce cash; it also "wasted" God's time. Common laborers had no moral right to drink tea with their wives, at least according to those who shared the opinions of Dr. Hamilton's traveling companion. Nevertheless, the practice was spreading.[42]

Not only did tea introduce potentially corrupting luxuries into yeoman households; it threatened to alter the relationship between men and women in equally subversive ways. The ramifications of tea-drinking among common farm folk of this period are eye-opening. First of all, respectable men and women did not normally drink together in a recreational way, except on major ceremonial occasions such as weddings and funerals. Men freely socialized with other men in the new public places then proliferating, such as taverns and inns, where they drank cider or punch spiked with cheap rum. The only women present, notably, were servers.[43] Meanwhile, women drank celebratory beverages together at their own occasions, such as lyings-in. The married daughter of Mary Cooper, for instance, was called out repeatedly to attend these obligatory gatherings. Tea-drinking, by contrast, brought the sexes into intimate social contact, requiring entirely new rituals.[44] Most important, tea promoted conversation in which the housewife could participate because she could sit down as she served. Tea-drinking in mixed company, therefore, significantly enlarged the acceptable sphere of social intercourse for ordinary farm women and made them, at least temporarily, equal company with men.[45]

The new emphasis on refined behavior within the family thus encouraged and applauded rather different attributes for the sexes than had been the rule in the early seventeenth century. It was part of what Bernard Bailyn posited as a "silent revolution" that took place in colonial society before independence, one that widened differences in family styles across social classes, diminished parental control, and produced a new conception of children not as embodiments of sin but as innocent and malleable creatures whose characters were molded by their upbringing.[46] All these changes were assuredly under way in eighteenth-century New England. But although housing interiors among yeoman families reveal that rural attitudes toward domestic arrangements were evolving, they cannot speak directly to issues of gender politics. To judge from marriage and birth records, traditional role expectations for women continued powerful. Most women still expected to marry (probably 92 percent of those born in 1750–1774 did so, compared with nearly 100 percent in 1650), and childbearing after marriage maintained its stiff pace.[47] Two rather different lines of inquiry offer considerable light here. The first is unconventional but suggestive, and that is looking at patterns of naming children for information about parental attitudes toward children and toward daughters versus sons. The second involves examining the treatment of wives and children in wills. Together, these two kinds of evidence indicate a new direction in family power relations.

Naming Children

In contrast to the seventeenth century, fewer and fewer children in the eighteenth century bore the forename of a parent or grandparent. Instead, they were given names of parents' siblings, of friends, of biblical figures, heroes, literary characters, or of nobody in particular. Although biblical names continued to dominate the birth registers well into the nineteenth century, their proportion of the total declined sharply after 1750 and continued to decline thereafter. The most fascinating change is the growing use of nontraditional names, especially for girls. These did not appear everywhere in rural New England, but tended to arise in some families and communities more than in others. Rhode Island families, for instance, who tolerated lower rates of literacy than their counterparts elsewhere, had long tended to stick with customary English names. They had shown none of the Puritan fondness for biblical hortatory names in the seventeenth century, nor did they in the next emulate the new taste for literary and poetical ones.[48]

The new names given girls were far more individualistic and venturesome than the more stolid ones burdening little boys. Some of the more interesting names given girls include Aletha and Althea (from the Greek, "truth"), Celia and Copelia, Artemisi and Aurelia, Diademia and Diana, Loren, Loranna and Lusanna, Orinda and Paulina.[49] Some are from Greek and Roman mythology, but others are poetic inventions. The sudden appearance of "Clarissa" in New England birth records in the 1750s points to another source of names for daughters: secular print media such as novels and magazines.[50] New names for boys tended toward surnames such as Smith, Chase ter, and Johnson, every bit as sober as the biblical Samuels, Davids, and Joshuas that continued to appear in the records. Although parents were becoming more playful in choosing names for daughters, they were also deliberately seeking to set their children apart, sons as well as daughters. The number of individual names in use by both sexes increased dramatically in the eighteenth century, as fewer and fewer children shared the five or ten most popular.[51]

The expanding diversity of names suggests a growing liberation of families from tradition. By choosing distinctive names for their children, parents were encouraging the growth of individual identity if not quite individualism itself. This trend, however, was accompanied by an increasingly marked divergence in the "weights" of the names given the two sexes. Parents bestowed sedate surnames on their boys while conferring nonserious, even fanciful, names on their girls. Indeed, there was a sharp rise in the use of diminutives (such as Dolly, Molly, Betty, Sally, and Fanny) among registered names for baby girls. Parents have always bestowed pet names on their offspring, who often retain them into adulthood. Mary Cooper, for instance, was called Molly by her husband. However, she was not Molly outside the family and would never have signed herself by that name. Thus, the use of nicknames in New England was not new, but inscribing them on birth and baptismal records was. It meant that Molly, Dolly, Polly, Betty, Sally, and Fanny would eventually be appearing on marriage records, church covenants, deeds and contracts, and all manner of other public documents, including witnesses' depositions in court trials, criminal complaints, petitions to the legislature, and probate records. A grown woman, some worthy matron like Mary Cooper, might end up signing a divorce petition or an estate account with a child's pet name. A few years down the road, a woman with a child's name, Dolley, would enter the White House as wife to one of the Virginian presidents.[52]

Inheritance Practices

Despite the possibility posed by the naming evidence that girls were receiving greater individual recognition and affection from their parents, the rise of unserious names for girls provokes concerns over trends in the image of women vis-à-vis men. On the one hand, families were becoming more child-centered, as naming practices and fathers' bequests in wills both suggest, and this may fairly be read as an abridgment of old-style patriarchy, just as Bailyn argues. But on the other hand, what the father was giving to the children, he first took from his wife. The same wills that show fathers' evenhandedness toward their daughters show husbands' growing skepticism about their wives' competence to manage estate affairs. This lack of confidence can be seen in testators' choices for executor and in the restrictions placed on widows' dowers. A family man contemplating writing a will faced three choices for executor: his wife, his son(s) or daughter if of legal age, or a friend outside the immediate family. The wills show that he was increasingly unlikely to appoint his wife. This tendency began as early as the 1660s in New Hampshire and Connecticut where husbands appointed others as executors while granting widows a third of the *income,* not the assets themselves.[53] In rural Suffolk County, in eastern Massachusetts, testators did not begin excluding their widows from acting as executors until later, but the direction had become pronounced there by the middle of the eighteenth century.

This trend was not unique to New England. The same inclination to exclude widows from control over family estates appeared in Chesapeake wills in the eighteenth century, suggesting that similar influences were at work in both regions. The explanation that comes first to mind is the problem posed by the fully mature farm or plantation that cannot be subdivided without damaging the productivity of the whole. Only about one out of five New England husbands in the eighteenth century bequeathed the home farm intact to a married son who was then to house and keep his mother. Most of the others gave the widow a third of the personal estate remaining after the payment of all debts and a third of the income from the real estate, which the heirs to that real estate (usually one or two sons) were supposed to pay. This annuity arrangement likewise made the widow dependent on her children, but the court would enforce payment if she sued, and she at least could choose her own living accommodations if the size of the annuity permitted.

Part and parcel of the growing disinclination of husbands to put their widows in charge of the estate was the penchant of testators to restrict wives' dower thirds to the period of their widowhood rather than for life. This measure was designed to prevent her from taking any of the estate into another marriage, where, because of the law of coverture, a stranger would gain control of it. She remained legally free to marry again, but at the cost of her thirds. Since by law she was entitled to her dower for life, she could go to court to contest her husband's restriction, but she would forfeit her rights to the personal estate by doing so. In most cases she would be better off financially by not remarrying, unless a very rich suitor came along who was indifferent to her handicap. The likelihood of remarriage for widows over the age of forty in the eighteenth century was, in any case, quite low; but for younger widows who were now single parents, prospects were much better and probably desirable for the sake of the children. Yet an astonishing proportion of younger men writing their wills in the eighteenth century sought to prevent their widows from finding another partner. Figure 8 contrasts the bequest decisions in the two centuries by young fathers in New England and the Chesapeake. The sample includes only testators married to their first

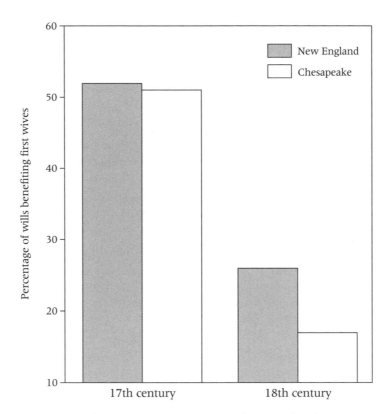

Figure 8. Share of first wives given more than dower and without restrictions in wills of young fathers, New England and the Chesapeake, seventeenth and eighteenth centuries (New England landowners) (Source: Lois S. Carr, "Inheritance in the Colonial Chesapeake," in *Women in the Age of the American Revolution,* ed. Ronald Hoffman and Peter J. Albert [Charlottesville: University Press of Virginia, 1989], p. 176; wills of young fathers from sample probate records reported in Gloria L. Main and Jackson T. Main, "The Red Queen in New England?" *William and Mary Quarterly* 56 [1999]: 148)

wives and whose children were all minors. Because their widows were presumably still young and burdened with young children, they were in the group most likely to remarry. As the bars in the graph make crystal clear, widows of young fathers in the seventeenth century enjoyed the full confidence of their husbands. They acted as sole executors of the estates and were free to take their children and the estate into a second marriage, if they chose. In the eighteenth century, widows of young fathers lost these rights. The data, arising as they do from two different regions in the British colonies, suggest that a new kind of gender bias had emerged in Anglo-America.

Why this radical shift in attitudes? The simple answer is that Parliament did it, passing a succession of statutes between 1660 and 1725 that both standardized and restricted dower rights across the realm in England. Probate practices in most of the colonies fell into line, with the consequence we have seen, that testators in both New England and the Chesapeake were placing their children's inheritance ahead of their mothers' traditional property rights. They were, in effect, denying that dower *was* a right.[54]

One can only speculate about the reasons for so stunning a shift in the colonies, since they were not bound to copy every detail of the parent country's inheritance practices.[55] Insofar as the great majority of the population was concerned, the conditions favorable to women in the seventeenth century no longer obtained. In the older settlements, land was now fully developed and expensive. With the frontier receding ever further over the horizon, hopeful young men followed after, leaving a surplus of marriageable women to compete for a shrinking pool of bachelors and widowers. Did such conditions cause a decline in female status?[56] The evidence assembled so far, such as that on naming, suggests a more complex process at work. The outmigration of young men, for instance, opened doors to new occupations and raised wages for young women.[57] First of all, husbands' doubts about their wives' financial capabilities reflected the growing complexity of commerce and credit litigation, which demanded a competence in arithmetic calculations that had never formed part of girls' customary schooling. Partly as a consequence, women's participation in the courts plummeted during the eighteenth century.[58] The commercializing nature of the yeoman's world rearranged the particles of gender honor along different magnetic lines. As men came to exercise virtue in new ways to accord with the demands of keeping good credit, so, too, did women. The refinement in manners described above reflected men's new needs, but emerging views of women's natural capabilities, physiological and psychological, complemented that process by celebrating wives more as mothers than as copartners in the family enterprise. The demands of the new standard of living added to the housewife's burden, yet emphasis on her motherly virtues distracted attention from her economic contributions to family well-being.

The story of how gender politics shifted in New England as Puritan patriarchy morphed into its pre-republican, "Enlightenment" form requires telling. England in the early seventeenth century was in social and economic flux. As men became anxious about their status vis-à-vis one another, their distrust and mockery of women intensified. The dominant themes of stage plays and street literature was the folly of women and their lascivious natures. The Bible, newly available in the vernacular, supplied plenty of ammunition, beginning with Eve's tempting of Adam. Medical theories of the day reinforced the Creation story, in which God fashioned woman from the rib of man in order to provide him with a companion. Women were thought to be inferior versions of men: smaller, weaker, less intelligent, more emotional and foolish. Their sexual organs supposedly paralleled men's but were too cool to be outside the body. The clitoris was a very little penis, but more demanding than the man's, and the uterus needed to be "refreshed" regularly with men's seed, or it would sicken with desire and the woman would go mad. Women, therefore, needed frequent orgasms and plenty of babies to thrive. Women's peculiar biology placed the burden of satisfying their needs directly on their husbands. A man who failed in his duty—and women could be insatiable—was vulnerable to her cheating. Men so feared shaming by an out-of-control woman that they preferred to err on the side of dominating her. To be ruled or fooled by a woman was far more shameful than to be duped by a dishonest rogue.[59]

These ideas about the female body and character go back to classical times and reemerged in Europe with the Scholastic translations of ancient manuscripts.[60] Early modern English society was in such flux that levels of trust had plummeted and institutional remedies were proving unreliable.[61] Among men and women emigrating to the New World, tensions eased when they set to work building farms together. It takes at least two to pioneer, after all, and marriageable women were in short supply. Women did not gain their freedom from coverture by moving to the colonies, but they did acquire higher status and greater esteem. One mark of this can be seen in the naming of the firstborn of each sex. In New England, mothers became free to name their firstborn daughters after themselves, an act of presumption they would not have dared in old England.[62]

English family institutions and gender politics were thus refashioned in the colonies in the face of the very high value of labor relative to land. Women and children gained leverage within the family, but men continued to hold the votes outside. To exercise control over sons in the potentially revolutionary regime created by high wages, men were vastly aided by the invention of the township system, which regulated access to land and provided fathers with substantial heritable claims by which to reward sons' loyalty. The opening of new towns tended to offset this source of patriarchal power, however, because they provided opportunities to sons lacking good prospects at home. So long as raw land was available and markets abroad continued to grow, new generations could be accommodated, but the Native American presence continued in force prior to 1675 so that their title claims moderated the pace of new town creation sufficiently to restrain further encroachments by grown children on parental rights. Altogether, social and gender relations in Puritan New England could remain healthy under these circumstances, and children continued to find it worth their while to defer to their parents.[63]

There were signs of trouble in Eden even before King Philip's War, but after Indian resistance to further expansion solidified, the people's equanimity evaporated. Ministers chastised the people for their sins, and they sought forgiveness in revivals and covenant renewals, but misfortunes continued to rain in the forms of a unilateral imposition of direct rule by the English crown, military setbacks, and persisting economic troubles. Given this unnerving state of affairs, it is little wonder that afflicted girls exposed a great Satanic conspiracy at Salem Village early in 1692, with hundreds accused, a turncoat minister and a Boston merchant among the alleged leaders, and nineteen hanged at the gallows.[64]

As King Philip's War had brought the first era to an end, the shamed reaction to Salem's terrible tragedy marked the beginnings of a new one. Superstition did not go away, and rationalism did not sweep the stage clean, but magistrates under the new imperial system lost their reforming zeal to make people behave. Judges no longer encouraged the prosecution of petty sexual misdemeanors, such as fornication between betrothed pairs. Fear of out-of-control sexuality subsided, and individual women began to appear in sermon texts as models of virtue. Ministers might rail, but magistrates had ceased to listen. The cases now crowding their court dockets more often concerned disputes between debtors and creditors living in different towns than quarrels between neighbors.[65]

The return of peace with France and its Abenaki allies reopened the frontier in New England, and the creation of new towns resumed quickly. The availability of good raw land annulled fathers' control over their grown sons, but patriarchy still bred tensions between the sexes. A persisting imbalance of power called for newer modes of justifying the continued subordination of women. A new feminine ideal took shape that complemented the increasingly visible shifts in male roles away from old-style sexual dominance of women to one of self-control, public responsibility, trustworthiness, and defense of female virtues. Given the direction of economic change toward greater use of credit in broader networks of transactions, the new emphasis on reliability and credibility as an appropriate basis for male honor appears understandable, indeed inevitable. Newer expectations of respectable women, on the other hand, favored a staggering load of virtues. From persons suspected of being emotionally unstable, lacking in judgment, and sexually insatiable, well-bred white women were now thought to be steeped in piety, sexually passive, extrasensitive, and especially kind to children and animals. The sweet little daughter would grow up to be a loving, self-sacrificing mother who was also a faithful wife to whom the harried husband could turn for comfort and moral support. She was not to meddle in the business of men, even though farm women still had to know how to run a house, manage a dairy, and keep up an acre of garden. The bad-girl image was relegated to women of color and those whites who got into trouble.[66]

Anglophone society on both sides of the Atlantic in the eighteenth century was moving away from old-style misogyny but not toward gender equality. Rather, the trend was to keep mothers out of property management. The ideas in circulation celebrating women's special talents for empathy and love increasingly placed the burden of sacrifice for family's sake on wives and mothers. Their sexuality was deemphasized as their maternal nature became the reputed source of their greater virtue. They were expected to surrender power over property, and the autonomy it conferred, for the greater good of their children. And this was the price they paid for a century's lull in the war between the sexes.

Mary Cooper's Long Island diary offers a real-life portrait of domestic life from which to begin an assessment of the impact of a century of social change on power relations within the family.[67] She was a better-than-middling farm wife who had slaves and who served tea to guests, but who was so overworked and made so frantic by financial worries that she had little time for the genteel female culture enjoyed by planters' wives of the upper classes in the South. The Coopers did not live like gentlefolk and apparently had no pretensions that way. On a trip with a female relative, Mary and her companion put up at a kind of boardinghouse where several "gentlemen" happened also to be staying. They were exceedingly "civil" toward them, she reported in some relief.[68]

Cooper's diary records an amazing succession of visitors for whom she cooked and cleaned. Most spent only a few hours or a few days, but some moved in for weeks at a time, giving the diary multiple story lines reminiscent of a television soap opera. Her little granddaughter, Sally Wright, stayed for months, much to Mary's dismay; and her daughter, Esther, moved in permanently when her marriage went sour. But then Esther's estranged husband followed her, hoping to reconcile, and they continued to quarrel while both lived under Mary's roof. When he finally moved out his goods, he didn't entirely remove himself: "Simon Cooper and his brother Joseph both seems to live here," she complained.

The females who lived with Mary helped with the work, but not enough to satisfy her. Once when she and her daughter were cleaning house together, Esther whined the whole time, to her mother's intense annoyance. Mary and Esther were not without help. One of the Cooper slaves, Frances, worked in the house and was very useful; but the others all worked for Mary's husband, Joseph, and lived in their own quarters. Mary had little authority over them: "I was mighty angry this morning becaus our peopel did not bring in the pumkins and they are all frose and spoiled."[69]

In addition to Mary's immediate duties toward her visitors and her family, she carried out many of the usual tasks of the farm wife: keeping a large kitchen garden, nursing new lambs in the spring, overseeing the hiving of the bees in June, drying cherries that month and apples in October and November, frying out fat from pork and beef, then making sausages and "souse," mincemeat, soap, and candles in December.

There are hints throughout the diary that Mary resented her husband for not being a better provider. When their debts became pressing, they mortgaged land and hired out her maid to collect her wages. Their cupboards were bare every summer until the crops come in, and Mary felt humiliated when she couldn't supply bread to passing boatmen or give her own family sufficient "vittels" to appease their appetites. Weak tea and dry crusts served for dinner on a number of occasions, as Mary pointedly informed her diary. And then Joseph groused when she served tea to guests and at one point denied her request for a turkey to celebrate their daughter's safe recovery from smallpox inoculation.[70]

At another point Mary became so exasperated with her family and with her continuing financial problems that she could not contain her emotions: "My heart is burnt with anger and discontent, want of every nesesary thing in life and in constant feare of gapeing credtors consums my strenth and wasts my days. The horrer of these things with the continuel cross of my famaly, like to so many horse leeches, prays upon my vitals."[71]

Mary Cooper's unhappiness was exacerbated by unbreakable ties of marriage to a man who bungled real estate deals, mismanaged the farm, and failed to keep the house in good repair. He did not share her interest in religion and ideas, nor did he treat her with the loving indulgence she had enjoyed from her father as she was growing up. That Mary did not fit comfortably into her role as housewife and mother, her diary makes clear. Her restlessness and spiritual independence repeatedly break through the descriptions of household affairs. When work did not keep her at home, she sallied forth to one or another of the religious meetings in town and heard all the visiting speakers, including Indian evangelists. And Mary did not hesitate to argue religion with family members or friends. Her own sister was a leader in organizing a local Baptist congregation that admitted blacks as members, including at least two of the Coopers' slaves. Indeed, blacks held their own prayer meetings at night at the Cooper farm and elsewhere, which Mary reported as matter-of-factly as she did their speaking up in church. For Mary, and apparently for many of her neighbors, the civil or racial status of blacks and Indians did not derogate from their equal standing in the eyes of God.

For Mary Cooper, who strove so determinedly to attend one or another of the four churches in Oyster Cove every sabbath day, religion offered intellectual stimulation as well as spiritual comfort, and drinking tea provided occasions for her to discuss her ideas with others. Mary's daily struggles with overwork and her troubles with her family may seem unremarkable to modern eyes, yet she lived under a legal system that gave her no real leverage against her husband's fecklessness. Although she could refuse to cosign deeds and mortgages, their creditors pestered her unmercifully. Unhappy as she was, Mary did not question the system, blaming instead her husband and children. Of the various influences on her mental outlook, the comfort she found in expressive religious exercises was probably foremost. Mary respected and adhered to many of the emerging standards of respectability, but the new sensibility that supposedly accompanied them had done nothing to empower her vis-à-vis her husband or her children. She remained under the rule of coverture and the sway of a male dominant ideology. Patriarchy had donned more fashionable clothes and had begun to dote on the children, but it was still patriarchy.[72]

Mary Cooper's world was a busier, more cosmopolitan place than when the Pilgrims first came ashore at Plymouth or when their grandchildren sallied forth to defend their homes against the grandsons of Massasoit's warriors. The Ninnimissinouk no longer posed a barrier or a threat. They and descendants of Africans did supply a significant fraction of the work force, but only in New England's saltwater communities. Elsewhere the children of farm families continued to provide the backbone of the agricultural and domestic manufacturing economy. When development engulfed the last remaining pockets of arable land in southern New England, the New England family system did not grind to a halt. The defeat of New France opened up the interior river valleys of northern parts of the region as well as the coast of Maine. Descendants of the original settlers headed west as well as north, carrying the New England family gospel to New Jersey, New York, and western Pennsylvania. And after the Revolution, the juggernaut rolled on. Their posterity spread across the lands of the Iroquois into the territories north of the Ohio conquered from the Shawnee and Delaware, Illinois and Miami, reaching westward into Wisconsin and Minnesota and all the way to the Willamette Valley of Oregon.

That gospel was a distinctive blend of personal piety, family labor, and congregational independence, aided by the township system of distributing land and regulating community life. It was a gospel forged under frontier conditions in which the original dwellers were expected to give up their land and scatter before the oncoming wave of the righteous.

Select Bibliography

Anderson, Robert Charles. *The Great Migration Begins: Immigrants to New England, 1620–1633.* 3 vols. Boston: New England Historic Genealogical Society, 1995.

Individual Family Genealogies

Genealogies of Rhode Island Families from Rhode Island Periodicals. 2 vols. Baltimore: Genealogical Publishing, 1983. Covers descendants of families who were not descendants of *Mayflower* passengers.

General Society of Mayflower Descendants. *Mayflower Families through Five Generations.* 5 vols. Plymouth, Mass., 1975–1991; plus the series Mayflower Families in Progress: John Billington, William Bradford, William Brewster, James Chilton, Francis Cooke, Edward Doty, Francis Eaton, Samuel Fuller, Richard More, Thomas Rogers, Henry Samson, George Soule, Myles Standish, Richard Warren, William White, and Edward Winslow. Multiple authors, 1975–.

Loomis, Elias. *The Descendants of Joseph Loomis Who Came from Braintree, England, in the Year 1638 and Settled in Windsor, Connecticut, in 1639.* 2d ed. New Haven: C. E. Tuttle, 1875.

New England Historical and Genealogical Register. Vols. 143–147 (1989–1993). Covers Rhode Island families who were not descendants of *Mayflower* passengers.

Phelps, Oliver S., and Andrew T. Servin. *The Phelps Family of America and Their English Ancestors . . .* 2 vols. Pittsfield, Mass., 1899.

White, Elizabeth Pearson. *John Howland of the Mayflower.* 2 vols. Camden, Maine: Picton Press, 1990, 1993.

Genealogical Histories of Towns

Bond, Henry. *Genealogies of the Families and Descendants of the Early Settlers of Watertown, Massachusetts . . .* 2d ed. 2 vols. in one. 1860; reprint, Boston: New England Historic Genealogical Society, 1978, 1981.

Blodgette, George Brainard, and Amos Everett Jewett. *Early Settlers of Rowley, Massachusetts. 1933;* reprint, Somersworth, N.H.: New England History Press, 1981.

Chamberlain, George Walter. *History of Weymouth*. Vols. 3 and 4, *Genealogy of Weymouth Families* (1932), reprinted as *Genealogies of the Early Families of Weymouth, Massachusetts*. Baltimore: Genealogical Publishing, 1984.

The History of Woodstock, Connecticut: Genealogies of Woodstock Families. 8 vols. Vols. 1–6 edited by Clarence W. Bowen. Norwood, Mass.: Plimpton Press, 1926–1935; vols. 7–8 edited by Donald Lines Jacobus and William Herbert Wood. Worcester, Mass.: American Antiquarian Society, 1943.

Jacobus, Donald Lines. *Families of Ancient New Haven*. 3 vols. 1923–1932; reprint, Baltimore: Genealogical Publishing, 1974. Includes Wallingford.

Merrill, Joseph. *History of Amesbury and Merrimac, Massachusetts*. Bowie, Md.: Heritage Books, 1978.

Stiles, Henry R., *The History of Ancient Windsor, Connecticut . . .* 2 vols. 1891, 1892; reprint, Somersworth, N.H.: New Hampshire Publishing, 1976.

Stiles, Henry R., and W. S. Adams. *The History of Ancient Wethersfield, Connecticut . . .* 2 vols. 1902, 1904; reprint, with a new foreword by John C. Willard, Somersworth, N.H.: New Hampshire Publishing, 1974–1975.

Town Vital Records

Vital Records of Charlestown, Massachusetts, to the Year 1850. Compiled by Roger D. Joslyn. Boston: New England Historic Genealogical Society, 1984.

Vital Records of Groton, Massachusetts, to the Year 1849. 2 vols. Salem, Mass.: Essex Institute, 1926, 1927.

Vital Records of Pepperell, Massachusetts, to the Year 1850. Compiled by George A. Rice. Boston: New England Historic Genealogical Society, 1985.

Notes

1. Native New England

1. Lawrence C. Wroth, *The Voyage of Giovanni da Verrazano, 1524–1528* (New Haven: Yale University Press, 1970), pp. 137–140.
2. Neil Jorgensen, *A Sierra Club Naturalist's Guide to Southern New England* (San Francisco: Sierra Club Books, 1978), pp. 88–89; Carolyn Merchant, *Ecological Revolutions: Nature, Gender, and Science in New England* (Chapel Hill: University of North Carolina Press, 1980), p. 30.
3. Jorgensen, *Sierra Club Guide*, p. 89; Peter C. Fletcher, *Soil Survey of Barnstable County, Massachusetts* (Washington, D.C.: U.S. Department of Agriculture, Soil Conservation Service, 1993), pp. 75, 212–222; William Cronon, *Changes in the Land: Indians, Colonists, and the Ecology of New England* (New York: Hill and Wang, 1983), p. 35. Bruce C. Daniels, in *The Connecticut Town* (Middletown, Conn.: Wesleyan University Press, 1979), drew on a statewide soil survey of 1939 to compile his county soil maps.
4. Cronon, *Changes in the Land*, pp. 28, 142.
5. W. M. Denivan, "The Pristine Myth: The Landscape of the Americas in 1492." *Annals of the Association of American Geographers* 82 (1992): 369–385; A. C. Cline and S. H. Spun, *The Virgin Upland Forest of Central New England: A Study of Old Growth Stands in the Pisgah Mt. Section of Southwestern New Hampshire Harvard Forest* (Petersham, Mass., 1942), quoted in Mitchell T. Mulholland, "Patterns of Change in Prehistoric Southern New England: A Regional Approach" (Ph.D. diss., University of Massachusetts, 1984), p. 335; Fletcher, *Soil Survey of Barnstable County*, p. 122.
6. Jorgensen, *Sierra Club Guide*, p. 53; Fletcher, *Soil Survey of Barnstable County*, p. 72.
7. Jean M. Grove, *The Little Ice Age* (London: Methuen, 1988), discusses the evidence. John Winthrop described heavy snows and the freezing of the Ipswich River on December 4, 1633, which prompted the editors to comment in a lengthy footnote on other evidences of severe winters and untimely frosts; *The*

241

Journal of John Winthrop, 1630–1649, ed. Richard S. Dunn, James Savage, and Laetitia Yeandle (Cambridge, Mass.: The Belknap Press of Harvard University Press, 1996), p. 105.

8. Roger Williams, *A Key into the Language of America,* ed. John T. Teunissen and Evelyn J. Hing (Detroit: Wayne State University Press, 1973), p. 157.

9. Edward Winslow, *Good Newes from New England* (London, 1623), reprinted in Alexander Young, ed., *Chronicles of the First Planters of the Colony of Massachusetts Bay from 1623 to 1636* (1846; reprint, Boston: Little, Brown, 1978), p. 577; Edward Johnson, *Johnson's Wonder-Working Providence, 1628–1651,* ed. J. Franklin Jameson (New York: Charles Scribner's Sons, 1910), p. 86.

10. Wroth, *Voyage of Verrazano,* pp. 136, 139. "I suppose, had you underwoods as we have in England, you should need house [no cattle] but such as you would use about your house for milke"; Emmanuel Downing to John Winthrop Jr. in 1632, *Winthrop Papers,* 6 vols. (Boston: Massachusetts Historical Society, 1929–1944), 4: 91.

11. Mary Rowlandson was a captive who accompanied a large group of Pokanoket and Narragansetts in the winter of 1675–76 as they continually shifted their habitations to evade English pursuit. Despite English destruction of their crops the previous summer, these Native Americans were able to live off the land. Ground nuts provided the winter staple, but the women could feed their families a variety of local plant resources, including the bark of a tree. *A Narrative of the Captivity, Sufferings, and Removes of Mrs. Mary Rowlandson* (Boston, 1682). Her *Narrative* has been conveniently reprinted in Alden T. Vaughan and Edward W. Clark, eds., *Puritans among the Indians: Accounts of Captivity and Redemption, 1676–1714* (Cambridge, Mass.: The Belknap Press of Harvard University Press, 1981), pp. 31–75.

12. A broad-scale shift to maize-centered agriculture emerged in eastern North America during the three centuries from A.D. 800 to 1100, but did not spread to the Northeast until women successfully adapted flint species to colder climates; Bruce D. Smith, "Origins of Agriculture in Eastern North America," *Science* 246 (1989): 1566–71; Patty Jo Watson and Mary C. Kennedy, "The Development of Horticulture in the Eastern Woodlands of North America: Women's Role," in *Engendering Archaeology: Women and Prehistory,* ed. Joan M. Gero and Margaret Conkey (Oxford: Basil Blackwell, 1991), pp. 255–275; Jeffrey C. Bendremer and Robert E. Dewar, "The Advent of Prehistoric Maize in New England," in *Corn and Culture in the Prehistoric New World,* ed. Sissel Johansessen and Christine A. Hastorf (Boulder: Westview Press, 1994), pp. 369–394.

13. Bendremer and Dewar, "The Advent of Prehistoric Maize," pp. 369–394; Dena F. Dincauze and Robert J. Hasenstab, "Explaining the Iroquois: Tribalization on a Prehistoric Periphery," in *Centre and Periphery: Proceedings of the World Archaeological Congress, September 1986,* ed. T. C. Champion (London: Unwin Hyman, 1987), pp. 67–87; Kathleen J. Bragdon, *Native People of Southern New England, 1500–1650* (Norman: University of Oklahoma Press, 1996), pp. 81–85.

14. Neil Depaoli, "Patterns of Settlement and Land Use: Contact Period (1500–

1620), Plantation Period (1620–1675)," in *Historic and Archaeological Resources of the Connecticut River Valley,* ed. James Bradley (Boston: Massachusetts Historical Commission, 1984), pp. 46–76; Peter F. Thornbahn, "Where Are the Late Woodland Villages in Southern New England?" *Bulletin of the Massachusetts Archaeological Society* 49 (1988): 46–57; Barbara E. Luedtke, "Where Are the Late Woodland Villages in Eastern Massachusetts?" ibid., pp. 58–65; David J. Bernstein, *Prehistoric Subsistence on the Southern New England Coast: The Record from Narragansett Bay* (San Diego: Academic Press, 1993); Jordan E. Kerber, "Where Are the Woodland Villages in the Narragansett Bay Region?" *Bulletin of the Massachusetts Archaeological Society* 49 (1988): 44–45 and 66–71; Peter Pagoulatos, "Late Woodland and Contact Period Land-Use Patterns in Rhode Island: Continuity and Change," *Bulletin of the Massachusetts Archaeological Society* 51 (1990): 69–82; Elizabeth A. Little, "Where Are the Woodland Villages on Cape Cod and the Islands?" *Bulletin of the Massachusetts Archaeological Society* 49 (1988): 72–82; Peter A. Thomas, "In the Maelstrom of Change: The Indian Trade and Cultural Process in the Middle Connecticut River Valley, 1635–1665" (Ph.D. diss., University of Massachusetts, 1979); idem, "Cultural Change on the Southern New England Frontier, 1630–1665," in *Cultures in Contact: The European Impact on Native Cultural Institutions in Eastern North America, A.D. 1000–1800,* ed. William W. Fitzhugh (Washington, D.C.: Smithsonian Institution, 1985), pp. 131–162; Kevin McBride and Robert Dewar, "Prehistoric Settlement in the Lower Connecticut River Valley," *Man in the Northeast* 22 (1981): 37–66; Kevin McBride, "The Development of the Household as an Economic Unit in the Lower Connecticut River Valley," *Man in the Northeast* 28 (1984): 39–49; Bragdon, *Native People of Southern New England,* pp. 80–101.

15. Verrazano at Narragansett Bay in 1524: "the fields extend for XXV–XXX leagues [75–90 miles]; they are open and free of any obstacles or trees, and so fertile that any kind of seed would produce excellent crops. Then we entered the forests, which could be penetrated even by a large army"; Wroth, *Verrazano,* p. 139; Gordon M. Day, "The Indian as an Ecological Factor in the Northeastern Forest," *Ecology* 34 (1953): 329–346. Captain Peirce wrote to John Winthrop: "The country on the west of the Bay of Naraganstt is all champaign [level plain] for many miles, but very stony, and full of Indians"; *Winthrop's Journal,* p. 133.

16. Cronon, *Changes in the Land,* pp. 35–48.

17. Bragdon, *Native People of Southern New England,* pp. 55–79.

18. David J. Bernstein, "Trends in Prehistoric Subsistence on the Southern New England Coast: The View from Narragansett Bay," *North American Archaeologist* 11 (1990): 321–352; idem, "Prehistoric Use of Plant Foods in the Narragansett Bay Region," *Man in the Northeast* 44 (1992): 1–13; idem, *Prehistoric Subsistence,* p. 50; Dean R. Snow, *The Archaeology of New England* (New York: Academic Press, 1980), p. 178.

19. Carl Bridenbaugh, *Fat Mutton and Liberty of Conscience: Society in Rhode Island,* 1636–1690 (Providence: Brown University Press, 1974), p. 12.

20. The manufacture of wampum beads supplied the Narragansetts with the means of trade and a lucrative partnership with the Mohawks of the Five Nations Confederacy; Neal Salisbury, "Indians and Colonists in Southern New England after the Pequot War: An Uneasy Balance," in *The Pequots in Southern New England: The Fall and Rise of an American Indian Nation,* ed. Laurence M. Hauptman and James D. Wherry (Norman: University of Oklahoma Press, 1990), pp. 86–87.

21. Williams, *A Key into the Language,* pp. 127–128; Cronon, *Changes in the Land,* pp. 43–53.

22. Two oval wigwams at Niantic, Connecticut, in 1761 measured 17 by 12 feet and 14 by 9 feet, respectively. Their heights were approximately 6 and 10 feet. William C. Sturtevant, "Two 1761 Wigwams at Niantic, Connecticut," *American Antiquity* 40 (1975): 437–444.

23. Bragdon, *Native People of Southern New England,* pp. 126–129; David Demeritt, "Agriculture, Climate, and Cultural Adaptation in the Prehistoric Northeast," *Archaeology of Eastern North America* 19 (1991): 195.

24. Demeritt, "Agriculture, Climate, and Cultural Adaptation," pp. 183–202 passim.

25. McBride and Dewar, "Prehistoric Settlement in the Lower Connecticut River Valley," pp. 37–66; "Where Are the Woodland Villages?" a forum published in the *Bulletin of the Massachusetts Archaeological Society* 49 (1988): 44–83.

26. Bragdon links land, inheritance, lineage, and kinship systems into a system centered on sachemship; *Native People of Southern New England,* pp. 130–183, especially 140–155.

27. Bragdon, drawing on Williams' *Key,* uses this as a general term signifying all the native peoples of southern New England. "Ninnuock, Ninnimissinnuwock, Eniskeetompauwog, which signifies Men, Folke, or People"; Williams, *Key into the Language,* p. 84.

28. Snow, *Archaeology of New England,* p. 33.

29. John Josselyn observed in 1638 an "Indian pinnace . . . made of birchbark, sewed together with the roots of spruce and white cedar . . . with a deck, and trimmed with sails"; *Account of Two Voyages to New-England,* ed. Paul J. Lindholdt (Hanover, N.H.: University Press of New England, 1988), p. 23; Neal Salisbury, *Manitou and Providence: Indians, Europeans, and the Making of New England, 1500–1643* (New York: Oxford University Press, 1982), p. 87.

30. Bert Salwen, "Indians of Southern New England and Long Island: Early Period," in *Handbook of North American Indians,* ed. William G. Sturtevant, vol. 15: *Northeast,* ed. Bruce G. Trigger, (Washington, D.C.: Smithsonian Institution, 1978), pp. 161–162; Ives Goddard, "Eastern Algonquian Languages," ibid., pp. 70–75.

31. Bernstein, *Prehistoric Subsistence,* p. 119.

32. Lynn Ceci, "The First Fiscal Crisis in New York," *Economic Development and Cultural Change* 28 (1979–80): 339–347.

33. Bernstein, *Prehistoric Subsistence,* p. 50.

34. Mary Rowlandson describes her mistress, the squaw sachem Weetamo, stringing wampum; *Narrative*, p. 61.

35. William S. Simmons, *Cautantowwit's House: An Indian Burial Ground on the Island of Conanicut in Narragansett Bay* (Providence: Brown University Press, 1970); P. A. Kelley and P. E. Rubutone, "Preliminary Interpretations from a Seventeenth-Century Narragansett Indian Cemetary in Rhode Island," in Fitzhugh, *Cultures in Contact*, pp. 117–119; Dena Dincauze, "A Capsule Prehistory of Southern New England," in Hauptman and Wherry, *The Pequots in Southern New England*, pp. 19–32; Ives Goddard and Kathleen J. Bragdon, *Native Writings in Massachusetts*, 2 vols. (Philadelphia: American Philosophical Society, 1988); William Scranton Simmons, *Spirit of the New England Tribes: Indian History and Folklore, 1620–1984* (Hanover, N.H.: University Press of New England, 1986).

36. The following discussion is heavily indebted to Bragdon, *Native People of Southern New England*, but my purposes and emphases differ from hers.

37. Thomas Morton, *New English Canaan; or, New Canaan, Containing an Abstract of New England* (1632; reprint, New York: Peter Smith, 1947). See Bragdon, *Native People of Southern New England*, p. 233.

38. Bragdon leans toward matrilineality and its ideology of collective relationships, multiple kin ties, and lineage or clan affiliations; *Native People of Southern New England*, p. 158.

39. Bragdon, *Native People of Southern New England*, pp. 107–129.

40. Simmons, *Cautantowwit's House*, pp. 44–47.

41. See Simmons, *Cautantowwit's House*, pp. 50–62; idem, *Spirit of the New England Tribes*, pp. 73–78; Bragdon, *Native People of Southern New England*, pp. 184–199.

42. Bragdon, *Native People of Southern New England*, p. 184; Simmons, *Spirit of the New England Tribes*, pp. 73–78. What follows again depends very heavily on Bragdon's work.

43. Bragdon, *Native People of Southern New England*, p. 133.

44. The geographic distribution of these cemeteries is closely associated with the centers of wampum manufacture and trade, according to ibid., p. 242.

45. Even-handedly summarized in ibid., pp. 231–247. Bragdon does not choose among them, nor does she present a new synthesis of her own, but offers a kind of codicil that links the burial of wealth with sacrifice intended to further community renewal. The goods buried with the dead did not represent sacrifices to appease an angry god, she argues, but courted a bountiful one, for in the spirit of coercive reciprocity, the greater the sacrifice, the greater the potential gain. The adornment of the individual who died was to persuade him or her to serve as an emissary or intermediary in seeking spiritual aid in revitalizing the community.

2. Newcomers

Epigraph: *A journal of the Pilgrims at Plymouth; Mourt's relation, a relation or journal of the English plantation settled at Plymouth in New England, by certain English adven-*

turers both merchants and others (1622), ed. Dwight B. Heath (New York: Corinth Books, 1963; hereafter *Mourt's Relation*).

1. Thomas Dermer, *To His Worshipfull Friend M Samuel Purchas, Preacher of the Word, at the Church a little within Tudgate,* (London, 1625), reprinted in G. P. Winship, ed., *Sailors' Narratives of Voyages along the New England Coast, 1524–1624,* (Boston: Houghton Mifflin, 1905); Gookin's report comes from *Historical Collections of the Indians in New England* (1674), Massachusetts Historical Society Collections, 1st ser., vol. 1 (Boston, 1792), p. 148. Neal Salisbury, *Manitou and Providence: Indians, Europeans, and the Makings of New England, 1500–1643* (New York: Oxford University Press, 1982), p. 267, cites the relevant literature up to that time. See also Arthur E. Speiss and Bruce D. Weiss, "New England Pandemic of 1616–1622: Cause and Archaeological Implication," *Man in the Northeast* 34 (1987): 71–72; Dean R. Snow and K. M. Lanphear, "European Contact and Indian Depopulation in the Northeast: The Timing of the First Epidemics," *Ethnohistory* 35 (1988): 15–33.

2. Salisbury, *Manitou and Providence,* p. 191.

3. As were Quakers in western New Jersey such as Mary Smith: "God's providence made room for us in a wonderful manner, in taking away the Indians"; quoted in Joan M. Jensen, *Loosening the Bonds of Womanhood: Mid-Atlantic Farm Women, 1750–1850* (New Haven: Yale University Press, 1986), p. 4. For New England, see William Bradford, *Of Plymouth Plantation, 1620–1647,* ed. Samuel Eliot Morison (New York: Alfred A. Knopf, 1952); John Winthrop, May 1634: "For the natives, they are near all dead of the smallpox, as the Lord hath cleared our title to what we possess"; *The Journal of John Winthrop, 1630–1649,* ed. Richard S. Dunn, James Savage, and Laetitia Yeandle (Cambridge, Mass.: The Belknap Press of Harvard University Press, 1996), p. 137.

4. Roger Williams, *The Correspondence of Roger Williams,* ed. Glenn W. LaFantasie, 2 vols. (Providence: Rhode Island Historical Society; and Hanover, N.H.: Brown University Press, University Press of New England, 1988), 1: 20.

5. Bradford, *Of Plymouth Plantation,* p. 59.

6. *A journal of the Pilgrims at Plymouth; Mourt's relation, a relation or journal of the English plantation settled at Plymouth in New England, by certain English adventurers both merchants and others* (1622), ed. Dwight B. Heath (New York: Corinth Books, 1963), pp. 16, 19–39; Bradford, *Of Plymouth Plantation,* pp. 58–61.

7. *Mourt's Relation,* p. 47; Thomas Dudley, "Letter to Lady Bridget, Countess of Lincoln, 12 and 28 March 1630/1," in *Letters from New England: The Massachusetts Bay Colony, 1629–1638,* ed. Everett Emerson (Amherst: University of Massachusetts Press, 1976), pp. 66–83; Bradford, *Of Plymouth Plantation,* p. 223, mentions scurvy.

8. *Mourt's Relation,* pp. 50–57; Bradford, *Of Plymouth Plantation,* pp. 79–84, 87–90. Salisbury's version stresses the fearful anticipation of the English, who had little experience with Indians; *Manitou and Providence,* pp. 113–116. But Stephen Hopkins of the *Mayflower* showed a good deal of knowledge about native ways on their scouting trips to Cape Cod and elsewhere on the mainland, as de-

scribed in *Mourt's Relation*. He may have been the Stephen Hopkins who was among a ship's company cast away on a Bermudan island in July 1609 and who made it to Virginia nine months later in two homemade boats. Hopkins' stay in Jamestown would have acquainted him with Powhatan's people. John D. Austin, *Stephen Hopkins*, vol. 6 of *Mayflower Families through Five Generations: Descendants of the Pilgrims who Landed at Plymouth, Mass., December 1620* (Plymouth, Mass.: General Society of Mayflower Descendants, 1992), p. 3.

9. Of approximately 500 members of the Leiden congregation, about 100 emigrated to Plymouth during the 1620s; Mark A. Peterson, "The Plymouth Church," *New England Quarterly* 66 (1993): 577.

10. *Mourt's Relation*, pp. 42–43; Isaac de Rasieres to Samuel Bloomaert, in *Narratives of New Netherland, 1609–1664*, ed. J. Franklin Jameson (New York: Barnes and Noble, 1909), pp. 111–113.

11. Charles M. Andrews, *The Colonial Period of American History*, 4 vols. (New Haven: Yale University Press, 1964), 1: 291; from calculations based on Robert Charles Anderson, *The Great Migration Begins: Immigrants to New England, 1620–1633*, 3 vols. (Boston: New England Historic Genealogical Society, 1995).

12. Based on inventories of estates recorded before 1675. The sample counties surveyed are Suffolk (which then included Boston's rural hinterland), Essex, and Hampshire in Massachusetts; New Haven, Fairfield, and Hartford in Connecticut; and Plymouth Colony. Excluded are Middlesex County in Massachusetts, New London County in Connecticut, Rhode Island, New Hampshire, and Maine.

13. Andrews, *Colonial Period*, 1: 396; *Encyclopedia of the North American Colonies*, 3 vols. (New York: Charles Scribner's Sons, 1993), 1: pt. 3, s.v. "Colonial Settings." The French, the Dutch, and the Swedes all built forts first and asked questions later. They attempted at all times to deal with native peoples from positions of strength.

14. Edward Johnson, *Johnson's Wonder-Working Providence, 1628–1652* [1653], ed. James Franklin Jameson (New York: Charles Scribner's Sons, 1910), p. 54.

15. E. A. Wrigley and Roger S. Schofield, *The Population History of England, 1541–1871: A Reconstruction* (Cambridge: Cambridge University Press, 1981), pp. 175, 186, 224; Henry A. Gemery, *Research in Economic History* 5 (1980): 215. Given the size of the English population, approximately 4 million in 1600 rising perhaps to 5 million by midcentury, this outmigration represented an extreme self-purging of its young, far greater proportionately than the numbers leaving France or the Netherlands, and exceeding even Spain's annual emigration.

16. Wrigley and Schofield, *Population History*, pp. 219–220: "It is likely that more Scots, Welsh, and Irish entered England than Englishmen went to settle elsewhere . . . It is therefore quite possible for there to have been a substantial emigration of Englishmen, say to the North American colonies, while net migration was modest."

17. Ibid., pp. 228, 260. See also revisions of Wrigley and Schofield in E. A. Wrigley, R. S. Davies, J. E. Oeppen, and R. S. Schofield, *English Population History from*

Family Reconstitution, 1580–1837 (New York: Cambridge University Press, 1997). For a detailed analysis of the Cambridge population project, see David Levine's review, "Sampling History: The English Population," *Journal of Interdisciplinary History* 28 (1998): 605–632.

18. Wrigley and Schofield, *Population History,* pp. 638–644. See also the reworking of these data by Peter H. Lindert, "English Population, Wages, and Prices: 1541–1913," in *Population and Economy: Population and History from the Traditional to the Modern World,* ed. Robert I. Rotberg, Theodore K. Rabb, Roger S. Schofield, and E. Anthony Wrigley (Cambridge: Cambridge University Press, 1986), pp. 49–74.

19. Joan Thirsk, ed., *Agricultural Change: Policy and Practice, 1500–1750,* vol. 3: *Chapters from the Agrarian History of England and Wales* (Cambridge: Cambridge University Press, 1990).

20. Keith Wrightson and David Levine, *Poverty and Piety in an English Village: Terling, 1525–1700* (New York: Academic Press, 1979); D. M. Palliser, *The Age of Elizabeth, 1546–1603* (London: Longman, 1983); Joyce Youings, *Sixteenth-Century England* (Harmondsworth: Penguin, 1983); Keith E. Wrightson, *English Society, 1580–1680* (London: Hutchinson, 1982); J. A. Sharpe, *Crime in Early Modern England, 1550–1750* (London: Longman, 1984).

21. Karen Ordahl Kupperman, "Climate and Mastery of the Wilderness," in *Seventeenth-Century New England,* ed. David D. Hall and David Grayson Allen (Boston: Colonial Society of Massachusetts, 1984), pp. 2–37.

22. The best summaries of the hard times are in J. Arnold Sharpe, *Early Modern England: A Social History, 1550–1760,* 2d ed. (London: St. Martin's Press, 1997); and Wrightson, *English Society.* Sharpe's discussion is the more pointed.

23. Richard Hakluyt, *Discourse of Western Planting* (London, 1584), reprinted in Karen Ordahl Kupperman, ed., *Major Problems in American Colonial History* (Lexington, Mass.: D. C. Heath, 1993), pp. 47–49.

24. Bradford, *Of Plymouth Plantation,* p. 195. The "Old Planters" at Salem planted tobacco as a commercial crop in the 1620s; *Suffolk Deeds,* 14 vols. (Boston: Rockwell and Churchill, 1880–1906), 1: 4. In 1652 Providence merchants sent tobacco to London by way of Boston, according to Howard Russell, *A Long Deep Furrow: Three Centuries of Farming in New England* (Hanover, N.H.: University Press of New England, 1976), p. 63. Inventories of farmers in the Connecticut Valley mention tobacco by the 1660s. Sarah, daughter of Daniel Belden, escaped the massacre at Deerfield in 1696 by hiding in the tobacco, according to Ruth Leighton Freeberg, in *The Ancestors and Descendants of Elijah Carr Belding and Capt. Levi Blake of Swanzey, New Hampshire, with Allied Lines* (n.p., 1971), p. 6.

25. A. P. Newton, *Colonizing Activities of the English Puritans* (New Haven: Yale University Press, 1914); Karen Ordahl Kupperman, *Providence Island, 1640–1641: The Other Puritan Colony* (Cambridge: Cambridge University Press, 1993).

26. Lorena S. Walsh and Russell R. Menard, "Death in the Chesapeake: Two Life Tables for Men in Early Colonial Maryland," *Maryland Historical Magazine* 59

(1974): 211–227; Darrett B. Rutman and Anita H. Rutman, "Of Agues and Fevers: Malaria in the Early Chesapeake," *William and Mary Quarterly* 33 (1975): 31–60; idem, "'Now-Wives and Sons-in-Law': Parental Death in a Seventeenth-Century Virginia County," in *The Chesapeake in the Seventeenth Century: Essays in Anglo-American Society*, ed. Thad W. Tate and David L. Ammerman (Chapel Hill: University of North Carolina Press, 1979), pp. 177–182.

27. Gloria L. Main, *Tobacco Colony: Life in Early Maryland, 1650–1720* (Princeton: Princeton University Press, 1982), pp. 97–100.

28. For example, Winthrop D. Jordan's *White over Black: American Attitudes toward the Negro, 1550–1812* (Chapel Hill: University North Carolina Press, 1968); and Richard S. Dunn, *Sugar and Slaves: The Rise of the Planter Class in the English West Indies, 1624–1713* (Chapel Hill: University of North Carolina Press, 1972), to which Hilary McD. Beckles would respond that the English did not treat white servants any better and that therefore historians place too much emphasis on the roles of "Africanness" and "blackness" and too little on the inhumanity of early capitalism. See Beckles, *White Servitude and Black Slavery in Barbados, 1627–1715* (Knoxville: University of Tennessee Press, 1989).

29. Kupperman, *Providence Island*, p. 338; Lorenzo Johnston Greene, *The Negro in Colonial New England, 1620–1776* (1942; reprint, New York: Atheneum, 1969), pp. 16–17.

30. Russell Robert Menard, "Economy and Society in Early Colonial Maryland" (Ph.D. diss., University of Iowa, 1975), p. 194.

31. John Smith argued that it was the "maine Staple" the region had to offer even though it was "a mean and base commoditie"; *Travels and Works of Captain John Smith, President of Virginia, and Admiral of New England, 1580–1631*, ed. Edward Arber (Edinburgh: John Grant, 1910), vol. 1, p. 194, quoted in Daniel Vickers, *Farmers and Fishermen: Two Centuries of Work in Essex County, Massachusetts, 1630–1830* (Chapel Hill: University of North Carolina Press, 1994), p. 86.

32. Kupperman, *Providence Island*, pp. 12–19.

33. Christopher Durston and Jacqueline Eales, "Introduction: The Puritan Ethos, 1560–1700," in *The Culture of English Puritanism, 1560–1700*, ed. Christopher Durston and Jacqueline Eales (New York: St. Martin's Press, 1996), pp. 1–31. Patrick Collinson emphasizes the gradualness of the process of Protestantizing the people in *The Birthpangs of Protestant England: Religious and Cultural Change in the Sixteenth and Seventeenth Centuries* (New York: St. Martin's, 1988). Collinson, *The Elizabeth Puritan Movement* (1967; reprint, Oxford: Clarendon Press, 1989), is the standard work on the origins of Puritanism, but Collinson has since deemphasized political polarity, finding considerable consensus in the movement as a whole. See his *The Religion of Protestants: The Church in English Society, 1559–1625* (Oxford: Oxford University Press, 1982).

34. R. H. Baker and Robin A. Butlin, *Studies of Field Systems in the British Isles* (Cambridge: Cambridge University Press, 1973).

35. Stephen Foster, *The Long Argument: English Puritanism and the Shaping of New England Culture, 1570–1700* (Chapel Hill: University of North Carolina Press,

1991), pp. 12–24, 95–104, 135–136; Patrick Collinson, "The English Conventi-
cle," in *Voluntary Religion,* ed. W. J. Sheils and D. Wood (Oxford: Oxford University Press, 1986), pp. 223–259.

36. Charles E. Banks, *The Winthrop Fleet of 1630* . . . (1930; reprint, Baltimore: Genealogical Publishing, 1972); Anderson, *The Great Migration Begins,* pp. xv–xvi.

37. One must group these geographic origins to make sense of them, and how one
cuts the pie inevitably shapes the pieces. With a good map of England in hand,
I assigned the immigrants' English counties of origin to larger regional group-
ings, using information on their field systems and economic structures supplied
in Baker and Butlin, *Field Systems;* Joan Thirsk, "The Farming Regions of England," in *The Agrarian History of England and Wales,* vol. 4: *1500–1640,* ed. Joan
Thirsk (Cambridge: Cambridge University Press, 1967), pp. 46–80; and Marjorie Keniston McIntosh's regional classification of 255 parishes on the basis of a
variety of factors, including the nature and number of misconduct cases by
presentment juries; McIntosh, *Controlling Misbehaviour in England, 1370–1600*
(Cambridge: Cambridge University Press, 1998). Given the very small proportions of immigrants originating in counties outside the southeastern triangle, I
grouped the central counties into a single region. "Other" includes Lancashire,
Wales, the Welsh border counties, and Ireland.

38. Virginia DeJohn Anderson, *New England's Generation: The Great Migration and the
Formation of Society and Culture in the Seventeenth Century* (Cambridge: Cambridge
University Press, 1991), pp. 4–5.

39. Alison F. Games analyzed all emigrants departing from London for the New
World in 1635. As many as 30 percent of those going to New England were
servants, far more than indicated in the R. Anderson and V. Anderson data.
The rest were heads of households and their dependents. As expected,
identifiable nuclear families made up only a tiny percentage of those going to
Virginia, but the Puritan migration to Providence Island bore a combination of
status groups about halfway in between Virginia's and New England's: 22 percent of those going there traveled in family groups, of whom 46 percent were
servants; Games, *Migration and the Origins of the English Atlantic World* (Cambridge, Mass.: Harvard University Press, 1999).

40. Recent English historians have found the term "Puritan," as applied to individuals, political positions, and ideology, so volatile and ambiguous in England in
this period that they now spell the adjective with a lower-case "p." I use "Puritan" as a synonym for "English" in southern New England outside Rhode
Island. Virginia DeJohn Anderson, "Migrants and Motives: Religion and the
Settlement of New England, 1630–1640," *New England Quarterly* 58 (1985):
339–383, articulates the argument most coherently, but see the rebuttal by David Grayson Allen, "The Matrix of Motivation," *New England Quarterly* 59
(1986): 408–418.

41. David Cressy, *Coming Over: Migration and Communication between England and
New England in the Seventeenth Century* (New York: Cambridge University Press,
1987).

42. The term "Builders of the Bay Colony" comes from Samuel Eliot Morison, *The*

Builders of the Bay Colony (Boston: Houghton Mifflin, 1930). The correspondence of John Winthrop with relatives and fellow travelers in England reflects the views of one who has jumped into the water and shouts "Come on in! The water's fine!" *Winthrop Papers,* 6 vols. (Boston: Massachusetts Historical Society, 1929–1944), vol. 3.

43. Most English clothing was of wool. Cotton was not yet grown in quantity anywhere within England's trading sphere, and linen from Holland was a luxury. Flax was only just beginning to be grown commercially in Ireland and Scotland. Silk was for aristocrats.

44. "Fields and Fences" forms the title of chapter 7 in William Cronon, *Changes in the Land: Indians, Colonists, and the Ecology of New England* (New York: Hill and Wang, 1983). Roger Williams addressed the words quoted in the text to Connecticut governor John Winthrop Jr., May 28, 1647; Williams, *Correspondence,* 1: 234.

3. Taking the Land

Epigraph: John Winthrop, *Winthrop Papers,* 6 vols. (Boston: Massachusetts Historical Society, 1929–1944), 3: 172.

1. William Cronon, *Changes in the Land: Indians, Colonists, and the Ecology of New England* (New York: Hill & Wang, 1983), pp. 141–142. William Wood greatly exaggerates both the quantity of hay ground and the quality of its grasses for fodder in *New England's Prospect* (1633), ed. Alden T. Vaughan (Amherst: University of Massachusetts Press, 1977), pp. 33–34.

2. William Bradford, *Of Plymouth Plantation, 1620–1647,* ed. Samuel Eliot Morison (New York: Alfred A. Knopf, 1952); Edward Winslow, *Good Newes from New England* (1648), reprinted in Alexander Young, ed., *Chronicles of the Pilgrim Fathers* (Boston: C. C. Little and J. Brown, 1846); Nathaniel Morton, *The New England's Memorial* (Plymouth: A. Danford, 1826).

3. John Winthrop to Sir Nathaniel Richard, May 1634, in *The Journal of John Winthrop, 1630–1649,* ed. Richard S. Dunn, James Savage, and Laetitia Yeardle (Cambridge, Mass.: The Belknap Press of Harvard University Press, 1996), p. 166; Winslow, *Good Newes,* p. 577; George G. Langdon Jr., *Pilgrim Colony: A History of New Plymouth, 1620–1691* (New Haven: Yale University Press, 1966); Bradford, *Of Plymouth Plantation,* pp. 238–244.

4. Wood, *New England's Prospect,* p. 79.

5. Gary Arthur Warrick, "A Population History of the Huron-Petun, A.D. 900–1850" (Ph.D. diss., McGill Univiersity, 1990), provides an excellent survey of the literature on disease mortality in northeastern North America and persuasively argues that this smallpox epidemic, which reached Upper Canada in 1634, was the first great epidemic of European disease to hit the interior.

6. *Winthrop Papers,* 4: 166–167, 147–149. "The Indians having only a natural right to so much land as they had or could improve, so as the rest of the country lay open to any that could and would improve it"; ibid., p. 349.

7. Keith Thomas, *Religion and the Decline of Magic: Studies in Popular Belief in Six-*

teenth- and Seventeenth-Century England (1971; reprint, Harmondsworth: Penguin, 1978); David D. Hall, *Worlds of Wonder, Days of Judgment: Popular Religious Beliefs in Early New England* (New York: Alfred A. Knopf, 1989); Barbara Donegan, "Providence, Chance, and Explanation: Some Paradoxical Aspects of Puritan Views of Causation," *Journal of Religious History* 11 (1981): 385–402; Michael P. Winship, *Seers of God: Puritan Providentialism in the Restoration and Early Enlightenment* (Baltimore: Johns Hopkins University Press, 1996), pp. 9–28. On Ninnimissinouk beliefs, see Kathleen J. Bragdon, *The Native People of Southern New England, 1500–1650* (Norman: University of Oklahoma Press, 1996), pp. 220–244; William S. Simmons, *Spirit of the New England Tribes: Indian History and Folklore, 1620–1984* (Hanover, N.H.: University Press of New England, 1986), pp. 73–79; Roger Williams, *The Correspondence of Roger Williams,* ed. Glenn W. LaFantasie, 2 vols. (Providence: Rhode Island Historical Society; and Hanover, N.H.: Brown University Press, University Press of New England, 1988), 2: 488–489, 577, 591–592, 675–676.

8. See the pathetic letter by the son of William Pond in Everett Emerson, ed., *Letters from New England: The Massachusetts Bay Colony, 1629–1638* (Amherst: University of Massachusetts Press, 1976); and Thomas Dudley's "Letter to Lady Bridget, Countess of Lincoln, 12 and 18 March 1630\1," ibid., pp. 66–83.

9. Based on information in Robert Charles Anderson, *The Great Migration Begins: Immigrants to New England, 1620–1633,* 3 vols. (Boston: New England Historic Genealogical Society).

10. Darrett Rutman, "Assessing the Little Communities of Early America," *William and Mary Quarterly* 48 (1986): 163–178.

11. John Frederick Martin, *Profits in the Wilderness: Entrepreneurship and the Founding of New England Towns in the Seventeenth Century* (Chapel Hill: University of North Carolina Press, 1991), pp. 131–141.

12. Examples are the founding towns of Salem, Watertown, Boston, and Dorchester.

13. These remarks are based on published town genealogies that identify the time of arrival of new residents. Alison F. Games, "Venturers, Vagrants, and Vessels of Glory" (Ph.D. diss., University of Pennsylvania, 1991), found postemigrant mobility very high among those arriving in New England from London in 1635. The four most popular destinations were, in order, Boston, Ipswich, Lynn, and Cambridge.

14. David Grayson Allen offers good contrasting descriptions of these two regions in *In English Ways: The Movement of Societies and the Transferral of English Local Law and Custom to Massachusetts Bay in the Seventeenth Century* (Chapel Hill: University of North Carolina Press, 1981); but see also David Hackett Fischer, *Albion's Seed: Four British Folkways in America* (New York: Oxford University Press, 1989), who likens the West Country to the American South.

15. Sumner Chilton Powell, *Puritan Village: The Formation of a New England Town* (Middletown, Conn.: Wesleyan University Press, 1963); Van R. H. Baker and Robert A. Butlin, *Studies of Field Systems in the British Isles* (Cambridge: Cambridge University Press, 1971).

16. Richard P. Gildrie, *Salem, Massachusetts, 1626–1683: A Covenant Community* (Charlottesville: University Press of Virginia, 1975); John J. Waters Jr., "Hingham, Massachusetts, 1631–1661," *Journal of Social History* 1 (1968): 351–370; idem, *The Otis Family in Provincial and Revolutionary Massachusetts* (Chapel Hill: University of North Carolina Press, 1968), pp. 14–19.

17. Paul R. Lucas, *Valley of Discord: Church and Society along the Connecticut River, 1636–1725* (Hanover, N.H.: University Press of New England, 1976), p. 38; Frank Thistlewaite, *Dorset Pilgrims: The Story of West Country Pilgrims Who Went to New England in the 17th Century* (London: Barrie and Jenkins, 1989).

18. Henry Bond, *Genealogies of the Families and Descendants of the Early Settlers of Watertown, Massachusetts,* vol. 1 (Boston: Little, Brown, 1855), pp. 995–1000, 1004–18.

19. Sylvia J. Bugbee, "'A Society of Continuance?' The Role Played by Kinship and Neighborhood in the Settlement of an Early New England Town" (M.A. thesis, University of Vermont, 1993), p. 25; Games, "Venturers, Vagrants, and Vessels of Glory," pp. 294–296, has a brief but excellent discussion of the 1635 immigrants from London who settled Roxbury.

20. Bugbee, "A Society of Continuance," pp. 101–106. Games found that married daughters were more likely to move than were parents or brothers; "Venturers, Vagrants, and Vessels of Glory," p. 257.

21. Games found that 60 percent of the London emigrants of 1635 had arrived as part of family groups, and many others traveled with friends and neighbors; ibid., p. 195.

22. Bugbee, "A Society of Continuance," pp. 134–136, 31; Robert Emmet Wall Jr., *Massachusetts Bay: The Crucial Decade, 1640–1650* (New Haven: Yale University Press, 1972); *Roxbury Land and Church Records,* Sixth Report of the Boston Record Commissioners (Boston, 1884), p. 76, quoted by Robert Charles Anderson in his sketch of minister John Eliot in *The Great Migration Begins: Immigrants to New England, 1620–1633,* 3 vols. (Boston: New England Historic Genealogical Society, 1995), 1: 630.

23. An earnest and vocal minority of the London immigrants in 1635 challenged the emerging orthodoxy and as a consequence found themselves moving repeatedly. Thirty-nine percent left the Bay Colony. An astonishingly high percentage left New England entirely; Games, "Venturers, Vagrants, and Vessels of Glory," p. 262.

24. Allen, *In English Ways,* pp. 184–204. About half the church members left Roxbury, according to Bugbee, "A Society of Continuance," p. 155.

25. *Roxbury Land and Church Records,* cited in Anderson, *The Great Migration Begins,* 1: 437.

26. Wealth comparisons based on deflated values from all surviving clerks' copies of probate inventories and accounts for 1661–1675 from Suffolk and Essex Counties in Massachusetts, Plymouth Colony, Rhode Island, New Haven Colony, and Hartford District, Connecticut. Thomas Hooker's petition is quoted in William DeLoss Love, *The Colonial History of Hartford: Gathered from the Original Records* (Hartford: privately published, 1914), p. 116.

27. Michael G. Hall, *The Last American Puritan: The Life of Increase Mather* (Middletown, Conn.: Wesleyan University Press, 1988), p. 30.

28. Stephen Innes, *Labor in a New Land: Economy and Society in Seventeenth-Century Springfield* (Princeton: Princeton University Press, 1983), pp. 14–16; Philip F. Gura, *A Glimpse of Sion's Glory: Puritan Radicalism in New England, 1620–1660* (Middletown, Conn.: Wesleyan University Press, 1984), pp. 304–322.

29. Allen, *In English Ways*, p. 119; Bond, *Genealogies of Watertown*, p. 983; Nathaniel Ward to John Winthrop Jr., December 24, 1635, *Winthrop Papers*, 3: 215.

30. Anderson, *Great Migration Begins*, pp. 1433–38.

31. Ibid., p. 1435.

32. Ralph J. Crandall and Ralph J. Coffman, "From Emigrants to Rulers: The Charlestown Oligarchy in the Great Migration," *New England Historic and Genealogical Society* 131 (1977): 3–27, 121–132, 207–213. Half of those who settled Charlestown in the 1630s left.

33. Martin, *Profits in the Wilderness*, pp. 46–110.

34. Ibid., pp. 131–148.

35. Kathleen Davidson March, "Uncommon Civility: The Narragansett Indians and Roger Williams" (Ph.D. diss., University of Iowa, 1985). Arnold later served as governor of Rhode Island and amassed some 5,000 acres in thirteen parcels scattered among four towns; Martin, *Profits in the Wilderness*, pp. 74, 307.

36. Bruce C. Daniels, *The Connecticut Town: Growth and Development, 1632–1790* (Middletown, Conn.: Wesleyan University Press, 1979), pp. 119–121.

37. Kenneth A. Lockridge terms Dedham "A Utopian Commune" in *A New England Town: The First Hundred Years: Dedham, Massachusetts, 1636–1736* (New York: W. W. Norton, 1970), pp. 4–5.

38. *Journal of John Winthrop*, pp. 168–170, 173; Michael Hall, *The Last American Puritan*, pp. 19–20.

39. Lockridge, *A New England Town*, pp. 24–30.

40. Lockridge says that 70 percent of the adult men in town in 1648 were members of the church; ibid., p. 31. According to another estimate, 60 percent of all men whose names appear in Dedham records were members of the church, roughly the same proportion as in neighboring Roxbury (62 percent) and Dorchester (63 percent), slightly less than in Charlestown (65 percent), but more than in Cambridge (56 percent) and Watertown (41 percent); Wall, *Massachusetts Bay*, p. 39.

41. Lockridge, *A New England Town*, p. 83. The map on page x shows the thirteen modern towns encompassed by the original Dedham town grant of 1637, an area of some 200 square miles. Dedham fought the incorporation of Natick in 1651 on its western side as a "Praying Town" for Christian Indians, probably because its location on the Charles involved choice land.

42. Martin, *Profits in the Wilderness*, pp. 149–161; Daniels, *The Connecticut Town*, p. 120; Lockridge, *A New England Town*, pp. 8–10.

43. Martin, *Profits in the Wilderness*, pp. 42, 51, 205. Martin points out that only

sixty-eight out of ninety-two taxpayers in 1663 were proprietors of common land in Dedham and that therefore only these sixty-eight were entitled to shares in Deerfield.

44. Martin, *Profits in the Wilderness,* pp. 186–216; Elizabeth Pearson White, *John Howland of the Mayflower,* vol. 2 (Camden, Maine: Picton Press, 1993), p. 18.

45. Sumner Chilton Powell, *Puritan Village: The Formation of a New England Town* (Garden City, N.Y.: Doubleday, 1963), pp. 102–129.

46. Ibid., pp. 119–123.

47. Ibid., pp. 152–170.

48. Ibid., pp. 160, 171–177.

49. Philip Greven, *Four Generations: Population, Land, and Family in Colonial Andover, Massachusetts* (Ithaca: Cornell University Press, 1970), pp. 132–133.

50. Virginia DeJohn Anderson, "King Philip's Herds," *William and Mary Quarterly* 51 (1994): 623–624.

4. Sexuality, Courtship, and Marriage

Epigraph: Abigail Young is quoted in *Mayflower Descendant* 15 (1914): 79.

1. The universality of the desire for children is the theme of an extensive literature by evolutionary biologists and their colleagues in related disciplines. See, for instance, the essays in Patricia Adair Gowaty, ed., *Feminism and Evolutionary Biology* (New York: Chapin and Hall, 1997); Jane B. Lancaster, Jeanne Altman, Alice S. Rossi, and Lonnie R. Sherrod, eds., *Parenting across the Life Span: Biosocial Dimensions* (New York: Aldine de Gruyter, 1987); and Mary Ellen Morbeck, Alison Galloway, and Adrienne L. Zihlman, eds., *The Evolving Female: A Life-History Perspective* (Princeton: Princeton University Press, 1997). For a parallel viewpoint but a different theoretical model, see Gary S. Becker, *A Treatise on the Family* (Cambridge, Mass.: Harvard University Press, 1991).

2. Laura Betzig, Monique Borgerhoff Mulder, and Paul Turke, eds., *Human Reproductive Behaviour: A Darwinian Perspective* (Cambridge: Cambridge University Press, 1988), provides a good introduction to the Darwinist side of the debate on human marital strategies, as do the essays in Morbeck, Galloway, and Zihlman, *The Evolving Female,* part 5, "Women in Human Societies," pp. 179–258; and the remarkable new synthesis by Sarah Blaffer Hrdy, *Mother Nature: A History of Mothers, Infants, and Natural Selection* (New York: Pantheon Books, 1999). On female choices for mates, see ibid., pp. 36–42. For a valuable introduction to the history of marriage and the family by historians, see Tamara K. Hareven, "The History of the Family and the Complexity of Social Change," *American Historical Review* 96 (1991): 95–124. Especially useful for Christian Europe are David Herlihy, "Family," *American Historical Review* 96 (1991): 1–16; and Martha C. Howell, "Herlihy's Families," *Journal of Interdisciplinary History* 28 (1998): 417–425. On early modern England, see Lawrence Stone, *The Family, Sex, and Marriage in England, 1500–1800* (New York: Harper & Row, 1977); Ralph Houlbrooke, *The English Family* (Cambridge: Cambridge University Press,

1982); and Alan Macfarlane, *Love and Marriage in England, 1300–1700* (Oxford: Blackwell, 1988). For more gender-sensitive discussions, see Laura Gowing, *Domestic Dangers: Women, Words and Sex in Early Modern London* (Oxford: Clarendon Press, 1996), especially chaps. 5 and 6; and Margaret R. Hunt, *The Middling Sort: Commerce, Gender, and the Family in England, 1680–1780* (Berkeley: University of California Press, 1996), especially chap. 6. For New England, Edmund S. Morgan, *The Puritan Family: Religion and Domestic Relations in Seventeenth-Century New England* (New York: Harper & Row, 1966), is the enduring classic study. Mary Beth Norton, *Founding Mothers and Fathers: Gendered Power and the Forming of American Society* (New York: Alfred A. Knopf, 1996), updates Morgan and adds a valuable comparative perspective emphasizing gender and power in marital relations. Two works continue to be influential on historians' interpretation of early New England families: John Demos, *A Little Commonwealth: Family Life in Plymouth Colony* (Oxford: Oxford University Press, 1970); and Philip J. Greven Jr., *Four Generations: Population, Land, and Family in Colonial Andover, Massachusetts* (Ithaca: Cornell University Press, 1970).

3. Roger Williams, *A Key into the Language of America*, ed. John J. Teunissen and Evelyn J. Hinz (Detroit: Wayne State University Press, 1973), p. 206.

4. William Wood, *New England's Prospect*, ed. Alden T. Vaughan (Amherst: University of Massachusetts Press, 1977), p. 99; Neal Salisbury, "Indians and Colonists in Southern New England after the Pequot War: An Uneasy Balance," in *The Pequots in Southern New England: The Fall and Rise of an American Indian Nation*, ed. Laurence M. Hauptman and James D. Wherry (Norman: University of Oklahoma Press, 1990), pp. 81–95; idem, *Manitou and Providence: Indians, Europeans, and the Making of New England, 1500–1643* (New York: Oxford University Press, 1982), pp. 150, 232–233.

5. Williams, *A Key into the Language*, pp. 205–209. I have taken the liberty of rearranging his statements for purposes of clarity. Wood and Edward Winslow likewise assert that husbands would punish their wife's lover and "put her away"; Wood, *New England's Prospect*, p. 100; Edward Winslow, *Relation* (1624), reprinted in Alexander Young, ed., *Chronicles of the Pilgrim Fathers of the Colony of Plymouth, from 1602 to 1624*, 2d ed. (1844; reprint, Baltimore: Genealogical Publishing, 1974), p. 349. See also Richard White, "What Chigabe Knew: Indians, Household Government, and the State," *William and Mary Quarterly* 52 (1995): 151–156.

6. Sara Mendelson and Patricia Crawford, *Women in Early Modern England, 1550–1720* (Oxford: Clarendon Press, 1998), pp. 18–30; Charles J. Hoadley, ed., *Records of the Colony and Plantation of New Haven, from 1638 to 1649* (Hartford: Case, Tiffany, 1857), October 18, 1654, p. 123.

7. Gowing, *Domestic Dangers*, p. 193; Edmund Leites, *The Puritan Conscience and Modern Sexuality* (New Haven: Yale University Press, 1986), pp. 75–76.

8. Martin Ingram, *Church Courts, Sex and Marriage in England, 1570–1640* (Cambridge: Cambridge University Press, 1988), chaps. 4 and 6; idem, "The Reform of Popular Culture? Sex and Marriage in Early Modern England," in *Popular Culture in Seventeenth-Century England*, ed. Barry Reay (New York: St. Martin's

Press, 1985), pp. 129–165; Lawrence Stone, *Uncertain Unions: Marriage in England, 1660–1753* (New York: Oxford University Press, 1991); idem, *Road to Divorce: England, 1530–1987* (New York: Oxford University Press, 1990), part 1; Susan Dwyer Amussen, *An Ordered Society: Gender and Class in Early Modern England* (Oxford: Basil Blackwell, 1988), chap. 2.

9. According to Cornelia Hughes Dayton, magistrates in New Haven courts were less than rigorous in applying the two-witness rule in cases of rape; Dayton, *Women before the Bar: Gender, Law, and Society in Connecticut, 1639–1789* (Chapel Hill: University of North Carolina Press, 1995), p. 60. County court records occasionally turn up cases of sexual behavior not anticipated by the laws. See, for instance, Norton, *Founding Mothers and Fathers,* p. 48, quoting Samuel Eliot Morison, ed., *Records of the Suffolk County Court, 1671–1680,* 2 vols. (Boston: Colonial Society of Massachusetts, 1933), 1: 49–351, 478–479.

10. Barbara B. Smuts, "The Evolutionary Origins of Patriarchy," *Human Nature* 6 (1995): 1–32; Jane Lancaster, "Evolutionary History of Human Parental Investment," in *Feminism and Evolutionary Biology: Boundaries, Intersections, and Frontiers,* ed. Patricia Adair Gowaty (New York: Chapman & Hall and International Thomson, 1997), pp. 475–476; Joan Frigole Reixach, "Procreation and Its Implications for Gender, Marriage, and Family in European Rural Ethnography," *Anthropological Quarterly* 71 (1998): 32–39.

11. Morgan, *The Puritan Family,* pp. 29–64; Norton, *Founding Mothers and Fathers,* pp. 62–77; *Records of the Court of Assistants of the Colony of Massachusetts Bay, 1630–1692,* 3 vols. (Boston: County of Suffolk, 1901–1928), vol. 2, part 2, p. 138. On divorce in early New England, see Norton, pp. 89–91; Nancy F. Cott, "Divorce and the Changing Status of Women in Eighteenth-Century Massachusetts," *William and Mary Quarterly* 34 (1977): 542–571; idem, "Eighteenth-Century Family and Social Life Revealed in Massachusetts Divorce Records," *Journal of Social History* 10 (1976): 20–43; Henry S. Cohn, "Connecticut's Divorce Mechanism, 1636–1969," *American Journal of Legal History* 14 (1970): 35–55. See also Marylynn Salmon, *Women and the Law of Property in Early America* (Chapel Hill: University of North Carolina Press, 1986), chap. 4; and D. Kelly Weisberg, "Under Great Temptations Here: Women and Divorce Law in Puritan Massachusetts," in *Woman and the Law: A Social Historical Perspective,* ed. D. Kelly Weisberg (Cambridge, Mass.: Schenkman, 1982).

12. Salmon, *Women and the Law of Property,* p. 60. Divorce cases in Massachusetts appear in *Records of Court of Assistants.* For instance, 3: 146 (1664) contains the petition of Sarah Helwis, née Hawthorn, whose husband was a mercenary in Ireland, had there married another woman, and had a child by her. The court declared Sarah freed from him and at liberty to remarry. In ibid., p. 253, there is a court order dated October 23, 1672, granting a divorce to Nanny, wife of Edward Nailer and daughter of John Wheelwright, on grounds of Edward's breach of the marriage covenant. He was forbidden to remain in Boston, a sentence that suggests he was the guilty party in the marriage, yet the court awarded him, as the father, custody of the children.

13. Lyle Koehler, *A Search for Power: The "Weaker Sex" in Seventeenth-Century New*

England (Urbana: University of Illinois Press, 1980); Dayton, *Women before the Bar,* app. 1, "Divorce Petitions, Connecticut and New Haven Colonies, 1639–1710," pp. 329–333, and her discussion in chap. 3.

14. The following pages deal with material taken from divorces and court cases about the sexual responsibilities of husbands and were written before the appearance of Thomas A. Foster's excellent article on the same topic, "Deficient Husbands: Manhood, Sexual Incapacity, and Male Marital Sexuality in Seventeenth-Century New England," *William and Mary Quarterly* 56 (1999): 723–744. My argument is much the same.

15. *Suffolk Deeds,* 14 vols. (Boston: Rockwell and Churchill Press, 1880–1906), 1: 83–84; Richard D. Pierce, ed., *Records of the First Church in Boston, 1630–1868* (Boston: Colonial Society of Massachusetts, 1961), pp. 46–49. Sarah had imbibed some radical religious ideas while in London, according to a letter by Stephen Winthrop, and she was admonished by the Boston church for "Irregular Prophesying in mixt Assemblies," a complaint similar to that made against Anne Hutchinson ten years earlier. Family information is from Robert Charles Anderson, *The Great Migration Begins: Immigrants to New England, 1620–1633,* 3 vols. (Boston: New England Historic Genealogical Society, 1995), 1: 582–587, who also reprints Dudley's will, codicils, and part of the letter from Keayne to Dudley, in which he also states, "she has unwived herself," and excerpts from other letters relating to the scandal. Thomas Dudley's will mentions no children by Sarah Pacy and awards her only a small annuity, to be paid by his other heirs, making no mention of her husband. According to a petition dated January 29, 1683/84, by Captain Nicholas Paige and Anna, his wife and sole heir of Captain Robert Keayne, Benjamin Keayne had died before his father, who wrote his will in 1653. His death would have freed her to remarry; Judith McGhan, ed., *Suffolk County Wills: Abstracts of the Earliest Wills upon Record in the County of Suffolk, Massachusetts* (Baltimore: Genealogical Publishing, 1984), pp. 65, 360.

16. *Records of Court of Assistants,* 3: 67 (1658). A year later she and Lane asked the governor to be remarried, a request that he declined to grant but said if the "Cause was removed" that had prompted the court to declare their marriage null, then the "Nullity was voyde"; Edmund S. Morgan, *A Boston Heiress and Her Husbands* (Boston: Colonial Society of Massachusetts, 1939), pp. 499–513. This is the same Anna who married Nicholas Paige and petitioned the court for the administration of her grandfather's estate in 1684. (See previous note.)

17. Hoadley, *Records of Colony of New Haven,* 2: 199–202. In Massachusetts, Margaret Bennet moved the court to annul her daughter's marriage on the grounds of her husband's "Insufficiency & her desire of being freed from him that hath nor cannot perform the duty or office of a husband to her." He had been asked if when he lay with his wife "there were any motion in him." He said yes "and for hours," but "when he turned to hir It was gone againe." The court declared that there was not sufficient ground to separate them but "advised them to a more loving & suitable Cohabitation one with the other & that all due phisicall meanes may be used"; *Records of Court of Assistants,* 3: 253 (1672).

18. Hoadley, *Records of Colony of New Haven*, 2: 209–212.

19. Middlesex County Court Records, County Court House, Charlestown, Mass., folder 42, group 3, cited by Morgan, *The Puritan Family*, p. 63.

20. Daniel K. Richter, *Ordeal of the Longhouse: The Peoples of the Iroquois League in the Era of European Colonization* (Chapel Hill: University of North Carolina Press, 1992), p. 20.

21. Adam Kuper, *The Chosen Primate: Human Nature and Cultural Diversity* (Cambridge: Cambridge University Press, 1994), p. 200. Kuper points out that even in societies in which women are assertive, sexually adventurous, and active economically on their own account, they do not control men or men's lives. In such societies, the sexes live separate lives.

22. See cases discussed in Gowing, *Domestic Dangers;* Ingram, *Church Courts, Sex and Marriage in England;* and Norton, *Founding Mothers and Fathers.*

23. Mendelson and Crawford, *Women in Early Modern England*, pp. 31–34. First quotation is from Keith Thomas, "The Double Standard," *Journal of the History of Ideas* 20 (1959): 216, 210; Gowing, *Domestic Dangers*, p. 192. Second quotation is from a marginal note in the Account Book of William and Thomas Richardson (1662–1702), dated November 1668, Newport Historical Society, Newport, R.I.; quoted in Carl Bridenbaugh, *Fat Mutton and Liberty of Conscience: Society in Rhode Island, 1636–1690* (Providence: Brown University Press, 1974), p. 100. Medical, religious, and popular ideas about women in early seventeenth-century England are explored at length by Anthony Fletcher, *Gender, Sex, and Subordination in England 1500–1800* (New Haven: Yale University Press, 1995), pp. 30–98. See the close, positive reading of *Aristotle's Masterpiece*, a popular late seventeenth-century sex manual that underwent many editions, by Roy Porter and Lesley Hall, in *The Facts of Life: The Creation of Sexual Knowledge in Britain, 1650–1950* (New Haven: Yale University Press, 1995), pp. 33–53. Fletcher and Porter would agree with Thomas Laquer, who argues that Europeans, including the English, did not so much view women as a separate or opposite *sex* but as lesser versions or analogues of men; Thomas Laqueur, *Making Sex: Body and Gender from the Greeks to Freud* (Cambridge, Mass.: Harvard University Press, 1990).

24. Mendelson and Crawford, *Women in Early Modern England*, pp. 23–25.

25. John Winthrop, *The Journal of John Winthrop, 1630–1649*, ed. Richard S. Dunn, James Savage, and Laetitia Yeandle (Cambridge, Mass.: Harvard University Press, 1996), p. 570.

26. Suzanne W. Hull, *Chaste, Silent, and Obedient: English Books for Women, 1475–1640* (San Marino, Calif.: Huntington Library, 1982).

27. "My Wife Will be my Master; Or, the Married Man's Complaint against his Unruly Wife . . ." (ca. 1640), quoted in Gowing, *Domestic Dangers*, p. 186.

28. Mary Astell, *Reflections upon Marriage*, 3d ed. (London: R. Wilkin, 1709), quoted in Hunt, *The Middling Sort*, p. 147. In her preface to this edition, Astell accepts the argument for the need for a final authority in the family. This, combined with women's physical weakness, she thinks, gives men their advantage. See Bridget Hill, ed., *The First English Feminist: Reflections upon Marriage and Other*

Writings by Mary Astell (New York: St. Martin's Press, 1986); Ruth Perry, *The Celebrated Mary Astell* (Chicago: University of Chicago Press, 1986).

29. Spelling in quotation slightly modernized for readability. They were to have ten pounds given them on their day of marriage, double to the eldest son. These are small sums relative to the inventory value of close to £500. Nathaniel Warren the elder was the eldest son of Richard Warren of the *Mayflower* and his wife Elizabeth, born 1617. He appointed his wife Sarah sole executrix but apparently did not trust her negotiating abilities; C. H. Simmons Jr., ed., *Plymouth Colony Records: Wills and Inventories, 1633–1669,* 2 vols. in 1 (Camden, Maine: Picton Press, 1996), June 29, 1667, 2: 463.

30. Adverse economic conditions in seventeenth-century England hindered poorer people from marrying, but improving economic conditions in the eighteenth century saw rising proportions doing so, and at younger ages; E. A. Wrigley and R. S. Schofield, *The Population History of England, 1541–1871: A Reconstruction* (Cambridge: Cambridge University Press, 1981), pp. 256–265.

31. *The Diary of Ralph Josselin, 1616–1683,* ed. Alan Macfarlane (London: Oxford University Press, 1976), p. 551 (January 1669/70).

32. Lawrence Stone, *The Family, Sex, and Marriage in England, 1500–1800* (New York: Harper & Row, 1977), pp. 30–36, 180–199, 293–297, 390–404.

33. Norton, *Founding Mothers and Fathers,* p. 64.

34. Hunt, *The Middling Sort,* p. 150; Gowing, *Domestic Dangers,* p. 157.

35. Alice Morse Earle published choice collections of these, but one suspects that many of them became embroidered with each retelling to suit the taste of new audiences; Earle, *Customs and Fashions in Old New England* (New York: C. Scribners, 1894).

36. Edward R. Lambert, *History of the Colony of New Haven, Before and After the Union with Connecticut . . .* (New Haven: Hitchcock & Stafford, 1838), pp. 137–138.

37. David Hackett Fischer, *Albion's Seed: Four British Folkways in America* (New York: Oxford University Press, 1989), p. 79; Laurel Thatcher Ulrich, *Good Wives: Image and Reality in the Lives of Women in Northern New England, 1650–1750* (New York: Alfred A. Knopf, 1982), pp. 122–123, locates the practice in the late eighteenth century.

38. Judges called on midwives to testify whether such babies were full-term or premature. Sexual misdemeanors made up 5 percent of court business in Middlesex County, Massachusetts. Roger Thompson, *Sex in Middlesex: Popular Mores in a Massachusetts County, 1649–1699* (Amherst: University of Massachusetts Press, 1986), p. 55; Hoadley, *Records of Colony of New Haven,* 1: 75 (August 5, 1642) and 77 (September 7, 1642). Roger Thompson says "too soon" meant seven months, but his only citation is to Cotton Mather, *Ratio Disciplinae Fratrum Nov-Anglicom* (Boston, 1726), p. 143.

39. If one defines premarital pregnancy as likely whenever a baby arrived earlier than 8.5 months after the marriage, an extreme definition that undoubtedly exaggerates its incidence, the average proportion of brides who were pregnant before 1670 was only about 7 out of 100. This proportion is significantly lower

than in England at this time, which was about 20 out of 100, albeit with great variability by region. (Town genealogies and vital records consulted for estimates of bridal pregnancy include New Haven, Guilford, Windsor, Weymouth, Rowley, Salisbury, and Watertown, plus Howland descendants in Plymouth Colony.) I have excluded marriages in which the interval between the marriage and the first recorded birth or baptism was longer than thirty-six months, on the grounds that such very long intervals were more likely a product of inadequate recordkeeping than of actual circumstances. About a third of the marriages in the period before 1690 went unrecorded, or the birth date or baptismal date of the first child was lacking. On bridal pregnancy in England, see Wrigley and Schofield, *Population History of England*, p. 254; and Paul Griffiths, *Youth and Authority* (Oxford: Oxford University Press, 1996), pp. 238–240.

40. Gowing, *Domestic Dangers*, chap. 5.
41. *Diary of Ralph Josselin*, p. 632 (June 2, 1681).
42. Ulrich, *Good Wives*, p. 119.
43. Morgan lists several cases among well-to-do families in which the children expressed themselves as ever dutiful to their parents' direction, but he nevertheless concluded that "parents and children had both to consent to a match and that in practice either might take the first steps to bring it about"; *The Puritan Family*, p. 86.
44. Ibid., pp. 31–32.
45. Charles William Manwaring, comp., *A Digest of Early Connecticut Probate Records*, 3 vols. (Hartford: R. S. Peck, 1906), 1: 91 (August 26, 1657). See the profile of Jeremy Adams and his family in Anderson, *The Great Migration Begins*, 1: 6–11. Almost a century later an angry parent was still attempting to control his child's marital choice by fiat. Joshua Hempstead recorded in his diary on February 9, 1746: "Christopher Stubbins hath Set on the Meetinghouse doorpost a Paper by him Signed forbiding any person to Joyn his Daughter Lydia in Mariage Covenant with a stranger (I dont Remember his name) to whom She was published Last Sunday"; *Diary of Joshua Hempstead from September, 1711 to November, 1758* (New London, Conn.: New London County Historical Society, 1901), p. 455.
46. W. C. Pelkly, ed., *Early Records of the Town of Providence*, 21 vols. (Providence: Snow & Farnham, 1892–1915), 6: 26–27 (February 9, 1681).
47. *Mayflower Descendant* 6 (1905): 169; and Simmons, *Plymouth Colony Records*, 1: 50.
48. Richard Dexter in Thompson, *Sex in Middlesex*, p. 35; Abigail Young in *Mayflower Descendant* 15 (1914): 79. This was in 1692, in Eastham, in Plymouth County.
49. Manwaring, *Connecticut Probate Records*, 1: 5.
50. The brides of Ephraim and Joseph were daughters of James Avery, to whom their father had contracted the service of their brother, Thomas, some ten years before; *The Diary of Thomas Minor, Stonington, Connecticut, 1653–1685* (New London, Conn.: Day, 1899), April 15, 1657; April 11, 1666; March 18, 1667; September 27 and November 26, 1662; and January 19, 1663. Clement and Fran-

ces had more children, including one only a year after the first, but Frances died December 6, 1672, six weeks after giving birth to another daughter. Clement remarried within ten weeks of her death.

51. Hunt, *The Middling Sort,* p. 151.

52. Although one might suppose that husbands were especially nice to wives from affluent and well-connected families, Hunt found horrific examples in England of men using physical violence or its threat as revenge for their disappointments with dowry payments or as blackmail for extorting more; Hunt, *The Middling Sort,* p. 154; Pelkly, *Early Records of Providence,* 3: 169–171.

53. *Mayflower Descendant* 7 (1906): 65. Young William was born in 1624 and died there in 1704. He and Alice married in 1650. She was born in England ca. 1627 and died in Plymouth in 1671. They had ten children together; Robert S. Wakefield and Lee D. van Antwerp, comps., *William Bradford of the Mayflower and His Descendants for Four Generations,* 4th ed. (Plymouth, Mass.: General Society of Mayflower Descendants, 1994), pp. 7–8. See also *Suffolk Deeds,* 2: 54 (ca. 1651), for the marriage portion given by Michael Metcalf to his son of the same name.

54. Nathaniel B. Shurtleff and David Pulsifer, eds., *Records of the Colony of New Plymouth in New England, 1620–1692,* 12 vols. (Boston: White, 1855–1861), vol. 12: *Deeds,* p. 61 (August 5, 1640). Godbertson, a hatter, and his second wife, Sarah Allerton, widow of John Vincent and of Degory Priest, married in Leiden in 1621 and arrived in Plymouth in 1623. She died without a will shortly after his death in 1633; Anderson, *The Great Migration Begins,* pp. 777–778. Captain Arthur Fenner gave his three daughters equal shares in a thirty-four-acre tract of land; Pelkly, *Early Records of Providence,* 4: 170–171 (July 31, 1688). Two of the three girls sold their shares for ten pounds apiece to merchant Gideon Crawford; George F. Dow, ed., *Records and Files of the Quarterly Courts of Essex County, Massachusetts, 1636–1686,* 9 vols. (Salem, Mass.: Essex Institute, 1911–1921), 5: 195, quoted in Anderson *The Great Migration Begins,* p. 567; Shurtleff and Pulsifer, *Records of New Plymouth,* 12: 53.

55. Boston inventory of Edward Winslow, January 19, 1682/83, Suffolk County Probate Records (microfilm), 9: 228, 116.

56. James Russell Trumbull, *History of Northampton, Massachusetts,* 2 vols. (Northampton, Mass.: Massachusetts Gazette Publishing, 1898, 1902), 1: 13–14. This statement is based on a mixed regional sample of probate records from New England dated 1710–1720, deflated to sterling. Both the sample and the deflating process are described in Gloria L. Main and Jackson T. Main, "The Red Queen in New England?" *William and Mary Quarterly* 56 (1999): 121–150. Exchange rates are in John J. McCusker, *Money and Exchange in Europe and America, 1600–1775* (Chapel Hill: University of North Carolina Press, 1978), p. 147. The Maryland comparison comes from Gloria L. Main, *Tobacco Colony: Life in Early Maryland* (Princeton: Princeton University Press, 1982). See also "A compt of Sundry Particulars I give to my dafter Mary that married Job Smith . . . as part of her portion," in Account Book of Capt. Jonathan Burnham,

Chebaco Parish, Ipswich, 1741, Peabody Institute, Salem, Mass. (unpaginated). Likewise, Hampshire County Probate Records (microfilm), 5 (1723–1733): 129 and 6 (1734–1749): 12, 65, 103, itemize wedding portions for daughters. Portions given the daughter of Silvanus and Jemima Allen in 1758 and to her husband are described in Elizabeth Pearson White, *John Howland of the Mayflower,* vol. 1 (Camden, Maine: Picton Press, 1990), pp. 589–590.

57. Except in the wills and settlements of early Connecticut (Hartford, Windsor, and Wethersfield), in which the distributions favored sons over daughters and older siblings over younger.

58. A darker view of seventeenth-century father-son relations appears in Philip J. Greven Jr., "Patriarchalism and the Family," in *Four Generations: Population, Land, and Family in Colonial Andover, Massachusetts* (Ithaca: Cornell University Press, 1970), pp. 72–102. Daniel Vickers, *Farmers and Fishermen: Two Centuries of Work in Essex County, Massachusetts, 1630–1850* (Chapel Hill: University of North Caroline Press, 1994), pp. 64–83, emphasizes the codependence and mutuality of fathers and sons. For more detailed analysis of this question, see Chapter 6 of this book.

59. John Ballantine Journal, October 17, 1769, and February 18, 1767, American Antiquarian Society, Worcester, Mass. The diary of Joshua Hempstead of Stonington does not mention large-scale wedding festivities until the 1750s. The entry for February 21, 1754, describes the wedding celebration of his grandson, Nathaniel Minor, to Ann Denison at Captain John Denison's, where the company was numerous: "more than 100 horses besides near neighbors that came on foot." They then rode up to his son Minor's place, where they stayed the rest of the day and were "entertained liberally with plumb cake and cheese and wine and other strong drink"; *Diary of Joshua Hempstead,* p. 624.

60. Among the 204 wedding dates used in the sample, November and February led, at 30 percent and 26 percent, respectively. The months with the fewest weddings were April, May, June, July, and August.

61. Median ages at marriage in New England were lower than the mean: for men, it remained at 25 except for 1675–1684, when it rose to 26, and for 1745–1774, when it fell to 24. The median age at marriage for women began at 20, rose to 21 in the last quarter of the seventeenth century, then rose to 22, where it stayed until 1745 before falling again to 21. For ages at marriage elsewhere in the colonies, see Fischer, *Albion's Seed,* pp. 76, 285, 487.

62. *Records of Court of Assistants,* vol. 2, part 1, p. 32 (April 1, 1633); Franklin Bowditch Dexter and Zara Jones Powers, eds., *New Haven Town Records,* 3 vols. (New Haven: Ancient Town Records, 1917–1962), 2: 427 (January 3, 1660). According to family and town genealogies, about 96 percent of daughters born in the seventeenth century and known to have survived to adulthood eventually married. That rate fell to 92 percent in the eighteenth century but may have been even lower, because genealogies are naturally biased toward women who show up in the records as a result of marrying and having chil-

63. John D. Cushing, ed., *The Laws of the Pilgrims: A Facsimile Edition of the Book of the General Laws of the Inhabitants of the Jurisdiction of New-Plimouth, 1674 & 1685* (Wilmington, Del.: M. Glazier, 1977).

64. Diary of John May, American Antiquarian Society; Samuel Lane, *A Journal for the Years 1739–1803,* ed. Charles L. Hanson (Concord: New Hampshire Historical Society, 1937); Minor, *Diary,* March 18, 1668. On May's and Lane's careers, see Chapter 8.

65. Gloria L. Main, "Gender, Work, and Wages in Colonial New England," *William and Mary Quarterly* 51 (1994): 39–66.

66. W. C. Rossiter, *American Population before the Federal Census of 1790* (Gloucester, Mass.: Peter Smith, 1966).

67. A similar instrument, the "joynture," is extremely rare in New England records. *Suffolk Deeds,* 2: 155, is a "Jointure Agreement between John Dwight and Henry Phillips," both of Dedham, dated 1653.

68. Zephaniah Smith, *A Digest of the Laws of the State of Connecticut,* 2 vols. (New Haven, 1822–23), 1: 28–29.

69. Only two-thirds of widows under forty remarried in the eighteenth century. Those forty and over tended not to remarry: 22 percent did so in the seventeenth century and only 10 percent in the eighteenth. These data are based on a subsample of first marriages using family genealogies listed in the Bibliography. These rates are lower than for modern women who separate, divorce, or are widowed, but the negative relationship between age and remarrying is the same.

70. After this ceremony and before saying their vows, "the sayd John Betts in Court renounced all Claymes & Interest to her estate, both Debts and Credits"; Manwaring, *Connecticut Probate Records,* 1: 183 (April 13, 1673).

71. Thompson, *Sex in Middlesex,* p. 43.

72. *Suffolk Deeds,* 7: 92 (1670); Suffolk County Probate Records, 7: 29 (1670). Joshua Hempstead wrote a bond and jointure for Samuel Fox, who "aged about 72 was published to Zipporah Bolles a maiden about 42"; *Diary,* p. 606 (April 19, 1753). In sample genealogies, 95 percent of widowers under age forty in the seventeenth century remarried, as did 55 percent of those forty and over.

73. Timothy Baldwin of Milford, January 31, 1665. Timothy's bequest to his wife's son was conditional on his being "obedient, etc."; Manwaring, *Connecticut Probate Records,* 1: 177.

74. "The four children of the Intestate by the sd Widow being intitled to an equal share with the mother in the aforesaid Two hundred and fifty pounds, the same is to be accounted to them accordingly towards their portions"; Settlement of the estate of the Rev. Mr. Samuel Willard, Suffolk County Probate Records, 16: 492 (October 28, 1708).

75. See the discussion of prenuptial agreements and marriage settlements by Amy Louise Erickson, *Women and Property in Early Modern England* (London: Routledge, 1993), p. 31. Erickson does not make clear, however, whether the

men had been married before or had children living, the situation that most often prompted such agreements in New England. New England examples: George F. Dow, ed., *The Probate Records of Essex County, Massachusetts, 1635–1681,* 3 vols. (1916–1920; reprint, Newburyport, Mass.: Parker River Researchers, 1988), 2: 23 (1666); Suffolk County Probate Records, 7: 323 (1673?); 9: 181 (1683); 13: 635 (1695); 16: 453 (1708); 17: 453 (1712); 19: 225 (1716); Nathaniel Bouton et al., eds., *Probate Records, Vols. 1–6,* vols. 31–40 of *Documents and Records Relating to the Province of New Hampshire,* 40 vols. (Concord, 1867–1941); citations are from a microfilm copy, New Hampshire State Archives, Concord, 2: 254 (1681); 4: 187–191 (1752); 16: 453 (1708); *Suffolk Deeds,* 35: 34 (1715).

76. Dow, *Essex County Probate Records,* 1: 81–82. Another example: William Wardell and Elizabeth Gillett, widow of John, signed a marriage contract prior to 1657, wherein it was agreed that she could bequeath her property by a will or at the marriage of her children, one of whom was only two years old at the time; Suffolk County Probate Records, 4: 176. See cases reported by Richard B. Morris, *Studies in the History of American Law, with Special Reference to the Seventeenth and Eighteenth Centuries* (New York: Octagon Books, 1974), pp. 135, 138, 387–388. The judges required assurance from the widow's new husband that he would give each of the children their inheritance as they came of age, and the bond he posted with sureties served part of the purpose of a prenuptial agreement; *Plymouth Colony Records,* 12: 33, quoted in Harriet Woodbury Hodge, comp., *John Billington of the Mayflower,* vol. 5 of *Mayflower Families through Five Generations* (Plymouth, Mass.: General Society of Mayflower Descendants, 1991), pp. 31–34. See *Mayflower Descendant* 19 (1918): 144, printed from Plymouth Colony Deeds, March 23, 1672, for promises made by William Tubbs Sr. of Duxboro "engaged unto Dorothy Soames of Scitutate." An example of a very simple form of protection for remarrying widows is the deed of disclaimer in *Suffolk Deeds,* 7: 214 (1671), signed by John Upham Sr. of Maldon prior to marriage with widow Katherine Holland.

77. Dow, *Essex County Probate Records,* 1: 395–397 (1650); another agreement between Thomas Fox and Ellen, "his wife that now is," that same year in Suffolk was very similar; *Suffolk Deeds,* 1: 118–119. Seven marriage contracts and prenuptial agreements, four of which were made in Boston, appear in ibid., vols. 12 and 13. A Wethersfield jointure, ca. 1685, appears in Manwaring, *Connecticut Probate Records,* 1: 55–56.

78. Dexter and Powers, *New Haven Town Records,* 1: 517 (April 1, 1662).

79. Remarriage penalties for widows became more common in the eighteenth century. Widows were normally appointed administrators and executors in cases in which all the children were under age, except in cases of insolvency. On remarriage, these women would surrender that bond, and their new husbands would post new ones. A son coming of age could petition the probate court to force his stepfather to give him his lawful share.

80. *The Diary of Samuel Sewall,* ed. M. Halsey Thomas, 2 vols. (New York: Farrar,

Straus and Giroux, 1973); Kenneth Silverman, *The Life and Times of Cotton Mather* (New York: Columbia University Press, 1985).

81. Lisa Wilson assesses the quality and character of New England marriages through diaries and correspondence in "A Marriage 'Well-Ordered': Love, Power, and Partnership in Colonial New England," in *A Shared Experience: Men, Women, and the History of Gender,* ed. Laura McCall and Donald Yacovone (New York: New York University Press, 1998), pp. 78–97. She believes that most were loving, companionate partnerships, chiefly because of wifely submission to the principle of male superiority.

82. Norton, *Founding Mothers and Fathers,* explores the ambiguity of ideological boundaries separating public and private jurisdictions of authority and responsibility in her first chapter and by means of case studies, pp. 240–277. Further cases are provided by Thompson, *Sex in Middlesex,* pp. 169–189. Dayton, *Women Before the Bar,* sees the eighteenth-century decline in court prosecution of family-related disputes as a loss for women, whereas Helena M. Wall, *Fierce Communion: Family and Community in Early America* (Cambridge, Mass.: Harvard University Press, 1990), regards the pro-active neighbor and magistrate as intrusive and destructive of privacy; see especially pp. 7–12.

83. Roger Williams, *Correspondence,* ed. Glenn W. LaFantasie, 2 vols. (Hanover, N.H.: Brown University Press and University Press of New England, 1988), 1: 156.

84. *Plymouth Colony Records,* 6: 190–191, 203; *Court of Assistants,* 2: 74 (October 6, 1635, and May 4, 1638). Another example of legal separate maintenance comes from Morris, *Studies in American Law,* pp. 139–140. Henry Sewall also stirred up a ruckus in the Newbury town meeting of 1638; David Grayson Allen, *In English Ways: The Movement of Societies and the Transferal of English Local Law and Custom to Massachusetts Bay in the Seventeenth Century* (Williamsburg, Va.: Institute of Early American History of Culture and Chapel Hill: University of North Carolina, 1981), p. 114. He was again before the Court of Assistants in 1640, and that same year a grand jury indicted Sewall for disturbing the worship and arguing with his pastor in church. Born in Coventry in 1576, he inherited considerable property, but both his father and his mother castigated him in their wills. See the biographical sketch in *The Diary of Samuel Sewall,* 2: 1072–74.

85. Cushing, *The Laws of the Pilgrims,* p. 28: "No man shall strike his wife or any woman her husband."

86. Demos, *A Little Commonwealth,* pp. 93–95; Norton, *Founding Mothers and Fathers,* p. 74.

87. G. Andrews Moriarty, "Herodias (Long) Hicks-Gardiner-Porter: A Tale of Old Newport," in *Genealogies of Rhode Island Families,* 2 vols. (Baltimore: Genealogical Publishing, 1983), 1: 599–607.

88. For instance, Peter Thacher Diary, typescript 1 (January 28, 1681), Massachusetts Historical Society, Boston, in which he states that "Mr. Davis" has been married thirty years and the Thachers are invited to their feast. Diaries and correspondence overwhelmingly testify to the marital satisfaction of their male

authors, according to Wilson, "A Marriage 'Well-Ordered,' " but such records tend to draw from the more privileged strata of colonial society. Chapter 8 considers this matter further, especially for the eighteenth century.

89. Daniel King's Diary, photocopy, Massachusetts Historical Society (original at Peabody Institute Library, Salem, Mass.). Joshua Hempstead, whose chronicles epitomize the stereotypical hard-working, stiff-upper-lipped Yankee, broke a thirty-year silence when he confided to his diary: "I was at home all day & did no work Remembering that this day 30 years my Dear Wife Departed this Life"; *Diary,* p. 465.

90. Colonel Joseph Pitkin's diary/memoir, 1695–1762, Connecticut State Archives, Hartford.

5. Bearing and Losing Children

Epigraph: *The Complete Works of Anne Bradstreet,* ed. Joseph R. McElrath Jr. and Alan P. Robb (Boston: Twayne, 1981), p. 37.

1. Laura Gowing, *Domestic Dangers: Women, Words, and Sex in Early Modern London* (Oxford: Clarendon Press, 1996), pp. 193–194.

2. Merry E. Wiesner, *Women and Gender in Early Modern Europe* (Cambridge: Cambridge University Press, 1993), pp. 46–50; Anthony Fletcher, *Gender, Sex, and Subordination in England, 1500–1800* (New Haven: Yale University Press, 1995), pp. 56–57, 104; Otho T. Beall Jr., "Aristotle's Master Piece," *William and Mary Quarterly* 20 (1963): 207–222; and see Porter's lengthy investigation of this advice manual in Roy Porter and Lesley Hall, *The Facts of Life: The Creation of Sexual Knowledge in Britain, 1650–1950* (New Haven: Yale University Press, 1995), pp. 33–53.

3. Judith K. Brown, "A Note on the Division of Labor by Sex," *American Anthropologist* 72 (1970): 1073–78; Alice S. Rossi, "Parenthood in Transition: From Lineage to Child to Self-Orientation," in *Parenting across the Life Span: Biosocial Dimensions,* ed. Jane B. Lancaster, Jeanne Altmann, Alice S. Rossi, and Lonnie R. Sherrod (New York: Aldine de Gruyter, 1987), especially pp. 54–71; Jane B. Lancaster, "Evolutionary History of Human Parental Investment," in *Feminism and Evolutionary Biology: Boundaries, Intersections, and Frontiers,* ed. Patricia Adair Gowaty (New York: Chapman & Hall: International Thomson, 1997), p. 473; Joan Frigole Reixach, "Procreation and Its Implications for Gender, Marriage, and Family in European Rural Ethnography," *Anthropological Quarterly* 71, (1998): 32–39.

4. Mammals that live in social groups are usually matrilineally organized: the daughters stay and the sons leave. Gregarious, socially skilled daughters who remain nearby will help each other out and gain a competitive advantage for their children. Evolutionarily speaking, then, the social skills and braininess of humankind appear to be inherited through the mother; Sharon Blaffer Hrdy, *Mother Nature: A History of Mothers, Infants, and Natural Selection* (New York: Pantheon Books, 1999), pp. 143–144.

5. Darwinians argue that natural selection has programmed humans to want chil-

dren. See, for instance, Richard Dawkins, *The Selfish Gene,* 2d ed. (New York: Oxford University Press, 1989). On medical ideas about the human body in early modern Europe and England, see Wiesner, *Women and Gender,* pp. 9–81; and Fletcher, *Gender, Sex, and Subordination,* p. 114.

6. Hester Thrale (1741–1821), *Thraliana: The Diary of Mrs. Hester Lynch Thrale,* ed. Katherine Balderstone, 2 vols., 2d ed. (Oxford: Clarendon Press, 1951), quoted by Linda Pollock in *Forgotten Children: Parent-Child Relations from 1500 to 1900* (Cambridge: Cambridge University Press, 1983), p. 389.

7. Michael MacDonald, *Mystical Bedlam: Madness, Anxiety, and Healing in Seventeenth-Century England* (Cambridge: Cambridge University Press, 1981).

8. Justus Forward Diaries, American Antiquarian Society, Worcester, Mass.

9. Inga Clendinnen, *Aztecs: An Interpretation* (Cambridge: Cambridge University Press, 1991), pp. 174–184.

10. Adrian Wilson, *The Making of Man-Midwifery: Childbirth in England, 1660–1770* (Cambridge, Mass.: Harvard University Press, 1995); Laurel Thatcher Ulrich, "'Living Mother of a Living Child': Midwifery and Mortality in Post-Revolution England," *William and Mary Quarterly* 46 (1989): 30; Peter Thacher Diary, Typescript 1, Massachusetts Historical Society, Boston, April 14, May 7 and 16, and June 3, 1680.

11. Wilson, *The Making of Man-Midwifery,* p. 25. "Father and I sitting in the great Hall, heard the child cry . . . Went home with the Midwife about 2 o'clock, carrying her Stool, whoes parts were included in a Bagg. Met with the Watch at Mr. Rocks Brew House, bad us stand, enquired what we were. I told the Woman's occupation, so they bad God bless our labours and let us pass"; *The Diary of Samuel Sewall, 1675–1729,* ed. M. Halsey Thomas, 2 vols. (New York: Farrar, Straus and Giroux, 1973), 1: 41 (April 2, 1677). Another diarist husband persistently struck a pose of laconic indifference to the process: "Got the midwife and women to my wife early in the morning and went in the afternoon and finished raising the meeting house. Oct 16. my wife delivered about 8 in the morning of a son and sold a cow to Wm Macneal of New Boston. Oct 17. Carried home the midwife which was Deacon Boyes wife and had not money to pay her"; *Diary of Matthew Patten of New Bedford, New Hampshire* (New Bedford, Mass.: Picton Press, 1993), October 15–17, 1755. After noting the general muster of officers and men the day before, Joshua Hempstead of Stonington, Connecticut, commented: "they were mustering the Weomen for Stephens Wife & before 9 of ye Clock she was safely d'd of a Daughter"; Joshua Hempstead, *Diary of Joshua Hempstead from September, 1711 to November, 1758* (New London: County Historical Society Collections, 1901), p. 467 (September 11–12, 1746).

12. Wilson, *The Making of Man-Midwifery,* pp. 30–31.

13. Peter Thacher Diary, Typescript 1, April 14, 1680. Samuel Sewall mentioned brewing "my Wives Groaning Beer," for her first lying-in; *Diary,* 1: 36.

14. Ibid., p. 38 (March 1, 1683). There were other things that could go badly wrong, such as sudden high blood pressure in the mother, producing a stroke.

Sewall reported: "Esther Kein at her Time, falls into Convulsion Fits, and dyes last Thorsday. No likelihood of the Child's being born"; *Diary,* 1: 87 (December 12, 1685).

15. Quoted in Ulrich, "'Living Mother of a Living Child,'" p. 32.

16. Ibid., p. 35.

17. Thacher Diary, Typescript 2, August 19, 1682.

18. Little is known about the practice of swaddling. Wilson, *The Making of Man-Midwifery,* bases his remarks on E. L. Lipton et al., "Swaddling, a Child Care Practice: Historical, Cultural and Experimental Observations," *Paediatrics,* suppl. 35 (1965): 519–567. Karin Calvert opens her book with a description of the midwife placing the newborn infant on her lap, firmly but gently molding the baby's body, stretching its legs and arms out full length, and then wrapping the entire form in linen bandages to keep the child firmly straight; Calvert, *Child in the House: The Material of Early Childhood, 1660–1900* (Boston: Northeastern University Press, 1992), pp. 19–38. All of this is based on a single Italian source from the fifteenth century that was published in English in the early seventeenth century. The purpose of this mummylike bandaging was to prevent bodily deformation caused by rickets, says Calvert, the true sources of which people did not understand. The evidence on swaddling in England is elusive and indirect; hence it is difficult to judge how widespread the practic was and whether it was as tight as this description seems to insist. In any event, the cost of the linen and the time-consuming nature of wrapping and unwrapping would seemingly have restricted its practice to well-off households.

19. Massachusetts Historical Society Collections, 1st ser., vol. 9 (Boston, 1900), p. 176.

20. Ross W. Beales Jr., "Nursing and Weaning in an Eighteenth-Century New England Household," in *Families and Children,* ed. Peter Benes (Cambridge, Mass.: Boston University Press, 1987), pp. 48–63.

21. *The Journal of Esther Edwards Burr, 1754–1757,* ed. Carol F. Karlsen and Laurie Crumpacker (New Haven: Yale University Press, 1984), p. 142 (August 7, 1755); Sewall, *Diary,* 1: 460 (January 16, 1702).

22. English diarist Nicholas Blundell wrote in 1704 that "my wife's month being now out we lay together." In 1655 John Stewkely, of Hampshire, England, wrote during his wife's pregnancy to Sir Ralph Verney that he "desired a man's society during his gander-month." Both are quoted in David Cressy, *Birth, Marriage, and Death: Ritual, Religion, and the Life-Cycle in Tudor and Stuart England* (Oxford: Oxford University Press, 1997), p. 204; Thacher Diary, Typescript 1 (April 14, May 7, May 16, June 3, 1680).

23. Roger Thompson, *Sex in Middlesex: Popular Mores in a Massachusetts County, 1649–1699* (Amherst: University of Massachusetts Press, 1986), p. 208. Midwife Martha Ballard's diary occasionally records the names and time of arrival of the "afternurse," who cared for the woman during lying-in; Ulrich, "'Living Mother of a Living Child,'" pp. 39–40.

24. Parkman and Orvall quoted in Barbara Hanawalt, *The Ties That Bound: Peasant*

Families in Medieval England (New York: Oxford University Press, 1989), p. 217; David Cressy, "Purification, Thanksgiving, and the Churching of Women in Post-Reformation England," *Past & Present* 141 (1993): 106–146. The Book of Common Prayer required that the child be baptized on the first or second Sunday after birth, according to Wilson, *The Making of Man-Midwifery,* p. 28. Genealogies of colonial New England families that report the dates of both birth and baptism normally show short lapses of only one or two weeks between them. Note that it was the midwife who bore Sewall's infants to church for baptism.

25. James Axtell, *Indian Peoples of Eastern America: A Documentary History of the Sexes* (New York: Oxford University Press, 1981), pp. 10–11, 17–24; Roger Williams, *A Key into the Language of America,* ed. John T. Teunissen and Evelyn J. Hing (Hanover, N.H.: Brown University Press and University Press of New England, 1988), pp. 117, 121, 207; John Oliver, *A Present for Teeming Women . . .* (London: Sarah Griffin for Mary Rothwell, 1663).

26. Keith Thomas, *Religion and the Decline of Magic: Studies in Popular Beliefs in Sixteenth- and Seventeenth-Century England* (Harmondsworth: Penguin, 1978), pp. 68–69; and Ulrich, "'Living Mother of a Living Child,'" p. 30.

27. Cornelia Hughes Dayton, *Women before the Bar: Gender, Law, and Society in Connecticut, 1639–1787* (Chapel Hill: University of North Carolina Press, 1995), p. 21.

28. Quoted in Mary Beth Norton, *Founding Mothers & Fathers: Gendered Power and the Forming of American Society* (New York: Alfred A. Knopf, 1996), p. 359. Hutchinson was excommunicated for heresy, however, and not for unwomanliness. Samuel Sewall, who was extremely status conscious, always referred to the midwife in his diary as "Mrs." or "Madame," titles of respect.

29. Wilson, *The Making of Man-Midwifery,* p. 32; Robert A. Erickson, "'The Books of Generation': Some Observations on the Style of the English Midwife Books, 1671–1764," in *Sexuality in Eighteenth-Century Britain,* ed. Paul-Gabriel Bouche (Manchester: Manchester University Press, 1982).

30. Thomas Walter Laqueur, *Making Sex: Body and Gender from the Greeks to Freud* (Cambridge, Mass.: Harvard University Press, 1996), chap. 5, "Discovery of the Sexes." Laqueur emphasizes that new anatomical knowledge did not create the new polarity; rather the underlying political relationships between men and women were changing, and the new knowledge was put to service in the cause of male political needs.

31. More accurate knowledge of anatomy did not alter the practice of general medicine, however, according to John Harley Warner, *The Therapeutic Perspective* (Cambridge, Mass.: Harvard University Press, 1986).

32. Ulrich, "'Living Mother of a Living Child,'" p. 46; idem, *A Mid-Wife's Tale: The Life of Martha Ballard, Based on Her Diary, 1785–1812* (New York: Vintage, 1991). White, middle-class, native-born women hired physicians for their confinements beginning quite early in the nineteenth century, according to Judith Walzer Leavitt, *Brought to Bed: Childbearing in America, 1750–1950* (New York:

Oxford University Press, 1986); and Sylvia D. Hoffert, *Private Matters: American Attitudes toward Childbearing and Infant Nurture in the Urban North, 1800–1860* (Urbana: University of Illinois Press, 1989). See also Jane B. Donegan, "'Safe Delivered,' But by Whom? Midwives and Men-Midwives in Early America," in *Women and Health in America: Historical Readings,* ed. Judith Walzer Leavitt (Madison: University of Wisconsin Press, 1984), pp. 302–317.

33. B. M. Willmott Dobbie, "An Attempt to Estimate the True Rate of Maternal Mortality, Sixteenth to Eighteenth Centuries," *Medical History* 26 (1982): 79–90, cited by Ulrich, "'Living Mother of a Living Child,'" p. 39. For data on more recent rates of maternal mortality, see Irvine Loudon, *Death in Childbirth: An International Study of Maternal Care and Maternal Mortality, 1800–1950* (New York: Clarendon Press, Oxford, 1992). Martha Ballard delivered 814 babies at the rate of about 30 per year from 1785 to 1812; Ulrich, "'Living Mother of a Living Child,'" p. 33. Wilson estimates that the average midwife's case load in rural areas of England may have been as few as 20 per year, given the sizes of the country villages in which they lived and performed; *The Making of Man-Midwifery,* p. 33. A study of midwives in Wisconsin, 1870–1915, found that active rural midwives attended only about 8 births per year; Charlotte G. Borst, *Catching Babies: The Professionalization of Childbirth, 1870–1920* (Cambridge, Mass.: Harvard University Press, 1995), p. 59.

34. Data on family size are from published genealogies listed in the Select Bibliography.

35. James W. Wood, *Dynamics of Human Reproduction: Biology, Biometry, Demography* (New York: Aldine de Gruyter, 1994), pp. 338–343, 368–370. Ethnographers report that women in field studies often begin weaning their child *because* they have become pregnant. See, for instance, Kim Hill and A. Magdalena Hurtado, *Ache Life History: The Ecology and Demography of a Foraging People* (New York: Aldine de Gruyter, 1996), p. 250. See also Paula A. Treckel, "Breastfeeding and Maternal Sexuality in Colonial America," *Journal of Interdisciplinary History* 20 (1989): 25–51; and Valerie Fildes, "On Breastfeeding in England," in *Women as Mothers in Pre-Industrial England: Essays in Memory of Dorothy McLaren,* ed. Valerie Fildes (London: Routledge, 1990); idem, *Breasts, Bottles and Babies: A History of Infant Feeding* (Edinburgh: Edinburgh University Press, 1986).

36. Articles in *Natural History* 106, no. 9 (November 1997), vividly describe differences between cultures, but field studies that monitored breastfeeding and noted the timing of the resumption of menses quickly discovered great variability within the group under study. In a study conducted among a noncontracepting group living on Java, field workers identified "high intensity" nursers versus "low intensity" nursers and found a median average difference of almost nine months in the timing of the onset of menses; Wood, *Dynamics of Human Reproduction,* pp. 339, 368–370. See also Barry Bogin, "Evolutionary and Biological Aspects of Childhood," in *Biosocial Perspectives on Children,* ed. Catherine Panter-Brick (Cambridge: Cambridge University Press, 1998), pp. 10–44; and Peter T. Ellison, "Breastfeeding, Fertility, and Maternal

Condition," in *Breastfeeding: Biocultural Perspectives,* ed. Patricia Stuart-Macadam and Katherine A. Detwyler (New York: Aldine de Gruyter, 1995), pp. 305–345.

37. On Native American practices in eastern North America, see examples in Axtell, *Indian Peoples of Eastern America;* Roger Williams, *A Key into the Language,* p. 206; and Daniel Gookin, *Historical Collections of the Indians in New England* (1674), Massachusetts Historical Society Collections, 1st ser., vol. 1 (Boston, 1792), pp. 141–226. Meredith F. Small, "Our Babies, Ourselves," *Natural History* 106 (November 1997): 42–51; Katherine A. Detwyler (quoted in ibid., p. 49) says: "Every study that includes the duration of breast-feeding as a variable shows that, on average, the longer a baby is nursed, the better its health and cognitive development." The World Health Organization, for instance, recommends two years or more of breast-feeding. Among preindustrial societies, those with dairy cows have far higher fertility rates than those without; Wood, *Dynamics of Human Reproduction,* p. 366. Thomas Malthus would have been intrigued by the idea that cows, not people, push human population growth.

38. Wood, *Dynamics of Human Reproduction,* p. 367. The energy demands of lactation far exceed those of pregnancy according to Michael Leon, "Somatic Aspects of Parent-Offspring Interactions," in *Parenting across the Life Span: Biosocial Dimensions,* ed. Jane B. Lancaster, Jeanne Altmann, Alice S. Rossi, and Lonnie R. Sherrod (New York: Aldine de Gruyter, 1987), pp. 85–110; R. V. Short, N. G. Blurton-Jones, and R. M. Sibley, "Testing Adaptiveness of Culturally Determined Behaviour: Do Bushmen Women Maximize Reproductive Success by Spacing Births Widely and Foraging Seldom?" in *Human Behaviour and Adaptation,* ed. N. G. Blurton-Jones and V. Reynolds (London: Taylor and Francis, 1978), pp. 135–157. Narragansett mothers were not as mobile as modern !Kung foragers, but they were not as sedentary as the English, and that difference was crucial. See also Mary Ellen Morbeck, Alison Galloway, and Adrienne L. Zihlman, eds., *The Evolving Female: A Life-History Perspective* (Princeton: Princeton University Press, 1997), p. 182.

39. Wood, *Dynamics of Human Reproduction,* chap. 6, discusses fetal loss and its effect on fecundability, pp. 239–277. Birth intervals in colonial Québec families averaged slightly shorter than in New England; Hubert Charbonneau et al., *The First French Canadians: Pioneers in the St. Lawrence Valley* (Newark, Del.: University of Delaware Press and London: Associated University Presses, 1993). See the discussion of birth intervals and breastfeeding in Richard T. Vann and David Eversley, *The British and Irish Quakers in the Demographic Transition, 1650–1900* (Cambridge: Cambridge University Press, 1992), pp. 146–170. English Quakers married three or four years later than New Englanders, quit childbearing two years earlier, but spaced their babies about same. Hence, among these Quakers, two or three fewer children were born over the course of a woman's reproductive cycle.

40. Darwinians argue that humans, like other animals, are programmed by natural selection for maximizing their reproductive success by rearing successful children who will themselves rear successful children. In a world of scarcity and

sudden death, men and women will have as many babies as they believe they can care for. The more secure and predictable their world, however, the more they will be inclined to limit the number of children in order to invest a greater proportion of their resources in the success of each; N. G. Blurton-Jones, "The Costs of Children and the Adaptive Scheduling of Births: Towards a Sociobiological Perspective on Demography," in *The Sociobiology of Sexual and Reproductive Strategies*, ed. Eckart Voland, Christian Vogel, and Anne E. Rasa (London: Chapman and Hall, 1989), pp. 265–282; P. W. Turke, "Evolution and the Demand for Children," *Population and Development Review* 15 (1989): 61–90. See also the essays in Laura Betzig, Monique Borgerhoff Mulder, and Paul Turke, eds., *Human Reproductive Behaviour: A Darwinian Perspective* (Cambridge: Cambridge University Press, 1988). Even the labor of quite a young child could contribute significantly to household income of farm families, according to Lee A. Craig, *To Sow One Acre More: Childbearing and Farm Productivity in the Antebellum North* (Baltimore: Johns Hopkins University Press, 1993), p. 80. Robert Fogel and Stanley Engerman estimated that slaves as young as eight years old in the antebellum South yielded their owners a positive return over costs; *Time on the Cross: The Economics of American Negro Slavery* (Boston: Little, Brown, 1974), pp. 74–77. On the economics of choice in reproduction, see Gary Stanley Becker, *A Treatise on the Family*, enl. ed. (Cambridge, Mass.: Harvard University Press, 1991); and Ramon Febrero and Pedro S. Schwartz, *The Essence of Becker* (Stanford, Calif.: Hoover Institution Press, 1995). A useful summary of this extensive literature can be found in Mark R. Rosenzweig and Oded Stark, eds., *Handbook of Population and Family Economics*, 2 vols. (Amsterdam: Elsevier, 1997), particularly the essay by Yoram Weiss.

41. On the usefulness of birth-interval data for family limitation studies, see Blurton-Jones, "The Costs of Children," pp. 265–282. For historical demographic studies using birth intervals as diagnostic tools for detecting deliberate timing or stopping of births, see Vann and Eversley, *Friends in Life and Death*, pp. 146–168; Charbonneau et al., *The First French Canadians;* Lee L. Bean, Geraldine P. Mireau, and Douglas L. Anderton, *Fertility Change on the American Frontier: Adaptation and Innovation* (Berkeley: University of California Press, 1990); Jenny Bourne Wahl, "New Results on the Decline in Household Fertility in the United States from 1750 to 1900," in *Long-Term Factors in American Economic Growth,* ed. Stanley L. Engerman and Robert E. Gallman (Chicago: University of Chicago Press, 1986), pp. 391–437. An excellent, thoughtful discussion of the demographic history of Western Europe is offered by Ron A. Lesthaeghe in two articles: "On the Social Control of Human Reproduction," *Population and Development Review* 4 (1980): 527–548; and "A Century of Demographic and Cultural Change in Western Europe: An Exploration of Underlying Dimensions," ibid., 9 (1983): 411–435.

42. Merry E. Wiesner provides a guide to men's attitudes toward women, sexuality, and sexual intercourse in early modern Europe in *Women and Gender,* pp. 9– 41. See also David D. Hall, *Worlds of Wonder, Days of Judgment: Popular Religious*

Belief in Early New England (Cambridge, Mass.: Harvard University Press, 1990), pp. 71, 77–78. Otho T. Beall furnishes a useful introduction to the literature of the times concerning sexual reproduction in "Aristotle's Master Piece in America," *William and Mary Quarterly* 20 (1963): 207–222. David Hackett Fischer argues that Quakers and Calvinists must have held very different attitudes toward sex because completed family size among Quakers in New Jersey and Pennsylvania was lower than among their Calvinist neighbors. Fischer believes that when Quakers stopped with five or six children, they had stopped having sex; *Albion's Seed: Four British Folkways in America* (Oxford: Oxford University Press, 1989), pp. 483–484, 498–502.

43. Daniel Scott Smith and J. David Hacker, "Cultural Demography: New England Deaths and the Puritan Perception of Risk," *Journal of Interdisciplinary History* 26 (1996): 367–392. By and large, people of the times were not in the habit of thinking in terms of *rates,* only in absolute numbers; Patricia Cline Cohen, *A Calculating People: The Spread of Numeracy in Early America* (Chicago: University of Chicago Press, 1982), pp. 15–46.

44. Robert Charles Anderson, *The Great Migration Begins: Immigrants to New England, 1620–1633,* 3 vols. (Boston: New England Historic Genealogical Society, 1995), 3: 2039–41. Samuel Sewall's *Diary* is filled with death notices accompanied by his comments on the circumstances, often expressing wonder verging on awe at the suddenness of death. As an earnest Puritan, he saw these deaths as evidence of God's warning hand.

45. See Richard M. Smith, "Some Issues Concerning Families and Their Property in Rural England, 1250–1800," in *Land, Kinship and Life-Cycle,* ed. R. M. Smith (Cambridge: Cambridge University Press, 1984), pp. 68–71. Alan Macfarlane, in *Marriage and Love in England: Modes of Reproduction, 1300–1848* (Oxford: Blackwell, 1986), argues that because people did not have as many children as was biologically possible, they were "choosing" to have fewer.

46. Inga Clendinnen, *Aztecs: An Interpretation* (Cambridge: Cambridge University Press, 1991).

47. Patrick Hanks and Flavia Hodges, *A Dictionary of First Names* (New York: Oxford University Press, 1990); Joan Comay and Ronald Brownrigg, *Who's Who in the Bible* (New York: Holt, Rinehart and Winston, 1980); Scott Smith-Bannister, *Names and Naming Patterns in England, 1538–1700* (Oxford: Clarendon Press, 1997); Richard D. Alford, *Naming and Identity: A Cross-Cultural Study of Personal Naming Practices* (New Haven: HRAF Press, 1988).

48. Hatevil M. Leighton, an eighth-generation Leighton who was born at Lubec, Maine, in 1828, died sometime after 1903, probably in an old people's home in Boston. He had changed his name to Hartwell long before; Perley M. Leighton, *A Leighton Genealogy: Descendants of Thomas Leighton of Dover, New Hampshire,* 2 vols. (Boston: New England Historic Genealogical Society, 1989), 1: 391.

49. St. Augustine argued that the baby who died without baptism was damned, for "The innocence of children is in the helplessness of their bodies, rather than any quality of soul"; quoted in David Herlihy, *Medieval Households* (Cambridge,

Mass.: Harvard University Press, 1985), p. 27. Cotton Mather argued that if children who were baptized died as infants, "They shall none of them be lost"; Mather, *Baptismal Piety*, quoted by Hall, *Worlds of Wonder, Days of Judgment*, p. 155. Hall, p. 284, also cites John Brand, *Observations on the Popular Antiquities of Great Britain* (London, 1849), p. 335, on the folk belief that unbaptized children were highly vulnerable to witches. William G. McLoughlin, *New England Dissent, 1630–1833: The Baptists and the Separation of Church and State*, 2 vols. (Cambridge, Mass.: Harvard University Press, 1971), 1: 28–32, clarifies the theological debate over infant baptism and its connection to Puritan covenantal theology.

50. Sewall, *Diary*, 1: 41–42, 45–46, 52, 87, 133, 175–176, 264, 283, 324, 460.

51. Christopher Jedrey, *The World of John Cleaveland: Family and Community in Eighteenth Century New England* (New York: W. W. Norton, 1974), pp. 77–78.

52. Darrett Rutman and Anita Rutman, *A Place in Time: Explicatus* (New York: W. W. Norton, 1984), chap. 7.

53. Richard Woodruff Price, "Child-Naming Patterns in Three English Villages, 1558–1740: Whickham, Durham; Bottesford, Leicester; and Hartland, Devon" (Master's thesis, Brigham Young University, 1987), pp. 73, 142–144; Michael F. Sekulla, "Patterns of Naming in the Parish of Dry Dayton, Cambridgeshire, 1550–1850" (Master's thesis, University of Leicester, 1993).

54. Sewall, *Diary*, 1: 39; Mary MacManus Ramsbottom, "Religious Society and the Family in Charlestown, Massachusetts, 1630–1740" (Ph.D. diss., Yale University, 1987). By the 1660s the proportion baptized among infants born in Dedham, Massachusetts, had fallen from 80 percent to 40 percent; Kenneth A. Lockridge, *A New England Town: The First Hundred Years* (New York: W. W. Norton, 1970), p. 34. The Massachusetts General Court did not vote in support of the clergy's recommendation until 1671, and its decision was not binding on the congregations; Robert G. Pope, *The Half-Way Covenant: Church Membership in Puritan New England* (Princeton: Princeton University Press, 1969), p. 67. The legislature of Connecticut never adopted the Half-Way Covenant; Paul R. Lucas, *Valley of Discord: Church and Society along the Connecticut River, 1636–1725* (Hanover, N.H.: University Press of New England, 1976), pp. 106–107.

55. John Demos, "Introduction: Family History's Past Achievements and Future Prospects," in *The American Family: Historical Perspectives*, ed. Jean E. Hunter and Paul T. Mason (Pittsburgh: Duquesne University Press, 1991), p. xix; Michael MacDonald, *Mystical Bedlam: Madness, Anxiety, and Healing in Seventeenth-Century England* (Cambridge: Cambridge University Press, 1981), p. 85; E. A. Wrigley, R. S. Davies, J. E. Oeppen, and R. S. Schofield, *English Population History from Family Reconstitution, 1580–1837* (New York: Cambridge University Press, 1997), p. 215. In New England, information about survivorship is available for only about half of the nearly 40,000 children born to the approximately 6,000 first marriages formed before 1776 in a sample of family and town genealogies drawn from about 200 towns in southern New England. Missing so many may have the effect of understating child mortality in these families. In late nine-

teenth-century America, nearly two out of ten children died before reaching their fifth birthday, considerably worse than my estimate for seventeenth-century New England; Samuel H. Preston and Michael R. Haines, *Fatal Years: Child Mortality in Late Nineteenth-Century America* (Princeton: Princeton University Press, 1991), pp. 3, 86.

56. John Hale, *A Modest Enquiry into the Nature of Witchcraft* (Boston, 1702), quoted in Carol F. Karlsen, *The Devil in the Shape of a Woman: Witchcraft in Colonial New England* (New York: W. W. Norton, 1987), p. 22. Parsons later denied being a witch. She was tried and acquitted of witchcraft but convicted of murder.

57. Thomas Minor, *The Diary of Thomas Minor, Stonington, Connecticut, 1653–1685* (New London, Conn.: Day, 1899).

58. Cotton's grandfather then went on to inform them further of the death on September 8 of their young daughter, Sarah, who had been staying with them, and the simultaneous arrival home of their son Josias, who was then so sick that they were despairing of his life as well; "Josiah Cotton of Plymouth in New England, Esq., Memoirs in Three Parts originally begun December 1, Anno 1726," Massachusetts Historical Society, pp. 56–57.

59. Sewall, *Diary,* 1: 87.

60. Ibid., p. 89.

61. Ibid., p. 117.

62. Ibid., p. 145.

63. Ibid., pp. 264–265. Sewall never says anything about his wife until she dies.

64. Ibid., p. 328.

65. On Edward Taylor (ca. 1644–1729) see the short biography in Samuel Eliot Morison, *The Intellectual Life of Colonial New England,* 2d ed. (New York: New York University Press, 1956), p. 235.

66. Philip Greven, *The Protestant Temperament: Patterns of Childrearing, Religious Experiences, and the Self in Early America* (New York: Alfred A. Knopf, 1977), pp. 30–31, 52–53; Sewall, *Diary,* 1: 249.

67. Kenneth Silverman, *The Life and Times of Cotton Mather* (New York: Columbia University Press, 1985), p. 76. Michael Hall indicates that Increase Mather, father of Cotton, involved himself very little with his children when they were young but concerned himself in the formal education of sons Cotton and Samuel as they got older. Increase did preach hellfire and damnation to six- and seven-year-olds in the meeting house; Michael G. Hall, *The Last American Puritan: The Life of Increase Mather, 1639–1723* (Middletown, Conn.: Wesleyan University Press, 1988), pp. 94–95, 138–140.

68. While he was in England on a visit, John Hull went to the town where his wife, Judith (Samuel Sewall's mother-in-law), was born, "and took her age out of the register, born September 3, 1626"; *Puritan Personal Writings: Diaries* (New York: AMS Press, 1983), discontinuous paging.

69. Daniel King Diary, photocopy, Massachusetts Historical Society (original at Peabody Institute Library, Salem, Mass.). King was born in 1704 and died in 1790. By midcentury, in Boston at least, a man with a dying child could pre-

sume on the sympathies of other men. A letter by Thomas Mason of Boston, written in 1749, arrived at the home of "Mr. Dolbear," a merchant, asking for an extension and addition to a loan. His daughter had fallen ill suddenly of a "Quinsey. It was seald in Heaven that she must Die, Die in full Strength, vigorous in Spirit, Sences Retaind to the Last Moment tho depried of Speech. Die at that very time that could affect those who was related to most, Die when most desirous they were of its life & when she had there Affection fixd entirely upon her"; Dolbeare Papers, Massachusetts Historical Society, box 2, October 23, 1749.

70. Ballantine Diary, American Antiquarian Society, August 13, 1760.

71. Justus Forward Diary, American Antiquarian Society, Belchertown, May(?) 28, 1766.

72. Experience Richardson Diary, typescript, Massachusetts Historical Society, pp. 8 (July 14, 1748), 22 (October 5 and 12, 1752), and 23 (December 15, 1752; February[?] 1753).

73. Ibid., pp. 24 (July 1, 1753) and 25 (October 6, 1753).

6. Childrearing and the Experience of Childhood

1. Ideas about the nature of childhood and the process of growing up have been converging toward a consensus among the diverse disciplines that study parenting and child development. Although they disagree about the precise nature of the effect of parents on the kind of adults their children become, all have come to appreciate the agency of children themselves in forging their own culture. Works that have been most influential in shaping my own ideas begin with Kim Hill and A. Magdalene Hurtado, *Ache Life History: The Ecology and Demography of a Foraging People* (New York: Aldine de Gruyter, 1996); Judith Rich Harris, *The Nurture Assumption: Why Children Turn Out the Way They Do* (New York: Free Press, 1998); Helen Morton, *Becoming Tongan: An Ethnography of Childhood* (Honolulu: University of Hawai'i Press, 1996); and the essays in Jane B. Lancaster, Jeanne Altmann, Alice S. Rossi, and Lonnie R. Sherrod, eds., *Parenting across the Life Span: Biosocial Dimensions* (New York: Aldine de Gruyter, 1987).

2. Harris, *The Nurture Assumption*, passim but especially chap. 4, "Separate Worlds." Robert Burton said in the early seventeenth century that it was odd and effeminate for men to play with their children; for a gentleman to appear in public with an infant in his arms caused great amazement. Reported in Anthony Fletcher, *Gender, Sex, and Subordination in England, 1500–1800* (New Haven: Yale University Press, 1995), pp. 86–87.

3. Barry Bogin, "Evolutionary and Biological Aspects of Childhood," in *Biosocial Perspectives on Children*, ed. Catherine Panter-Brick (Cambridge: Cambridge University Press, 1998), pp. 10–37; Mary Ellen Morbeck, Alison Galloway, and Adrienne L. Zihlman, eds., *The Evolving Female: A Life-History Perspective* (Princeton: Princeton University Press, 1997). Field studies of nonhuman primates

have proven enormously valuable for understanding the physical aspects of human childhood. Jane Goodall's methods of close analysis of every form of visible chimpanzee behavior, combined with laboratory analysis of the bodies of deceased individuals whose biographies are known, has helped to refine our knowledge about the relationships among nutrition, size, age, and social and reproductive success in primate bands and family groups. The study of modern human societies applies the same exacting, time-consuming methods of observation and notetaking. The founder of this approach is Nancy Howell, *Demography of the Dobe !Kung* (New York: Academic Press, 1979). Because of her work, the !Kung of the Kalihari are the best known of these societies, but there are now many more such group studies, all of them, unfortunately for the historian of New England, in tropical and subtropical regions of the world. No traditional societies remain in areas of temperate forests. For a handy summary, see the bibliography in James W. Wood, *Dynamics of Human Reproduction: Biology, Biometry, Demography* (New York: Aldine de Gruyter, 1994).

4. Suzanne Gaskins, "How Mayan Parental Theories Come into Play," in *Parents' Cultural Belief Systems: Their Origins, Expressions, and Consequences,* ed. Sara Harkness and Charles M. Super (New York: Guilford Press, 1996), pp. 350–352.

5. Beatrice Blyth Whiting and Carolyn Pope Edwards, *Children of Different Worlds: The Formation of Social Behavior* (Cambridge, Mass.: Harvard University Press, 1988), especially chap. 3; Harris, *The Nurture Assumption,* pp. 91–92, 160–165, 179–180.

6. Hill and Hurtado, *Ache Life History,* passim.

7. And one full year later than the children of the Kalahari !Kung people studied by Nancy Howell.

8. Hill and Hurtado, *Ache Life History,* pp. 221–222.

9. Among the Chewong of the Malay Peninsula rain forest, "children voluntarily detach themselves from their parents well before they reach their teens." They join a peer group of older children of the same sex. "Adults cease to teach actively unless approached by a child requiring specific guidance"; S. Nancy Howell, "From Child to Human: Chewong Concepts of Self," in *Acquiring Culture: Cross-Cultural Studies in Child Development,* ed. Gustav Jahoda and I. M. Lewis (London: Croom Helm, 1988), pp. 147–169, quoted by Harris, *The Nurture Assumption,* p. 161.

10. Ache marriages are fragile, and spouses are free to seek new ones. If the child's father no longer cohabits with her mother, she may go a little hungrier than usual until Mother takes a new partner. Many traditional societies rely on chiefs to redistribute the products of the hunt or tributary gifts to the tribe, but even among these the ideal of equality exists side by side with a system in which the allocator retains a little more for his own family. See Laura Betzig, "Redistribution: Equity or Exploitation?" in *Human Reproductive Behaviour: A Darwinian Perspective,* ed. Laura Betzig, Monique Borgerhoff Mulder, and Paul Turke (Cambridge: Cambridge University Press, 1988), pp. 49–64.

11. Roger Williams, *A Key into the Language of America*, ed. John T. Teunissen and Evelyn J. Hing (Detroit: Wayne State University Press, 1973), p. 115.

12. P[ierre] de Charlevoix, *Journal of a Voyage to North-America*, 2 vols. (1761), quoted in James Axtell, ed., *Indian Peoples of Eastern America: A Documentary History of the Sexes* (New York: Oxford University Press, 1981), pp. 15–16.

13. Father Gabriel Sagard speaking of Algonquians and Hurons in Axtell, *Indian Peoples of Eastern America*, p. 6.

14. Williams, *Key into the Language*, p. 128; "it is almost incredible what burthens the poore women carry of Corne, of Fish, of Beanes, of Mats, and a childe besides"; p. 121.

15. Lidia Standish, a witness in a court trial, described herself as "a mother of many children my selfe and have Nursed many"; quoted in John Demos, *A Little Commonwealth: Family Life in Plymouth Colony* (New York: Oxford University Press, 1970), p. 133 n. 5, from Davis Scrapbooks, Pilgrim Hall, Plymouth, Mass., vol. 3, p. 12. In Robert Gibbs's Account Book (Boston), American Antiquarian Society, Worcester, Mass., Goody Cooke was credited eighteen shillings for "sucking ye child 9 weeks." Samuel Sewall usually noted the names of the first women to nurse his newborns; *The Diary of Samuel Sewall, 1674–1729*, ed. M. Halsey Thomas, 2 vols. (New York: Farrar, Straus and Giroux, 1973). That nursing children shared their mothers' beds is indicated in numerous references, most vividly in the case of Elizabeth Wells, who stated in Middlesex County court in Massachusetts that she had "left a boy of two years in bed & rann away up to London with her breasts full of milk"; quoted in Roger Thompson, *Sex in Middlesex: Popular Mores in a Massachusetts County, 1649–1699* (Amherst: University of Massachusetts Press, 1981), p. 25. In another court case, a housewife testified that she had tried to talk a nocturnal male visitor out of entering her bed: "She told him he would hurt the child"; ibid., p. 75. On breast-feeding practices in eighteenth-century New England, see Ross Beales, "Nursing and Weaning in an Eighteenth-Century New England Household," in *Families and Children*, ed. Peter Benes (Cambridge, Mass.: Boston University Press, 1987), pp. 48–63. On the other hand, Thomas Hatch of Scituate and his wife left their six-month-old child for several days with the baby's older sister; Samuel Eliot Morison, ed., *Records of the Suffolk County Court, 1671–1680*, 2 vols. (Boston: Colonial Society of Massachusetts, 1933), 2: 45 (July 1, 1680).

16. Hill and Hurtado, *Ache Life History*, p. 249; Williams, *Key into the Language*, p. 149.

17. Barbara A. Hanawalt, "Childrearing among the Lower Classes of Late Medieval England," *Journal of Interdisciplinary History* 8 (1977–1978): 1–22, determined from coroners' records that the most common cause of untimely death for babies a year old or less was being burned in their cradles. John Winthrop tells of such a tragedy at Concord: two children were left home alone, one in a cradle; the other accidentally set a haystack by the door on fire, "whereby the hay and house were burned and the child in the cradle before they came from the

meeting"; *The Journal of John Winthrop*, ed. Richard S. Dunn, James Savage, and Laetitia Yeandle (Cambridge, Mass.: Harvard University Press, 1996), p. 352. According to the Peter Thacher Diary, typescript 2, Massachusetts Historical Society, Boston, p. 45, a maidservant took Thacher's son Oxenbridge to Boston for treatment of rickets. This was the second trip. The doctor bled him in the ears and prescribed some special drink, not identified in the diary; cited in Karin Calvert, "Children in American Family Portraiture, 1670 to 1810," *William and Mary Quarterly* 39 (1982): 89–113. Calvert's *Children in the House: The Material Culture of Early Childhood, 1600–1900* (Boston: Northeastern University Press, 1992), argues that fear of rickets (and of its deformative effects) created a culture of infant care that sought straightness of body and limbs by mechanical, external force: swaddling; narrow, deep-sided cradles in which babies were tightly laced down; and stays. The sources she cites on the use of stays are neither English nor American, however. "Children's stays" appear only very occasionally in the probate inventories of rural New England, but since few items appertaining to children occur anyway, their absence is not decisive. However, the fact that they fail to show up in rural storekeepers' accounts of the eighteenth century leads to the conclusion that farm families rarely, if ever, employed them.

18. Probably few people in the past ever slept alone. An English girl, Anne Clifford, at age thirteen mentions in her diary that her mother was angry with her for her disobedience and "commanded that I should lie in a chamber alone, which I could not endure, but my cousin Frances got the key of my chamber and lay with me"; Linda A. Pollock, *Forgotten Children: Parent-Child Relations from 1500 to 1900* (Cambridge: Cambridge University Press, 1983), p. 147. Minister Ebenezer Parkman wrote in his diary: "Now we are intirely alone having no Servant nor any one in the House. Our Loneliness gives Scope for Thought. God Sanctifie our solitude"; *The Diary of Ebenezer Parkman, 1703–1782: First Part, 1719–1755*, ed. Francis G. Walett (Worcester, Mass.: American Antiquarian Society, 1974), pp. 32–33.

19. Nathaniel B. Shurtleff and David Pulsifer, eds., *Records of the Colony of New Plymouth in New England, 1620–1692*, 12 vols. (Boston: White, 1855–1891), vol. 6: *Court Orders*, p. 45 (July 1, 1680). Pollock reports a number of such "overlay" accidents in American diaries; *Forgotten Children*, pp. 135–137.

20. *Early Records of the Town of Providence*, 21 vols. (Providence: Snow & Farnham, 1892–1915), 5: 252–254.

21. Minister Ebenezer Parkman reported, "Memorable Deliverance of my little Hannah. The Cellar Door was left open, and She in her Go-Cart, pitched down, and went to the bottom—yet without any great Hurt. To God our preserver be all Glory!" Ebenezer Parkman Diary, American Antiquarian Society, December 28, 1758. Hannah Parkman was born February 9, 1758, so she was less than eleven months old when this misadventure took place.

22. Joseph Green, "Diary," in *Puritan Personal Writings: Diaries* (New York: AMS

Press, 1983), p. 222 (April 12, 1703): "Carryed my mother and Nanny to Wenham, and Ben carryed my wife. I left my wife and Nanny and came home to wean John."

23. Valerie A. Fildes has searched the European literature for information on the age of weaning and found 18–24 months the most often mentioned in the literature of the seventeenth and eighteenth centuries, although English diaries and correspondence of the aristocracy and the educated classes report generally shorter periods, ranging from 6 to 36 months in the seventeenth century (cases number fourteen, eight from one diary alone, with a mean of 15 months) and 1 to 37 in the eighteenth (cases number eighteen, with a mean of 10.5 months); Fildes, *Breasts, Bottles and Babies: A History of Infant Feeding* (Edinburgh: Edinburgh University Press, 1986), pp. 353, 355. Ross Beales has culled the long diary of Ebenezer Parkman of Westborough, Massachusetts, for all the available information related to childbearing and weaning in his household. The ages at which the children were weaned varied from 10 to 20 months. In every case but one, the weaning took place during the spring-to-early-fall season, when cows were in milk; Beales, "Nursing and Weaning," p. 63.

24. Barbara Welles-Nystrom, "Scenes from a Marriage: Equality Ideology in Swedish Family Policy, Maternal Ethnotheories, and Practice," in Harkness and Super, *Parents' Cultural Belief Systems,* pp. 192–213.

25. Whiting and Edwards, *Children of Different Worlds,* pp. 155–157. Harris observes that among modern children, "even three-year-olds identify themselves as girls or boys"; *The Nurture Assumption,* p. 219. When John Demos describes the dress of colonial children as "the same sort of clothing that was normal for adults," he sees this as yet another indicator of negative adult attitudes toward the child: from "his earliest years he was expected to be—or to try to be—a miniature adult"; Demos, "The American Family in Past Time," *American Scholar* 43 (1974): 428. It is true that colonial children lived their lives amidst adults, but diaries suggest that they were appreciated for themselves as children. In some modern European societies such as Italy, children accompany parents everywhere and are involved in all the family doings, including late evening meals. The young child enjoys the hullabaloo, gets tired, falls asleep, and is carried off to bed. In these cultures, adults are not expecting children to behave like themselves and are fully able to enjoy their company.

26. Parents in modern Singapore, for instance, place their infants, toddlers, and preschoolers with professional caretakers "until the children are old enough to benefit from the care of their parents around 6 or 7 years of age"; Ake Sander, "Images of the Child and Childhood in Religion," in *Images of Childhood,* ed. C. Philip Hwan, Michael E. Lamb, and Irving E. Sigel (Mahwah, N.Y.: Lawrence Erlbaum Associates, 1996), pp. 14–26.

27. Sagard, quoted in Axtell, *Indian Peoples of Eastern America,* p. 7.

28. Williams, *A Key into the Language,* pp. 115–116. Daniel Gookin in 1674 said of the Indians he knew: "The men and women are very loving and indulgent to

their children"; *Historical Collections of the Indians in New England* (1674), in Massachusetts Historical Society Collections, 1st ser., vol. 1 (Boston, 1792), pp. 141–227.

29. Quoted in Axtell, *Indian Peoples of Eastern America,* p. 34. It is noteworthy that this eighteenth-century Jesuit could speak of "nature" as a positive force in the upbringing of children.

30. *Works of Anne Bradstreet,* ed. John Harvard Ellis (1867; reprint, New York: P. Smith, 1932), p. 151, quoted in Edmund S. Morgan, *The Puritan Family: Religion and Domestic Relations in Seventeenth-Century New England* (1944; reprint, New York: Harper & Row, 1966), p. 93.

31. See the discussion of "evangelical" childrearing practices by Philip Greven in *The Protestant Temperament: Patterns of Child-Rearing, Religious Experience, and the Self in Early America* (New York: Alfred A. Knopf, 1977), pp. 28–38. Greven emphasizes "breaking of the will" as distinctive to this type of discipline, but a historically deeper search of the literature tempers this extreme view.

32. Patrick Collinson, *Godly People: Studies on English Protestantism and Puritanism* (London: Hambledon Press, 1983); idem, *The Religion of Protestants: The Church in English Society, 1559–1625* (Oxford: Oxford University Press, 1982); Morgan, *The Puritan Family,* pp. 65–86.

33. The origins of Puritan social thought and of the "spiritualization of the household" can be found in Catholic humanism. Emphasis on early religious education and on the mother's role, the great deference due from the child to the parent, and the importance of reasoning with the child, all can be found in Catholic writers, as is demonstrated in Richard Whytford, *A Werke for Householders,* ed. James Hogg (Salzburg: Institut fur Anglistek and Amenhanistek, Salzburg Universitat, 1979). Text taken from the copy in the Bodleian Library, Oxford, dated 1530, "newly corrected & prynted agayne."

34. Puritan works on family discipline repeated these ideas. For instance, Ezekias Woodward (1590–1675) claimed that the child imitates by example, and so the parent is the young child's book, school, and church; Woodward, *A Sons Patrimony and Daughters Portion* (London: T. Underhill, 1643); the original is in the University of Illinois Library and is published on microfilm in "Early English Books, 1641–1700." For Puritan attitudes toward children and childrearing, see C. John Sommerville, *The Discovery of Childhood in Puritan England* (Athens: University of Georgia Press, 1992).

35. Woodward, *Sons Patrimony and Daughters Portion,* pp. 40–52.

36. Whytford, *Werke for Householders,* pp. 30–31. Woodward says much the same thing a hundred years later: "if he spares his child, he kills it." But "A Parent carried in a passion, cannot mingle his corrections with instructions, and where that mixture is not, there is no Discipline; for that is true Discipline when the child smarts from the hand, and learns from the tongue." He also affirms with Whytford, however, that "the more force the less good"; *Sons Patrimony and Daughters Portion,* p. 27.

37. Whytford, *Werke for Householders,* pp. 31–32.

38. Woodward in 1643 consigns responsibility for the child's earliest years to the mother and the nurse. In bringing up the child, he says, the mother is "charged with the head," but both the father and mother are "charged with the heart"; ibid., p. 2. When urging parents to be active disciplinarians, he does not distinguish between parental roles. Londoner Samuel Pepys left most of the disciplining of servants to his wife, particularly so in the case of young women; Fletcher, *Gender, Sex, and Subordination,* pp. 213, 216.

39. John D. Cushing, comp., *The Earliest Laws of the New Haven and Connecticut Colonies, 1639–1673* (Wilmington, Del.: M. Glazier, 1977), p. 87. The year was 1672.

40. Pollock, *Forgotten Children,* p. 392; Robert V. Smucker, "Puritan Attitudes toward Childhood Discipline, 1560–1634," in *Women as Mothers in Pre-Industrial England,* ed. Valerie Fildes (London: Routledge, 1990), pp. 108–121; Anthony Fletcher and John Steveson, eds., *Order and Disorder in Early Modern England* (Cambridge: Cambridge University Press, 1985), pp. 1–40; Susan D. Amussen, "Gender, Family and the Social Order, 1560–1725," ibid., pp. 196–217; Fletcher, *Gender, Sex, and Subordination,* pp. 3–29, 401–407; Pollock, *Forgotten Children,* p. 144. Shulamith Shahar agrees with Pollock that "it is . . . highly doubtful whether any 'emotional revolution' has occurred in the attitude of parents to their children"; *Childhood in the Middle Ages,* trans. Chaya Galain (London: Routledge, 1990), p. 3. Harris, *The Nurture Assumption,* summarizes a half-century of studies in hereditary genetics based on identical and fraternal twins that tends to support Pollock's conclusions. If our genes are responsible for 50 percent of the variation in our temperaments, as these studies confirm, and if our temperaments shape our day-to-day responses to our children, then advice manuals can have only a limited impact on childrearing practices. Cultural attitudes toward children and their nature would have to change before parents could effectively redirect their energies. The eighteenth century witnessed the beginnings of such a change, as discussed in Chapter 9.

41. Pollock, *Forgotten Children,* p. 146.

42. Dee in ibid., p. 148.

43. Mildmay in Pollock, *Forgotten Children,* p. 147; Norwood in ibid., p. 148; Newcome in ibid., p. 149; Heywood in ibid., p. 150. Pollock finds many examples in early diaries of parents who favored one child over the rest, usually without realizing it, and occasionally "spoiling" that child beyond redemption.

44. Ralph Houlbrooke, *The English Family* (Cambridge: Cambridge University Press, 1982), pp. 180–181.

45. Margo Todd, *Christian Humanism and the Puritan Social Order* (Cambridge: Cambridge University Press, 1987), emphasizes the continuity between Catholic humanists and English Protestant social thought and argues that Puritans should be seen as evangelists who earnestly strived to practice the virtues of the spiritualized household they preached to others.

46. Quoted and elucidated in Demos, *A Little Commonwealth,* pp. 134–135; and David E. Stannard, *The Puritan Way of Death: A Study of Religion, Culture and Social Change* (New York: Oxford University Press, 1977), p. 49.

47. Morgan, *The Puritan Family,* p. 103.

48. Greven, *The Protestant Temperament,* pp. 22–55.

49. *The Works of John Robinson,* ed. Robert Ashton, vol. 1 (Boston, 1851), pp. 246–247, quoted in Demos, *A Little Commonwealth,* p. 101; Cotton Mather, *Diary of Cotton Mather,* ed. Worthington Chauncey Ford, Massachusetts Historical Society Collections, 7th ser., vol. 7 (Boston, 1912), p. 204. Mather did not approve of Indians: "They are very lying Wretches, and they are very lazy Wretches, and they are out of measure indulgent unto their Children; there is no Family Government among them"; Mather, *Great Examples of Judgment and Mercy* (1697), reprinted in *Magnalia Christi Americana* (London, 1702), bk. 6, p. 35, quoted in Richard Gildrie, *The Profane, the Civil, & the Godly: The Reformation of Manners in Orthodox New England, 1679–1749* (University Park: Pennsylvania State University Press, 1994), p. 143.

50. Quoted in Greven, *The Protestant Temperament,* pp. 32–33.

51. *The Journal of Esther Edwards Burr, 1754–1757,* ed. Carol F. Karlsen and Laurie Crumpacker (New Haven: Yale University Press, 1984), pp. 84 (January 24, 1755) and 95 (February 28, 1755). Burr clearly left the business of childcare and discipline to his wife, and she would have been surprised at his interference with her hitting the little girl. This incident provides evidence that the division of labor within the household empowered the wife and mother as well as burdening her.

52. Ibid., p. 195 (April 16, 1756).

53. The "Indian girle" has no name or identity other than this; Peter Thacher Diary, typescript 1, Massachusetts Historical Society, p. 234 (August 18, 1679). In 1683 he whipped his boy servant, Ephraim, for lying, and on another occasion administered a "talking-to" to an older lad, Thomas Swift: "I talked roundly to [him] about lying and being unfaithful in my businees about breaking up ground for hours"; Thacher Diary, typescript 2, pp. 37–38 (February 1 and 23).

54. George Dow, ed., *Essex County Court Records,* 4 vols. (Boston, 1914), 2: 247; Franklin Bowditch Dexter and Zara Jones Powers, eds., *New Haven Town Records,* 3 vols. (New Haven: Ancient Town Records, 1917–1962), 1: 284–285, quoted by Mary Beth Norton, *Founding Mothers and Fathers: Gendered Power and the Forming of American Society* (New York: Alfred A. Knopf, 1996), p. 51.

55. Sagard, quoted in Axtell, *Indian Peoples of Eastern America,* pp. 35–36.

56. My thoughts on child development have been heavily influenced by Harris, *The Nurture Assumption,* chap. 10, "Gender Rules," citing dozens of studies of modern and traditional cultures. See also Whiting and Edwards, *Children of Different Worlds,* especially pp. 155–157.

57. Pierre de Charlevoix, quoted in Axtell, *Indian Peoples of Eastern America,* pp. 33–34; David Zeisberger in ibid., p. 42; Fox woman in ibid., pp. 64–65. The quotation is from Sagard in ibid., p. 36. These descriptions of the differences in rear-

ing boys and girls are strikingly similar to David Hackett Fischer's depiction of gender roles and childrearing among pioneer families of the southern backcountry in *Albion's Seed: Four British Folkways in America* (New York: Oxford University Press, 1989), pp. 675–680, 687–690. Although Fischer attributes this behavior to customs brought over from the borderlands between Celt and English in Great Britain, Indian folkways may have provided some of the inspiration.

58. Nehemiah Wallington (1598–1658), in Pollock, *Forgotten Children*, p. 147; Hanawalt, "Childrearing among the Lower Classes," p. 22.

59. Ross W. Beales Jr., "Boys' Work on an Eighteenth-Century New England Farm," in *The American Family: Historical Perspectives*, ed. Jean E. Hunter and Paul T. Mason (Pittsburgh: Duquesne University Press, 1991), pp. 75–89.

60. Harris, *The Nurture Assumption*, p. 160.

61. Roger Schofield, "Dimensions of Illiteracy, 1750–1850," *Explorations in Entrepreneurial History* 10 (1973): 437–454; idem, "The Measure of Literacy in Pre-Industrial England," in *Literacy in Traditional Societies*, ed. Jack P. Goody (Cambridge: Cambridge University Press, 1968), pp. 311–325; David Cressy, *Literacy and the Social Order: Reading and Writing in Tudor and Stuart England* (New York: Cambridge University Press, 1980), pp. 2, 128–129.

62. The standard works on early New England schools and school laws are Walter Herbert Small, *Early New England Schools* (Boston: Ginn, 1914); Harlan Updegraff, *The Origin of the Moving School in Massachusetts* (New York: Teachers College, Columbia University, 1908); George Leroy Jackson, *The Development of School Support in Colonial Massachusetts* (1909; reprint, New York: Columbia University Press, 1969). Geraldine Joanne Murphy, "Massachusetts Bay Colony: The Role of Government in Education" (Ph.D. diss., Radcliffe College, 1960), proved the most useful for the seventeenth century. See also Charles J. Hoadley, ed., *Records of the Colony and Plantation of New Haven, from 1638 to 1649* (Hartford: Case, Tiffany, 1857), February 25, 1641–42. On Harvard graduates and their jobs, see Samuel Eliot Morison, *Harvard College in the Seventeenth Century*, 2 vols. (Cambridge, Mass.: Harvard University Press, 1936).

63. Jackson, *School Support*, p. 69; Robert Middlekauff, *Angels and Axioms: Secondary Education in Eighteenth-Century New England* (New Haven: Yale University Press, 1963), p. 15. Watertown's record was one of steady support until the 1680s, when the town dropped Latin. A four-year hiatus was ended in 1690, when the town voted to keep a school according to law.

64. Dexter and Powers, *New Haven Town Records*, 1: 99 (November 17, 1651) and 111–112 (March 11, 1652).

65. Ibid., pp. 48 (October 3, 1650) and 68, 74 (1651).

66. Charles J. Hoadley, ed., *Records of the Colony or Jurisdiction of New Haven, 1653 to the Union* (Hartford: Case, Lockwood, 1858), pp. 376 (May 30, 1660) and 407–408 (1661). Different towns worked out different schemes for complying with the law. Most combined a subsidy to the schoolmaster paid by town taxes with a pension in charge, and a few supplemented these with rental income of

land that had been set aside to support the school. Murphy, "Massachusetts Bay Colony," states that in the first decade, all eight of the hundred-family towns complied with the school laws but only one-third of the fifty-family towns maintained petty schools according to the laws. Thereafter, as new towns grew to the minimum stipulated size, they tended to disregard both requirements.

67. Peter Thacher Diary, typescript 1, pp. 226 (September 24, 1681) and 234 (October 27, 1681); Charles William Manwaring, comp., *A Digest of Early Connecticut Probate Records*, 3 vols. (Hartford: R. S. Peck, 1906), 1: 186 (October 18, 1668); Morison, *Harvard College*, 1: 404–407; Lawrence Cremin, *American Education: The Colonial Experience, 1607–1783* (New York: Harper & Row, 1970), pp. 180–182. Cremin acknowledges these troubles but concludes nevertheless that "By 1650, schooling as an institution had been firmly transplanted." Part of Harvard's problem may have been associated with the declining prestige of ministers. Only four of the Harvard class of 1671 went on to take a second degree, the usual qualifying degree for ministers. Only three students were in residence in the fall of 1674, and only one of the class of 1674 went on to graduate. Samuel Sewall was one of those graduates who went into business instead of the ministry, although this decision seems to have nagged at his conscience the rest of his life.

68. John Langdon Sibley, *Biographical Sketches of the Graduates of Harvard*, vol. 1 (New York: John Reprint, 1967), p. 330; Morison, *Harvard College*, 1: 332. Morison quotes the report of the synod of 1679, written by Increase Mather: "now when we are become many, and more able than at our Beginning, that Society [Harvard?] and other Inferior Schools are in such a Low and Languishing state." Morison estimates the average size of the graduating classes between 1676 and 1683 at slightly over four per year; ibid., pp. 404–407, 423.

69. Signatures offer a straightforward index of the simplest writing skills, providing a way of comparing at least minimum levels of these skills across time and space. These were more advanced skills than reading primers and were generally taught at school or by the minister to sons of the more affluent residents; Schofield, "Dimensions of Illiteracy" and "Measure of Literacy in Pre-Industrial England"; Cressy, *Literacy and the Social Order*, chap. 2. According to Locke, the child was to begin by learning to read and write as painlessly as possible in his native tongue, using the traditional progression from hornbook to primer to Psalter to Bible; *Some Thoughts Concerning Education* (ca. 1685), in *The Educational Writings of John Locke*, ed. James L. Axtell (New York: Cambridge University Press, 1968), p. 260. *The New England Primer*, first published in 1690, combined the hornbook (alphabet and syllabarium) with primer, the Lord's Prayer, the Creed, the Decalogue, and an "authorized catechism"; Cremin, *American Education*, p. 394. Samuel Sewall of Boston sent his children to dame schools to learn how to read at ages four and five and listened to them read from the Bible beginning at age eight. He sent Samuel to Boston Latin School at that age and to writing school at age ten; Sewall, *Diary*, 1: 100, 121, 130, 167, 358.

70. These data appear in Gloria L. Main, "An Inquiry into When and Why Women Learned to Write in Colonial New England," *Journal of Social History* 24 (1991): 579–589.
71. Whiting and Edwards, *Children of Different Worlds,* chap. 3, describe childraising patterns in six cultures.
72. Patricia Crawford, "The Sucking Child: Adult Attitudes to Child Care in the First Year of Life in Seventeenth-Century England," *Continuity and Change* 1 (1986): 41–42.
73. Hanawalt, "Childrearing among the Lower Classes," p. 22.
74. I. K. Ben-Amos, *Adolescence and Youth in Early Modern England* (New Haven: Yale University Press, 1994), pp. 40–47; Margaret Spufford, "First Steps in Literacy: The Reading and Writing Experiences of the Humblest Seventeenth-Century Spiritual Autobiographers," *Social History* 4 (1979): 414–415; Hugh Cunningham, "The Employment and Unemployment of Children in England c. 1680–1850," *Past and Present* 126 (1990): 115–150.
75. Whiting and Edwards, *Children of Different Worlds,* chap. 3, distinguish between training commands and reprimands, the former used in those societies in which women have heavy subsistence work loads and are genuinely in need of their children's assistance. The latter characterize cultures in which mothers want their children to be busy and useful but are unsure how best to make them so. Boys in these cultures are far less cooperative, according to the authors.
76. See Harris' marvelous chapter in *The Nurture Assumption,* "In the Company of Children," pp. 146–182.
77. When minister Peter Thacher moved himself and his family to Barnstable in 1679, "many people and families" came to help them move into their new quarters. In gratitude, he gave out rum and cider and a book of his father's sermons to each family. Because he was a minister, he himself did not participate in the work, however; Diary, typescript 1, p. 189. Locke was to argue that children of pauper parents should be sent to a working school at the age of three to inure them to habits of hard labor; Hugh Cunningham, *Children and Childhood in Western Society since 1500* (London: Longman, 1995), pp. 21–27. Daniel Defoe welcomed textile manufacturing because children aged four or five could earn their own bread by such work; ibid., p. 32.
78. Ann Kussmaul, *Servants in Husbandry in Early Modern England* (Cambridge: Cambridge University Press, 1981); Shurtleff and Pulsifer, *Records of Colony of New Plymouth,* vol. 11: *Laws,* p. 38 (1641); Joseph Merrill, *History of Amesbury and Merrimac, Massachusetts* (1880; reprint, Bowie, Md.: Heritage Books, 1978), p. 199.
79. Peter Laslett has estimated that 27 percent of children aged fifteen were fatherless in early modern England; "Parental Deprivation in the Past: A Note on Orphans and Step Parenthood in English History," in *Family Life and Illicit Love in Earlier Generations: Essays in Historical Sociology,* ed. Peter Laslett (Cambridge: Cambridge University Press, 1977), p. 162 n. 4 and pp. 162–165,

80. Scot's will is in Manwaring, *Connecticut Probate Records,* 1: 33 (November 6, 1643). Turner's will is in Suffolk County Probate Records (microfilm), 1: 103, and his inventory is in ibid., 3: 9. Peverly's will is in Nathaniel Bouton et al., eds., *Probate Records, Vols. 1–6,* vols. 31–40 of *Documents and Records Relating to the Province of New Hampshire,* 40 vols. (Concord, 1867–1941), 2: 89; Carl Bridenbaugh, *Fat Mutton and Liberty of Conscience: Society in Rhode Island, 1636–1690* (Providence: Brown University Press, 1974), p. 77.

81. Suffolk County Probate Records, 6: 587; Dexter and Powers, *New Haven Town Records,* 1: 89 (1651). Bunell's family occasionally required assistance thereafter, and the town sought to bind out another of the boys: "It was said that the boy . . . will be spoyled for want of govermt. [because he] for want of due nurture grows rude and offensive"; ibid., pp. 112, 129.

82. Dexter and Powers, *New Haven Town Records,* 1: 162 (February 1, 1653). Another servant boy in New Haven was accused of burning down his master's barn. When questioned, the boy described frequent beatings: "when the oxen went not right" his master "would knock him"; Hoadley, *Records of Colony of New Haven,* 2: 169 (1656).

83. John Hull, "Diary," in *Puritan Personal Writings: Diaries,* p. 153; Sewall, *Diary,* 1: 34; Peter Thacher Diary, typescript 1 (October 21, 1682) and typescript 2 (November 20, 1682); Lawrence Hammond Diary, Massachusetts Historical Society (April 23, 1688); Joseph Green, "Commonplace Book," in *Puritan Personal Writings: Autobiographies and Other Writings* (1938; reprint, New York: AMS Press, 1983), p. 252.

84. Lorenzo Johnston Greene, *The Negro in Colonial New England* (1942; reprint, New York: Atheneum, 1969), pp. 34, 93–95, 101–104, 110–120.

85. Graves Family Account Book, Connecticut State Archives, Hartford.

86. Joseph H. Smith, ed., *Colonial Justice in Western Massachusetts (1639–1702): The Pynchon Court Record . . .* (Cambridge, Mass.: Harvard University Press, 1961), p. 294 (September 20, 1680). Most young servants in the Chesapeake were immigrants rather than native-born, and were usually without parents or kin to protect them, circumstances that probably account for the difference between the two regions in the limitations placed on masters. According to Maryland law, orphans who were bound out were to be taught a trade, and justices of the Orphans' Court were supposed to inquire yearly into the welfare of all orphan children. See Lois Green Carr, "The Development of the Maryland Orphans' Court, 1654–1715," in *Law, Society, and Politics in Early Maryland,* ed. Aubrey C. Land, Lois Green Carr, and Edward C. Papenfuse (Baltimore: Johns Hopkins University Press, 1977), pp. 43–44.

87. *Diary of Joshua Hempstead from September, 1711 to November, 1758* (New London, Conn.: New London County Historical Society, 1901), p. 462.

88. *The Diary of Thomas Minor, Stonington, Connecticut, 1653–1685* (New London, Conn.: Day, 1899), p. 61 (November 20, 1664): "Manaseth is to be with Thomas Bell for 6 mos at 18s per month including diet, washing, lodging."

89. Sewall, *Diary,* 1: 314; 2: 1085. His daughter Betty at age fifteen was likewise

sent to live with a sewing mistress in Charlestown (1: 359). A reconstitution of the households in Salem Village in 1692 by Paul Boyer and Stephen Nissenbaum shows numerous young girls living as maids with families to whom they were often but not invariably related; *Salem Possessed: The Social Origins of Witchcraft* (Cambridge, Mass.: Harvard University Press, 1974).

90. Morgan, *The Puritan Family,* pp. 76–78. Morgan also reports the case of Sarah Gibbs, who behaved "very sinfully and disorderly," so the Particular Court of Connecticut ordered "that Shee should bee put to service"; *Records of the Particular Court of Connecticut,* Connecticut Historical Society Collections, vol. 22 (Hartford, 1929), p. 97.

91. English Puritan minister Ralph Josselin (1616–1683) threatened his younger son with disinheritance for his continued disobedience. "I should allow him nothing except he tooke himselfe to bee a servt; if he would depart and live in service orderly, I would allow him 10/- yearly"; *The Diary of Ralph Josselin, 1616–1683,* ed. Alan Macfarlane (London: Oxford University Press for the British Academy, 1976), quoted in Pollock, *Forgotten Children,* p. 149.

92. Harris, *The Nurture Assumption,* pp. 91–92, 160–166; Whiting and Edwards, *Children of Different Worlds,* pp. 150–158; Gaskins, "Mayan Parental Theories," pp. 360–362.

93. The tools for these activities were common items in probate inventories, as were Bibles.

94. Children's activities among Native Americans are described in Axtell, *Peoples of Eastern America.* Harvest celebrations are described in Wood, *New England's Prospect,* p. 105; Williams, *A Key into the Language,* p. 231; and Gookin, *Historical Collections,* p. 153.

95. Rye and oats could be scythed without damaging the heads, but wheat would shatter and so had to be held up with one hand and sickled with the other. Women did not sickle as fast as men, but they tended to do it more carefully, losing fewer grains in the process; Harriet Bradley, *Men's Work, Women's Work: A Sociological History of the Sexual Division of Labor in Employment* (Minneapolis: University of Minnesota Press, 1989), pp. 77–85.

96. See Judith Harris on small, mixed-age play groups in nonindustrialized agricultural societies in *The Nurture Assumption,* pp. 90–94, and on larger age-peer groups in modern Western societies, pp. 161–182. John Cotton, *A Practical Commentary, or An Exposition with Observations, Reasons and Uses upon the First Epistle Generall of John* (London, 1656), p. 124, quoted in Morgan, *The Puritan Family,* p. 66. On the other hand, minister John Norton believed that "Idleness in youth is scarcely healed without a scar in age." "Life is but short," he pointed out; John Norton, *Abel Being Dead yet Speaketh* (London, 1658), p. 9, quoted in Morgan, *The Puritan Family,* p. 66. Hempstead, *Diary,* p. 617 (November 29, 1753). On one occasion memorable for its near uniqueness, Samuel Sewall took his own children and four others on a sail and a picnic to an island in Boston Harbor. There they dined on "a Turkey and other Fowls: had a fair wind home"; Sewall, *Diary,* p. 182.

97. A notable consequence of militia training days can be discovered by tracking back nine months from the dates of birth of babies born to newlyweds; Thompson, *Sex in Middlesex*, pp. 20, 41; and data from town genealogies and vital records on marriages and births of first children (cited in Chapter 4, note 39).

98. "Josiah Cotton of Plymouth in New England, Esq., Memoirs in Three Parts originally begun December 1, Anno 1726," Massachusetts Historical Society, pp. 58–61.

99. Ruth Wallis Herndon, "Research Note: Literacy among New England's Transient Poor, 1750–1800," *Journal of Social History* 29 (1996): 963–965.

100. Sewall, *Diary*, p. 119.

7. Youth and Old Age

1. Quoted in Roger Thompson, *Sex in Middlesex: Popular Mores in a Massachusetts County, 1649–1699* (Amherst: University of Massachusetts Press, 1986), p. 88.

2. Ibid.

3. William Gouge, *Of Domesticall Duties* (Amsterdam: Theatrum Orbis Terrarum, 1622), pp. 545–547, quoted in Paul Griffiths, *Youth and Authority* (Oxford: Oxford University Press, 1996), p. 49.

4. Thompson, *Sex in Middlesex*, p. 209, quoting from Martin Ingram, "Ecclesiastical Justice in Wiltshire, 1600–1640" (Ph.D. diss., Oxford University, 1976), p. 239.

5. J. M. Beattie, *Crime and the Courts in England, 1660–1800* (Princeton: Princeton University Press, 1986); Edgar J. McManus, *Law and Liberty in Early New England: Criminal Justice and Due Process, 1620–1692* (Amherst: University of Massachusetts Press, 1993); Bradley Chapin, *Criminal Justice in Colonial America, 1606–1660* (Athens: University of Georgia Press, 1983); Joseph H. Smith and Thomas G. Barnes, *The English Legal System: Carryover to the Colonies* (Los Angeles: University of California Press, 1975); Edwin Powers, *Crime and Punishment in Early Massachusetts, 1620–1692* (Boston: Beacon Press, 1966); N. E. H. Hull, *Female Felons: Women and Serious Crime in Colonial Massachusetts* (Urbana: University of Illinois Press, 1987).

6. According to Paul Griffiths, historians of early modern France and Italy have reported finding secret youth organizations, but no parallels have yet been found in England, leading people to doubt the importance of "youth culture" there; *Youth and Authority*, pp. 169–174.

7. Thompson, *Sex in Middlesex*, pp. 90–96; Griffiths, *Youth and Authority*, p. 49.

8. Clifford K. Shipton's biographies of Harvard graduates supply many hilarious examples of wild times at the college; *New England Life in the 18th Century: Representative Biographies from Sibley's Harvard Graduates* (Cambridge, Mass.: Harvard University Press, 1963).

9. Ralph Houlbrooke, *The English Family, 1450–1700* (New York: Longman, 1982), p. 173; Ann Kussmaul, *Servants in Husbandry: Early Modern England* (Cambridge: Cambridge University Press, 1981); Griffiths, *Youth and Authority*, p. 7;

Ilana Krausman Ben-Amos, *Adolescence and Youth in Early Modern England* (New Haven: Yale University Press, 1994), pp. 39–47; Laura Gowing, *Domestic Dangers: Women, Words and Sex in Early Modern London* (Oxford: Clarendon Press, 1996), p. 192.

10. Gloria L. Main and Jackson T. Main, "The Red Queen in New England?" *William and Mary Quarterly* 61 (1999): 121–150.

11. Anthony Fletcher, *Gender, Sex, and Subordination in England, 1500–1800* (New Haven: Yale University Press, 1995), p. 89.

12. In England the minimum age for departing apprenticeship was twenty-four for males and twenty-one for women, or less if they married; Griffiths, *Youth and Authority*, pp. 60, 5.

13. Character references submitted on behalf of a young single man who was principal in a court case, quoted by Thompson in *Sex in Middlesex*, p. 84.

14. Griffiths, *Youth and Authority*, pp. 30, 66, 73.

15. Diary of John May, American Antiquarian Society, Worcester, Mass.; Samuel Lane, *A Journal for the Years 1739–1803*, ed. Charles L. Hanson (Concord: New Hampshire Historical Society, 1937); excerpts from the diary of Jabez Fitch published in occasional issues of the *Mayflower Descendant*. Later portions of this diary are in the Peter Force Papers, Library of Congress, Washington, D.C.; earlier ones are in the manuscript collections of the Bailey/Howe Library at the University of Vermont.

16. Ruggles, Suffolk County Probate Records (microfilm), 12: 272; Bullen, ibid., 11: 177; Beal, ibid., 18: 428; Whiton, ibid., 72: 307. Joseph Olmsted of East Hartford debited his son Joseph Jr. for yearly boarding from 1695 through 1699 and credited him for various kinds of work beginning in 1688, such as driving plow, weeding corn, making hay, and weaving; Joseph Olmsted Account Book, American Antiquarian Society.

17. Daniel Vickers, *Farmers and Fishermen: Two Centuries of Work in Essex County, Massachusetts, 1630–1830* (Chapel Hill: University of North Carolina Press, 1994), pp. 64–72.

18. Immigrant Emanuel Downing was convinced that the high level of wages would not decrease for generations: "Our Childrens Children will hardly see this great Continent filled with people, soe that our servants will still desire freedome to plant for themselves and not stay but for verie great wages"; Emanuel Downing to John Winthrop (1645), 6 vols. (Boston: Massachusetts Historical Society, 1929–1944), 4: 38.

19. Median ages at first marriage are calculated from the sample of town and family genealogies listed in the Select Bibliography.

20. Gloria L. Main, "Gender, Work, and Wages in Colonial New England," *William and Mary Quarterly* 41 (1994): 39–66. Carol Karlsen has speculated that the inherited property of young single adults, especially of women, did not go through probate but was appropriated and distributed by relatives without legal supervision; Carol Frances Karlsen, *The Devil in the Shape of a Woman: Witchcraft in Colonial New England* (New York: W. W. Norton, 1987), p. 83. Inven-

tories of estates belonging to single women are indeed scarce but not entirely absent from the records. In a sample of probate records used by Main and Main, "Red Queen in New England?", there were 131 such inventories for the period 1630–1774, of which 52 mentioned real as well as personal estate. With only a handful of exceptions, these were small estates. There were 2,371 inventoried estates of single men in the sample, a ratio of 18 to 1.

21. *Suffolk Deeds,* 14 vols. (Boston: Rockwell and Churchill Press, 1880–1906), 1: 199; Charles J. Hoadley, ed., *Records of the Colony and Plantation of New Haven, from 1638 to 1649* (Hartford: Case, Tiffany, 1857), pp. 13, 130.

22. "Josiah Cotton of Plymouth in New-England, Esq. Memoirs: in Three Parts originally begun December 1, Anno 1726," manuscript, Massachusetts Historical Society, p. 219.

23. Josiah Cotton, "Cotton Genealogy," in ibid.

24. Ibid., p. 213. He and his wife had four sons born and died in four years, 1720–1723. Although the son born in 1724, Josiah II, survived, none did so thereafter.

25. Ibid., p. 227.

26. Ibid., p. 161; John Langdon Sibley, *Biographical Sketches of the Graduates of Harvard* (New York: Johnson Reprint, 1967), pp. 4, 401–402.

27. Diaries indicate that maid's work was normally performed by young, unmarried girls, often kin, who seldom stayed more than three months at a time. There were few female indentured servants available, except for Indian girls after King Philip's War.

28. Probate accounts disclose that daughters were more likely than sons to accept this role.

29. The rise in the median ages at death was more impressive: from sixty-four to seventy for men and from sixty-five to sixty-nine for women.

30. An English writer of the seventeenth century described old age as that time in life when "all the abilities of the mind shall be decayed"; Thomas Powell, *Beauty, Vigour and Strength of Youth* (1676), pp. 57–59, quoted in Griffiths, *Youth and Authority,* p. 50.

31. See John Demos, "Old Age in Early New England," in *Turning Points: Historical and Sociological Essays on the Family,* ed. John Demos and Sarane Spece Boorcock (Chicago: University of Chicago Press, 1978), pp. 279–285, on the status of elderly by sociologists. Status depends on power, whether earned or ascribed. The source of legitimate power varies from one society to another but is often associated with wealth, which may have been inherited or personally accumulated by selling special services, control over special knowledge, or dealing in rare goods that are especially prized.

32. Kathleen Bragdon says nothing about old age or elders but quotes Roger Williams on the Narragansetts, who, he said, had a governmental structure paralleling that described in the Old Testament for the ancient kingdom of Israel: kings, priests, and prophets. Kings rule; priests perform and manage their worship, and their "wise men and old men of which number the priests are also

... they make solemne speeches and orations, or Lectures to them, concerning Religion, Peace, or Warre and all things"; *A Key into the Language of America,* ed. John T. Teunissen and Evelyn J. Hing (Detroit: Wayne State University Press, 1973), p. 192.

33. Kathleen J. Bragdon, *Native People of Southern New England, 1500–1650* (Norman: University of Oklahoma Press, 1996), p. 123.

34. In her memoir about her captivity, Mary Rowlandson tells a hilarious story about her Indian master, Quanopin, a sachem of the Narragansetts. Rowlandson identified three wives, each of whom kept her own separate household: the "old" one, who was kind and nurturing; the second one, the queenly Weetamo, who disliked and resented Rowlandson; and a young wife, mother to two small children, who lived at a distance from the others. One day after drinking, the old sachem got a little randy but was repulsed by Weetamo. When he called Rowlandson into his presence, she feared for her honor, but he offered her no insult, as she put it, and eventually settled for his old wife, who cheerfully accommodated him. Mary Rowlandson, "The Soveraignty and Goodness of God" (1682), in *Puritans among the Indians: Accounts of Captivity and Redemption, 1676–1724,* ed. Alden T. Vaughan and Edward W. Clark (Cambridge, Mass.: The Belknap Press of Harvard University Press, 1981), pp. 29–76.

35. Bragdon, *Native People of Southern New England,* pp. 107–115, 175–183.

36. S. Kelly Robinson and Patricia E. Rubestone, "Preliminary Biocultural Interpretations from a Seventeenth-Century Narragansett Indian Cemetery in Rhode Island," in *Cultures in Contact: The Impact of European Contacts on Native American Cultural Institutions, A.D. 1000–1800* (Washington, D.C.: Anthropological Society of Washington, 1985), pp. 117–119.

37. Massachusetts Historical Society Collections, 1st ser., vol. 9 (Boston, 1800), pp. 168–169.

38. Daniel Vickers, *Farmers and Fishermen,* pp. 64–77.

39. Accounts of administration in probate records and private account books from late in the seventeenth century contain occasional references to leasing and rental arrangements, most often single fields or houses by the year and not the complete operating farm. The Pynchon family papers contain numerous references to tenants in the upper Connecticut River Valley, an unusual state of affairs in New England; Stephen Innes, *Labor in a New Land: Economy and Society in Seventeenth-Century Springfield* (Princeton: Princeton University Press, 1983).

40. Retirement contracts were relatively common in medieval and early modern England, according to Barbara A. Hanawalt, *The Ties That Bound: Peasant Families in Medieval England* (New York: Oxford University Press, 1989), p. 225; and Houlbrooke, *The English Family,* p. 189, who surveyed the evidence and discovered that the majority of elderly married people of both sexes (i.e., those aged sixty and over) lived with unmarried children but only 5 percent lived with children who were married.

41. William Gouge in *Domesticall Duties* advised: "God hath so disposed everyones severall place as there is not anyone, but in some respect is under another";

quoted by Griffiths, *Youth and Authority*, p. 67. English magistrates and ministers, as well as writers, maintained the "patriarchal fiction" about the family as a "little commonwealth," in which the male head of household exercised a magisterial function over all those under his care.

42. Henry Elkins to son Gershom, 1667, in Nathaniel Bouton et al., eds., *Probate Records, Vols. 1–6*, vols. 31–40 of *Documents Relating to the Province of New Hampshire* (Concord, 1867–1941), 1: 95; Elkins to "son" Abraham Harding (probably a son-in-law), in W. C. Pelkly, ed., *Early Records of the Town of Providence*, 21 vols. (Providence: Snow & Farnham, 1892–1915), 4: 93; Joseph Jones to Ephraim Jones, 1718, Suffolk County Probate Records, 21: 109; John Hurd and Debro Hurd to son-in-law Nathaniel Gold of Harwich in 1717, *Mayflower Descendant* 16 (1915): 219; Samuel Bullen and wife Experience of Medfield to her nephew Stephen Sabin, in Suffolk County Deeds, Suffolk County Courthouse, Boston, 35: 49 (1718).

43. Zephine Humphrey, *The Story of Dorset* (Rutland, Vt.: C. E. Tuttle, 1924), pp. 90–91. A pioneer of Norway, New York, left a memoir that included stories about Dorset, and this was among them.

44. Daniel Rogers, *Matrimoniall Honour: or the Mutuall Crowne and Comfort of godly, loyall, and chaste Marriage* (London, 1642), quoted in Houlbrooke, *The English Family*, p. 190.

45. Houlbrooke, *The English Family*, p. 189.

46. *Suffolk Deeds*, 1: 199 (1650).

47. *Mayflower Descendant* 3 (1902): 67 (1678).

48. Suffolk County Probate Records (microfilm), 6: 436 (1678), the will of John Gill, yeoman, who also left to his daughter Rebecca, wife of Joseph Belcher, and to their six children the house and land they lived in; Bouton et al., *New Hampshire Probate Records*, 2: 306 (will written 1685 and proved 1686).

49. Houlbrooke, *The English Family*, p. 192. Seventeenth-century English censuses show that only 5 percent of the elderly who were living independently had grandchildren living with them without their parents, and that these grandparents tended to be among the more well-to-do.

50. Unpublished research by Jackson T. Main, who kindly supplied his conclusions.

51. Based on laws and probate cases in the colonies mentioned for the period before 1690.

52. The earliest example of this kind of will that I have seen is that drawn by the wealthy William Moulton of Hampton, New Hampshire, in 1663; Bouton et al., *New Hampshire Probate Records*, 1: 66. See also the settlement of the estate of William Savel of Braintree in Suffolk County Probate Records, 6: 64.

53. George Dow, ed., *The Probate Records of Essex County, Massachusetts, 1635–1681*, 3 vols. (1916–1920; reprint, Newburyport, Mass.: Parker River Researchers, 1988), 1: 185–186. When the widow of John Fuller remarried in 1672, the probate court supervised the division of Fuller's real and personal estate, including the widow's dower, and then the widow transferred her dower lands

to her son in exchange for seven pounds per year for life. The court ordered
that the real estate in question be "bound for the performance" of that agreement; ibid., 2: 57–60; quotation p. 60.

54. The key change in Massachusetts law with respect to dower came in a law of
1701, "where no division can be made by metes and bounds, so as a woman
cannot be endowed of the thing itself, she shall be endowed thereof . . . a third
part of the rents, issues, or profits." Who determined when an estate was not
divisible? In Massachusetts, the judge of probate appointed a committee of the
town where the decedent owned the property in question to make that judgment. In every case where this judgment was recorded by the clerk of probate,
the conclusion of the townsmen was that the property was indivisible, relegat-
ing the widow from manager to annuitant dependent on a contract with the
heir. The literature on dower in England and the colonies is extensive and
technical. For England, the most comprehensive work is Amy Louise Erickson,
Women and Property in Early Modern England (London: Routledge, 1993); but see
criticisms by Lawrence Stone, *Uncertain Unions: Marriage in England, 1660–1753*
(Oxford: Oxford University Press, 1992), p. 14 n. 5, who cites Susan Staves,
Married Women's Separate Property in England, 1660–1833 (Cambridge, Mass.:
Harvard University Press, 1990). See also the discussion of men's wills by Keith
Wrightson, "Kinship in an English Village: Terling, Essex 1500–1700," in *Land,
Kinship and Life-Cycle,* ed. Richard M. Smith (Cambridge: Cambridge University
Press, 1984), pp. 313–332, an interpretation of Terling wills that is strikingly
similar to my reading of early New England wills. For New England, one begins
with George L. Haskins, who is especially strong on Massachusetts and Plym-
outh Colony, in "The Beginnings of Partible Inheritance in the American Col-
onies," *Yale Law Journal* 51 (1942): 1280–1315; idem, *Law and Authority in
Early Massachusetts: A Study in Tradition and Design* (New York: Macmillan,
1960); idem, "The Legal Heritage of Plymouth Colony," *University of Pennsylvania Law Review* 110 (1962): 847–859; Richard B. Morris, *Studies in the History of
American Law,* 2d ed. (New York: Columbia University Press, 1964); and
Marylynn Salmon, who treats New Haven and Connecticut in *Women and the
Law of Property in Early America* (Chapel Hill: University of North Carolina Press,
1986). The conclusions in the text rest on my own studies of the practices of all
these colonies plus New Hampshire.

55. Urban widows lived in a much more accommodating milieu. London's inheritance rules were the most generous in England toward women. In Boston,
widows and married women entered business freely. The earliest female storekeeper did business out of her house: Elizabeth Hubbard, widow, kept seventy
pounds' worth of "wares" in her lower room, which perhaps fronted on the
street. Her estate had thirty pounds in debts receivable and seventy-five
pounds in debts payable; Suffolk County Probate Records, 2: 36 (February 6,
1644). A Mrs. Stolyon, whose husband was still alive, bought a share in the
ship built by New Havenites in 1644 and drove a hard bargain retailing cloth;
Hoadley, *New Haven Colony Records,* 1: 147, 171; Halifax Jones, likewise of New

Haven, freely did business on her own account and even challenged her husband's creditor's attempt to attach a boat she had sold; ibid., 2: 121. C. Dallett Hemphill used Essex County (Mass.) court records to show the extent to which women were knowledgeable about the possessions and financial affairs of their families; Hemphill, "Women in Court: Sex Role Differentiation in Salem, Massachusetts, 1636–1683," *William and Mary Quarterly* 39 (1982): 164–175.

56. Sarah Warren Prince Osborne's story appears in Karlsen, *Devil in the Shape of a Woman*, p. 243; and in Paul Boyer and Stephen Nissenbaum, *Salem Possessed: The Social Origins of Witchcraft* (Cambridge, Mass.: Harvard University Press), pp. 193–194. Karlsen treats the sexual accusations as unsubstantiated gossip and lays emphasis on the dispute over land between Sarah and her sons. See Dow, *Essex County Probate Records*, 2: 401–402. Because, under English common law, however, a wife could be barred from her dower rights if she had deserted her husband or committed adultery, Osborne's neighbors may have thought she lost her dower rights if she cohabited with her servant before marrying him.

57. Cotton Mather, *The Old Man's Honour: Addresses to Old Men, and Young Men and Little Children* (Boston, 1690). One wonders if his father, Increase, was causing gossip back in England, where he was lobbying for the restoration of Massachusetts' original charter.

58. Suffolk County Deeds, 35: 8. Elizabeth Ellis, widow, mortgaged property to Elizabeth Phillips and Abigail Philips, spinsters, for L300, due in one year, canceled two years later; ibid., p. 28.

59. For a description of changes in the New England economy and currency-related problems in the eighteenth century, see Main and Main, "The Red Queen in New England?"

60. John Duffy, *Epidemics in Colonial America* (Baton Rouge: Louisiana State University Press, 1953), pp. 164–165; William H. McNeill, *Plagues and Peoples* (Garden City, N.Y.: Doubleday, 1976), pp. 52–53.

61. Diphtheria is caused by a bacillus, scarlet fever by a streptococcus infection; Duffy, *Epidemics in Colonial America*, pp. 113–114. According to a contemporary pamphlet reporting fatalities in New Hampshire in 1735–36, four out of five victims of the throat distemper were under age ten, and fewer than one out of a hundred were over age thirty; ibid., p. 119.

62. Duffy, *Epidemics in Colonial America*, pp. 206–207, 218–222. Of thirteen towns from southern New England included in this study, Rowley showed the lowest proportion of children surviving per family, only 73 percent for the period 1620–1775, compared to lows of 77 and 78 percent in Weymouth, on the coast south of Boston in Massachusetts; in Woodstock, in the interior of northeastern Connecticut; and in Wallingford, north of New Haven in Connecticut. Elsewhere the average share of children surviving ranged from 80 to 87 percent. The town samples contain sufficient data on which to calculate the proportion of children surviving to adulthood or marriage for only 45 percent of the fami-

lies, so that even a slight bias in reporting would swamp these figures. See the Select Bibliography for the town and family genealogies included in this study.

63. Duffy, *Epidemics in Colonial America*, gives many examples of medical treatments utilized by the colonists. For contemporary reports, see William Wood, *New England's Prospect*, ed. Alden T. Vaughan (Amherst: University of Massachusetts Press, 1977); Roger Williams, *A Key into the Language;* and John Josselyn, *John Josselyn, Colonial Traveler: A Critical Edition of Two Voyages to New England*, ed. Paul J. Lindholdt (Hanover, N.H.: University Press of New England, 1988). Medical theories and practices in colonial Massachusetts are described in Philip Cash, Eric H. Christianson, and J. Worth Estes, eds., *Medicine in Colonial Massachusetts 1620–1820* (Boston: Colonial Society of Massachusetts, 1980); Cotton Mather, *The Angel of Bethesda*, ed. Gordon W. Jones (Barre, Mass.: American Antiquarian Society and Barre Publishers, 1972); Laurel Thatcher Ulrich, "The Living Mother of a Living Child," *William and Mary Quarterly:* 27–50. See also essays in Peter Benes, ed., *Medicine and Healing* (Boston: Boston University Press, 1992). Samuel Sewall occasionally mentions herbal remedies in his diary, such as spirits of lavender to be taken with figs, "that food and Physick might go together"; *The Diary of Samuel Sewall, 1675–1729*, ed. M. Halsey Thomas, 2 vols. (New York: Farrar, Straus and Giroux, 1973), 1: 141, 594.

64. Williams, *A Key into the Language*, chap. 21; Bragdon, *Native People of Southern New England*, pp. 240–244. For contrary arguments, see Elise M. Brenner, "Sociopolitical Implications of Mortuary Ritual Remains in 17th-Century Native Southern New England," in *The Recovery of Meaning: Historical Archaeology in the Eastern United States*, ed. Mark P. Leone and Parker B. Potter Jr. (Washington, D.C.: Smithsonian Institution, 1988), pp. 147–182. For other contemporary observations on Indian religion and funerary customs, see Thomas Morton, *New English Canaan; or, New Canaan, Containing an Abstract of New England* (1632) (New York: Peter Smith, 1947), p. 27; Wood, *New England's Prospect*, pp. 100–102; and Daniel Gookin, *Historical Collections of the Indians of New England* (1674), Massachusetts Historical Society Collections, 1st ser., vol. 1 (Boston, 1792), p. 20.

65. On attitudes among the English in New England toward supernatural actions in the natural world, see David D. Hall, *Worlds of Wonder, Days of Judgment: Popular Religious Beliefs in Early New England* (New York: Alfred A. Knopf, 1989), particularly chap. 2; Richard Godbeer, *The Devil's Dominion: Magic and Religion in Early New England* (New York: Cambridge University Press, 1992); and Michael Winship, *Seers of God: Puritan Providentialism in the Restoration and Early Enlightenment* (Baltimore: Johns Hopkins University Press, 1996).

66. Peter Benes, *The Masks of Orthodoxy: Folk Gravestone Carving in Plymouth County, Massachusetts, 1689–1805* (Amherst: University of Massachusetts Press, 1977), pp. 35–36; Mary Cooper, *The Diary of Mary Cooper: Life on a Long Island Farm, 1768–1773*, ed. Field Horne (New York: Oyster Bay Historical Society, 1981), p. 54.

67. Quoted in Benes, *Masks of Orthodoxy,* p. 227.
68. David E. Stannard, *The Puritan Way of Death: A Study in Religion, Culture and Social Change* (New York: Oxford University Press, 1977), pp. 72–95.
69. Benes, *Masks of Orthodoxy,* p. 35; Gordon Geddes, *Welcome Joy: Death in Puritan New England* (Ann Arbor: UMI Research Press, 1981), pp. 146–149.
70. Clare Gittings, *Death, Burial and the Individual in Early Modern England* (London: Croom Helm, 1984), pp. 67–74. Because of the sacred fate of the body, it was against the law in England to dissect corpses. Thus medical schools had to hire grave robbers to acquire them for research and classes in anatomy. According to Gittings, the general public developed such a horror of these practices that when Parliament forbade Christian burial for murderers in the eighteenth century, crowds of rioters would prevent their corpses from being carried off to medical schools.
71. See Gittings, *Death, Burial and the Individual,* pp. 110–118; and David Cressy, *Birth, Marriage and Death: Ritual, Religion and the Life-Cycle in Tudor and Stuart England* (Oxford: Oxford University Press, 1997).
72. Geddes, *Welcome Joy,* p. 11, provides the biblical bases for Christian ideas about death. Medieval scholarship shifted attention away from the resurrection and Judgment day to the situation of the soul when released into eternity. It could go to hell, purgatory, or heaven, depending on the spiritual state in which the individual died. Saying masses and praying for the souls of the dead was deemed efficacious by Catholics for getting souls out of purgatory, but Reformed Protestants, including Puritans, did not believe in purgatory. It was their negative reaction to the idea that good works by humans could earn them dispensations from God that brought Puritans to emphasize the absoluteness of God's gift of salvation.
73. David Watters, *"With Bodilie Eyes": Eschatological Themes in Puritan Literature and Gravestone Art* (Ann Arbor: UMI Research Press, 1981), p. 10.
74. Ibid., p. 35.

8. Transitions: The Narragansetts

1. Alfred W. Crosby, *Ecological Imperialism: The Biological Expansion of Europe, 900–1900* (Cambridge: Cambridge University Press, 1986).
2. Kathleen J. Bragdon, *Native Peoples of Southern New England, 1500–1650* (Norman: University of Oklahoma Press, 1996), pp. 107–115, 179–181; Peter T. Ellison, "Breastfeeding, Fertility, and Maternal Condition," in *Breastfeeding: Biocultural Perspectives,* ed. Patricia Stuart-Macadam and Katherine A. Dettwyler (Hawthorne, N.Y.: Aldine de Gruyter, 1995), pp. 305–345; Sarah Blaffer Hrdy, *Mother Nature: A History of Mothers, Infants, and Natural Selection* (New York: Pantheon Books, 1999), pp. 183–188, 193–200. Skeletons recovered from precontact Narragansett graves show good nutritional status, whereas later burials exhibit bone effects of widespread tuberculosis, arthritis, osteoporosis, nonspecific infections, vitamin C deficiencies, and tooth caries; Paul A. Robin-

son, Marc Kelley, and Patricia E. Rubertone, "Preliminary Interpretations from a Seventeenth-Century Narragansett Indian Cemetery in Rhode Island," in *Cultures in Contact,* ed. William W. Fitzhugh (Washington, D.C.: Smithsonian Institution, 1985), pp. 117–119.

3. James W. Wood, *Dynamics of Human Reproduction: Biology, Biometry, Demography* (New York: Aldine de Gruyter, 1994), pp. 31–32; Hubert Charbonneau et al., *The First French Canadians: Pioneers in the St. Lawrence Valley* (Newark, Del.: University of Delaware Press; London: Association of University Presses, 1993); Robert Ross, *Beyond the Pale: Essays on the History of Colonial South Africa* (Middletown, Conn.: Wesleyan University Press, 1993); Lee L. Bean, Geraldine P. Mineau, and Douglas L. Anderton, *Fertility Change on the American Frontier: Adaptation and Innovation* (Berkeley: University of California Press, 1990).

4. Bean, Mineau, and Anderton, *Fertility Change on the American Frontier,* p. 67. A high-fertility response by humans to fill "empty" or vacated space has been exhibited more recently by the Yanomama tribes of Venezuela and Brazil, who have been expanding to fill an ecological vacuum left by the postcontact depopulation of neighboring peoples. See Wood, *Dynamics of Human Reproduction,* p. 32. Robert Charles Anderson offers an excellent thumbnail sketch of John Winthrop in *The Great Migration Begins: Immigrants to New England, 1620–1633,* 3 vols. (Boston: New England Historic Genealogical Society, 1995), 3: 2039–41.

5. According to reports from Jacques Cartier and others in the sixteenth century, the St. Lawrence Valley had been populated by Iroquoisan speakers who farmed the best lands along the river from Lake Erie to the Gaspé. These Native Americans were gone when Samuel de Champlain founded New France in the early seventeenth century. Archaeologists and anthropologists have been understandably intrigued by the mystery of this disappearance. Was it precipitated by war with the Huron or the Mohawk or by a virulent epidemic introduced by Europeans? Whatever the reason, French colonists of the St. Lawrence did not have to treat with current residents in order to make use of its prime agricultural sites.

6. Neal Salisbury, "Indians and Colonists in Southern New England after the Pequot War: An Uneasy Balance," in *The Pequots in Southern New England: The Fall and Rise of an American Indian Nation,* ed. Laurence M. Hauptman and James D. Whery (Norman: University of Oklahoma Press, 1990), pp. 81–95.

7. Darrett B. Rutman, *Husbandmen of Plymouth: Farms and Villages in the Old Colony, 1620–1692* (Boston: Beacon Press for Plimoth Plantation, 1967).

8. Salisbury, "Indians and Colonists," p. 89.

9. John Frederick Martin, *Profits in the Wilderness: Entrepreneurship and the Founding of New England Towns in the Seventeenth Century* (Chapel Hill: University of North Carolina Press, 1991), pp. 51–52.

10. Martin, *Profits in the Wilderness,* pp. 53–56; Richard S. Dunn, *Puritans and Yankees: The Winthrop Dynasty of New England, 1650–1717* (New York: W. W. Norton, 1971), pp. 70, 186, 202; Sydney V. James, *Colonial Rhode Island: A History* (New York: Charles Scribner's Sons, 1975), pp. 85–113. As early as 1645, Emanuel

Downing wrote to John Winthrop Jr. about the benefits to be won by making war on the Narragansetts: "If upon a Just warre the lord should deliver them into our hands, wee might easily have men women and children enough to exchange for Moores, which wilbe more gaynefull pilladge for us then we conceive"; *Winthrop Papers,* 6 vols. (Boston: Massachusetts Historical Society, 1929–1944), 5: 38–39.

11. Richard S. Dunn, "John Winthrop, Jr., and the Narragansett Country," *William and Mary Quarterly* 13 (1956): 68–86.

12. Peter A. Thomas, *In the Maelstrom of Change: The Indian Trade and Cultural Process in the Middle Connecticut River Valley, 1635–1665* (New York: Garland Press, 1990), p. 395; Dean R. Snow, *The Iroquois* (Oxford: Blackwell, 1994), pp. 116–121; *The Correspondence of Roger Williams,* ed. Glenn W. LaFantasie, 2 vols. (Hanover, N.H.: Brown University Press and University Press of New England, 1988), 2: 556–570, 594–604.

13. Williams, *Correspondence,* 2: 614–616; Dunn, "John Winthrop, Jr.," p. 72; idem, *Puritans and Yankees,* pp. 159–160.

14. Gloria L. Main and Jackson T. Main, "The Red Queen in New England?" *William and Mary Quarterly* 58 (1999): 121–150.

15. Williston Walker, *Creeds and Platforms of Congregationalism* (New York: Scribner's Sons, 1893; Boston: Pilgrim Press, 1960), p. 431.

16. Stephen Saunders Webb, *1676: The End of American Independence* (New York: Alfred A. Knopf, 1984), pp. 239–242; and Daniel K. Richter, *The Ordeal of the Longhouse: The Peoples of the Iroquois League in the Era of European Colonization* (Chapel Hill: University of North Carolina Press, 1992), pp. 135–137.

17. Douglas Leach, *Flintlock and Tomahawk: New England in King Philip's War* (New York: W. W. Norton, 1966); James David Drake, "Severing the Ties That Bind Them: A Reconceptualization of King Philip's War" (Ph.D. diss., University of California at Los Angeles, 1996); Eric Spencer Johnson, "'Some by flatteries and others by threatenings': Political Strategies among Native Americans of Seventeenth-Century Southern New England" (Ph.D. diss., University of Massachusetts, 1993). Peace with Canada came with the Treaty of Utrecht in 1713, but peace with the Abenaki and their partners was not fully restored until the Five Nations undertook full pacification of British borders in a treaty agreement with the British in 1722; Richter, *The Ordeal of the Longhouse,* pp. 236–254.

18. Suffolk County Probate Records (microfilm), 8: 23, undated; Neal Salisbury, *Manitou and Providence: Indians, Europeans, and the Makings of New England, 1500–1643* (New York: Oxford University Press, 1982), p. 52; Leach, *Flintlock and Tomahawk,* pp. 243, 247; Webb, *1676,* pp. 221–244.

19. George D. Langdon Jr., *Pilgrim Colony: A History of New Plymouth, 1620–1691* (New Haven: Yale University Press, 1966), pp. 181–182; Ian K. Steele, *War Paths: Invasions of North America* (New York: Oxford University Press, 1994), pp. 107–108; Sherburne F. Cook, "Interracial Warfare and Population Decline among the New England Indians," *Ethnohistory* 20 (1973): 1–24.

20. Daniel Mandell, "'To Live More like My Christian English Neighbors': Natick Indians in the Eighteenth Century," *William and Mary Quarterly* 48 (1991): 552–

556; Harold W. Van Lonkhuyzen, "A Reappraisal of the Praying Indians: Acculturation, Conversion, and Identity at Natick, Massachusetts, 1646–1730," *New England Quarterly* 62 (1990): 420–440. Jean M. O'Brien explains how the Natick Indians lost the land and their autonomy in *Dispossession by Degrees: Indian Land and Identity in Natick, Massachusetts, 1650–1790* (Cambridge: Cambridge University Press, 1997). See the census summaries in Evarts B. Greene and Virginia D. Harrington, *American Population before the Federal Census of 1790* (1932; reprint, Gloucester, Mass.: Peter Smith, 1966), pp. 61–69.

21. Greene and Harrington, *American Population*, pp. 14–17, 48–59; William S. Simmons, "Narragansett Identity Persistence," in *Hidden Minorities: The Persistence of Ethnicity in American Life*, ed. Joan H. Rollins (Washington, D.C.: University Press of America, 1981), p. 37. Simmons estimated that there were fewer than seventy Narragansetts remaining after the war and believes all were forced into long terms of indentured servitude.

22. Suffolk County Probate Records, 13: 439; ibid., 15: 415; W. C. Pelkly, ed., *Early Records of the Town of Providence*, 21 vols. (Providence: Snow & Farnham, 1892–1915), 17: 266–277.

23. Frances Manwaring Caulkins, *History of Norwich, Connecticut, from the Settlement in 1600 to January 1874* (Hartford, 1866), p. 279.

24. Suffolk County Probate Records, 14: 446; ibid., 17: 198.

25. George Dow, ed., *Essex Country Probate Records*, 3 vols. (Salem, Mass.: Essex Institute, 1917) 3: 328. Peter Thacher Diary, Typescript 1, Massachusetts Historical Society, Boston, June 12, August 18, and September 11, 1679, and February 4 and April 8, 1680. After moving to Milton, Thacher continued to use Indian labor there and still retained an Indian girl servant; ibid., July 10 and August 7, 1682; Pelkly, *Early Records of Providence*, 5: 267; Hampshire County Probate Records (microfilm), 3: 138. Joseph Green, minister of Salem Village and successor of the notorious Samuel Parris of witchcraft fame, purchased an Indian woman named Flora at Salem in 1708, but she was probably foreign-born; Joseph Green, "Commonplace Book," in *Puritan Personal Writings: Diaries* (New York: AMS Press, 1983), various paging; *Diary of Joshua Hempstead from September, 1711 to November, 1758* (New London, Conn.: New London County Historical Society, 1901), p. 465.

26. "Josiah Cotton of Plymouth in New-England, Esq. Memoirs: in Three Parts originally begun December 1, Anno 1726," manuscript, Massachusetts Historical Society; Daniel Mandell, *Behind the Frontier: Indians in Eighteenth-Century Eastern Massachusetts* (Lincoln: University of Nebraska Press, 1996), map on frontispiece.

27. Daniel F. Vickers, "The First Indian Whalemen of Nantucket," *William and Mary Quarterly* 40 (1983): 560–583; Edward Byers, *The Nation of Nantucket: Society and Politics in an Early American Commercial Center, 1660–1820* (Northeastern University Press, 1987), pp. 94–100; Plymouth Colony agreed to raise 200 soldiers, including 50 Indians, for a campaign against Quebec; Langdon, *Pilgrim Colony*, p. 211; Mandell, *Behind the Frontier*, p. 102.

28. Mandell, *Behind the Frontier*, pp. 30–36, 102–104, 182–186.

29. The next Rhode Island census, in 1731, listed 1648 "Negroes," not "blacks" as in 1708, and 985 Indians. Both groups concentrated in the southern coastal towns. Connecticut censuses mentioned Indians only once, in 1756, during the Seven Years' War; Greene and Harrington, *American Population,* pp. 59, 63.

30. Greene and Harrington, *American Population,* pp. 62–63. See also Paul R. Campbell and Glenn W. LaFantasie, "Scattered to the Winds of Heaven—Narragansett Indians, 1676–1880," *Rhode Island History* 37 (1978): 67–83; Ruth Wallis Herndon and Ella Wilcox Sekatu, "The Right to a Name: The Narragansett People and Rhode Island Officials in the Revolutionary Era," in *After King Philip's War: Presence and Persistence in Indian New England,* ed. Colin G. Calloway (Hanover, N.H.: Dartmouth College, University Press of New England, 1997), pp. 114–143; Jean M. O'Brien, "'Divorced' from the Land: Resistance and Survival of Indian Women in Eighteenth-Century New England," ibid., pp. 144–161; Thomas L. Doughton, "Unseen Neighbors: Native Americans of Central Massachusetts: A People Who Had 'Vanished,'" ibid., pp. 207–230; and Jack D. Forbes, *Black Africans and Native Americans* (Oxford: Oxford University Press, 1988), pp. 88, 199–208. Philip D. Morgan reports similar white responses in the South to Indians with "African" features; *Slave Counterpoint: Black Culture in the Eighteenth-Century Chesapeake and Lowcountry* (Chapel Hill: University of North Carolina Press, 1998), pp. 479–480.

31. Campbell and LaFantasie, "Scattered to the Winds of Heaven," p. 69.

32. Laura E. Conkey, Ethel Boissevain, and Ives Goddard, "Indians of Southern New England and Long Island: Late Period," in *Handbook of North American Indians,* ed. William Sturtevant, vol. 15: *Northeast,* ed. Bruce Trigger (Washington, D.C.: Smithsonian Institution, 1978), pp. 277–289. The state of Rhode Island abolished the Narragansett reservation in 1880; William S. Simmons, "Red Yankees: Narragansett Conversion in the Great Awakening," *American Ethnologist* 20 (1983): 253–271. What follows rests heavily on Simmons' work and interpretation.

33. Quoted in Simmons, "Red Yankees," p. 260.

34. Ibid., p. 261.

35. *Boston Gazette,* September 1–8, 1735.

36. Hempstead, *Diary,* pp. 342, 360, 377, 380; Park's letter is quoted in Simmons, "Red Yankees," p. 261.

37. On the career of John Davenport see Harry S. Stout, *The New England Soul: Preaching and Religious Culture in Colonial New England* (Oxford: Oxford University Press, 1986), p. 202. All quotations in text are from Simmons, "Red Yankees," p. 262.

38. Joseph Fish, pastor of the church in North Stonington, accused New Lights of being "false teachers and their followers, [who] are of a *lower class*"; quoted in Simmons, "Red Yankees," p. 265. Frederic Denison, *Westerly and Its Witnesses . . .* (Providence: J. A. and R. A. Reid, 1878), p. 80, quoted in Simmons, "Red Yankees," p. 262.

39. Simmons, "Narragansett Identity Persistence," p. 44.

40. Ibid., p. 48.

41. Simmons, "Red Yankees," pp. 263–266; Williams, *A Key into the Language of America*, ed. John T. Teunissen and Evelyn J. Hing (Detroit: Wayne State University Press, 1973), pp. 191–192.

9. Transitions: The English

1. *The History of Woodstock, Connecticut: Genealogies of Woodstock Families*, 8 vols., vols. 1–6 ed. Clarence W. Bowen (Norwood, Mass.: Plimpton Press, 1926–1935), vols. 7–8 ed. Donald Lines Jacobus and William Herbert Wood (Worcester, Mass.: American Antiquarian Society, 1943), 7: 422. The Diary of John May is in the American Antiquarian Society.

2. Thomas Minor, *The Diary of Thomas Minor, Stonington, Connecticut, 1653–1685* (New London, Conn.: Day, 1899).

3. John May Diary, pp. 29–30. He also paid Mr. Carpenter's wife six pounds on account and five shillings to her for butter.

4. Early in the diary he describes "digging clay and filling walls" as part of his work for Lieutenant Bridge.

5. The "French town" was probably Oxford, Massachusetts, fifteen miles from Woodstock, first settled by about thirty families of Huguenot refugees in 1686, attacked and dispersed in 1695–1696, and resettled in 1699. The town was reorganized in 1713 after another abandonment in 1704; Jon Butler, *The Huguenots in America: A Refugee People in New World Society* (Cambridge, Mass.: Harvard University Press, 1983), pp. 60–64; Peter Whitney, *The History of the County of Worcester, in the Commonwealth of Massachusetts* (Worcester, Mass.: Isaiah Thomas, 1793), p. 83.

6. April 19, 1712: "helpt C[ousin] Lyon plow, he had my oxen and mare." April 23: "C[ousin] Lyon helpt me plow with his oxen and plow."

7. After shaving shingles for the roof of his new barn, he laid a thousand of them in a single day, July 3, 1716. He recorded selling a hog in 1727 that weighed 260 pounds, the largest I have encountered in any record outside a newspaper report.

8. His new customers were in Worcester County, of which Woodstock was a part until 1738, when authorities moved Connecticut's border northward, putting Woodstock into Windham County, Connecticut.

9. Thomas Minor stated in 1654 that his father-in-law, Walter Palmer, had given him two oxen and four cows, which were then worth far more in real terms than in John May's time; *Diary of Thomas Minor* (1899), p. 7.

10. "A World of Fields and Fences" is the memorable title of chapter 7 in William Cronon, *Changes in the Land: Indians, Colonists, and the Ecology of New England* (New York: Hill & Wang, 1983), pp. 127–158.

11. Two-wheeled carts still greatly outnumbered wagons in probate inventories at the outbreak of the American Revolution.

12. Unpublished research by the author in the probate records of sample counties of rural New England.

13. Gloria L. Main, "Gender, Work, and Wages in Colonial New England," *William and Mary Quarterly* 51 (1994): 39–66.

14. From 1662 to 1684 there were thirteen inventories in the file of probated estates from sample regions (excluding Boston) that listed seventeen slaves. Three of the slaves were in New Haven/Milford, five were in Hartford/Middletown, three were in Wethersfield, five were in New Hampshire in the Portsmouth/Dover area, and one in Dedham, six miles from Boston. There were no slaves in the inventories in Ipswich and Rowley, in Essex County (but there were a few in Newbury and Salem), or in Plymouth Colony.

15. W. S. Rossiter, *A Century of Population Growth, 1790–1900* (1909; reprint, Baltimore: Genealogical Publishing, 1967), pp. 149–169.

16. Gloria L. Main and Jackson T. Main, "The Red Queen in New England?" *William and Mary Quarterly* 56 (1999): 123–150.

17. Ibid., pp. 131–135.

18. "Working smarter" is how Jan de Vries puts it in "The Industrial Revolution and the Industrious Revolution," *Journal of Economic History* 54 (1994): 249–270.

19. *A Journal for the Years 1739–1803 by Samuel Lane of Stratham, New Hampshire*, ed. Charles Lane Hanson (Concord: New Hampshire Historical Society, 1937). Includes his memoir.

20. The house was torn down by Lane's son Jabez early in the nineteenth century, according to Charles B. Nelson, *History of Stratham, New Hampshire, 1631–1900* (Somersworth, N.H.: New Hampshire Publishing, 1965).

21. This paragraph draws on a vast and richly suggestive literature beginning with Norbert Elias, *Über den Prozess der Zivilsation: The Civilizing Process*, 2 vols., trans. Edmund Jephcott (New York: Pantheon Books, 1982); Philippe Ariès, *Centuries of Childhood* trans. Robert Baldick (New York: Alfred A. Knopf, 1962); and Lawrence Stone, *The Family, Sex, and Marriage in England, 1500–1800* (New York: Harper & Row, 1977). James Deetz argues that the Renaissance influences that transformed English architecture in the late seventeenth century manifested a profoundly new view of the world; *In Small Things Forgotten: The Archaeology of Early American Life*, rev. ed. (New York: Doubleday/Anchor, 1996), pp. 62–67.

22. Michael P. Steinitz, "Landmark and Shelter: Domestic Architecture in the Cultural Landscape of the Central Uplands of Massachusetts in the Eighteenth Centry" (Ph.D. diss., Clark University, 1988). He points out (p. 99) that in 1729 the Massachusetts General Court required that houses in new towns be a minimum of eighteen feet square and seven feet stud (ceiling height).

23. Houses in the Worcester survey built before 1740 were only one or two rooms in size, oriented to maximum light and heat from the sun; ibid. J. S. Wood and Michael P. Steinitz argue that most colonial New Englanders lived in low-ceilinged, one- and two-room houses devoid of the charms imagined by their imitators at the end of the nineteenth century; "A World We Have Gained:

House, Common, and Village in New England," *Journal of Historical Geography* 18 (1992): 105–120. On the 1798 Federal Census of Housing, see Lee Soltow, *The Distribution of Wealth and Income in the United States in 1798* (Pittsburgh: University of Pittsburgh Press, 1989).

24. Steinitz, "Landmark and Shelter," p. 168.

25. Ibid., pp. 165–167.

26. The Cushing farmstead in Hingham, Massachusetts, provides an excellent example of the evolving New England farmhouse. It was originally built in the summer of 1679 and remodeled and rebuilt several times thereafter. Cary Carson's drawings of the structure in 1679 and circa 1762 can be seen in his essay "The Consumer Revolution in America: Why Demand?" in *Of Consuming Interest: The Style of Life in the Eighteenth Century,* ed. Cary Carson, Ronald Hoffman, and Peter J. Albert (Charlottesville: University Press of Virginia for the United States Capitol Historical Society, 1994), pp. 559–562.

27. Ebenezer Parkman, *Diary* (Worcester, Mass.: American Antiquarian Society, 1978), pp. 63, 84. In light of the fact that the federal tax on housing in 1798 based assessments on the number and size of windows, this incident is a telling one.

28. The tensions implied by combining formal assertions of respectability with folksy hospitality are visible in many nineteenth-century farmhouses surviving in Maine today. They have formal front doors facing the road, but these are never used. Often there is nothing but lawn between the granite doorstep and the road. One goes around to the side, as the path or walk clearly indicates. The front door and a clean, well-furnished parlor establish the respectability of the family, but apparently to force guests to use them would be both wasteful and impolite.

29. Richard Bushman sees something more profound in decorative changes: "When the householder covered the beams of the room with a smooth ceiling, moved cooking and sleeping functions to another space, narrowed the fireplace and installed a mantel, when he placed a broad stair in a passage by itself and thought about decorating door and window frames and installing sash windows, then that person indicated a wish to transform his environment and presumably himself along with it . . . After crossing that boundary, a person became alert for every little clue to proper behavior"; *The Refinement of America: Persons, Houses, Cities* (New York: Alfred A. Knopf, 1992), p. 185. I part company with Bushman on this issue. I see no boundary crossed nor any transformation sought in dressing up a new house that retains the old room layout.

30. Gloria L. Main, "Probate Records as a Source for Early American History," *William and Mary Quarterly* 32 (1975): 89–99; idem, "The Correction of Biases in Colonial American Probate Records," *Historical Methods Newsletter* 8 (1974): 10–18.

31. Mary Ellin D'Agostino, "Household Stuffe: Material Culture and Identity in the Seventeenth-Century Anglo-Colonial World" (Ph.D. diss., University of California at Berkeley, 1998). For a bold foray into the ways of seeing by *makers* of

artifacts, see Robert Blair St. George, *Conversing by Signs: Poetics of Implication in Colonial New England Culture* (Chapel Hill: University of North Carolina Press, 1998).

32. Robert Blair St. George, "'Set Thine House in Order': The Domestication of the Yeomanry in Seventeenth-Century New England," in *New England Begins: The Seventeenth Century,* ed. Jonathan L. Fairbanks and Robert F. Trent, 3 vols. (Boston: Boston Museum of Fine Arts, 1982), 2: 168, describes yeoman dining in the late seventeenth century. On the basis of their counts of shards uncovered in excavations, archaeologists insist that probate inventories seriously undercount the amount of ceramic- and glassware present in "ordinary" households. That may be, but if the very perceptible rise in the number of ceramic and glass items in the eighteenth-century inventories is real, the dearth in the seventeenth century must be equally real.

33. Joseph Green, "Commonplace Book," in *Puritan Personal Writings: Autobiographies and Other Writings* (New York: AMS Press, 1938), variable paging. "Major Vaughan" was probably William, born ca. 1641, who had been apprenticed to Sir Josiah Child of London, merchant, and was first recorded in New England in 1664, or his son, George, who became lieutenant governor of New Hampshire and died in 1724 an immensely wealthy man. Both Vaughans were influential merchants. See their biographies in Sybil Noyes, Charles Thornton Libby, and Walter Goodwin Davis, *Genealogical Dictionary of Maine and New Hampshire* (1928–1939; reprint, Baltimore: Genealogical Publishing, 1972, 1976, 1979, 1983, 1988), p. 704.

34. Featherbeds and bedding had grown cheaper in real terms. They were more expensive than milk cows until the Seven Years' War, when the prices of all farm animals abruptly rose. The prices of sheeting and other textiles at the end of the colonial period were almost a third less in sterling value than they had been in 1700.

35. Ruth Schwartz Cowan, *More Work for Mother: The Ironies of Household Technologies from the Open Hearth to the Microwave* (New York: Basic Books, 1983), pp. 16–39.

36. "Middling" refers to the range of male decedents' estates between the thirtieth and eightieth percentile in the frequency distribution of total estate wealth in each period, in which the records of each age group have been reweighted to conform to the estimated age distribution of the male population living at the time. The county sample is described in Main and Main, "The Red Queen in New England?" p. 148. Lane bought his clock in 1747 and a watch in 1748; *Journal,* pp. 32–33. Lane's politics were not ordinary either. He had Tory leanings during the Revolution and was a firm Federalist afterward.

37. Pehr Kalm, *The America of 1750; Peter Kalm's Travels in North America . . .,* 2 vols. (New York: Wilson-Erickson, 1937), 1: 612–614. Simon Schama emphasizes the religious anxieties of Dutch Calvinists: "When food, lust, sloth, indolence, and vain luxury were subdued by the domestic virtues–sobriety, frugality, piety, humility, aptitude and loyalty–they were deprived of their dirt, which is to say, their capacity for inflicting harm or jeopardizing the soul"; *The Embarrass-*

ment of Riches: An Interpretation of Dutch Culture in the Golden Age (Berkeley: University of California Press, 1988), p. 388. Forms of consumption associated with family and domestic life were, however, "sentimentalized" as "comforts" by both English and colonists, writes Joyce Appleby in "Consumption in Early Modern Social Thought," in *Consumption and the World of Goods,* ed. John Brewer and Roy Porter (New York: Routledge, 1993), p. 169.

38. Sara F. Matthews Grieco, "The Body, Appearance, and Sexuality," in *A History of Women in the West,* vol. 3: *Renaissance and Enlightenment Paradoxes,* ed. Natalie Zemon Davis and Arlette Farge (Cambridge, Mass.: The Belknap Press of Harvard University Press, 1993), pp. 46–55; Keith Thomas, "Cleanliness and Godliness in Early Modern England," in *Religion, Culture and Society in Early Modern Britain: Essays in Honour of Patrick Collinson,* ed. Anthony Fletcher and Peter Roberts (Cambridge: Cambridge University Press, 1994), pp. 78–80, argues for the interaction of religion and the developing culture of good manners. Covering much of the same ground, Richard Bushman sidesteps religious ideas but accepts "piety" as part of the package, in *The Refinement of America,* pp. 79–80. For instance, he describes Eleazar Moody's *The School of Good Manners* (Boston, 1715) as an immensely popular book of piety and etiquette that went through more than a dozen printings and was a plagiarism of a book printed in London in 1595, which was itself a translation of a French book published in 1564, which was probably Italian in origin; ibid., p. 31.

39. Epidemics of "throat distemper" between 1735 and 1760 (diphtheria and/or scarlet fever) mowed down the children, but life expectancy rose substantially for adults. Mean age at death for men rose from fifty-nine in the seventeenth century to over sixty-two in the eighteenth, and from fifty-nine to sixty-two for women, according to genealogies listed in the Select Bibliography, after weighting by area to maintain consistent representation.

40. Thomas, "Cleanliness and Godliness," pp. 56–83; Richard L. Bushman and Claudia L. Bushman, "The Early History of Cleanliness in America," *Journal of American History* 74 (1988): 1213–38; *The Diary of Mary Cooper: Life on a Long Island Farm, 1768–1773,* ed. Field Horne (New York: Oyster Bay Historical Society, 1981). Cooper complains frequently of being dirty and tired; the two conditions went together. For instance, on March 11, 1769, she wrote: "Sat[urday] and no clothes to wear to meeten, dirty and distressed." A few weeks later she wrote: "Sabbath—dirty, fretted, tired, no clothes ironed—forct to stay home."

41. Carl Bridenbaugh, ed., *Gentleman's Progress: The Itinerarium of Dr. Alexander Hamilton, 1744* (Chapel Hill: University of North Carolina Press, 1948), p. 55.

42. Christopher J. Berry, *The Idea of Luxury* (Cambridge: Cambridge University Press, 1994), is a good place to explore English anxieties over these issues. Dr. Alexander Hamilton made fun in his journal of a would-be gentleman, a "clownish blade, much addicted to swearing, at the same time desirous to pass for a gentleman . . . he would have us know that he had good linnen in his bags, a pair of silver buckles, silver clasps and gold sleeve buttons, two Holland

shirts, and some neat night caps; and that his little woman att home drank tea twice a day"; Bridenbaugh, *Gentleman's Progress,* pp. 13–14.

43. David W. Conroy, *In Public Houses: Drink and the Revolution of Authority in Colonial Massachusetts* (Chapel Hill: University of North Carolina Press, 1995). Farmers found these places so necessary to their well-being that they played important roles in securing and keeping licences for their favorite watering holes.

44. Diaries of educated men, such as those by John Ballantine, minister of Westfield, Massachusetts, in the Connecticut Valley, or Jabez Fitch, of northeastern Connecticut, report frequent visiting and tea-drinking in the 1750s and 1760s. The original of John Ballantine's diary is apparently lost, but a printed copy is at the American Antiquarian Society. Jabez Fitch's diaries are scattered. Two from 1775 and 1776 are in the Library of Congress; additional portions are in the Bailey/Howe Library at the University of Vermont. Transcriptions of portions have appeared sporadically in the *Mayflower Descendant* since 1899.

45. The courtesy literature is succinctly reviewed by Bushman, *The Refinement of America,* pp. 31–43. Of fundamental importance for understanding long-term change in western European rules of social behavior is Norbert Elias, *The History of Manners,* vol. 1 of *The Civilizing Process.* Appleby argues that because new consumer goods encouraged self-expression, their increasing accessibility also opened up new avenues for rebellion by youth and women; "Consumption in Early Modern Social Thought," p. 172.

46. Bernard Bailyn, *Education in the Forming of American Society: Needs and Opportunities for Study* (Chapel Hill: University of North Carolina Press, 1960), pp. 15–36.

47. Statements on marital behavior and childbearing are based on the genealogies listed in the Select Bibliography.

48. Gloria L. Main, "Naming Children in Early New England," *Journal of Interdisciplinary History* 27 (1996): 16.

49. Celia is from Shakespeare's *As You Like It;* Artemisi presumably comes from Artemis, the Greek goddess of the moon and of hunting. Diana is her Roman equivalent. Patrick Hanks and Flavia Hodges, *A Dictionary of First Names* (New York: Oxford University Press, 1990), pp. 59, 28, 84. The others also seem to be classically inspired.

50. Of more than 5,100 daughters recorded between 1750 and 1775 in the family genealogies listed in the Select Bibliography, there were only 7 occurrences of "Clarissa," all but one born to Connecticut couples. Jay Fliegelman reports that newspaper advertisements attest to the popularity of the novel by Samuel Richardson but its first American imprint did not appear until 1772. Every surviving edition was abridged, he says, "in such a way as to render it an unadulterated polemic against parental severity"; *Prodigals and Pilgrims: The American Revolution against Patriarchal Authority, 1750–1800* (Cambridge: Cambridge University Press, 1982), pp. 81–82.

51. "The slow retreat from biblical names did not become a rout until the early decades of the nineteenth century," cautions Daniel Scott Smith in "Continuity

and Discontinuity in Puritan Naming: Massachusetts, 1771," *William and Mary Quarterly* 51 (1994): 69. The ten most popular names, such as Joseph, Samuel, and John for boys and Mary, Hannah, and Sarah for girls, fell from more than half of names in use for children not named for parents or grandparents in the seventeenth century to 22 percent for boys and 39 percent for girls in 1750–1774; Main, "Naming Children in Early New England," p. 19.

52. The relative number of diminutives continued to increase among girls born in 1775–1799, but I do not mean to exaggerate their implications for the status of women. They were not a tidal wave. Out of the nearly 2,500 nonlineally named daughters in the data file born in 1740–1775, fewer than 7 percent were given diminutives as their official names.

53. Connecticut Valley towns originally placed decisions concerning distributions of intestate estates in the hands of commissioners to decide in a case-by-case manner. Their decisions favored older sons over younger ones and all sons over daughters; Charles William Manwaring, comp., *A Digest of Early Connecticut Probate Records*, 3 vols. (Hartford, 1906); vol. 1, spanning 1636 to 1677, lists forty-six distributions to widows and children of married men who died intestate. The inheritance laws passed by Connecticut (before the merger with New Haven Colony) also denied wives any veto over their husbands' dealings in family lands. This meant that a Connecticut man was free to deed over the farm to his sons, if he so chose, and his wife could be left with one-third of whatever was left after paying debts and court charges. Of all the probate jurisdictions in New England, Connecticut (not New Haven Colony) treated married women the worst. See Marylynn Salmon, *Women and the Law of Property in Early America* (Chapel Hill: University of North Carolina Press, 1986), pp. 58–76.

54. George Lee Haskins, *Law and Authority in Early Massachusetts: A Study in Tradition and Design* (New York: Macmillan, 1960); idem, "Reception of the Common Law in Seventeenth-Century Massachusetts: A Case Study," in *Law and Authority in Colonial America*, ed. George Billias (Barre, Mass.: Barre Publishers, 1965), p. 20, reprinted with revisions from the *University of Pennsylvania Law Review* 97 (1949): 842–53; Salmon, *Women and the Law of Property;* Carole Shammas, Marylynn Salmon, and Michel Dahlin, *Inheritance in America from Colonial Times to the Present* (New Brunswick, N.J.: Rutgers University Press, 1987), chap. 1; and Lois Green Carr, "Inheritance in the Colonial Chesapeake," in *Women in the Age of the American Revolution,* ed. Ronald Hoffman and Peter J. Albert (Charlottesville: University Press of Virginia, 1989); John D. Cushing, ed., *The Laws of the Pilgrims: A Facsimile Edition of the Book of the General Laws of the Inhabitants of the Jurisdiction of New-Plimouth, 1672 and 1685* (Wilmington, Del.: M. Glazier, 1977); William H. Whitmore, ed., *The Colonial Laws of Massachusetts, Reprinted from the Edition of 1672, with the Supplements through 1686* (Boston, 1887); J. H. Trumbull, ed., *Colonial Records of Connecticut Prior to the Union with New Haven Colony, May, 1665* (Hartford, 1850); John D. Cushing, ed., *The Earliest Laws of the New Haven and Connecticut Colonies, 1639–1673* (Wilmington, Del.: M. Gla-

zier, 1977); John D. Cushing, ed., *The Earliest Acts and Laws of the Colony of Rhode Island and Providence Plantations, 1647–1719* (Wilmington, Del.: M. Glazier, 1977). See also Charles M. Andrews, *The Connecticut Intestacy Law* (New Haven: Yale University Press, 1933); Charles J. Hoadly, comp., *Records of the Colony and Plantation of New Haven, from 1638 to 1649* (Hartford: Case, Tiffany, 1857); idem, *Records of the Colony or Jurisdiction of New Haven 1653 to the Union, Together with the New Haven Code of 1656* (Hartford: Case, Lockwood, 1858); John T. Farrell, "The Early History of Rhode Island's Court System," *Rhode Island History* 9 (1950): 14–25, 65–71, 103–117. In a case from Hampton, New Hampshire, in the 1660s, the probate judge made a distinction in his rules for the distribution of an intestate estate wherein the widow was to administer the bulk of the estate even after her son reached his majority so long as she stayed a widow. If she remarried, then she was to have her thirds, and the son was to have the lands at her marriage or her death. The same decision marks a similar case in Portsmouth; Nathaniel Bouton et al., eds., *Probate Records, Vols. 1–6*, vols. 31–40 of *Documents and Records Relating to the Province of New Hampshire*, 40 vols. (Concord, 1867–1941); 1: 51, 52, 60, 81. Wills and administrations of estates from the following sources supplied the evidence on inheritance practices: Manwaring, *Connecticut Probate Records; Plymouth Colony Records*, vol. 1: *Wills and Inventories, 1633–1669*, ed. (Camden, Maine: Picton Press, 1996); *Suffolk County Wills: Abstracts of the Earliest Wills upon Record in the County of Suffolk, Massachusetts* (Baltimore: Genealogical Publishing, 1984); *The Early Records of the Town of Providence*, 21 vols. (Providence: Snow & Farnham City Printers, 1896–1915); George Dow, ed., *The Probate Records of Essex County, Massachusetts, 1635–1681*, 3 vols. (1916–1920; reprint, Newburyport, Mass.: Parker River Researchers, 1988); typescripts of Plymouth probate records to the year 1691 on deposit at Pilgrim Hall, Plimouth Plantation, Plymouth, Mass.; and the manuscript clerks' copies in bound folios of Suffolk, Hampshire, and Worcester Counties, Massachusetts, and of New Haven Colony. Early Rhode Island's difficulties in adjudicating inheritance and dower issues can be viewed in the Providence town records. The reform impulse died a quick death there because legislative representatives could not muster sufficient authority to pass clear and binding laws. They passed the buck to the town councils, whose members constantly resorted to published works on English common law.

55. Connecticut's laws concerning inheritance were challenged in English courts in two long-running cases. In neither case was the outcome sufficiently clear-cut to call forth action by either courts or Parliament to overturn Connecticut law; Andrews, *The Connecticut Intestacy Law.*

56. Alexander Keyssar, "The Problem of Widowhood in Eighteenth-Century Massachusetts," *Perspectives in American History* 8 (1974): 83–119.

57. Main, "Gender, Work, and Wages," p. 48.

58. Cornelia Hughes Dayton, *Women before the Bar: Gender, Law, and Society in Connecticut, 1639–1789* (Chapel Hill: University of North Carolina Press, 1995); Kathleen M. Brown, *Good Wives, Nasty Wenches, and Anxious Patriarchs: Gender,*

Race, and Power in Colonial Virginia (Chapel Hill: University of North Carolina Press, 1996); Cynthia A. Kierner, *Beyond the Household: Women's Place in the Early South, 1700–1835* (Ithaca: Cornell University Press, 1998).

59. Joy Wiltenburg, *Disorderly Women and Female Power in the Street Literature of Early Modern England and Germany* (Charlottesville: University Press of Virginia, 1992), pp. 47–48, 176–177. On medical theories about women's bodies, see Evelyne Berriot-Salvadore, "The Discourse of Medicine and Science," in Davis and Farge, *History of Women*, pp. 348–387; Thomas Walter Laqueur, *Making Sex: Body and Gender from the Greeks to Freud* (Cambridge, Mass.: Harvard University Press, 1990), chap. 2; Anthony Fletcher, *Gender, Sex, and Subordination in England, 1500–1800* (New Haven: Yale University Press, 1995), pp. 30–59, 376–400; and Sara Mendelson and Patricia Crawford, *Women in Early Modern England, 1550–1720* (Oxford: Clarendon Press, 1998), pp. 18–33, 58–74.

60. Angus McLaren, *A History of Contraception, from Antiquity to the Present Day* (Oxford: Basil Blackwell, 1990), chaps. 1 and 5.

61. Ibid., p. 390; Susan Dwyer Amussen, *An Ordered Society: Gender and Class in Early Modern England* (Oxford: Basil Blackwell, 1988), pp. 134–176.

62. Main, "Naming Children in Early New England," p. 4.

63. John Frederick Martin, *Profits in the Wilderness: Entrepreneurship and the Founding of New England Towns in the Seventeenth Century* (Chapel Hill: University of North Carolina Press, 1991); Neal Salisbury, "Indians and Colonists in Southern New England after the Pequot War: An Uneasy Balance," in *The Pequots in Southern New England: The Fall and Rise of an American Indian Nation*, ed. Laurence M. Hauptman and James D. Wherry (Norman: University of Oklahoma Press, 1990), pp. 81–95.

64. The literature on the Salem witchcraft trials is vast. Among the most important are Paul Boyer and Stephen Nissenbaum, *Salem Possessed: The Social Origins of Witchcraft* (Cambridge, Mass.: Harvard University Press, 1974); Carol Frances Karlsen, *The Devil in the Shape of a Woman: Witchcraft in Colonial New England* (New York: W. W. Norton, 1987); and Bernard Rosenthal, *Salem Story* (Albany: SUNY Press, 1992).

65. Roger Thompson, *Sex in Middlesex: Popular Mores in a Massachusetts County, 1649–1699* (Amherst: University of Massachusetts Press, 1981); Mary Beth Norton, *Founding Mothers and Fathers: Gendered Power and the Forming of American Society* (New York: Alfred A. Knopf, 1996); Dayton, *Gender before the Bar*; Bruce H. Mann, *Neighbors and Strangers: Law and Community in Early Connecticut* (Chapel Hill: University of North Carolina Press, 1987); Laurel Thatcher Ulrich, "'Vertuous Women Found': New England Ministerial Literature, 1668–1735," *American Quarterly* 28 (1976): 20–40. Arguments about changing gender attitudes in England are in Amussen, *An Ordered Society*, pp. 176–189; Fletcher, *Gender, Sex, and Subordination*, pp. 376–413; and G. J. Barker-Benfield, *The Culture of Sensibility: Sex and Society in Eighteenth-Century Britain* (Chicago: University of Chicago Press, 1992), all clearly summarized by Susan Kingsley Kent in *Gender and Power in Britain, 1640–1990* (London: Routledge, 1999).

66. This transmutation in the views of women's nature is most explicit in English novels and magazines, but Porter and Hall emphasize the relative absence of misogyny in the most popular printed source of reproductive and sexual lore in the colonies, *Aristotle's Masterpiece;* Roy Porter and Lesley Hall, *The Facts of Life: The Creation of Sexual Knowledge in Britain, 1650–1950* (New Haven: Yale University Press, 1995), pp. 33–53. Lisa Wilson accents domesticity and continuity in male gender roles in New England in her reading of diaries and correspondence in *"Ye Heart of a Man": The Domestic Life of Men in Colonial New England* (New Haven: Yale University Press, 1999). John Adams praised Mrs. John Hancock in a pointed letter to Abigail, because "She avoids talking upon Politics"; Elaine Forman Crane, "Political Dialogue and the Spring of Abigail's Discontent," *William and Mary Quarterly* 56 (1999): 763. Gender attitudes among New England's elite in the eighteenth century were undoubtedly much more directly influenced by imperial affairs than was true for those in the yeoman ranks, whose narrow economic horizons shielded them to some degree from changing ideological fashions in urban capitals.

67. The town of Oyster Bay is on the north shore of Long Island, opposite Stamford, Connecticut. The area was originally settled from Connecticut, and Mary herself describes a visit to relatives there. Although New York City served as the major entrepôt for the area, New England was its cultural and religious hearth.

68. The remark about the gentlemen: Cooper, *Diary,* p. 2. Gentility in Virginia: Kathleen M. Brown, *Good Wives, Nasty Wenches, and Anxious Patriarchs: Gender, Race, and Power in Colonial Virginia* (Chapel Hill: University of North Carolina Press, 1996); and Kierner, *Beyond the Household.*

69. Cooper, *Diary,* p. 44.

70. Cooper, *Diary:* Joseph's financial difficulties, p. 30; pays fifteen pounds on mortgage, p. 58; repairs on house, for which they hold a "chopping frolic" and Mary must cook for the workmen, pp. 20, 25–29; incident with boatmen: p. 45; weak tea and dry crusts: pp. 14, 25; difficulty getting food for dinner: pp. 16, 17, 19, 23, 24; Joseph fretting because they drink tea: p. 13; turkey incident: p. 26.

71. Ibid., p. 18.

72. Linda K. Kerber, "Beyond Roles, Beyond Spheres: Thinking about Gender in the Early Republic," *William and Mary Quarterly* 46 (1989): 565–585.

Index